RETHINKING PROJECT MANAGEMENT FOR A DYNAMIC AND DIGITAL WORLD

RETHINKING PROJECT MANAGEMENT FOR A DYNAMIC AND DIGITAL WORLD

EDITED BY
DARREN DALCHER

Routledge
Taylor & Francis Group

First published 2022
by Routledge
6000 Broken Sound Parkway #300, Boca Raton, FL 33487

and by Routledge

2 Park Square, Milton Park, Abingdon, Oxon, OX14 4RN

Routledge is an imprint of the Taylor & Francis Group, an informa business

ISBN: 9781032133126 (hbk)
ISBN: 9781032133119 (pbk)
ISBN: 9781003228615 (ebk)

DOI: 10.1201/9781003228615

Typeset in Times New Roman
by DerryField Publishing Services, LLC

Trademarks Used in This Book

Contents

Contents   *vii*

List of Figures and Tables   *xiii*

About the Editor   *xv*

Contributing Authors   *xvii*

Introduction   1

Rethinking the Future of Project Management   2

Darren Dalcher

    Predicting the Future   3

    But Is It Really All About Technology?   4

    Looking Forward to Post-Industrial Development   6

    The Emergence of the Project Society   8

    The Challenge of Now and the Person of Tomorrow   11

    The Future Is Here Already   13

    Advances in Project Management   15

    Guiding Principles for Future Leading   16

    References   18

Chapter 1: Quality   23

The Quest for Supreme Performance: Benchmarking to Save Lives   24

Darren Dalcher

    The Power and Potential Impact of Benchmarking   25

    Looking Elsewhere: From Racing Cars to Saving Lives   27

    Directing the Lean Quality Management Revolution   29

    Benchmarking Reprised   30

    Progressing Beyond the Benchmarking Paradox   31

    References   32

Lean Quality in Construction Project Delivery—A New Model and Principles   33

John Oakland and Marton Marosszeky

Construction Industry Challenges and Solutions   33
Lean Quality: A New Model for Improved Outcomes in the Construction Sector   33
The Principles of Lean Quality in Construction   35
Values and Long-Term Philosophy   37
Conclusions   40
References   40

Chapter 2: Communication   41
Communicating Beyond Our Hidden Assumptions   42
Darren Dalcher

Exploring the Context   42
The Peril and Power of Hidden Assumptions   43
New Insights in Communicating Project Management   45
References   46

Communicating Project Management: A Participatory Rhetoric for Development Teams   48
Benjamin Lauren

Communicating Leadership, Positionality, and Identity   49
Introducing The Gardener   50
Introducing The Chef   53
Comparing Communication Values of The Gardener and The Chef   56
Leadership Identity as Rhetorical Performance   57
References and Further Reading   59

Chapter 3: Teams   61
From Teams and Teamwork to Teaming   62
Darren Dalcher

The Difference Between Groups and Teams   63
The Dynamic Dysfunctions of Teams   63
The Return of Trust   64
Who Is Packing Your Parachute?   66
Creative Teams   68
Teaming for Success   70
References   72

Leading Brainy Teams   74
Peter Cook

Brain Based Enterprises   74
Leading Brainy Teams   77
Summary   80
References   81

Chapter 4: Leadership   83

The Followership Advantage: Reconfiguring Leadership for Success   84
Darren Dalcher

    What Worked Before?   84
    Beyond Toxic Leadership   85
    Empowering Followers   87
    Asking the Impossible   88
    Turn the Ship Around   89
    The Way Forward: I Intend to . . .   90
    The New Management: Human-Centred Systems   91
    Postheroic Leadership Is Here   92
    Repositioning Leadership and Followership   93
    References   94

Human-Centred Management: A Systemic Interrelation   96
Roland Bardy

    The Four Perspectives   97
    Interrelating the Four Perspectives Through Multi-Stakeholder Dialogues   102
    References   109

Chapter 5: Life Cycle   113

Organising for Project Work: Thinking Beyond Project Delivery   114
Darren Dalcher

    Why Life Cycles?   114
    Rethinking Project Management   115
    Reflecting on the Shape, Efficacy, and Purpose of Life Cycles   116
    The Problem with Shared Practice   118
    The Death of Common Sense?   119
    Turning Knowledge into Action   120
    Reflection Reprised: Looking at Impacts   121
    The Demise of Project Delivery   123
    References   124

The Project Framework: Understanding Gates and Stages   125
Robert Buttrick

    Projects as Vehicles of Change   125
    Gates and Stages   127
    The Project Framework   131
    Some Key Questions   134
    How Can I Apply the Framework?   138
    Summary   141
    References   141

Chapter 6: Portfolios   143
Organising for Success in Project Portfolios, Initiatives and Strategies   144
Darren Dalcher

Portfolios: Definitions and Strategies   144
Portfolios: Why and Where?   146
One Portfolio, or More?   148
The Case for Strategic Initiatives   151
Potential Principles for Collecting Projects and Programmes Into a Portfolio   153
Rethinking Project Portfolio Success   154
References   158

Strategic Goal Alignment and Portfolio Stakeholder Management   162
John Wyzalek

An Example and Some Definitions   163
Strategic Goal Alignment for Managing a Portfolio and Its Stakeholders   164
Conclusion   165
References   166

Chapter 7: Entrepreneurship   167
The Entrepreneurship Turn: Repositioning Projects as Successful Ventures   168
Darren Dalcher

What Is This Thing Called Entrepreneurship?   168
How Project Management Lost Its Way   170
Reflecting on the Loss of Direction   172
And How We Can Find It Again—Repositioning Projects Alongside
Entrepreneurship   174
References   176

Effectual Project Management: Thinking Like an Expert Entrepreneur   179
Laura Mathiaszyk, Christine Volkmann and Stuart Read

The Most Complex of Them All?   179
Corporate Projects and Entrepreneurial Projects   179
What Expert Entrepreneurs Learn   181
Effectuation Principles   181
Effectual Decision-Making in Project Management   182
Empirical Study of Effectuation in Project Management   183
Measures   184
Discussion   187
From Experts to Experts   189
References   190

Chapter 8: People 193

Building from the Inside: The Power of Social Organising 194
Darren Dalcher

Putting Your People First 194
A Journey to Change 195
Creating Positive Organisations 197
The Power of Social Organisations 198
References 198

Social Process for Project Leaders 200
Ian Macdonald, Catherine Burke and Karl Stewart

Tim's Story 201
Manager and Project Leader Roles 202
Getting It Right 203
Team Leadership and Team Membership 205
Conclusion 210
References 210

Chapter 9: Hacking 211

Hacking Innovation: Revisiting Teams, Productivity and Limits 212
Darren Dalcher

The Mythical Man-Month: Mixing Effort and Progress 212
Mind What You Wish For . . . 214
Reimagining the Computer at IBM 215
Managing the Massive Project 216
Learning the Lessons 218
The Emergence of the Hacker: Where Do Hackers Come From? 220
Taking Stock: Hackers Gallery 222
Hacker Communities 224
What Are the Wider Implications for Innovation and for Projects? 226
Is Hacking Ready to Take the Next Big Step? 227
References 229

How to Herd Cats: The Art of the Hacker Paradigm Leadership 232
Tim Rayner

Hacker Paradigm Leadership 233
Be a 'Chief Experimenter' 239
References 246

Chapter 10: Stewardship   **249**

Taking Responsibility for Our Actions: Why It Is Time to
Think About Stewardship   **250**
Darren Dalcher

    Love Unchained   250
    Extending Our Scope of Interest   252
    The Case for Stewardship   253
    Product Stewardship   255
    Stewardship Reprised   256
    References   258

A Strategic Approach to Product Stewardship   **260**
Helen Lewis

    Introduction   260
    Drivers for Product Stewardship   260
    Product Stewardship Policy and Strategies   264
    Conclusions   269
    References   270

Chapter 11: Knowledge   **273**

The Mind of the Maker: Making Sense of Knowledge   **274**
Darren Dalcher

    So, Why Manage Knowledge?   274
    Engaging with the Mind of the Maker   275
    Managing Knowledge in Project Environments   277
    Learning to Work with Knowledge   278
    References   279

Through the Knowledge Lens: KM Adventures in Project-Land   **281**
Judy Payne, Eileen J. Roden and Steve Simister

    KM Principles, the KM Context and KM Scope   281
    Context Factor: Strategic KM Purpose   285
    Context Factor: Project Delivery Method   286
    Project Type   288
    Is That All There Is to KM?   292
    References   292

Conclusion   **293**

Rebooting Project Management for a Brighter Future   **294**
Darren Dalcher

    References   297

Index   **299**

List of Figures and Tables

Figure 1.1   New Framework for Lean Quality Management   35

Figure 1.2   A New Framework for the Principles of Lean Quality in Construction   38

Figure 3.1   War of the Worlds   76

Figure 4.1   Interrelations Between the Ethical, the Social, the Economic,
             and the Institutional   97

Figure 4.2   Katz and Kahn Open System Model   103

Figure 5.1   Select the Right Projects to Support Your Strategy.   126

Figure 5.2   Managing the Risk.   127

Figure 5.3   Address All Aspects of the Project in Parallel.   127

Figure 5.4   A Typical Stage.   128

Figure 5.5   The Three Decisions Required at Each Gate.   129

Figure 5.6   The Project Framework as a Bar Chart.   130

Figure 5.7   The Project Framework in Diagrammatic Form.   133

Figure 5.8   Bad Practice Depictions of Project Frameworks.   137

Figure 6.1   Project Portfolio Success Triangle   157

Figure 7.1   Contrast of Traditional Waterfall, Agile and Entrepreneurial
             Project Approaches   180

Figure 7.2   Gender of Sample   185

Figure 7.3   Age of Sample   185

Figure 7.4   Main Effects of Effectuation/Causation and Hard/Soft Success Outcomes   185

Figure 7.5   Moderating Effects of Complexity on the Relationship Between
             Effectuation/Causation and Hard/Soft Success Outcomes   186

Figure 9.1   The Code and Fix Cycle   220

Figure 10.1 Three Steps Towards a Product Stewardship Strategy   261

Figure 10.2 Examples of Product Stewardship Strategies   265

Figure 10.3 Environmental 'Lock-In' over a Product's Development Cycle   267

Figure 10.4 Producer Responsibility Strategies for Product Recovery   268

Figure 11.1 The KM Context: Clusters and Factors   283

Figure 11.2 Project Types   288

Table I.1	Principle-Driven Mapping of Topics and Coverage	17
Table 2.1	Comparing Value of The Gardener and The Chef	57
Table 3.1	Team Dynamics Checklist Inspired by Project Aristotle Findings	67
Table 5.1	Rethinking Project Management, Proposed Directions for Future Research	116
Table 5.2	A List of Alternative Gate Names	135
Table 5.3	How the Different Project and Activities Fit the Project Framework	140
Table 7.1	Effectuation and Causation Principles	182
Table 8.1	Complementary Authorities of Leaders and Team Members	206
Table 9.1	Hackers Gallery—A Representative Sample	223
Table 10.1	Prioritising Social Issues	265
Table 11.1	KM Principles and Underlying KM Fundamentals	282
Table 11.2	Summary of Context Factors	284
Table 11.3	Knowledge and KM in Extreme Linear and Iterative Project Life Cycles	287
Table C.1	Mapping of New Focal Areas—Central to Future Project Management Thinking	296

About the Editor

Professor Darren Dalcher, PhD (Lond), HonFAPM, FRSA, FCMI, FBCS, CITP, SMIEEE, SFHEA, MINCOSE

Professor Darren Dalcher holds a Chair in Strategic Project Management at Lancaster University Management School. He is a senior academic with a successful track record of consulting and collaborating with businesses, charities, professional associations and governmental organisations. He works to foster interactive dialogue about the integration of successful practice with theoretical research in the management of projects. He is a Visiting International Scholar at InnoLab, University of Vaasa and holds visiting appointments at the universities of Warwick, Drexel, WU (Vienna University of Economics and Business), Reykjavik and the Supply Chain Academy. He is the founder and Director of the National Centre for Project Management (NCPM), an interdisciplinary centre of excellence operating in collaboration with industry, government, academia, third-sector organisations and the learned societies.

Following industrial and consultancy experience in managing technology projects, Professor Dalcher gained his PhD from King's College, London, for his work on continuous delivery, dynamic feedback and extended project life cycles. In 1992, he founded an IEEE taskforce focused on learning from systems failures. He is active in numerous international committees, standards bodies, steering groups and editorial boards. He is heavily involved in organising international conferences and has delivered many keynote addresses and tutorials. He has written over 400 papers, articles and book chapters and published over 30 books. His work has been translated into French, German, Italian, Spanish, Portuguese, Russian and Chinese. He is Editor-in-Chief of Wiley's *Journal of Software: Evolution and Process,* and Editor of the *Routledge Frontiers in Project Management* book series, featuring cutting-edge research in managing projects, strategic initiatives and change.

He has built a reputation as leader and innovator in the area of practice-based education and reflection in project management and has designed, developed and launched the UK's first professional doctorate in project management, alongside an extensive suite of executive and professional master's programmes and diplomas. He was named by the Association for Project Management as one of the top 10 influential experts in project management and has also been voted *Project Magazine*'s Academic of the Year for his contribution in 'integrating and weaving academic work with practice'. He has been chairman of the influential APM Project Management Conference for an unprecedented five years, expanding the scope of the event, setting consecutive attendance records, bringing together the most influential speakers, exploring the boundaries and interactions of the profession and forging cross-disciplinary dialogue.

He received international recognition in 2010 with his appointment as a member of the PMForum International Academic Advisory Council. In October 2011 he was awarded a prestigious lifetime Honorary Fellowship from the Association for Project Management for outstanding contribution to the discipline of project management.

He is a very popular speaker and is regularly invited to deliver lectures and courses at many international institutions. He has won multiple awards and prizes, including, most recently, Best Paper Award from the British Academy of Management in 2015, CMI's Management Articles of the Year competition in 2016, Outstanding Paper Award in the Emerald Literati Network Awards for Excellence in 2017, and *PMWJ* Editor's Choice Awards in 2017, 2018, 2019 and 2020. His research interests focus on rethinking project success and the concept of agility, especially in the context of strategy and innovation, as well as considering the role of process in relation to maturity and capability, process improvement, systems engineering, decision-making, change management, ethics, complexity, knowledge management, responsible project management and reflective practice.

Professor Dalcher is an Honorary Fellow of the Association for Project Management, a Chartered Fellow of the British Computer Society, a Senior Fellow of the Higher Education Academy, a Fellow of the Chartered Management Institute and the Royal Society of Arts, a Senior Member of the IEEE, and a Member of the Project Management Institute, the British Academy of Management, the International Council on Systems Engineering and the Agile Business Consortium. He sits on numerous senior research and professional boards, including the PMI Academic Insight Team, the International Advisory Council of *PM World Today,* the CMI Academic Council, the British Computer Society Fellows Advisory Group, and the APM Group Ethics and Standards Governance Board.

He is the Academic Advisor and co-Editor of the highly acclaimed 7th edition of the *APM Body of Knowledge,* released to mark the formal award of Royal Charter to the Association for Project Management and the establishment of the project management profession. The new edition transforms projects thinking and practice by positioning project management in an organisational perspective and focusing on the delivery of beneficial change and strategic transformation through projects, programmes and portfolios.

Contributing Authors

Roland Bardy is owner of BardyConsult in Mannheim, Germany, where he mainly engages in management education, and he serves as Executive Professor of General Management and Leadership at Florida Gulf Coast University. Born in Vienna, Austria, in 1942, where he received his MBA in 1969, and he received his PhD (in econometrics) from Heidelberg University, Germany, in 1974. He worked in Finance and Administration of BASF SE, the German multinational chemicals manufacturer, for about 30 years until 1999. Then he took up teaching and consulting at Goizueta Business School, Emory University, at Fachhochschule Worms (Germany) and in various Swiss and Austrian MBA programmes. His areas are accounting, supply-chain management, leadership and business ethics. He promotes the philosophy and implementation of responsible development, accountability and sustainability through, among others, the Wittenberg Center for Global Ethics. Residing both in Mannheim, Germany, and in Naples, Florida, Roland is privileged to experience both US and European developments in business and academia. He has published, in English and in German on management accounting, leadership and business ethics.

Catherine Burke is Associate Professor of Public Administration, Emerita, University of Southern California, Price School of Public Policy, where she taught classes for over 30 years at the doctoral, master's and undergraduate levels. Her research focuses on organisations and systems design, management theory and leadership. She has been a consultant to Southern California Edison, the cities of Los Angeles and Pasadena, and the Congressional Office of Technology Assessment. She conducted two day-long training seminars for the command staff of LAPD in a programme created by Chief Bernard Parks, discussing leadership, systems and organisation structures that could be used in police departments. Her publications include *Innovation and Public Policy* and articles in various academic journals. She was a Director at Commonwealth Aluminium in Kentucky.

Robert Buttrick has a successful track record for building project management excellence in major organisations and as a contributor to project management methods, best practice and standards. He a UK Principal Expert working on the development of national and international project management standards, for which he received a Distinguished Service Certificate from BSI (British Standards Institute). He was an author of the 2017 edition of PRINCE® and the lead developer for the UK government's project delivery standard. He is a Member of the Chartered Institute of Marketing, a Chartered Engineer and an Honorary Fellow of the Association for Project Management. Robert is currently an independent author, a consultant and a Visiting Teaching Fellow at the University of Warwick.

Peter Cook is a unique hybrid of scientist, business academic and musician, blending hard analytical thinking with a creative twist that comes from the arts in his work at Human Dynamics and the Academy of Rock. His books are acclaimed by Professor Charles Handy, Tom Peters and Harvey Goldsmith CBE, and he writes for Sir Richard Branson's Virgin group. Peter was responsible for leading pharmaceutical innovation teams to bring the world's first treatment for HIV/AIDS and human insulin into being. He also performs with a variety of music legends, including Meatloaf's singer and Ozzy Osbourne's guitarist, learning from the boardroom to the boardwalk. Peter brings MBA business thinking into intimate contact with parallel ideas from the worlds of music and science in his work.

Benjamin Lauren is an Assistant Professor of Experience Architecture in the Department of Writing, Rhetoric, and American Cultures at Michigan State University, where he serves as Assistant Director of the MA in Digital Rhetoric and Professional Writing and as a HUB for Innovation in Learning and Technology Fellow. His book *Communicating Project Management: A Participatory Rhetoric for Development Teams* was published in the ATTW Series by Routledge. The book makes an argument that project managers must communicate to facilitate participation in project work, particularly in the context of networked organisations. Ben's work has been published in journals such as *Technical Communication*, *Transactions on Professional Communication* and *Computers and Composition*.

Helen Lewis runs her own consulting business, providing research and strategic advice to a range of industry and government clients on product stewardship and packaging. She is an Adjunct Professor with the Institute for Sustainable Futures (ISF) at the University of Technology Sydney and a consultant to the Australian Packaging Covenant Organisation (APCO). IN 2017 Helen co-founded the Product Stewardship Cluster to promote knowledge sharing and collaboration between product stewardship organisations. Helen has written widely on product stewardship and corporate social responsibility, including several books. She published *Product Stewardship in Action* in 2016 and is a co-author of *Packaging for Sustainability* (2012) and *Design + Environment* (2001). She has a PhD in product stewardship and is a Fellow of the Australian Institute of Packaging.

Ian Macdonald is a chartered psychologist who graduated with Honours from Brunel University in London. He was an academic staff member at Brunel and continues to be associated there, both as a consultant and as a Lifetime Honorary Fellow. His PhD thesis was about the development of identity of people with learning difficulties through work. Ian is Founder and Director of Macdonald Associates, an international organisational consultancy established in 1983. He is a director of BIOSS International Ltd. He is also an honorary fellow at Brunel University, teaches at Surrey Business School and works with NHS Was and Welsh government. Over the past 30 years, Ian's consultancy work has included many different countries, cultures and types of organisations, from indigenous communities to financial services, from mining to the Church, from smelting aluminium in Siberia and Australia, to psychology services in Denmark. He continues to work across all sectors.

Marton Marosszeky is a civil engineer. His career spans road construction, structural design, academic teaching and research and, most recently, consulting in the implementation of lean production thinking and TQM in construction and as a durability engineer. He retired as a professor of construction management from UNSW in 2006. He is recognised as an international leader in the lean construction community and most recently participated in two high-level workshops in India and was an invited keynote speaker at the Lean Construction Institute of India 2019 conference. He has also worked in Canada, Russia, Singapore, Malaysia and the US, helping major project teams and company executives to adopt lean thinking in building construction, infrastructure and the oil and gas sector. He is widely published in the areas of process improvement and concrete technology.

Laura P. Mathiaszyk is a social entrepreneur and founder of the Eco- and Adventure Travel Business TRAIL.VIEW. In addition, she manages projects supporting cultural diversity, integration and women's empowerment. Her doctoral research at the Schumpeter School of Business and Economics, University of Wuppertal (Germany), focussed on effectuation. Building on her consultancy experience, her thesis offers an investigation of how effectuation helps corporations deal with uncertainty.

John Oakland is Chairman of the Oakland Group and Head of its Research and Education Division, The Oakland Institute. He is also Emeritus Professor of Business Excellence and Quality Management at Leeds University Business School. For over 40 years he has taught and consulted in all aspects of quality management, business excellence and performance improvement to thousands of organisations. He has directed several large research projects in Europe which have brought him into contact with a diverse range of organisations. His research work on the quality management requirements of industry and commerce has been widely acknowledged and published. He has directed several large research projects in Europe, funded by the British Government and EU programmes, which have brought him into contact with a diverse range of organisations. He is author of several bestselling books, including *Total Organisational Excellence* and *Statistical Process Control* and co-author of *Total Quality Management and Operational Excellence* and *Total Construction Management*. He has written hundreds of research papers, articles and reports on various topics in these fields. Professor Oakland is a Fellow of the Chartered Quality Institute and was the first winner of the CQI International Honorary Award in 2017. In addition to being a Chartered Quality Professional, he is also a Fellow of the Royal Statistical Society, Member of the American Society for Quality and Hon. Life Member of the Research Quality Association.

Judy Payne works as an independent consultant, practitioner, reluctant academic and educator specialising in knowledge management, collaborative working and learning. Her work is positioned firmly on the boundaries between academia and practice. Not the most comfortable place to be, but there's such a huge gap between the two that there's a lot of bridging to be done. Judy chairs the BSI Knowledge Management Standards Committee and is a member of the ISO® working group that developed the Knowledge Management standard published in 2018. She co-founded and co-chairs the APM Knowledge SIG. She contributed new knowledge management sections to *APM Bok7*, the sixth edition of the Project Management Institute's *PMBOK® Guide* and the Axelos P3O® Manual and is the author of articles published in journals including *KM Review, Organisations and People, Strategic HR Review, Assets, Project,* and *HR Magazine.* With Vanessa Randle, Judy also produces short whiteboard animation videos, including a series of 'Courageous Conversations' published by APM.

Tim Rayner teaches Leadership, Teams & Scalability in the MBA (Entrepreneurship) programme at UTS Business School. He is the author of *Hacker Culture and the New Rules of Innovation* (2018) and the award-winning short film 'Coalition of the Willing' (2010). Tim works with leaders and teams on entrepreneurial capacity development, cultural alignment, and lean startup best practice. He runs design sprints with Hello Again, a solution design agency in Byron Bay, Australia.

Stuart Read is a Professor at the Atkinson School of Management, Willamette University. His research is focused on effectuation. Derived from practices employed by expert entrepreneurs, effectuation is a set of heuristics that describe how people make decisions and take action in situations of true uncertainty. As uncertainty is pervasive across all aspects of firms, markets and organisations, his work on effectuation applies to, and has been published in, a variety of disciplinary areas.

Eileen J. Roden is an experienced PMO and PPM consultant. She works with individuals and organisations, often at the executive level, to improve their delivery capability. She works across a wide range of industry sectors, including transport, finance, pharmaceuticals, defence, utilities and the public sector. As lead author of P3O® Best Management Practice, Eileen is a recognised expert in the implementation and development of PMOs and influencer in the development of the PMO profession. Her work includes the establishment of the leading PMO training organisation, PMO Learning, building on the success of the sister companies of PMO Flashmob and the PMO Conference. Her passion for all things PMO is underpinned by 17 years' practitioner experience, 14 years' consultancy and training experience along with a range of academic and professional qualifications.

Steve Simister is a consultant and university lecturer in project, programme and portfolio management. His specialism is in assisting clients to scope and define project requirements within a strategic business need framework. He has experience in most business sectors and has been involved in all stages of project life cycles. Steve is deputy chair of MS2, the BSI committee for project management. He has contributed to various ISO standards on project management including ISO:21500. He is a Chartered Project Professional with APM and co-founded the APM Knowledge SIG.

Karl Stewart is a mining engineer spending most of his working life in leadership positions. He spent four years as an internal managerial consultant developing a thorough understanding of the theory underpinning the leadership of people in organisations and the systems that facilitate that activity. He created and implemented these ideas as Managing Director of Comalco Smelting. He was President of the Australian Mines and Metals Association for several years. After leaving Comalco Smelting, he worked as a consultant to banks, aluminium, mining, finance and metallurgical industries. He also served eight years as Chairman of a medium-sized construction company based in Queensland.

Christine Volkmann is a Professor at the Schumpeter School of Business and Economics, University of Wuppertal (Germany), and head of the UNESCO Chair in Entrepreneurship and Intercultural Management. She is also a director of the Institute for Entrepreneurship and Innovations Research (IGIF) and executive committee member of the interdisciplinary Jackstädt Research Center for Entrepreneurship and Innovation. Her research focusses on Social Entrepreneurship, Entrepreneurial Ecosystem, Academic Entrepreneurship, Entrepreneurial Leadership and International Entrepreneurship.

John Wyzalek is a commissioning editor at Taylor & Francis, the editorial assistant for *International Journal for Managing Projects in Business*, and a post-doctoral researcher affiliated with the University of Quebec at Montreal. He is also a teaching assistant at Montclair State University, Montclair, New Jersey. He earned a Doctoral of Business Administration degree at SKEMA Business School, Lille, France, where he studied portfolio and stakeholder management.

Introduction

Rethinking the Future of Project Management

Darren Dalcher

What is the future of project management? Project management has recently been recognised as a profession in the UK with the formal award of a Royal Charter to the professional association, encouraging a rethink around the role, potential and impacts of projects. With the change in role and status comes additional responsibilities and a need to reflect on project work in general and to consider the future evolution of the profession. Cast your mind forward half a century and ask yourself: How will future projects be organised, sponsored and governed? What new practices are likely to be needed? What new ideas and concepts will shape the future of project management? What will be different about how organisations utilise and realise projects? Where will the new ideas and approaches come from?

Welcome to this edited volume featuring key ideas and perspectives on the development of the profession which aims to address some of these questions. This book is concerned with the rethinking of project management to ensure it is ready to assume a more central role in a more uncertain and turbulent world. It aims to explore new trends, promising ideas and novel concepts that will play a part in shaping thinking, reflection and practical action in the project, programme and portfolio space. Some commentators argue that basic project management has not changed fundamentally over the past five decades, while others point to significant advances and repositioned ideas and concepts that can make momentous differences to how projects are conceived, executed and governed and how they deliver beneficial value, change and transformation to organisations. The writing in this volume endeavours to refresh the thinking around projects and to offer new perspectives and enriched conversations that can underpin and enable a new future for project management work in increasingly dynamic and digital settings.

While there are many new publications and books focused on project management, we recognise that it can sometimes be difficult to know where to look and what to follow, especially when seeking fresh insights and enlightened perspectives. Finding a starting point for examining and exploring the future of project management can be difficult. Moreover, identifying key concepts and ideas, especially in new domains, is time-consuming and labour-intensive. This volume, therefore, offers a sampling of some of the best and most innovative writing centred on projects, people, teams, portfolios, change and innovation.

The content is divided into 11 main areas that extend beyond the scene setting and historical perspective offered through this introductory chapter. Each area is explored from two distinct perspectives. First, an introductory narrative sets the scene and explains the context, typically focusing on the key ideas and main thinkers or revisiting seminal writings. The areas explored often borrow from other disciplines or perspectives, and the writing tries to address an important question, explore paradoxes, highlight new insights or review progress to date. Second, the main guest-authored segment of the chapter features new ideas, ways of thinking or perspectives. Readers are strongly encouraged to pursue the additional sources listed in the chapters, which can offer further insight and detail. The seminal works indicated in the introductory narrative are also worth re-visiting.

The chapters in this collection bring together leading authorities on a diverse range of themes that are relevant to managing, leading and directing projects. Topics include benchmarking, lean quality, communicating, assumptions, teams and teamwork, followership, organising for project work, project frameworks, project portfolios and strategic initiatives, strategic alignment, entrepreneurship, putting people first, social processes, rethinking progress, hacker paradigm, community, stewardship and knowledge management.

The volume offers an introduction to a range of brand new and established ideas. It also introduces different perspectives and ways of thinking, as well as a host of new writers, thinkers and scholars from other domains and areas. The main aims of the collection are to reflect on and summarise the state of practice; to propose new extensions and additions to existing practice; to distil new insights and to provide a way of sampling a range of the most promising concepts, approaches, perspectives and styles of writing from leading thinkers and practitioners; and to encourage readers to engage with new communities, ideas, concepts and thought and value systems for the future.

Predicting the Future

Although project management is a newly recognised profession, it deals with a number of significant challenges. We seem to operate in an unprecedented and dynamic environment, rife with change, innovation and turbulence. Moreover, projects, by their very nature, tend to push boundaries, encourage novelty and demand engagement with the uncertain and the unknown. Indeed, projects reflect our organised impulse to constantly amend, shape, improve and define our context. So, if projects result from an insatiate demand for meaningful change, what would the future of project management entail beyond the expectation of doing more with less, only quicker? Furthermore, how can future projects overcome the challenges and come to terms with an increasingly dynamic and digital future?

The idea that *'prediction is very difficult, especially about the future'* is attributed to Niels Bohr.[*] Humans have long sought to become more comfortable with the unknown by gaining a glimpse of the future through prophecy, interpretation, extrapolation, forecasting and occasionally, even resorting to fortune telling, but the future ultimately resists accurate assessments. In some ways, it might be simpler to try to focus on emerging, promising new technologies; however, even that would require envisioning these future technologies in use, their potential impact on how things might be carried out, and how society will engage with and be rearranged, reorganised and restructured around them.

The allure of new technology can prove irresistible. Bernard Marr (2020: 1) asserts that *'[We] have never lived in a time of faster and more transformative technological innovation [as] incredible technologies like artificial intelligence, blockchains, smart robots, self-driving cars, 3D printing and advanced genomics . . . have ushered in a new industrial revolution'*. The combinations of technologies that he invokes appear to be overwhelming, encompassing machine learning, smart devices, big data, smart places, facial recognition, autonomous vehicles, drones, digital platforms, genomics and nanotechnologies. Segars (2018) similarly identifies seven core technologies—pervasive

---

[*] https://quoteinvestigator.com/2013/10/20/no-predict/

computing, wireless mesh networks, biotechnology, 3D printing, machine learning, nanotechnology, and robotics—as the drivers of the new revolution that will alter commerce, health care, learning and the environment, thereby reshaping our world.

There are many additional promising technologies and developments. The Future Today Institute (FTI, 2020) catalogues as many as 400 emerging technological trends across 31 industries that are ready to enter the mainstream and fundamentally disrupt business, geopolitics and everyday life. In contrast, Brown (2020) focuses on the six key digital technologies of artificial intelligence (AI), distributed ledgers and blockchain, the Internet of Things, autonomous machines, virtual and augmented reality, and 5G communication, which are positioned as fundamentally critical to business growth over the coming decade.

The promise of new technology in an increasingly digitalised and connected world is immense. Indeed, Marr (2020) predicts that the conjoining of the new technologies will become the driving force of the next industrial revolution, mirroring the respective roles of steam, electricity and computers in enabling previous revolutions. Schwab (2017) refers to the 'Fourth Industrial Revolution' as the fusing together of the physical, technological and biological worlds that will impact disciplines, economies and industries. Diamandis and Kotler (2020) observe that technology is accelerating far more quickly than anyone could have imagined. Their thesis is that the convergence of so many waves of exponentially accelerated technologies will herald the fundamental transformation of complete industries.

But Is It Really All About Technology?

However, it is not clear that the multiplicity of emerging technologies and their convergence will aggregate into a greater and more prominent positive shift. AI, for example, is projected to transform entire businesses and industries, as well as many human jobs (Brynjolfsson & McAfee, 2014; Kolbjørnsrud et al., 2016; Marr, 2020). New technology often brings about a wishful optimism about increased productivity and the potential for transformation. Research predicts significant changes to the workplace and the position, tasks and roles of individuals in light of advances in AI (see, for example, Susskind & Susskind, 2015; Brynjolfsson & Mitchell, 2017; Frey & Osborne, 2017). Yet, Davenport (2018) counsels caution, noting that AI offers solid, rather than spectacular, business value, given that such technologies are destined to augment, rather than replace, human workers, as smart machines work alongside smart people.

Marcus and Davis (2019) qualify the achievements in the field of AI, noting that they have been limited to relatively closed systems with fixed sets of rules rather than addressing open-ended and ever-changing contexts. Funk (2020) similarly predicts that despite the growing hype, AI will take years to significantly boost economic performance and therefore forecasts a gradual evolution rather than a transformative revolution. Moreover, Gibbons (2019) demonstrates that the more technologically enabled workplaces become, paradoxically, the greater their need for humanising business and emphasising aspects such as community, purpose, connection, empathy, relationships and trust.

Substituting people with technology is not merely an exercise in efficiency and economics (Pfeffer, 2020: 73). Managers utilise their contextual knowledge of organisational history and culture as well as their empathy and ethical reflection in deriving their human judgements

(Kolbjørnsrud et al., 2016), whilst the models and algorithms underpinning big data choices tend to be opaque, unregulated and incontestable—often reinforcing discrimination (O'Neil, 2016). Indeed, Birkinshaw (2020: 26–27) notes that while AI can improve the quality of decisions, it also creates new risks and blind spots, including analysis paralysis, loss of contextual understanding, and loss of differentiation, thereby impacting the value of strategic thinking.

> *Even though many observers think of AI as a potentially liberating force, my analysis suggests it is more likely to serve as a constraint on the actions of executives and the activities of the firm* (Birkinshaw, 2020: 33).

Pfeffer (2020) emphasises the importance of human sustainability and well-being at the very core of organisational performance. This challenges the focus on efficiency of resource utilisation enabled through new technology. Hyman (2018) pushes the point further, maintaining that the common narrative about technological revolution is seriously flawed:

> *But this narrative is wrong. The history of labor shows that technology does not usually drive social change. On the contrary, social change is typically driven by decisions we make about how to organize our world. Only later does technology swoop in, accelerating and consolidating those changes* (Hyman, 2018).

The revised narrative acknowledges that it was not technology that altered the world, but what came before it. The Industrial Revolution, which originated in Northern England in the 19th century, only became possible through a series of social changes, referred to by historians as the *industrious revolution*. The *industrious revolution* sets the scene for and places the Industrial Revolution in its broader historical context (De Vries, 1994; Clark & Van Der Werf, 1998; De Vries, 2008; Allen & Weisdorf, 2011). The wider setting only became possible as independent farmers and tradesman congregated in civil centres, thereby enabling manufacturers to gather them under one roof, divide, supervise them and pay them wages. Anderson maintains that Manchester became the cradle of the Industrial Revolution because it had the distinct advantages of ample free space and relaxed building laws, which made it possible to build factories alongside housing for the workers (2012: 42). Such household-based resource reallocation increased the supply of organised labour and of marketed commodities, as well as the demand for the goods (De Vries, 1994: 249).

> *In the Industrious Revolution, manufacturers gathered workers under one roof, where the work could be divided and supervised. For the first time, home and work were separated. Workers no longer controlled how they worked, and received a wage, not the profits of their efforts* (Hyman, 2015).

The shift from rural workers, including some local craftsmen engaged in cottage industry production, to urban labourers (Hyman, 2015; 2018), offered the precursor and context for the economic acceleration that became possible through the enabling technology of the Industrial Revolution (De Vries, 2008). Indeed, Hyman (2018) asserts that the creation of factory technology was possible only because the social change had already taken hold and people's relationship with work had been transformed. The revolutionary nature of the Industrial Revolution is therefore closely entwined with the antecedent social conditions that both predated and enabled it. In other words, it was not technology which changed the world, but the change in the human and social condition that ultimately enabled the emerging technology to accelerate and enhance development.

Looking Forward to Post-Industrial Development

It is often said that with the aid of the new emerging technologies we are entering a second machine age. So, given a revised understanding of the previous machine age, what would be at the core of the next revolution?

Hyman (2015) asserts that once again the re-organisation of people and society would underpin the advent of a new technological age. Yet, this time around the move would seem to be in the opposite direction, away from the factories and organised structures, and towards more remote and smaller practice-based settings, and occasionally new forms of home working.

> *In this second revolution, the employee receiving a regular wage or salary has begun to disappear, replaced by independent contractors, consultants, temps, and freelancers. On the one hand, there will be remarkable opportunities for people to create, to produce, in satisfying and profitable new ways. This revolution will decouple manufacturing from the factory, and services from the office. Every small producer can reach the global market. We can return to the home workshop. We can use 3-D printers to produce niche products at small scale* (Hyman, 2015).

Hyman (2015) maintains that it is not the technologies that merit attention, even though they will further reinforce an industrious revolution, but the people—the emerging social dislocation and the resulting impacts on their lives. Hyman (2018) reframes the social rearrangement and the move out of factories, which has been in train for around 50 years, as a *second industrious revolution*, underpinning and enabling the creation of the gig economy and the emergence of the service economy. As an aside, instability in the wake of the recent Covid-19 pandemic draws attention to the social vulnerability accompanying the glut of flexible, temporary and freelance jobs and the need for state intervention to secure social well-being when the economy and the opportunities for work decline suddenly or disappear altogether.

Hyman's reframing chimes with the notion of a *post-industrial society* (Bell 1967; 1973; 1976), reflecting a shift from an economy dominated by manufacturing towards a society in which the service sector generates more wealth and prosperity than does manufacturing. The sociological shift implies changes in norms, values and structures of society and its individual members. The shift away from manufacturing may necessitate outsourcing of some activities and the inevitable development of global links and supply chains. Given the reduced need for physical proximity to the manufacturing plant, citizens can begin to disperse, whilst the availability of communication technology and digital collaboration platforms allows increased distancing from co-workers as well as outsourced suppliers.

Post-industrial society benefits from the development of dispersed and flexible manufacturing and creativity away from the metropolis and traditional manufacturing centres. As a result, society increasingly cultivates a growing cadre of individual practitioners, small practices and networks of connected professionals operating in local and distributed settings. Authors such as Bosworth (2010) draw attention to the 'commercial counterurbanisation'—the growth of rural business migrating away from urban centres as rural communities are stimulated by inward migration. Decoupling from the physical industrial workplace also facilitates the emergence and development of a *creative class* composed of scientists, engineers, knowledge workers, intellectuals and artists enabling the establishment of a flourishing creative economy (Florida 2002; 2006; 2019; Rindermann & Thompson, 2011) or a gig economy featuring independent contractors and consultants (Friedman, 2014; De Stefano, 2016; Prassl, 2018).

In a similar vein, Anderson (2012) identifies the development of a burgeoning maker economy, fuelled by widely available new technologies that have become accessible to craftsmen and enthusiasts. The *maker movement* liberates innovation and enables entrepreneurship as makers can act as producers, increasing entrepreneurship rates, catalysing advanced manufacturing, and spurring economic development (Browder et al., 2019: 459). Anderson pinpoints a distinct shift as entrepreneurs decoupling themselves from established manufacturing centres discover new ways to create, invent and collaborate whilst minimising the requirement for expertise, equipment and the prohibitive cost of large-scale manufacturing (2012: 17).

The shift to digital making enables the maker economy to relocate small-scale manufacturing and start-ups to lesser urban centres and gentrified local communities, thereby encouraging new forms of balancing of living and working (Wolf-Powers et al., 2017; Doussard et al., 2018; Smith, 2020). Makers often congregate in maker spaces, workspaces where likeminded people, typically with complementary skills, get together to make things (Hatch, 2013; Davies, 2017). The resulting impacts emphasise the creation of new pockets of excellence, the democratisation of doing and making, and the resulting development of regional and national networks of capable makers and doers.

Post-industrial society embodies a stage in a society's development that extends beyond manufacturing, when knowledge becomes a significant and highly valued form of capital. Indeed, Lindgren (2012) foresees a transition from an industry and service economy towards a thought-driven economy where efficient production plants are replaced by thought cells and thought productivity as the new generators of wealth. In the foreword to the second edition of his book, *The Coming of the Post-Industrial Society*, Bell (1999) identifies fundamental changes to the nature of work that typify the post-industrial society (which are slightly paraphrased, relabelled and refreshed):

- **Focus.** Shift from manufacturing and the production of goods to the provision of services.
- **Occupation.** Blue collar work is replaced with professional and technical employment, as skills become valued.
- **Position.** Property and education are valued above privilege, enabling social mobility.
- **Capital.** Beyond financial capital; greater interest in human capital and the emergence of social capital, connections and social networks.
- **Technology.** Use of intellectual technology to support and enable intelligent decision-making.
- **Infrastructure.** While the industrial society was reliant on transportation, post-industrial society needs effective communication infrastructure.
- **Value.** A shift from a labour theory of value (emphasising labour-saving activities) to knowledge-intensive activity, where knowledge creates value, and provides the source for both innovation and growth, and may even extend and allow for the economics of increasing returns.

The idea of a post-industrial society represents an opening of society utilising scientific and technological advances to establish the conditions for reducing and eliminating the long-established class inequality (see, for example, Touraine, 1971), enabling creativity and the creation of a skilled population and sharing prosperity. Detaching occupation from the location of the work, or the factory, will ultimately enable the re-emergence of independent craftsmen and the development of small local and regional-based practices. The appearance of sophisticated technology platforms distributes the location further afield, ultimately allowing global competition, cooperation and collaboration across a range of traditional boundaries.

Technology alone is devoid of the power to transform, as it must be closely entwined to changes and advances in the society that may utilise it and benefit from its new potential. In a post-industrial society the old models of management and work organisation become obsolete. Indeed, Hamel (2007: 254) concludes that after decades of operating as a post-industrial society, we are on the verge of shifting into a *post-managerial*, or perhaps even, a *post-organisational* society, as management work is distributed out to those on the periphery. How might such post-industrial trends translate to the context of project management? Arup (2017), in association with University College London (UCL) and the Association for Project Management (APM), identifies a set of seven trends and challenges that will have a direct bearing on the future of project management, encompassing:

- Globalisation and virtual teams, operating across regional borders and time zones
- Open innovation culture, using external complementary knowledge to generate products and ideas
- Diversity of workforce, making people of all ages, skills and cultures available
- Gig economy, connecting businesses to new freelancers, independent consultants and service providers
- Changing corporate culture, requiring new leadership styles, flatter hierarchies and more flexible working arrangements
- Automation and human–machine collaboration, offering new possibilities for collaboration, creativity and productivity in the workplace
- Digital (construction) technologies, offering the potential to address the growing scale and complexity of projects

The new trends offer a range of fresh opportunities in a post-industrial setting. The first four, or even five, trends relate to the diversification and opening of markets and the economy, as befitting a post-industrial, or even a post-organisational, society experiencing significant social transformation. The last three enable and facilitate new ways of working, new mindsets and novel technologies, thus empowering project managers to make intelligent decisions, experiment and work in new ways and attempt ever more demanding endeavours. Together they enable projects to continue to push the boundaries and deliver novelty through deployment at an ever-increasing pace and scale.

The Emergence of the Project Society

Organising for the new realities of projects requires fundamentally new ways of thinking, rationalising, organising and operating. From business as usual, to disruption, to the new normal, tools and techniques on their own offer an insufficient basis for explaining or enabling current challenges, future trends or the potential and promise of project management. Projects act as the economic engines of our times, requiring a rethinking of their wider role and impact (Nieto-Rodrigues, 2019). According to the Project Management Institute (PMI, 2020) we are shifting into a project economy, one where business is increasingly utilising projects to handle work and solve problems:

> In many ways, **the organization is its projects**—led by a variety of titles, executed through a variety of approaches, and focused unwaveringly on delivering financial and societal value. This is what we call The Project Economy (PMI, 2020: 1).

The Industrial Revolution and the industrious revolution displayed strong underpinning economic activity and driving rationale. In a post-industrial society, ambitious new projects drive the change and innovation appetite for society at large. The first out of the four chapters comprising the 7th edition of the *APM Body of Knowledge* (2019) is written primarily for those leaders within organisations who have decisions to make about the role of projects, programmes and portfolios. Accordingly, the main focus of that first quarter of the body of knowledge for the profession is on the available options and the strategic decisions required to underpin and enable beneficial organisational change:

> *Organisations operate in a dynamic context, full of uncertainty, novelty and turbulence. Projects, programmes and portfolios are introduced in order to enhance performance, bring about change and enable organisations to adapt, improve and grow. Project-work therefore represents intentional investment in development, enhancement and improvement* (APM, 2019: 3).

Conceivably, the same can also be said about society at large, especially in light of the required multitude of responses to the Covid-19 pandemic, all presenting as urgent project interventions. The shifts and challenges in a post-industrial society identified by Bell (1999) are often addressed through projects; meanwhile, many of the new occupations that are emerging emphasise project work, and the resulting investment in change is also structured and managed through projects (APM, 2019).

> *The projectification of business and working life is ongoing and strong. The movement goes beyond traditional project-oriented sectors such as construction, consultancy, media and entertainment. Project thinking is spreading to most parts of society, including industrial enterprises, governmental organizations, educational institutions, and volunteer groups. Not only do people relate to project organizing in their working lives, but they even think and speak of their daily lives in project terms* (Lundin et al., 2015: ix).

The term *project society* has been used to refer to specific changes in the organisation of work and business activity required to transition from the industrial society, especially as the boundary and location of activities change (Lundin et al., 2015), or to the more fundamental form, activity and unit—the project—as the key to making sense of and engaging with the surrounding world (Jensen, 2012).

Perhaps a more significant use of the link to society comes from the work of social scientists, contending that risk had become a dominant feature of society that has replaced wealth production as the means of measuring decisions (Beck, 1992). Risk society recognises that a new system of articulations surrounding risk has emerged in multiple domains. Moreover, in Beck's critical formulation, contemporary society is dominated by technical risk and its reflexive consideration. In modern society, risk leads to political conflicts that are no longer focused on the distribution of wealth, converging instead on the distribution of risk. The notion of a risk society is recognised as one of the most influential concepts of social analysis in the late 20th century, recasting and shaping public debates in risk and ecological politics. Giddens positions *risk society* as a society increasingly preoccupied with the future, which generates the notion of risk (Giddens & Pierson, 1998; Giddens, 1999). Seismic shifts in the relationships between the social and the natural necessitate refreshed ways of reconceiving society and constructing a new narrative (Mythen, 2004).

> *A new kind of capitalism, a new kind of global order, a new kind of politics and law, a new kind of society and personal life are in the making which both separately and in context are clearly*

distinct from earlier phases of social evolution. Consequently, a paradigm shift in both the social sciences and in politics is required (Beck, 2000: 81).

The power of the re-conceptualisation established by Beck and Giddens lies in offering an alternative sociological imagination for investigating the dynamics of contemporary society and describing the emergence of a new ethos: the development of a collective identity and the formation of communities united by increasing vulnerabilities, or relationships, to the main phenomena being investigated (Ekberg, 2007: 343). Ekberg articulates six unique parameters of the risk society:

1. The omnipresence of risk and the emergence of a collective risk consciousness
2. The emergence of a new understanding of risk
3. The proliferation of contested, conflicting or contradictory risk definitions, which create obstacles to effective risk communication
4. The emergence of reflexivity as an individual and institutional response to risk issues and risk events
5. The inverse relationship between risk and trust, accounting for why the public has lost trust in traditional gatekeepers
6. The politics of risk (p. 344)

Conceivably, the same approach and treatment could also be applied to projects and by implication to the manner in which society organises for, around and in response to projects. The majority of the parameters could easily be converted to account for project discourse and consider contemporary challenges and interpretations (cf. Dalcher, 2016). Projects and initiatives increasingly feature in many strands of discourse around progress and improvement and in a diversity of domains and endeavours, reflecting a range of social activities, capabilities, practices and experiences. Indeed, the social production of wealth and progress is closely related to the social production of projects as instruments for achievement.

If the notion of a risk society refers to the way that a modern society preoccupied with the future organises in response to risk, perhaps it is time to re-arrange our thinking around opportunity and innovation as the drivers of progress. Such a reorganisation can begin to address the role of projects, as well as programmes, portfolios, strategic initiatives and other endeavours, as the drivers of development and change.

A much-needed reorganisation can also play an important part in recognising the duality of using the ubiquitous notion of projects as both instruments of exploration, especially in new, uncertain and turbulent contexts, as well as the chief means of exploiting, consolidating and delivering growth in better understood settings. The duality distinguishes projects as instruments for experimenting, buying information and engaging with the unknown, from projects as a way to harness existing and understood conditions. Organised portfolios of projects can allow a balancing between the different types of projects driven by organisational appetite, immediate needs, changing circumstances and situational conditions.

Projects are able to progress the discourse around development. Beck contends that the concept of risk refers to the practices and methods by which the future consequences of institutional and individual decisions are controlled in the present. Projects offer the counter position and the technical and organisational domain whereby individual and institutional decisions in the present manufacture the conditions that constrain, define and realise ambition in the future. The intensifying need for a longer-term perspective and the inclusion of considerations regarding use, value and benefits offer an alternative frame for considering the extended implications of proposed interventions in terms of deployment, governance and future use. In this fashion, projects provide the discipline to develop the blueprint for the future, whilst increasingly also encouraging working backwards from that future to establish the states that lead there from the present and fostering a growing sense of stewardship and responsibility for impacts and outcomes. This informed perspective could therefore underpin the notion of a project society operating within a project economy to empower and enable individuals to act as independent and distributed project agents, workers and practitioners collaborating and competing using powerful new technologies in a new modern context in order to conquer new boundaries and constraints, deliver novel undertakings and drive fresh achievements.

The Challenge of Now and the Person of Tomorrow

Rethinking and repositioning are always demanding, especially in volatile and turbulent times as we seek new ways of engaging, working, and collaborating. The application of new technologies, tools and techniques only offers partial gains as we endeavour to make sense of a rapidly transforming environment and develop fundamentally novel ways of organising and thriving in a precipitously changing and highly demanding setting. Ultimately, many challenges still remain as we seek to make sense of a transitioning and fluctuating context.

In 1969, US psychologist Carl Rogers (1980) surveyed a rapidly changing landscape and formulated the idea of the *world of tomorrow* to capture the dramatic shift to a transformed new world. Rogers foresaw challenges, as well as opportunities, and therefore encouraged a new focus on the *person of tomorrow*, who would be expected to inhabit that world. The person of tomorrow could therefore be expected to grow through development and therapy to transcend the vagaries of a turbulent world and grasp the promise of the future that arises.

Alvin Toffler (1970) similarly contends that society is undergoing an enormous structural change which overpowers people. Toffler's book, *Future Shock*, released in 1970, has become a perennial best seller, with over six million copies sold and multiple translations into other languages. The notion of *future shock*, which can be broadly defined as 'too much change in too short a period of time', overwhelms people, resulting in shattering stress and disorientation. Toffler contends that the majority of social problems are symptoms of future shock, as society struggles to adjust to rapid post-industrialisation. Future shock erases known certainties and familiar aspects, replacing them with unprecedented new conditions, where past history becomes questionable and past habits and approaches no longer apply. Perhaps some of the events witnessed in the aftermath of the Covid 19 pandemic are a new form of *present shock*, an accelerated period of rapid shifts and changes resulting from a perceived immediate threat that shakes and transforms society with immediate effect, destabilising known certainties and established methods and diminishing the safety of the known or the familiar.

Extending on Rogers's work, O'Hara and Leicester frame humanity's present and future predicament in terms of three emergencies—emergent trends that are gathering pace and threaten to overwhelm society (2019: 13):

- **The real emergency.** The incipient breakdown of systems we used to take for granted, encompassing a growing range of familiar challenges including democratic governance, decision-making, the economy, ecological balance, poverty, inequality, social care,

healthcare, education, sustainability, clean water, replacing fossil fuels, climate change, and the list goes on . . .
- **Conceptual emergency.** The pervading sense of cognitive dissonance experienced when the explanations and the core concepts we have relied upon to make sense of the world no longer seem be fit for purpose, adequate or sufficient.
- **Existential emergency.** The cumulative effects of the real and conceptual emergencies as they manifest themselves at the level of the human being, individually and collectively. As a result, shared narratives and patterns of life that hold communities and societies together fray and unravel, until '. . . *societies become incoherent and fragmented, we experience "culture wars, a loosening of cultural solidarity and a loss of faith in shared institutions'* (Ibid.).

Toffler (1996: *iix*) maintains that not since the dawn of the Industrial Revolution have managers had more to learn, and unlearn, whilst also being subjected to a profusion of diverse and confusing advice. Toffler re-invokes the term *de-massification* (first used by Toffler, 1980) to recognise an accelerating trend beyond mass production, mass distribution, mass media and socioeconomic homogeneity. Toffler considers organised agriculture as forming the first wave, concerned with converting the earth's resources into wealth, followed by the wave of industrialisation characterised by mass production, drive for larger markets and the creation of bureaucratic organisations. The incoming de-massification is powered by knowledge, generating waves of economic, technical and social change that will force businesses to challenge norms, conventions and received wisdoms ranging from vertical integration to economies of scale, hierarchies and command and control models, as a new paradigm fit for a new age emerges (1996: *ix*).

Crises and emergencies provide an excellent motivation for overhauling and rearranging mindsets and perspectives and preparing to engage with new thinking. The sense of emergency—real, conceptual and existential—often arises where paradigms fray and shatter, and thought systems, philosophies and orthodoxies that have outlived their usefulness, are challenged by new alternatives, fit for new times and changing conditions. Many commentators maintain that our culture, society and economy are in flux.

> *Every few hundred years in Western history there occurs a sharp transformation. We cross what in an earlier book I called a 'divide'. Within a few short decades, society rearranges itself—its world view; its basic values; its social and political structure; its arts; its key institutions . . . We are currently living in such a transformation. It is creating the Post-capitalist society* (Drucker, 1993: 1).

Drucker (2002: 165) foresees the emergence of the *Next Society*, which will be characterised by the currency and economy of knowledge, resulting in a society that is:

- Borderless, because knowledge travels more effortlessly than money
- Upwardly mobile, so that opportunities are available to everyone
- Open to failure, as well as success, as anyone can acquire the means of production, especially the knowledge, but not everyone can win

Drucker (2001: 245) positions innovation and entrepreneurship at the very core of the *Next Society*, especially given that theories, values and artefacts of the human mind age and rigidify until they become 'afflictions'. Drucker (Ibid.) maintains that innovation and entrepreneurship are needed to keep any society, economy, industry, public service or business flexible and self-renewing. The value of innovation and entrepreneurship arise from their pragmatic, tentative and opportunistic nature. Harvesting such opportunities requires purpose, but with direction, and under control. Drucker therefore calls for an entrepreneurial society, one in which innovation and entrepreneurship are recognised as normal, steady and continual, which he predicts will prove a major turning point in history.

Just as management has become the specific organ of all contemporary institutions, and the integrating organ of our society of organizations, so innovation and entrepreneurship have to become an integral life sustaining activity in our organizations, our economy, our society (Drucker, 2001: 245).

The coming of the entrepreneurial society introduces a number of fundamental challenges that Drucker identifies:

Planning does not work. Planning is incompatible with an entrepreneurial society or economy (p. 246). Whilst Drucker concedes that innovation needs to be purposeful and entrepreneurship has to be managed, he maintains that innovation, almost by definition, has to be decentralised, ad hoc, autonomous, specific and microeconomic. He advocates for small, tentative and flexible reactions in response to opportunities that emerge close to the ground and to the unexpected.

Systematic abandonment. Policies and actions become obsolete relatively quickly. Drucker recognises a need for more rapid change and therefore advocates for 'sunset laws' that allow for governmental agencies and public laws to lapse after certain periods unless they are specifically re-enacted.

Challenge for individuals. In order to exploit new opportunities, there is a constant need for continual learning and relearning. Education for a particular task or engagement is too limiting. There is therefore a need for individuals to take responsibility for and organise their own learning and continuous development. This challenges societal assumptions about schooling and learning (p. 248).

The constant need for refresh, and the response to emerging opportunities as the new entrepreneurial, societal and economic mantra, mandate a growing interest in projects as instruments for experimentation, discovery and exploration. It implies embedding projects within all aspects of society and recognising the needs and values of communities in order to test, discover and benefit from technological and knowledge-induced opportunities. By utilising technology and knowledge as the infrastructure that enables networks and relationships to develop beyond the boundary of physical proximity, it becomes possible to reimagine what can be achieved and to benefit from the global abundance and diversity of skills, capabilities, connections and innovation that will define the person of tomorrow and empower the emergence of the next society.

The Future Is Here Already

Recognising the potential for a momentous shift leads to a slew of critically important questions: What shape will this new emerging society assume? If we are free to release ourselves from industrial structures, manufacturing plants and cities, what other forms of organisation will emerge? How will we work? Which of our models will survive? What values will become essential in a reorganised world? What do we need to do in order to liberate future makers, reinvigorate creativity and foster responsible and sustainable entrepreneurship and innovation?

How do we prepare and develop the *person of tomorrow*? What knowledge, skills and capabilities will they require? And, of course, what will be the implication for project work?

The challenges expressed through the set of questions are clearly enormous, yet the answers may lie in utilising modestly small hacks and proven local innovation rather than hoping for big, bold and beautiful new transformational solutions. New innovations do not emerge as fully formed solutions. The industrious revolution did not materialise overnight. Progress transpires one modest step at a time, as innovation is established through iterative experimentation and development at a localised level. Walking in the proverbial fog, characterised by turbulence and constant change, entails a series of little, tentative steps required to make sense of the unfamiliar terrain and establish a strategy for determining a sensible way forward. It is particularly telling that during the recent Covid-19 global pandemic, what has worked effectively across most of the world seems to be a series of simple, straightforward and well-understood techniques for maintaining hygiene, minimising contact and establishing separation: Hand washing, using sanitisers and gels, cleaning and sterilising common areas, wearing protective equipment, facial coverings, physical distancing, shielding the vulnerable, isolation, lockdowns, and quarantines all date back across a multitude of bygone epidemics (see, for example, Starr, 2006; Wallis, 2006; Gawande, 2007; Smith, 2007; Fleming, 2020; Spitale, 2020; Strasser & Schlich, 2020). Continuous and appropriate application of proven good practice can build up momentum and make a significant difference over time, albeit in increasingly more unfamiliar and demanding settings. Similar patterns can be established at local, global and universal levels to create significant impacts, even if magic solutions cannot be found.

> *If the time comes when our culture tired of endless homicidal feuds, despaired of the use of force and war as a means of bringing peace, becomes discontent with the half-lives its members are living, only then will our culture seriously look for alternatives. And when they do they will not find a void... They will realize that there are ways, already tried out on a small scale, of enhancing learning, of moving towards new values, of raising consciousness to new levels* (Rogers, 1980: 205).

Many good solutions, as noted by Rogers, relate to re-visiting culture, values, learning, reflection and reflexivity. Poole (2016) maintains that countless old ideas that were mocked or ignored for centuries are storming back to the cutting edge of research and practice, increasingly informing the way we lead our lives and offering answers to the problems of the present. Research then can benefit from exploring long-neglected thinkers and re-visiting different domains and contexts in search of new, yet partly established potential answers. Indeed, Victor Hugo reasoned that *'an invasion of armies can be resisted, but not an idea whose time has come'*.

Rethinking implies thinking about an idea again, changing how one thinks about something, reassessing the viability of a notion or option, or repositioning an idea. Poole begins his discourse with the story of the *hummingbirds*, a fleet of electric taxis plying their trade across the streets of London for just over a decade at the end of nineteenth century, offering a cleaner, cheaper and smaller alternative transport technology (2016: 1). The commissioner of the Metropolitan Police was a strong supporter and approved the potential of the development to solve the increasing traffic problems of London. Similar services existed in Paris, Berlin and New York, but they all rapidly disappeared as horse-drawn cab drivers complained about the competition; large oil reserves were discovered, resulting in a substantial tumble in petroleum prices; and mass manufacturing of gasoline-powered cars offered significantly cheaper alternative technology. The idea of electric cars has resurfaced in recent times with Elon Musk along with numerous established car manufacturers and many other start-ups and innovators competing to re-position it as a viable and responsible alternative.

The history of civilisation holds a great potential, particularly in terms of experiments and alternative thinking patterns. Human culture and society could be richly informed by narratives of past debates, intellectual struggles and practical competitions offering a fertile ground for recycled and repurposed fresh ideas and approaches. Moreover, combining pre-existing concepts can lead to the composition of novel ideas and be particularly effective in identifying and developing brand new opportunities (Young, 2003; Atkinson, 2014). The potential for underpinning a forthcoming revolution, therefore, lies not in retransforming all thought patterns, but in intelligently offering a constellation of pragmatic and feasible approaches, techniques and tools developed and rehearsed through extensive practice and experience that are ready to be re-considered, embraced and championed.

So, where do we find the seeds for meaningful and sustainable innovations that can be applied in order to rethink and refresh the future of project work? The authors selected to feature in this volume rise to the challenge and prepare the groundwork by bringing together findings and results from a range of disciplines and perspectives, emphasising practical insights, working approaches and deeper consideration of people, teams and societal concerns in the context of projects.

Advances in Project Management

The majority of the individual chapters were selected from the best articles that have been featured in the 'Advances in Project Management' series of articles published in the *PM World Journal*. Many have been significantly expanded and updated for the book. The main purpose of the series is to make the ideas and principles of the key knowledge and skills areas required to effectively manage projects more accessible. 'Advances in Project Management' was introduced in order to improve understanding and project capability further up the organisation, amongst strategy and senior decision makers and amongst professional project and programme managers. Our ambition has always been to provide project sponsors, project management leaders, practitioners, scholars and researchers with thought-provoking, cutting-edge information that combines conceptual insights with interdisciplinary rigour and practical relevance, thus offering new insights and deeper understanding of key areas and approaches.

In order to identify the potential authors, a wide range of books and resources have been consulted. Contributions were selected on the basis of their individual merit, usefulness and applicability. The chapters offered here feature many leading practitioners, researchers and expert leaders and highlight concepts, ideas and tools that will be of benefit to practicing project and change managers. Indeed, many of the individual authors in this volume may be pushing the boundaries of knowledge and practice and are radically involved in facilitating the new future of project thinking and project management practice.

To this end, the individual chapters aim to:

1. Share and embrace new ways of thinking around the future and the challenges faced by project and programme managers.
2. Identify and focus on *key* aspects of project, programme and portfolio management.
3. Offer practical case examples of how novel applications have been tackled in a variety of industries.

4. Provide access to appropriate new models in these areas as they emerge from either academic research or practical application.

In other words, the book endeavours to provide those people and organisations who are involved with the development in project management with the kind of structured information that will inform their thinking, their practice and improve their decisions. Featured contributions have not been limited to a particular community, country or association to ensure that a wide variety of insights, angles and perspectives into the future of project management work are covered.

Guiding Principles for Future Leading

Project management is practiced in many different sectors and environments. Such a mixture of perspectives allows for the emergence of alternative and novel ideas and ways of thinking. Many of the new ideas were developed in different sectors, and it is important to find a shared platform to present and highlight the impacts of such innovations and recognise their potential for reinvigorating current thinking and engendering new insights. This publication offers such a shared environment, which will be of use to practitioners regardless of where they are based and whatever the geography of the projects that they are running.

- The book offers a rich variety of ideas, lessons and insights that are ready to be shared and adopted. The topics emphasise key areas required to improve the delivery of projects and programmes in a wide range of environments and contexts. The experts and authors come from a variety of backgrounds and bring organisational, psychological, sociological, or other influences they can share. Others are scientists, engineers, architects, entrepreneurs and experts in coaching, strategy, innovation, leadership, quality, human behaviour, organisational dynamics, systems thinking, complexity and transformational change. The value of the publication is in integrating the multitude of insights and perspectives and offering the opportunity to discuss, engage and adapt the ideas through an intellectual diversity of lenses and viewpoints.
- There are many different recipes to prepare for a more turbulent and unpredictable future and to consider and address the challenges highlighted earlier. The individual contributions in the book are divided by core areas, but it might be useful to position and underline how they relate to wider principles concerned with the future of work and organisations. Østergaard (2018) codifies five guiding principles for navigating and leading organisations operating within modern contexts and entrepreneurial societies in a sustainable and responsible fashion (his key principles are reproduced in bold, with summarised and expanded contextual explanations below):
  1. **People first.** People orientation in a human-to-human context—out of recognition that interactions, decisions and transactions hinge around people and relationships, thereby encouraging deeper focus on self, employees, customers, community, society.
  2. **Purpose, meaning, sensemaking and value creation.** Purpose enables us to focus our engagement and understand the core identity of both individuals and organisations; meaningfulness and sensemaking in tasks are powerful motivators for engagement, allowing individuals to create meaningful value and contribute to their context.

3. **Continuous innovation and experimentation.** Experimentation, testing and adaptation are essential for making sense of and flourishing in a fast-changing world; this calls for curiosity, creativity, innovation, strategic initiatives, acceptance of mistakes and continuous experimentation applied in relation to self, employees, organisation, business and customers.

4. **An insatiable drive for results.** Making a difference via a resilient drive for tangible results through products, processes and projects and for intangible ones related to relationships, people and teams, thus balancing financial, social, production and global concerns.

5. **Everybody has the opportunity to take a lead.** Distributing leadership power to those who have the ability, skills, motivation and desire to lead, especially given the greater prevalence of networked teams and the need to distribute engagement force and decision power.

All of these principles would seem to have a direct impact on the future of project management work, and it might be useful to consider the set of principles as an underlying framework for considering the new trends and challenges in a project-intensive world. The scope and richness of the discussion offered throughout the book can thus be mapped against the five principles to provide an alternative representation of key issues and perspectives and how they match against the five key principles enumerated above. Table 1 provides a preview of many of the main topics and a glimpse of the coverage offered through a principle-driven topical mapping.

A key takeaway from the mapping exercise is the multi-dimensional connections amongst the elements and the networks and webs of influence that work across and beyond the principles. It is encouraging to see the list of topics lining up against the full set of principles. Intriguingly, many of the topics and most of the chapters cut across and address the five guiding principles, offering multidimensional reflection on the essential dimensions related to project work. The ideas on offer throughout the book are not always new, but the insightful re-arrangements and conceptual reorganisations presented by the authors facilitate unique modes of addressing and

Table I.1 Principle-Driven Mapping of Topics and Coverage

Principle	Coverage and Areas
People first	Assumptions, communication, teams, teaming, trust, psychological safety, leadership, followership, stakeholders, human-centred management, multi-stakeholder dialogues, positive organisations
Purpose, meaning, sensemaking and value creation	Assumptions, strategic initiatives, strategic goal alignment, entrepreneurship, effectuation, social organisations, hacker communities, stewardship, knowledge lens, context
Continuous innovation and experimentation	Benchmarking, portfolios, entrepreneurship, effectuation, hacking innovation, hacker paradigm, knowledge management
Drive for results	Benchmarking, supreme performance, lean quality, life cycle, project framework, gates, portfolio success, goal alignment, portfolio stakeholders, decision-making, product stewardship
Leadership	Followership, leadership, teaming, strategic stakeholder management, social process, positive organisations, hackers

building the various elements needed for re-thinking, refreshing and enabling the future of project management.

An increasingly borderless, upwardly mobile and entrepreneurial society requires a revamped and revitalised project perspective that is more dynamic, adaptive, and reflective. *Rethinking Project Management for a Dynamic and Digital World* makes a powerful and original statement equipping project leaders and managers with new approaches and frameworks for an increasingly demanding world, in which the traditional methods, models and mindsets no longer suffice. The authors share experiences from many domains and distil the fundamentals for marshalling a world concerned with people, communities and value, by deploying innovation, rethinking purpose and acting responsibly. The collection thus offers an invaluable new resource for informed managers looking to engage with the latest thinking and research and for researchers seeking to reflect on how the discipline us changing.

Ultimately, the management of projects offers an exciting space for sharing, collaboration and exploration. The ambition, scale and scope of many of the new endeavours and challenges attempted by modern civilisation are breathtaking. But an injection of new insights and approaches, especially in regard to the future of projects and their integration into society and various communities, is desperately needed. Many of our authors will not regard themselves as futurists, but they are able to expertly guide new conversations and offer the new perspectives and mindsets imported from other terrains and cultures which are needed for initiating fundamentally different and meaningful conversations about potential futures. Together we can continue to develop and grow by embracing innovative skills and perspectives and improving the state of practice. We encourage readers who have been inspired or who would like to share their insights and ideas with the wider community to get in touch with the editor (d.dalcher@lancaster.ac.uk). We look forward to continuing the dialogue about enduring success in projects, programmes and portfolios and shaping the future of project thinking and practice in an emerging post-industrial project society.

Darren Dalcher
Lancaster, UK

References

Allen, R. C., and Weisdorf, J. L. (2011). Was there an 'industrious revolution' before the Industrial Revolution? An empirical exercise for England, c. 1300–1830. *The Economic History Review, 64*(3), 715–729.

Anderson, C. (2012). *Makers: The New Industrial Revolution.* London, UK: Random House.

APM (2019). *APM Body of Knowledge.* (7th Ed.). Murray Webster, R., and Dalcher, D. (Eds). Princes Risborough, UK: Association for Project Management.

Arup, (2017). *Future of Project Management.* London, UK: Arup.

Atkinson, I. (2014). *The Creative Problem Solver: 12 Tools to Solve any Business Challenge.* Harlow, UK: Pearson UK.

Beck, U. (1992). *Risk Society: Towards a New Modernity.* London, UK: SAGE Publications.

Beck, U. (2000). The cosmopolitan perspective: Sociology of the second age of modernity. *The British Journal of Sociology, 51*(1), 79–105.

Bell, D. (1967). Notes on the post-industrial society (II). *The Public Interest, 7,* 102.

Bell, D. (1973). *The Coming of Post-Industrial Society: A Venture in Social Forecasting.* New York, NY: Harper Colophon Books.

Bell, D. (1976). The coming of the post-industrial society. *The Educational Forum, 40*(4), 574–579.

Bell, D. (1999). *The Coming of Post-Industrial Society: A Venture in Social Forecasting.* New York, NY: Basic Books.

Birkinshaw, J. (2020). What Is the value of firms in an AI world? In: J. Canal and F. Heukamp (Eds.), *The Future of Management in an AI World,* 23–35. Cham, Switzerland: Palgrave Macmillan.

Bosworth, G. (2010). Commercial counterurbanisation: An emerging force in rural economic development. *Environment and Planning A, 42*(4), 966–981.

Browder, R. E., Aldrich, H. E., and Bradley, S. W. (2019). The emergence of the maker movement: Implications for entrepreneurship research. *Journal of Business Venturing, 34*(3), 459–476.

Brown, S. (2020). *The Innovation Ultimatum: How Six Strategic Technologies Will Reshape Every Business in the 2020s.* Hoboken, NJ: John Wiley & Sons.

Brynjolfsson, E., and McAfee, A. (2014). *The Second Machine Age: Work, Progress, and Prosperity in a Time of Brilliant Technologies.* New York, NY: W. W. Norton & Company.

Brynjolfsson, E., and Mitchell, T. (2017). What can machine learning do? Workforce implications. *Science, 358*(6370), 1530–1534.

Clark, G., and Van Der Werf, Y. (1998). Work in progress? The industrious revolution. *The Journal of Economic History, 58*(3), 830–843.

Dalcher, D. (2016). Rethinking project practice: Emerging insights from a series of books for practitioners. *International Journal of Managing Projects in Business, 9*(4), 798–821.

Davenport, T. H. (2018). *The AI advantage: How to put the artificial intelligence revolution to work.* Cambridge, MA: MIT Press.

Davies, S. R. (2017). *Hackerspaces: Making the Maker Movement.* New York, NY: John Wiley & Sons.

De Stefano, V. M. (2016). The rise of the 'just-in-time workforce': On-demand work, crowd work and labour protection in the 'gig-economy'. *Comparative Labor Law and Policy Journal, 37*(3), 471–504.

De Vries, J. (1994). The Industrial Revolution and the industrious revolution. *Journal of Economic History, 54*(2), 249–270.

De Vries, J. (2008). *The Industrious Revolution.* Cambridge, UK: Cambridge University Press.

Diamandis, P. H., and Kotler, S. (2020). *The Future Is Faster Than You Think: How Converging Technologies Are Transforming Business, Industries, and Our Lives.* New York, NY: Simon & Schuster.

Doussard, M., Schrock, G., Wolf-Powers, L., Eisenburger, M., and Marotta, S. (2018). Manufacturing without the firm: Challenges for the maker movement in three US cities. *Environment and Planning A: Economy and Space, 50*(3), 651–670.

Drucker, P. F. (1993). *Managing in Turbulent Times.* London, UK: Butterworth-Heinemann.

Drucker, P. F. (2001). *The Essential Drucker.* Oxford, UK: Butterworth-Heinemann.

Drucker, P. F. (2002). *Managing in the Next Society.* Oxford, UK: Butterworth-Heinemann.

Ekberg, M. (2007). The parameters of the risk society: A review and exploration. *Current Sociology, 55*(3), 343–366.

Fleming, A. (2020). Keep it clean: The surprising 130-year history of handwashing. *The Guardian.* 18 March. https://www.theguardian.com/world/2020/mar/18/keep-it-clean-the-surprising -130-year-history-of-handwashing

Florida, R. (2002). *The Rise of the Creative Class*. New York, NY: Basic Books.

Florida, R. (2006). The flight of the creative class: The new global competition for talent. *Liberal Education, 92*(3), 22–29.

Florida, R. (2019). *The Rise of the Creative Class Revisited*. New York, NY: Basic Books.

Frey, C. B., and Osborne, M. A. (2017). The future of employment: How susceptible are jobs to computerisation? *Technological Forecasting and Social Change, 114*, 254–280.

Friedman, G. (2014). Workers without employers: Shadow corporations and the rise of the gig economy. *Review of Keynesian Economics, 2*(2), 171–188.

FTI, (2020). *Tech Trends Report*. (13th Annual Ed.). New York, NY: Future Today Institute.

Funk, J. (2020). Expect evolution, not revolution: Despite the hype, artificial intelligence will take years to significantly boost economic productivity. *IEEE Spectrum, 57*(3), 30–35.

Gawande, A. (2007). *Better: A Surgeon's Notes on Performance*. New York, NY: Metropolitan.

Gibbons, P. (2019). *Impact: 21st Century Change Management, Behavioural Science, Digital Transformation and Future of Work*. Boston, MA: Phronesis Media.

Giddens, A., and Pierson, C. (1998). *Conversations with Anthony Giddens: Making Sense of Modernity*. Stanford, CA: Stanford University Press.

Giddens, A. (1999). *Runaway World: How Globalization Is Reshaping our Lives*. London, UK: Profile Books.

Hamel, G. (2007). *The Future of Management*. Boston, MA: Harvard Business Press.

Hatch, M. (2013). *The Maker Movement Manifesto: Rules for Innovation in the New World of Crafters, Hackers, and Tinkerers*. New York, NY: McGraw Hill Professional.

Hyman, L. (2015). The future of work: The second industrious revolution. *Pacific Standard*, August 3. Accessed 13 July, 2020. https://psmag.com/economics/the-future-of-work-the-second-industrious-revolution

Hyman, L. (2018). It's not technology that's disrupting our jobs. *New York Times*, August 18. Accessed 12th July, 2020. https://www.nytimes.com/2018/08/18/opinion/technology/technology-gig-economy.html

Jensen, A. F. (2012). *The Project Society*. Aarhus, DK: Aarhus University Press.

Kolbjørnsrud, V., Amico, R., and Thomas, R. J. (2016). How artificial intelligence will redefine management. *Harvard Business Review, 2*, 1–6.

Lindgren, M. (2012). *21st Century Management: Leadership and Innovation in the Thought Economy*. London, UK: Palgrave Macmillan.

Lundin, R. A., Arvidsson, N., Brady, T., Ekstedt, E., and Midler, C. (2015). *Managing and Working in Project Society*. Cambridge, UK: Cambridge University Press.

Marcus, G., and Davis, E. (2019). *Rebooting AI: Building Artificial Intelligence We Can Trust*. New York, NY: Vintage.

Marr, B. (2020). *Tech Trends in Practice: The 25 Technologies That Are Driving the 4th Industrial Revolution*. Chichester, UK: John Wiley & Sons.

Mythen, G. (2004). *Ulrich Beck: A Critical Introduction to the Risk Society*. London, UK: Pluto Press.

Nieto-Rodriguez. (2019). *Lead Successful Projects*. London, UK: Penguin Business.

O'Hara, M., and Leicester, G. (2019). *Dancing at the Edge*. (2nd Ed.). Axminster, UK: Triarchy Press.

O'Neil, C. (2016). *Weapons of Math Destruction: How Big Data Increases Inequality and Threatens Democracy*. New York, NY: Broadway Books.

Østergaard, E. K. (2018). *The Responsive Leader: How to Be a Fantastic Leader in a Constantly Changing World*. London, UK: LID Publishing.

Peppler, K., and Bender, S. (2013). Maker movement spreads innovation one project at a time. *Phi Delta Kappan, 95*(3), 22–27.

Pfeffer, J. (2020). The role of the general manager in the new economy: Can we save people from technology dysfunctions? In: J. Canal and F. Heukamp (Eds.), *The Future of Management in an AI World* (pp. 23–35). Cham, Switzerland: Palgrave Macmillan.

PMI (2020). Ahead of the curve: Forging a future-focused culture. *Pulse of the Profession*. Newton Square, NJ: Project Management Institute.

Poole, S. (2016). *Rethink: the Surprising History of New Ideas*. London, UK: Simon & Schuster.

Prassl, J. (2018). *Humans as a Service: The Promise and Perils of Work in the Gig Economy*. Oxford, UK: Oxford University Press.

Rindermann, H., and Thompson, J. (2011). Cognitive capitalism: The effect of cognitive ability on wealth, as mediated through scientific achievement and economic freedom. *Psychological Science, 22*(6), 754–763.

Rogers, C. R. (1980). The world of tomorrow, and the person of tomorrow. In: C. R. Rogers (Ed.), *A Way of Being*, 339–356. New York, NY: Houghton Mifflin.

Schwab, K. (2007). *The Fourth Industrial Revolution*. New York, NY: Currency.

Segars, A. H. (2018). Seven technologies remaking the world. *MIT Sloan Management Review, 58*, 1–19.

Smith, R. (2007). Social measures may control pandemic flu better than drugs and vaccines. *British Medical Journal, 334*(7608): 1341.

Smith, T. S. (2020). 'Stand back and watch us': Post-capitalist practices in the maker movement. *Environment and Planning A: Economy and Space, 52*(3), 593–610.

Spitale, G. (2020). COVID-19 and the ethics of quarantine: A lesson from the Eyam plague. *Medicine, Health Care, and Philosophy, 23*(4), 1–7.

Starr, I. (2006). Influenza in 1918: Recollections of the epidemic in Philadelphia. *Annals of Internal Medicine, 145*(2), 138–140.

Strasser, B. J., and Schlich, T. (2020). A history of the medical mask and the rise of throwaway culture. *The Lancet, 396*(10243), 19–20.

Susskind, R. E., and Susskind, D. (2015). *The Future of the Professions: How Technology Will Transform the Work of Human Experts*. Oxford, USA: Oxford University Press.

Toffler, A. (1970). *Future Shock*. New York, NY: Bantam Books.

Toffler, A. (1980). *The Third Wave*. New York, NY: William Morrow Press.

Toffler, A. (1996). Foreword. In: R. Gibson (Ed.). *Rethinking the Future: Rethinking Business, Principles, Competition, Control & Complexity, Leadership, Markets and the World*. London, UK: Nicholas Brealey.

Touraine, A. (1971). *The Post-Industrial Society: Tomorrow's Social History: Classes, Conflicts and Culture in the Programmed Society, 6813*. New York, NY: Random House.

Wallis, P. (2006). A dreadful heritage: Interpreting epidemic disease at Eyam, 1666–2000. *History Workshop Journal, 61*(1), 31–56.

Wolf-Powers, L., Doussard, M., Schrock, G., Heying, C., Eisenburger, M., and Marotta, S. (2017). The maker movement and urban economic development. *Journal of the American Planning Association, 83*(4), 365–376.

Young, J. W. (2003). *A Technique for Producing Ideas*. New York, NY: McGraw-Hill.

Chapter 1

Quality

The Quest for Supreme Performance: Benchmarking to Save Lives

Darren Dalcher

According to the *Oxford English Dictionary,* the verb *benchmark* implies *'evaluating something by comparison with a standard'*. In practice, it often entails a direct assessment of business processes, procedures and performance metrics and outcomes against those applied by industry or sector leaders in order to understand why market leaders are successful, or against other organisations in a similar position or of a similar size and expertise, in order to provide a reading about the current performance level of the organisation.

Benchmarks emerge out of the pursuit of 'best practice' implying an intention to copy or replicate what is considered to be superior performance. Benchmarks provide a disciplined approach and a reference point for determining one's current position from which measurements could be made or a basic standard and reference point against which others could be compared.

Reference points have long been used to determine position or encourage performance improvement. Land surveyors might be familiar with the idea of a benchmark, a distinctive mark made on a wall, rock or building which serves as a reference point in determining the current position and altitude in topographical surveys and tidal observations (Bogan & English, 1994: 3). Reference points are used elsewhere: Following the mass production and standardisation of rifles and cartridges in the mid-1800s, the marksman became the uncertain variable. Gun factories would therefore fix the rifle in a bench, making it possible to fire the rifle multiple times and determine the spread, introducing the idea of benchmarking weapons as used in both the gun factory and the ammunition factory to find the best combination of rifle and ammunition, without necessarily accounting for the foibles of the rifleman.

McGrath and Bates suggest that Fredrick Taylor used the concept of a benchmark at the beginning of the 20th century to identify excellent performers in the factory by putting a chalk mark on their benches (2017: 192). Taylor had utilised time and motion studies to identify good performers (Dalcher, 2017: 3). The mark on the bench could thus identify staff whose output or working practices should merit emulating, and McGrath and Bates (2017) propose that this rather crude method has evolved into rather more sophisticated benchmarking tools and procedures.

In the 1970s benchmarking became a widely accepted term. However, companies such as Xerox® applied it in a narrow way that focused primarily on comparisons with one's main competition to assess performance against the best in class, invoking the practice of competitive benchmarking (Camp, 1989). Competitive benchmarking entails comparison of company standards with those of leading rivals (Hindle, 2008: 15).

Yet, benchmarking is not a panacea, and it needs to be applied with judicious intellect and some degree of caution:

> All too often benchmarking is carried out by semi committed managers, without the use of predetermined measures, and without the proper tools for analysis and presentation. Unquestionably, many benchmarking projects end in dismay, a futile exercise often justifiably portrayed by onlookers as industrial tourism, comparing apples with pears. Even when performed in a structured way, the 'they're different from us syndrome' prevents benchmarking from leading for changes for the better. Furthermore, competitive sensitivity can stifle the free flow of information, even within an organization (ten Have et al., 2003: p. 24).

Nonetheless, benchmarking has been utilised for a range of diverse and varied purposes, including (Bogan & English, 1994):

- Setting and refining strategy
- Reengineering work processes and business systems
- Continuous improvement of work processes and business systems
- Strategic planning and goal setting
- Problem solving
- Education and idea enrichment
- Market performance comparisons and evaluations
- Catalyst for change
- A utilitarian tool

The Power and Potential Impact of Benchmarking

For an early example of benchmarking, Bogan and English note that in the 1800s British textile mills were best in class. American mills, in contrast, were relatively immature. New England industrialist Francis Cabot Lowell wanted to improve and upgrade local capability and modernise business technology. International trade was severely impacted by the 1807 embargo, leading Lowell to the inevitable conclusion that the local manufacturing basis in the US needed to be strengthened. In June 1810 he embarked on a two-year visit to Scotland and England, paying particular attention to the spinning and weaving technologies that he was able to observe by travelling around Scotland and Lancashire.

> Lowell travelled to England where he studied the manufacturing techniques and industrial design of the best British mill factories. He saw that the British plants had much more sophisticated equipment but the British plant layouts did not effectively utilize labor. In short there was room for improvement (Ibid.: 1).

Upon his return to the US, Francis Lowell proceeded to build his factory by replicating the use of technology that he observed in the British mills. However, it was designed to be significantly less labour intensive than the British facilities. In 1814 he established the Boston Manufacturing

Company and built its first mill beside the Charles River in Waltham, Massachusetts. The plant housed an integrated set of technologies that could deal with the full life cycle of converting the raw cotton to the finished product in one place. Its success was immediate and enormous, but it rapidly depleted the waterpower of the Charles River. To expand the enterprise, the plant was moved north to the banks of the more powerful Merrimack River. Following Lowell's death, this new mill centre became known as Lowell, Massachusetts. By 1840, this new industrial city had become the second largest city in America and was recognised as the largest manufacturing centre in the whole country.

The dynamic growth and impact on the wider industry is attributed to Lowell's ability to creatively adapt and further improve practices observed in the world's leading mills. Lowell has been able to identify and copy patterns that were sufficient to transform mills in the US from small facilities to integrated production facilities. By upgrading and strengthening the identified gaps and shortfalls, he was further able to establish industrial manufacturing in the northeast region of the US.

From a Benchmark to Benchmarking for Further Development

Industry has clearly progressed from Taylor's notion of marking a bench with a piece of chalk in order to identify a good performer that can pace others, towards recognition of effective practices that merit emulation and further improvement as exemplified by Lowell.

A key shift is in progressing from simple metrics and measures towards the observation of processes. This is perhaps best represented by the shift from a hand-written benchmark towards benchmarking, a more observational activity concerned not merely with gauging operating statistics, but also with identifying effective practices.

Benchmarking represents a positive, intentional and proactive process preoccupied with the search for improvement and superior performance. The Japanese have a special word *dantotsu*, which means striving to be the 'best of the best'. Being the best of the best incorporates the essence of what benchmarking is really about—a continuous search to become best of the best that is innovatively applied and can lead to a true focus on uncovering developmental insights and gaining and sustaining superiority.

Searching for dantotsu is innovatively applied as new approaches, perspectives and ideas are explored through a fresh pair of eyes. Such benchmarking can open up new possibilities for transformative innovation and the importation of good practices and methods to deliver new superior performance.

In 1912 Henry Ford observed men cutting up meat whilst on a tour of a Chicago slaughterhouse. The carcasses were hanging on hooks mounted on a monorail; after each worker performed his job, they would push the carcass to the next station, allowing the next bit of work to commence. Ford was inspired by the production-line dynamics and was interested to consider its potential application to his line of work.

Less than six months later, the world's first assembly line at the Ford Highland Park Plant started producing magnetos. The idea that would ultimately revolutionise car manufacturing was first observed in a completely different industry, in the meat packing warehouses in Chicago.

Ford explained his vision in the following way:

> *The man who places the part will not fasten it. The man who puts in the bolt does not put in the nut, and the man who starts the nut will not tighten it. . . . We started assembling a motor car in a single factory* (Ford, 1924: 27).

Looking Elsewhere: From Racing Cars to Saving Lives

Is it possible to learn from experts in other disciplines? Indeed, can we improve our own practices by watching other professionals ply their trade?

Racing and medicine are not normally reckoned to have a lot in common. Formula One racing offers many thrills to viewers and fans. But apparently it can also offer instructive lessons in process improvement.

Doctors in the UK's Great Ormond Street Hospital for Children NHS Trust's Surgical and Intensive Care Unit have long realised that there was an urgent need to speed up the handover process of patients moving from the operating theatre to the intensive care unit (ICU) following heart surgery. A normal transfer could take about 30 minutes as wires and tubes are untangled and unplugged, while a number of handover conversations could be taking place before the patient is transferred to the care of the ICU.

Following a particularly demanding 12-hour emergency transplant, two exhausted senior surgeons were unwinding by watching a Formula One race in the staff common room. They were struck by the contrasts between the somewhat chaotic process of transferring patients and the highly coordinated activities of the 20-member crew of engineers and mechanics who change the car tyres, fill it with petrol, clear the air intakes and correct any flaws, allowing the car to clear the pit within seven seconds. Indeed, the mechanics appeared to be using a highly coordinated, efficient and disciplined process.

Intrigued by the need for a highly ordered and controlled handover process and the slick execution observed in real time on the television screens, they invited McLaren and Ferrari racing managers to benchmark processes. Hospital surgeons went to the pits in the British Grand Prix and met Ferrari's technical managers in Italy. Ferrari's technical managers agreed to come over to the hospital and observe and reflect on their handover procedures.

One of the key lessons was that the racing environment was actually more safety conscious and process oriented than the medical context. The fast and fiery world of Formula One had developed stringent procedures and lines of responsibility that simply did not exist in the medical equivalent. At the end of an operation, the patient is transferred from the safe surgical environment onto a trolley that is then taken down a cold corridor towards intensive care without the dedicated equipment and with little monitoring. Within the span of 15 minutes all the technology and support systems are transferred twice (Sower et al., 2008: 173). The transition is difficult and requires a large team engaged through multiple stages and steps, not unlike the racing maintenance team.

While doctors deal with a variety of emergencies, the bulk of the preparation comes from their original training and the experience they accumulate over time. Existing procedures had involved operating on a solid table, which included all the vital connections to equipment. Following the operation, all equipment would be unplugged and a hand-operated ventilator utilised for transferring the patient out of theatre, into the lift, and along the corridor towards intensive care.

Teamwork is essential to success. In racing, teams try to optimise activities and minimise the time wasted when a car is away from the racing track. Many procedures are carried out concurrently with different teams taking control of different activities and small units dealing with each component of the racing car.

The team of doctors was originally convinced that their processes were optimal, as many of them had been following the same procedures for many years. However, the racing experts filmed the doctors at work. When they analysed the tapes and had time to reflect on their actions, they were shocked to realise the lack of structure in what they were doing. The reflection enabled the team to identify bottlenecks and areas for improvement. Moreover, it revealed that the medical specialists were not acting as a unified team. Junior doctors and nurses did not feel able to challenge, identify concerns or express their views.

Observing the process in action carries an enormous value. Formula One teams spend a lot of time rehearsing their procedures, making sure they do not infringe on the work of other specialists and watching recordings of themselves at work. Suggestions for improvements are fed into this process and trialled with a view to creating additional improvements. Shaving seconds or hundredths of seconds is meaningful, but avoiding delays and not getting in the way of other teams is even more crucial to ensure that the overall objective of getting the car back on the road in minimum time is still on track.

Improvement offers benefits to the organisation, thereby resulting in added value. Process improvement is about adopting a process-centric approach and maintaining a holistic view that will enable the 'improvers' to see the wood for the tree. Looking from outside and reflecting can often highlight deeply enshrined flaws and quirks. In order to continue to improve, we need to keep an open mind while remembering the ultimate purpose for improvement. The technical managers pointed out that performance is not about assembling the best collection of technical experts and asking them to perform. Performing as a team requires practice. Moreover, getting a collection of experts to work together requires them to become a team.

The racing experts observed the hospital's current procedures and advised the medical team on how to turn a relatively chaotic and noisy process into an optimised process, with each member of the team knowing their role at every given moment. The input from the pit technicians led to a major restructuring of the patient handover procedures (Catchpole et al. 2007, 2010; Sower et al., 2008), which included the adoption of a new protocol, the elaboration of new checklists and the development of training and rehearsals designed to improve performance in practice. The key to the transformation was in adopting the systematic discipline from Formula One. The protocol identified the leader through the process (the anaesthetist); provided detailed procedures and checklists for each stage of the handover; specified task allocation, rhythm and communication patterns; and even included a detailed diagram of the patient surrounded by staff, so all team members could recognise their station, which identified their exact position and their precise tasks.

While the hospital team may never be able to overhaul a patient inside 10 seconds like the racing engineers, they managed to trim down and optimise the handover procedures, hopefully saving lives in the process. They were also able to continue the search for improvement and continue to gaze, reflect upon and explore other aspects of the business.

What started initially as a fanciful idea of turning a hospital procedure into a Formula One arena had ultimately become a benchmarking and learning exercise that allowed highly experienced practitioners to learn how to work together as an efficient team. Borrowing processes from other disciplines and, indeed, applying a fresh pair of eyes to well-established routines has been instrumental in radically transforming patient handover following heart surgery.

While this was a small initiative introduced by individuals, the results have proved to be very encouraging. The mean and number of errors and handover omissions have been significantly reduced, and enhanced communication has resulted in improved teamwork and a reported improvement to patient safety. The unit reported a four-time reduction in mistakes, moving from poor to good on a number of standard performance measures.

The success of the initiative generated a growing appetite for further improvement. The partnership between the medical team and the engineers has now been in place for over a decade. Crucially, they continue to innovate and experiment with new technologies. Some of the new areas include the use of analytics and big data to monitor performance, utilisation of predictive technologies, fault monitoring and intervention and the development of 3D printing, as well as recognising the value of rehearsing and modelling in improving procedures (Massey-Beresford, 2016). The collaboration has also given the medical team license to begin to explore additional areas and ask new questions that can lead to further improvements.

By daring to look for expertise away from their main specialism, doctors have thus been able to radically improve the outputs and outcomes associated with their handover procedures. Using expertise honed while maintaining and servicing cars, experts were able to identify bottlenecks and fine-tune procedures required to operate in entirely different domains, create better-performing teams, and improve their resulting performance, proving that innovation sometimes lies where you least expect it.

Directing the Lean Quality Management Revolution

But such informed initiatives are few and far between. Meanwhile, the need for improvement in most sectors and projects continues apace, requiring new approaches for rethinking quality management. The following section by John Oakland and Marton Marosszeky draws on the new edition of their text *Total Construction Management: Lean Quality in Construction Project Delivery*, published by Routledge. Oakland and Marosszeky (2017) adopt a broader focus that lean quality brings to all aspects of organising and managing. They acknowledge that the traditional product-based paradigm does not offer a sufficiently broad or robust perspective to support continuous performance improvement and offer new insights and perspectives. Their work thus endeavours to provide the basis and the platform for progressing the conversation and honing practice in the area.

Benchmarking, lean management and other quality initiatives have offered multiple approaches and alternative perspectives for improving organisational performance. Oakland and Marosszeky are interested in exploring the wider foundations underpinning the range of approaches. While the different approaches appear to present distinct theories, they expose the commonalities and provide a guided tour through the strengths and values embedded in the different approaches. In doing so, they expose and compare the different dialects that unfold in what they view as an enormous jigsaw puzzle. They are thus able to document a comprehensive approach to improving organisational performance through an emphasis on quality.

Oakland and Marosszeky explore recent developments around TQM, quality awards, and lean management, thereby explaining the language of performance improvement. Quality thinking provides the basis for uncovering the assumptions and ideas underpinning the various quality trends. More importantly, Oakland and Marosszeky develop a new framework for lean quality management, which provides a starting point for making sense of new developments and introducing a new perspective for approaching lean management and quality improvement concepts in organisational settings. Exploring the foundations of different approaches to quality highlights a set of central principles that underpin thinking, offering the potential to improve performance and enhance quality. The underpinning principles enable organisations to re-focus their culture, values and philosophy; adopt a longer-term perspective; develop exceptional people and robust networks; drive to achieve quality; and encourage investment in planning to enhance reliability and flexibility.

A key strength of the work is in the focus on underpinning principles, which enable the merit and direction of each approach to be explored. The principles emphasise many of the underpinning values, including aspects such as: long-term vision and philosophy, the creation of a cooperative culture and structure, utilisation of creative resource, a focus on creating customer value as the driver for continuous improvement and maintaining a commitment to lean quality from top management throughout the organisation. Pulled together, many of the principles provide the agenda required for an ongoing quest for continuous improvement and the ongoing development that such approaches advocate.

Benchmarking Reprised

> *All Good to Great companies began the process of finding a path to greatness by confronting the brutal facts about the reality of their business. When you start with an honest and diligent effort to determine the truth of your situation, the right decisions often become self-evident.*[*]
>
> —Jim Collins

Benchmarking clearly fits within the continuous improvement and value delivery framework applied by organisations. Oakland and Marosszeky identify a number of external drivers for benchmarking, including (p. 227):

- Customers continually demanding better quality, lower prices, shorter lead times
- Competitors seeking a strategic advantage
- Legislation which places greater demands for improvement

The internal drivers, include (Ibid.):

- Targets which merit improvement
- Technologies, such as BIM (building information modelling), which drive fundamental changes in processes
- Self-assessment results providing opportunities to learn from the adoption of good practices

Oakland and Marosszeky define benchmarking as *'the continuous process of identifying, understanding and adapting best practice and processes that will lead to superior performance'* (Ibid.).

Oakland and Marosszeky observe that organisations progress through four different focus points related to benchmarking (p. 229):

- Initially, attention is concentrated on competitive products or services.
- Subsequently, the focus shifts to industry best practices.
- Consequently, the real breakthroughs begin to occur as the organisation becomes concerned with total business performance across all functions and aspects.
- Ultimately, there is a focus on processes and true continuous improvement.

Superior performance remains the objective of modern process improvement. The move from products to processes, and from benchmarks and metrics, to processes and practices thus chimes

---

[*] Collins, J. (2001). *Good to Great: Why Some Companies Make the Leap and Others Don't.* Harper Business.

with the development in understanding and applying benchmarking to support organisational growth and improvement described earlier in this chapter.

Progressing Beyond the Benchmarking Paradox

All successful companies are constantly benchmarking their competition. They have to know what they have to match up with day-in and day-out if their company is going to be successful.*
— *James Dunn*

Benchmarking is fluid and dynamic, requiring attention to relative performance and to the changing circumstances and conditions. For example, a retailer that shifts attention from sales through their high street shops towards greater presence on the internet should become less concerned with the accessibility of their physical shops, the ability to park near them and the delivery-to-car service that they offer. Their new focus would probably include the accessibility and appeal of their web portal, the performance of their delivery company and the effectiveness of the search algorithms employed when looking for the service, the company or their products. Benchmarking therefore needs to acknowledge that the relative importance of performance shifts with time.

However, we are often limited by past behaviours and acknowledged, idealised and celebrated past patterns whose value decays over time, thus creating a benchmarking paradox.

The benchmarking paradox: Identified best practices are often fossilised and ossified within organisations. As soon as you identify a good practice and mandate its use, the organisation risks institutionalising it and codifying it into a bureaucratic dogma that can arrest future development and rigidly obfuscate any further attempts at improvement. Indeed, mandating best practices can become a force against innovation and improvement, for bureaucracy and innovation operate at distinctly different levels and seek to achieve different, and often contradictory, objectives and outcomes.

Other challenges may also persist:

Nonaka and Takeuchi present some tough challenges to Western managers and organizational theoreticians. They question whether Peter Senge's work on the learning organization does not continue the Cartesian split between mind and body, something they feel has plagued Western thought for several centuries. They also question the West's notion of 'best practices' and 'benchmarking' because they believe it is not enough to just learn about other ways of doing something. Instead, companies need to actively process what they are learning to make it their own. And they question our approach to the virtual corporation that easily combines the knowledge of the company, supplier and customer (Savage, 1996: 138)

Best practices offer limited and temporary value unless it is considered in context and assessed for continued relevance. Nonaka and Takeuchi (1995) thus advocate a better combination of action and reflection to drive the knowledge creating processes by translating tacit to explicit knowledge. They also recognise the role of culture and values in shaping the organisation and the individuals within it. Their main contention is that Japanese firms are successful because they are innovative; they continue to make new knowledge, incorporating ideals, values and emotions, and

---

* https://www.peerviewdata.com/blog/10-quotes

use it with speed and flexibility to produce successful products and technologies. Therein lies the true essence of innovation through benchmarking, in direct contrast with defensive conservatism.

Benchmarking should therefore remain an *evergreen* process, one that is allowed to renew and regenerate as the organisation seeks to develop and innovate as part of a continuous improvement discipline. Ultimately, the best practices are those that pave the way for the next level of continuous improvement by becoming a step forward and a milestone to development and higher achievements, rather than a millstone which can arrest further refinement and growth. Superior performance can thus build on rapid and changing insights, take advantage of emerging understanding and continue to innovate and challenge the organisation to do even better on its perpetual journey towards supreme performance and sustained excellence.

References

Bogan, C. E., and English, M. J. (1994). *Benchmarking for Best Practices: Winning Through Innovative Adaptation*. New York, NY: McGraw Hill.

Catchpole, K. R., De Leval, M. R., McEwan, A., Pigott, N., Elliott, M. J., McQuillan, A., MacDonald, C., and Goldman, A. J. (2007). Patient handover from surgery to intensive care: Using Formula 1 pit-stop and aviation models to improve safety and quality. *Pediatric Anesthesia, 17*(5), 470–478.

Catchpole, K., Sellers, R., Goldman, A., McCulloch, P., and Hignett, S. (2010). Patient handovers within the hospital: Translating knowledge from motor racing to healthcare. *BMJ Quality & Safety, 19*(4), 318–322.

Camp, R. C. (1989/2006). *Benchmarking: The Search for Industry Best Practices That Lead to Superior Performance*. Milwaukee, WI: ASQC/Quality Resources.

Dalcher, D. (2017). What has Taylor ever done for us? Scientific and humane management reconsidered. *PM World Journal, 6*(4) 1–11.

Ford, H., and Crowther, S. (1924). *My Life and Work: In Collaboration with Samuel Crowther*. New York, NY: First World Library.

Hindle, T. (2008). *Guide to Management Ideas and Gurus*. London, UK: Economist Books.

Masse-Beresford, H. (2016). The benefits of a business partnership. *The Telegraph,* 21 April.

McGrath, J., and Bates, B. (2017). *The Little Book of Big Management Theories: . . . And How to Use Them*. London, UK: Pearson UK.

Nonaka, I., and Takeuchi, H. (1995). *The Knowledge-Creating Company: How Japanese Companies Create the Dynamics of Innovation*. Oxford, UK: Oxford University Press.

Oakland, J. S., and Marosszeky, M. (2017). *Total Construction Management—Lean Quality in Construction Project Delivery*. Oxford, UK: Routledge.

Savage, C. M. (1996). *Fifth Generation Management: Integrating Enterprises Through Human Networking*. London, UK: Butterworth-Heinemann.

Sower, V. E., Duffy, J. A., and Kohers, G. (2008). Ferrari's Formula One handovers and handovers from surgery to intensive care. In: *Benchmarking for Hospitals: Achieving Best-in-Class Performance Without Having to Reinvent the Wheel*, 171–190. Milwaukee, WI: ASQ Press.

ten Have, S., ten Have, W., and Stevens, F. (2003). *Key Management Models: The Management Tools and Practices That Will Improve Your Business*. London, UK: Pearson Education.

Lean Quality in Construction Project Delivery—A New Model and Principles

John Oakland and Marton Marosszeky

Construction Industry Challenges and Solutions

All industries are undergoing rapid change under the pressure of technological innovation and changing client needs. The construction sector is no exception—the past 10 years have seen accelerating globalisation, a demand for larger and more complex projects, and a requirement for them to be delivered in ever shorter timeframes. Meanwhile, clients of the industry are increasingly concerned that this sector is not keeping pace with the rates of improvement seen in other sections of the economy. In addition, in this sector, the rate and cost of errors in quality and safety have been too slow to improve.

In today's construction industry, many among clients, designers and contractors are seeing BIM as the silver bullet that will transform the industry. We are convinced that this position is misguided. BIM provides the basis for improved communications within the design team and with external stakeholders, and it provides support for solution optimisation in both the design and construction stages of projects. However, it is no more than a very powerful enabling technology. The authors contend that it is the philosophical foundations of lean quality that will underpin the coming transformation of this sector globally, significantly improving productivity and increasing the industry's potential for value creation for its customers. This viewpoint provides a foundation for organisational excellence across entire supply chains, it offers a powerful new perspective for policy makers, and helps to create the organisational prerequisites necessary for the effective deployment of technologies such as BIM.

Lean Quality: A New Model for Improved Outcomes in the Construction Sector

Pressure from clients and governments as well as commercial competitive pressures have continued to force leading organisations in the construction sector to differentiate themselves on the basis of customer focus, overall product and process quality, cost of products and services and value creation for clients.

In response to these pressures, senior management in leading design and construction organisations worldwide are embracing the philosophy and principles of what we have now called *Lean Quality*. Often approaching the overall task from different perspectives, some adopt frameworks of performance measurement and benchmarking, others use the goal of continuous improvement while others choose to follow the values and concepts of lean construction. We see these as different perspectives through different lenses of the same broad objective—improving performance in all the activities of a business.

Traditionally, in conversations about quality, the building and construction sector has had a natural orientation towards product quality. Given the complexity of its organisational relationships and traditional craft-based processes, most of the construction quality literature reflects this product focus, providing either a guide to compliance with the ISO9001 quality system standards or pragmatic advice on tools for the control of quality. However, lead organisations in every area of the building and construction industry have recognised that the broad focus that *Lean Quality* brings to all aspects of organising and managing is as relevant to building and construction as it is to the manufacturing and service sectors. Furthermore, teachers and researchers in building and construction have recognised that a traditional product-centred paradigm does not provide a sufficiently broad and robust basis for performance improvement within the sector.

Many books on the application of lean thinking are based on the tools of lean. Our book *Total Construction Management—Lean Quality in Construction Project Delivery* (Oakland & Marrosszeky, 2017) is designed to provide organisations within the sector a broad and robust conceptual platform on which to build their overall process improvement endeavours. Our approach integrates and places into a unified perspective the many seemingly disparate management innovations of the past 20 years into *Lean Quality*.

Increasing the satisfaction of customers and stakeholders through effective goal deployment, cost reduction, productivity and process improvement through lean systems has proved to be essential for organisations to stay in operation and to remain or become competitive. Lean quality is far wider in its application than assuring product or service quality—it is a way of managing organisations and their supply chains so that every aspect of performance, both internally and externally, is improved.

The book is based on a further development of John Oakland's well-known TQM model (2014), as shown in Figure 1.1—improving *Performance* through better *Planning* and management of *People* and the *Processes* in which they work. The core of the model will always be performance in the eyes of the customer, but this has been extended to include performance measures for all the stakeholders. This new core still needs to be surrounded by *commitment* to quality and meeting customer requirements, *communication* of the quality message, and recognition of the need to change the *culture* of most organisations to create lean quality. These are the *soft* foundations which must encase the hard management necessities of planning, people and processes. To this we have added *continuous improvement in all processes and outcomes,* as this is now such a key aspect of every successful organisation's operations and a focus on *maximising value for all customers.*

This new lean quality model, based on the extensive work done during the last century, provides a simple framework for excellent performance, covering all angles and aspects of an organisation and its operation. Performance is achieved using a 'business excellence' approach (see BQF, 2000, 2002; EFQM, 2018; NIST, 2018) and by planning the involvement of people in the improvement of processes by focusing on value creation for customers and by driving continuous improvement in all processes and outcomes:

- **Planning.** Developing and deploying policies and strategies; setting up appropriate partnerships and resources; designing in quality

Figure 1.1   New Framework for Lean Quality Management (*Source:* Oakland, J. S., and Marosszeky, M. [2017]. *Total Construction Management—Lean Quality in Construction Project Delivery*. Oxford, UK: Routledge.)

- **Performance.** Establishing a performance measurement framework—a 'balanced score-card' for the organisation; carrying out self-assessment, audits, reviews and benchmarking
- **Processes.** Understanding, managing, design and redesign; quality management systems; continuous improvement
- **People.** Managing the human resources; culture change; teamwork; communications; innovation and learning

Driving all of this to ensure successful implementation is, of course, effective leadership and commitment. This framework can be used then to set out the essential steps for the successful implementation of *Lean Quality* and its management.

The Principles of Lean Quality in Construction

Lean can be characterised in terms of the lean ideal, principles, and methods or tools. The lean ideal is to provide a custom product or service, exactly fit for purpose, delivered as required with no waste. It describes the ideal outcome from a service or product.

Lean principles, on the other hand, are the beliefs or rules that guide the actions that support the achievement of the ideal. These are not a prescriptive set of rules; rather, they are guidelines to inform thinking about the way forward, either at the individual or organisational level.

The methods and tools of lean are the how—these are practices that have been proven to be productive in moving towards the lean ideal. However, it is important to understand that a fundamental tenet of lean thinking is that this is not a rule-bound approach. Every organisation and every situation has its unique characteristics; the lean approach is to use the lean principles and practices (tools or methods) to guide action. Lean is a path, and the milestones are progress towards the achievement of the ideal.

In this section, we propose a set of principles specifically designed to guide enterprises in the construction sector towards the implementation of a lean business framework. The importance of adopting a clear set of principles should not be underestimated—this defines the values which will guide an organisation in its development. These principles are in large part very similar to the lean frameworks that have been successfully adopted in the manufacturing and service industries. However, there are some principles that are particularly relevant to organisations in the construction sector.

Because much of the construction sector is faced with the challenge of designing, fabricating and erecting unique facilities, every project offers the prospect for design and construction optimisation. The lean quality approach builds on the process approach and brings into focus the continuous search for opportunities for improvements in customer service, efficiency and the elimination of waste. This is as applicable to design processes as it is to fabrication and construction.

Jeffrey Liker, a leading researcher and teacher within the lean movement, in his groundbreaking book *The Toyota Way* (2004), structured his approach around the 14 principles of the Toyota Way, arranged in four groupings:

1. Long-term philosophy.
2. The right process will produce the right results.
3. Add value to the organisation by developing your people and partners.
4. Continuously solving root problems drives organisational learning.

Liker's principles address the broad organisational issues as well as the detailed processes of production in more detail:

1. Adopt a long-term philosophy.
2. Strive for continuous flow.
3. Use pull systems.
4. Level out workload.
5. Stop to fix problems.
6. Standardise tasks.
7. Use visual control.
8. Only use reliable technology.
9. Grow leaders who understand work.
10. Develop exceptional teams and people.
11. Respect external partners.
12. Go see for yourself.
13. Slow decisions by consensus, implement rapidly.
14. Become a learning organisation.

We have built on Liker's approach and expanded it, referring to the contributions of other leading thinkers in the lean construction community of researchers and practitioners.

In contrast to Liker, Lauri Koskela (1992, 2002) focused his attention on the principles of production systems. Early on Koskela (1992) proposed the following principles for the improvement of production processes:

1. Systematically focus on customer value.
2. Focus control on the whole process.
3. Balance improvement in flow and conversion.
4. Simplify processes.

5. Reduce the share of non–value-adding work.
6. Reduce variability.
7. Increase output flexibility.
8. Reduce cycle time.
9. Benchmark.

Later Koskela (2000) analysed in detail the wide-ranging principles that underpin theories of production, and he developed an integrated Transformation-Value-Flow (TVF) view of production, which is underpinned by the following three high level principles:

1. Transformation—getting production realised efficiently
2. Flow—elimination of waste (non–value-adding activities)
3. Value—elimination of value loss (achieved value relative to best possible value)

While this broad set of principles was based on the manufacturing literature and demonstrated that the principles of lean in manufacturing are applicable in the construction environment, it did not reflect much of the construction-specific thinking developed by the community of researchers and practitioners in the lean construction movement.

Ballard (2016), in a chapter on lean construction, turned his attention to the unique characteristics of construction, and he introduced four new principles which reflect the particular characteristics of the modern construction process:

1. Allow money and resources to move across contractual and organisational boundaries in search of the best project-level investment.
2. Improve the predictability of near-term work load to drive efficiency and reliability of operations.
3. Drive the design to realise an optimum, fit-for-purpose product design within the cost constraints of the customer.
4. Involve upstream players in downstream processes to realise innovative and efficient design and construction solutions.

We present a synthesis of these ideas in the context of their application to lean quality in the delivery of capital projects. Our framework is set out in the mind map of Figure 1.2 (on next page), which is consistent with the model which we proposed in Figure 1.1. In this framework, the three P's (*Planning, People and Processes*) are clearly articulated, while *Performance* and the three C's of *Communication, Culture* and *Commitment* are all included in the foundation category of Values and Long-Term Philosophy. For the purposes of this section, we will expand only on Principle 1, the foundations concerned with the underpinning values and long-term philosophy.

Values and Long-Term Philosophy

Basing management decisions on a long-term philosophy will ensure stability and sustainability. It is essential to create a cooperative culture with long-term supply chain relationships and to structure agreements to allow for flexibility in response to changes that may occur during project delivery. Visible leadership commitment to lean quality values and processes will ensure compliance by the rest of the workforce, including the supply chain, and lead to the development of a skilled and well-trained workforce that seeks continuous improvement based on learning and

Figure 1.2   A New Framework for the Principles of Lean Quality in Construction. (*Source:* Oakland, J. S., and Maroszeky, M. [2017]. *Total Construction Management—Lean Quality in Construction Project Delivery.* Oxford, UK: Routledge.)

reflection. Essential to continuous improvement is stability in corporate values and leadership. Principle 1 is broken down into five sub-principles which are expanded and described below.

Principle 1.1 Adopt a principled long-term philosophy—Create constancy of purpose

To ensure stability and sustainability, determine a long-term vision and mission based on your values and aspirations. Companies that practice lean quality are values based and ethically driven enterprises which seek to maximise their contribution to their customers, their employees, their supply chain partners, and the communities in which they operate.

Principle 1.2 Create a cooperative organisational culture and structure within the supply chain

Large, complex construction projects require close collaboration across all disciplines and companies in the supply chain to achieve optimum outcomes. The lead companies, designers, contractors and clients must build a culture of open communication and collaboration to ensure that downstream fabricators and constructors are involved in the design development and optimisation process. Innovation across disciplinary boundaries requires an open collaborative culture. Commercial frameworks should be designed to encourage such collaboration to occur.

Principle 1.3 Utilise the collective resources of the project team in the most effective and efficient manner possible

Organisational and commercial structures should be designed to permit the most effective and efficient use of collective resources on a project. This should enable resources to be shared across contractual and organisational boundaries to achieve the most efficient deployment of collective resources. As projects increase in complexity and uncertainty, the up-front relationship between work scope and compensation becomes more tenuous. Changes in scope during the project become more likely and with them the need to renegotiate work scope and cost. This principle addresses the need for flexibility in the use of all resources, ensuring that they are used in the most efficient manner possible.

Principle 1.4 Focus on creating customer value—Drive continuous improvement in all things and eliminate non–value-adding activities

A key aspect of lean quality is that targets are set for key inputs and outcomes, and performance is measured as a means of driving continuous improvement. Furthermore, everyone in the organisation is tasked with looking for waste, non–value-adding activities that can be modified or eliminated, as they do not add value to the end customer.

Principle 1.5 Maintain commitment to lean quality from the top leadership throughout the organisation

Lean quality is a committed, long-term approach to doing business. It is not a short-term fix. Lean quality drives incremental improvement in all the key aspects of a business and focusses the organisation on continuously improving customer value. It is essential that leadership at all levels in an organisation is visibly committed to the long-term values and processes of lean quality.

Conclusions

The long-term perspective embedded through the different principles encourages responsible consideration of resources and people offering value to the organisation. We see *Lean Quality* as providing the fundamental building blocks for the management of any organisation, and, hence, people working in every part of each organisation need to understand this broad perspective. This section outlines a comprehensive approach to the management of any business enterprise—one that has been used successfully by many design- and construction-based organisations throughout the world.

References

Ballard G. (2016). Lean Construction. In: T. Netland, and D. Powell (Eds.). *The Routledge Companion to Lean Management.* New York, NY: Routledge

BQF. (2000/2002). *The Model in Practice; The Model in Practice 2.* London, UK: British Quality Foundation.

EFQM. (2018). *The EFQM Excellence Model.* Brussels, BE: European Foundation for Quality Management.

Koskela, L. (1992). Application of the new production philosophy to construction. *CIFE Technical Report, #72.* Stanford, CA: Stanford University.

Koskela, L. (2002). *An Exploration Towards a Production Theory and Its Application to Construction.* PhD Dissertation. VTT Publication 408.

Liker, J. (2004). *The Toyota Way.* New York, NY: McGraw Hill.

NIST. (2018). USA Malcolm Baldrige National Quality Award, Criteria for Performance Excellence. Gaithersburg, MD: National Institute of Standard and Technology.

Oakland, J. S. (2014). *Total Quality Management and Operational Excellence—Text with Cases.* Oxford, UK: Routledge.

Oakland, J. S., and Marosszeky, M. (2017). *Total Construction Management—Lean Quality in Construction Project Delivery.* Oxford, UK: Routledge.

Chapter 2

Communication

Communicating Beyond Our Hidden Assumptions

Darren Dalcher

Communication is recognised as essential to successful projects (Dalcher, 2012), and indeed for almost any human endeavour. Moreover, one of the most commonly recorded complaints about the performance of organisations and teams relates to their inability to communicate or to the lack of knowledge regarding the intentions of the executive group. The 2013 *Pulse of the Profession Report* (PMI, 2013) contends that one in five projects is unsuccessful due to ineffective communication. The report further affirms that a typical project manager should be spending 90 percent of their time communicating.

Given the critical role of communication in projects, is there anything new to say about communicating?

When describing communication, there is a temptation to focus on the message being sent, the channel that is being utilised or the underpinning technology. *Merriam-Webster* accordingly describes communication as *'a process by which information is exchanged between individuals through a common system of symbols, signs or behavior'*.

However, communication entails a lot more. The *Oxford English Dictionary* defines communication as: 'the imparting or exchanging of information by speaking, writing or using some other medium', including 'a letter or message containing information or news; the successful conveying or sharing of ideas and feelings; and social contact'. *Oxford* traces the use of the phrase *communication* to Late Middle English, with a derivation from Old French *counicacion*, and the Latin *communicatio(n-)*, originating from the verb *communicare,* meaning 'to share'.

The idea of sharing is more powerful than the single direction implied by *imparting,* or even the mutually bi-directional association enabled through *exchanging.* Indeed, the *Cambridge Dictionary* refers to communication as *'the process of sharing information, especially when this increases understanding between people or groups'.* The *Collins English Dictionary* duly notes that communicating can extend beyond mere information to encompass ideas or feelings.

Conveying meaning, increasing understanding and sharing ideas and feelings extend beyond the typical core knowledge and skills taught to managers and leaders and should therefore merit further consideration regarding the potential, place and role of communication.

Exploring the Context

Communication is not a smooth process that is constituted by recipient design and intention recognition, as is often implied by the different theories (Kecskes, 2010: 50). Firstly, there is a need to account for the internal representations of external things, whilst many of our thoughts are not represented in the external world (Rapaport, 2003: 401). Secondly, we do communicate with others (p. 402).

> *When you and I speak or write to each other, the most we can hope for is a sort of incremental approach toward agreement, toward communication, toward common usage of terms* (Lenat et al., 1995: 45).

The context both constrains and aids the transmission of meaning, especially in unclear, unstructured and ambiguous situations (Dalcher, 2016). Actors do not have access to each other's thoughts and must instead be content to interpret the communication actions and gestures that they perceive. Kecskes (2010: 51) proposes that the speaker's knowledge involves constructing a model of the hearer's knowledge, while the hearer's knowledge includes constructing a model of the speaker's knowledge. Both models are constructed so that they remain relevant to the given situational context as it is understood by each of the two parties. Rapaport (2003: 402) observes that *'in order for two cognitive agents to communicate successfully, whether about an internal thing or an external thing, they must be able to detect misunderstandings and correct them by negotiating'*.

Communication can be viewed as the result of the interplay between intention and attention (Kecskes, 2010: 58). Communication also implies a degree of acceptance and manipulation (Grammer et al., 1997), as well as other observable manifestations of a relationship (Watzlawick et al., 2011: 4). Watzlawick et al. assert that rather than focus on a piece of communication, attention should be paid to the effect that the receiver's reaction has on the sender, and hence on the sender-receiver relationship, as mediated by communication.

Meaning is socially constructed and context sensitive and is the emerging result of the cooperation between the parties during the course of communication (Kecskes, 2010: 51). Communication should thus be perceived as a trial-and-error process that is co-constructed by participants (p. 69). Kecskes posits a socio-cognitive position that implies that the speaker and hearer are both equal participants in the communication process as they both produce and interpret, whilst being part of a dynamic process (p. 58). Yet, what is recovered is not always what was intended.

> *We almost always fail. . . . Yet, we almost always nearly succeed: This is the paradox of communication. Its resolution is simple: Misunderstandings, if small enough, can be ignored. And those that cannot be ignored can be minimized through negotiation* (Rapaport, 2003: 402).

But what would happen if the misunderstandings and mismatches remain hidden and elude detection? Similarly, what happens when opportunities for meaningful communication are not exploited?

The Peril and Power of Hidden Assumptions

On Friday evening, July 17, 1981, the lobby of the newest hotel in Kansas City was crowded with dancers, and the walkways above were packed with spectators tapping to the rhythm of the music. The evening ended with the catastrophic collapse of the two packed walkways onto the crowded lobby below. In the mayhem, 114 people were killed and around 200 injured. The Hyatt Regency became known as the worst structural tragedy in the history of the United States. The plaintiffs' claims following the collapse amounted to more than three billion dollars, also the largest-ever claim in a structural failure case.

The 1981 collapse of Kansas City's Hyatt Regency Hotel occurred because the contractor was unable to procure threaded rods sufficiently long to suspend a second-floor walkway from a roof truss, settling instead on hanging it from a fourth-floor walkway using shorter rods. The architectural designers relied on the strength of the long rods for their design (and implicitly assumed that they could be obtained). The procurement process proceeded downstream in a staged fashion: When the contractors could not obtain the rods needed (and were unable to go back to alter the architectural design or to assess the implications of the change), they 'assumed' that the alternative would suffice. The impact of the late decision was that the fourth-floor walkway was designed and delivered according to the original plan, but in practice, it had to be able to handle its own load as well as that of the lower walkway.

A key problem was the lack of communication between the designers and fabricators. The designers were not aware of the difficulty in obtaining the right size rods, while the fabricators did not understand the critical role of the rods. The separation of 'planning' from 'doing' (Dalcher, 2017; 2019) precluded the possibility of finding out about the implementation problems during the early stages and of sharing the design rationale with the later stages. Such linear separation weakens the basis of development by hiding some of the knowledge that is generated throughout the process and effectively sealing it, or concealing it, within a single phase. More crucially, the information was not available for critical risk assessment, as neither the original rationale nor the physical constraints uncovered by the fabricators were recorded. In this case, neither party recorded their assumptions. However, the increased focus on the recording of design rationale and assumptions enables more effective risk assessment of the implications of assumptions and opens the potential for the identification of resulting complications likely to be encountered in later stages.

Communication between the different stakeholders is essential. Ideologies, beliefs and assumptions tend to remain implicit and 'unargued' while participants are unable, or unwilling, to spell out their positions. All approaches used in development and management embody certain assumptions while omitting other considerations. In some cases, the context is misunderstood, in others it is incorrectly identified. In yet other situations, some relevant aspects may be missing, or changes may simply invalidate previous understanding. Regardless of the reason, unless the understanding is communicated, it cannot be shared and utilised.

A key to communication lies in understanding the personal frames, or perspectives, of participants. Frames encompass assumptions and perceptions, which are never registered. In complex design situations, this calls for an explicit framework for addressing assumptions and rationales. Adopting an adversarial approach encourages designers to re-examine their assumptions and their validity. Such a framework would call for:

- Identification and recording of assumptions and rationale
- Avoidance of premature closure and early commitment to a final course of action
- Encouragement of diversity and multiplicity of perspectives
- Adoption of explicit risk analysis procedures aimed at challenging the assumptions
- Challenging of assumptions and decisions in light of new and contradictory information
- Willingness to learn through reflection and to make the necessary revisions and corrections

The communication around the Hyatt Regency Hotel was downstream, one directional and partial. There were no opportunities to expand the communication, identify critical key assumptions, or make the conversation two sided and dialogical. As projects proceed downstream, it is often difficult to pause and reflect, and therefore it is essential to record the rationale for decisions and choices, especially for future reference.

Canadian philosopher Marshall McLuhan noted that most of our assumptions outlive their usefulness. The Hyatt Regency Hotel disaster also serves as a reminder of the destructive power of hidden assumptions. Effective communication and risk management require the establishment of a clear and shared context. The key issue is in challenging the right (or rather the 'wrong') assumptions. Hidden assumptions thus become the driving force that needs to be exposed, explored and challenged. The adoption of a more adversarial stance which can be used to expose underpinning assumptions relies on developing an emphasis on the situational context of the problem, the changing nature of the process and the substantial amount of hidden and tacit understanding and skills of stakeholders and participants. Many psychologists define learning as the detection and correction of error. Avoiding the collapse of buildings, and for that matter, the well-publicised failures of IT systems and other critical projects, may ultimately require a more active approach to uncovering and managing the context and the hidden assumptions that key players bring to a situation.

New Insights in Communicating Project Management

US management author guru Peter Drucker wryly observed that 'the most important thing in communication is hearing what isn't said'.* So how do we begin to listen for what is not being said? Indeed, does communication allow us to uncover the hidden assumptions? Moreover, is our stance or position always laden with additional information, and if so, how do we begin to unpack and explore it?

It is clearly important to understand project managers and recognise what baggage and assumptions they may harbour. The next section, by Benjamin Lauren, is extracted from his book *Communicating Project Management: A Participatory Rhetoric for Development Teams*, published by Routledge. As projects become more central to societal endeavours, Lauren makes a case for a deeper understanding of project management as a collaborative practice. His work offers a glimpse of how experienced project managers encourage and support teams and how they understand, interact with and negotiate the increasingly complex facets of modern projects.

Lauren opens up new avenues for inquiry into the work of experienced project managers. Given the paucity of scholarly exploration of the dynamics of project management practice, it is encouraging to consider new perspectives that might derive fresh insights and new ideas that could invigorate the principles and practice of project management. His position recognises a major assumption underpinning project practices that project management is about making teams efficient by using tools and processes.

Recognising that project managers have other roles makes it possible to consider alternative positions and emphasise different aspects. Lauren's focus is on positioning project managers as 'writers': people who assemble words and figures, prepare agendas and coordinate networks. Indeed, if most of project managers' work revolves around writing (or 90% communication), perhaps it is time to consider new perspectives for understanding the value, assumptions and emphases embedded within the role. Such a perspective may offer new ways of influencing team dynamics, leading and developing individuals and supporting teams.

---

* https://www.oxfordreference.com/view/10.1093/acref/9780191826719.001.0001/q-oro-ed4-00012211

As we have already established, the need to communicate is an essential part of project management; however, very little scholarly effort has been invested in studying communication within the context of projects. Lauren's chief interest is in *'the role of participation in communicating project management as a means for understanding it as writing—as a designed system of communication that has great influence over how people work'* (2018: 3).

At a time when projects are increasingly decentralised and agile and lean approaches offer alternative arrangements and organisational structures, it might be interesting to renew the focus on project managers by considering their role in communicating throughout projects.

Lauren boldly embraces a renewed paradigm for project work that progresses from a fixation with efficiency towards a growing recognition of the need to accommodate people, politics and social arrangements. The new perspective revolves around participation as an alternative position, which emphasises the role of communication. A participative approach enables a rethinking of project management and its ability to support and develop teams and individuals.

Lauren explores two alternative metaphors used to describe leadership in different project settings. The metaphors uncover different approaches and value sets, enabling a comparison of the communication and leadership styles that each one supports. The approaches appear to be both constrained and defined by the values of leadership and perspectives on development held by the different leaders. Each of the metaphors can be said to be underpinned by specific values and norms that reflect the particular lens or leadership perspective. Much like the assumptions explored earlier, patterns of behaviour are also enfolded into particular views and perspectives. Uncovering the associated values provides insightful context for understanding leadership and communication in the workplace, whilst offering new food for thought for developing fresh theoretical and pragmatic perspectives for improving project communicating and developing a better basis for understanding and supporting project practice.

British author and biologist Rupert Sheldrake observed that *'the sciences are being held back by assumptions that have hardened into dogmas, maintained by powerful taboos. I believe that the sciences will be regenerated when they are set free'.* Similar sentiment can be observed regarding the assumptions, dogma and taboos underpinning the state of project management practice. The theoretical and pragmatic basis of the discipline would benefit from fresh thinking into project communicating, stakeholders, benefits and many other new areas. The new work around participation and communicating in projects offers a great potential for challenging our hidden assumptions, reflecting on our paradigms and regenerating, revitalising and refreshing our understanding of effective project practice.

References

Dalcher, D. (2012). The art of communication. *PM World Journal, 1*(4), 1–4.

Dalcher, D. (2016). On the importance of context: Why situational awareness remains an essential focus. *PM World Journal, 5*(12), 1–6.

Dalcher, D. (2017). What has Taylor ever done for us?: Scientific and humane management reconsidered. *PM World Journal, 6*(4), 1–11.

Dalcher, D. (2019). *Managing Projects in a World of People, Strategy and Change.* Abingdon, UK: Routledge.

---

* https://www.oxfordreference.com/view/10.1093/acref/9780191826719.001.0001/q-oro-ed4-00012211

Grammer, K., Filova, V., and Fieder, M. (1997). The communication paradox and possible solutions. In: A. Schmitt, K. Atzwanger, K., Grammer, and K. Schäfer (Eds.). *New Aspects of Human Ethology,* 91–120. Boston, MA: Plenum Press.

Kecskes, I. (2010). The paradox of communication: Socio-cognitive approach to pragmatics. *Pragmatics and Society, 1*(1), 50–73.

Lauren, B. (2018). *Communicating Project Management: A Participatory Rhetoric for Development Teams.* New York, NY: Routledge.

Lenat, D., Miller, G., and Yokoi, T. (1995). CYC, WordNet, and EDR: Critiques and responses. *Communications of the ACM, 38*(11), 45–48.

PMI (2013). *Pulse of the Profession In-Depth Report: The High Cost of Low Performance: The Essential Role of Communications.* Newton Square, PA: Project Management Institute. May.

Rapaport, W. J. (2003). What did you mean by that? Misunderstanding, negotiation, and syntactic semantics. *Minds and Machines, 13*(3), 397–427.

Watzlawick, P., Bavelas, J. B., and Jackson, D. D. (2011). *Pragmatics of Human Communication: A Study of Interactional Patterns, Pathologies and Paradoxes.* New York, NY: W. W. Norton and Company.

Communicating Project Management: A Participatory Rhetoric for Development Teams

Benjamin Lauren

There are two metaphors I've come across used to describe leadership philosophy at the project team level. The first, offered by Demacro and Lister (1999), suggests that teams can be grown but not built. This leadership approach describes project managers who cultivate the conditions for teams to succeed as a member of a team. The second approach was described by Lammers and Tsvetkov (2008), and it positioned project managers as chefs because they must deliver successful project results consistently. The chef, they argue, uses 'industry standard processes' to achieve these results. Chefs tend to have a more complicated power relationship with the team, as they are very clearly responsible for managing its processes and procedures.

Leadership models in project management offer important insight into communication practices. This excerpt from Chapter 4 of my book *Communicating Project Management: A Participatory Rhetoric for Development Teams* (Lauren, 2018) explores leadership at the project level by embodying the two metaphors of gardening and cooking to understand how these leadership values influence the approach to communicating. Through a closer examination of two of the participants, this excerpt explains how leadership values influence communication at the project level and to what extent they shape invitations to participate in project work.

To study the relationship between leadership and communication, the excerpt will lean heavily on examining the communication of two participants. The first participant I call 'The Gardener' because she tends to communicate in ways that focus on growing and cultivating the growth of people to help a team succeed. Meanwhile, I refer to other participant as 'The Chef' because he tends to focus on making and assembling, usually through industry standard practices, the kinds of resources and people needed to successfully complete a project. As the excerpt will explain, their individual positionality on the team also influences how they perform leadership. Given these metaphors, how each participant approaches communicating project management is very different, even though they work toward the same goals: to complete project work successfully and to make space for people to participate.

The excerpt begins by reviewing leadership in project management. Then, it introduces The Gardener and presents the data from our work together, which illustrates her approach to growing and contributing to project teams. After that, I introduce The Chef, and I explain how his approach to communicating focuses on following proven recipes for success. Next, the excerpt explores how their leadership approaches are linked to specific ways of communicating; how they give presence to certain values. Finally, the section ends by describing the role of leadership identity as a form of rhetorical performance.

Communicating Leadership, Positionality, and Identity

As a scholarly interest and workplace practice, leadership contains a broad range of topic areas. For example, there are a number of books that focus on how to best lead (such as Asghar, 2014; Maxwell, 2007) or attempt to teach students to be effective leaders (Northouse, 2015; Kouzes & Posner, 2017). Often the published work in leadership traverses academic and practitioner spheres. Particularly useful is Higgs's (2003) work, which assembled a trajectory of leadership research in a western tradition, including the trends and schools of thought emerging since the ancient Greeks. In his article, he argued that scholarship in leadership tends to struggle with its paradigm, oscillating between a focus on personality or behaviour (p. 274).

A focus on leadership personality asserts, for example, the importance of an individual's character and charisma, whereas a focus on behaviour is concerned with how leadership can be developed as a skillset. Higgs explains, *'A personality-based paradigm would argue for selection as being the main focus, whereas a behaviour-based one would argue for development. In essence this is the debate around whether leaders are born or made'* (p. 274). This excerpt seeks to add to this conversation to argue that leadership at the project level is a kind of rhetorical performance that is based on a set of implicit values that shape communication activities.

In this view of leadership, communicating project management is both situational and contextual, but also reliant on the positionality of the project manager in the group. When a team shares in project management work, the positionality is different than when a person is hired to act exclusively as a project manager. As Amidon and Blythe (2008) learned from interviewing communication managers, *'Those who reveal a situated, contingent notion of agency [. . .] understand that their ability to act often comes not from autonomy but from their position within a larger group'* (p. 21). In other words, positionality of the project manager influences how they lead, and also, how they perform their identity as a leader.

While Amidon and Blythe (2008) are quick to dispel the notion that identity is fixed, they also understand it to be situated in the workplace and linked to personal and professional experiences (such as education and training). Similarly, in their study of the online forum *Science Buzz*, Grabill and Pigg (2012) explained, *'identity is often synonymous with authority due to their ongoing presence in the conversation, their rhetorical skill, and their status in relation to the site'* (p. 116). In other words, in online forums identity is performed 'in small, momentary, and fleeting acts' (p. 101) and is leveraged to *'create argumentative space by shaping how the conversation unfolds and enables the exchange of information and knowledge'* (p. 101).

In comparable ways, project managers, via organisational networks, enact agency by shaping conversations and activities to create a space for project work to get done using analogue and digital means (that is, using information communication technologies and during face-to-face meetings). A project manager's agency is awarded through interactions, through building relationships and trust via communication activities.

When leadership is expressed as a kind of performance of identity and positionality, it becomes clearer that leadership arises out of rhetorical situations that circle project work. To help illustrate this idea, I turn to Biesecker (1989), who described the rhetorical situation as *'an event that makes possible the production of identities and social relations'* (p. 126). Her treatment of the rhetorical situation suggests that leadership identities are not fixed—that *'the rhetorical event may be seen as an incident that produces and reproduces the identities of subjects and constructs and reconstructs linkages between them'* (p. 126).

Through these linkages people build relationships and trust as they work on projects. In other words, by assuming our leadership identity is not fixed—that it is constantly in a state of transformation—rhetorical events or incidents can be transformative to how someone perceives their role as a leader. Biesecker's (1989) ideas connect with Drucker's (2009) thoughts that the most powerful way of communicating as a manager is tied to shared experience. It is through communicating—through designing approaches to making space—that leadership is performed. Consequently, it is also through communicating that the values of a leader are exposed.

Introducing The Gardener

Project managers who lead as gardeners are cultivating conditions for teams to grow together as individuals and as a collective. They do this work positioned inside the team—as an equal member of the team. When DeMarco and Lister (1999) discussed the agricultural metaphor in *Peopleware,* they were reflecting on their own struggle to develop a prescriptive approach to creating what they called a 'jelled' team. As they wrestled with how to best make teams jell, they concluded, *'You can't make teams jell. You can hope they will jell; you can cross your fingers; you can act to improve the odds of jelling—but you can't make it happen. The process is much too fragile to be controlled'* (Demarco and Lister, 1999: 143). As they asked what could be done to create the circumstances teams needed to jell, the authors noted they needed to change their terminology. *'We stopped talking about* building *teams and talked instead of* growing *them'* (p. 143). As it turns out, the metaphor of gardening is also not new to professional and technical communication either. The gardening leadership model for project management values team building and developing people, and as a result, a gardener approach is more appropriate for shared control over leadership and internal processes. In a cultivation model, project management is treated as a more democratic process that requires frequent input from people on the team.

When the research for this excerpt began, The Gardener had just started a new job at an automotive company designing infotainment experiences. Her title was Senior User Experience Designer. When I asked how she was involved in managing or leading project work, she explained how she did so from inside the team: *'Here at my new position we don't have project managers specifically. . . . I like things to be really well defined and scheduled, and I like to plan, and I like being able to do that as much as I want with my own parts of the project'.* She did qualify this statement with an important point that she was not the team lead, though she had an informal role in how the work of her team was done.* She explained how she participated in project management: *'Some of the stuff that I do naturally, like scheduling things and laying out timelines, or taking more detailed notes. I have been sharing that somewhat—almost to get a sense of how much other people appreciate it and if other people find it helpful'.*

Given that The Gardener was new to the company and team, her approach made sense because she was looking for ways to add value to her surroundings. She wanted to fit in, but also to make an impact inside of the organisation. She explained one way she was adding value to project work—which had influenced how it was being managed—was building a shared calendar. She felt that by creating timelines in this calendar, she could help other people on the team see the

---

* Leading parts of projects and initiatives is something we saw reflected in the interviews because some products involve multiple project teams.

dependencies of the project. She explained the team had previously used a slideshow template, but that it wasn't visible enough. She translated that information into something she felt was more effective and thought, 'Hey, I can do it in this way, and I can share it with them, and if it's appreciated, then I can kind of manage that piece of things, or it can be adopted by everybody, and then we can all kind of manage that piece'. In the end, she explained that the team adopted her approach to scheduling and making dependencies visible.

The Gardener described the approach to project management at her company as waterfall, but with some agile elements practiced only by her team. This structure made sense because she worked for an automotive company, and much of her team's work had to do with people's experience in the car—perhaps the most flexible space of an automobile. The Gardener explained, 'We do design thinking as an approach to problem solving, and there have been discussions with my team in particular about trying to incorporate some of the methods of those methodologies', such as a Kanban board. To potentially help facilitate some of this transition, The Gardener practiced using a Kanban board to guide her own work but did not introduce it as a collaboration tool with her team during data collection.

Leadership Values of The Gardener

The communication I observed via experience sampling were events such as negotiating buy-in to project timelines, defining scope of a user interface, beginning a community-based project, assembling a team presentation and discussing design outcomes. These communicative events did not define The Gardener, but they did illustrate her values as a leader: to cultivate the conditions that would lead her team to individual and collective growth.

That is, for her team to *jell*, to use DeMarco and Lister's term. And she approached that work positioned as an equal member of her team, taking the lead where and when it made sense for her to do so. Importantly, participating in this way was intuitive for her because it aligned with her personality, but it was also a reaction to her situation as a new employee and to her perception of the organisation as a context for project work. Further, the data showed there were clear communication practices associated with the values of The Gardener as a leader. I describe the values here and provide examples from the communication events she reported. While these values are not all encompassing of gardeners as leaders, they demonstrate how one person inhabits the role in the ways she communicates with people on project teams.

Value 1: Teach Methods of Effective Collaboration

The Gardener frequently mentioned the importance of modelling behaviour or teaching others how to effectively collaborate on her team and those surrounding her team in the organisation. For her, modelling desirable behaviour was an instructional act, which she did by demonstrating specific kinds of action and occasionally embracing inaction to construct effective boundaries. She further explained during an interview that 'I am a firm believer in that you teach people how to treat you'.

Several reporting events demonstrated The Gardener working to teach people how to treat her or how she hoped her behaviour would influence others. For example, she reported receiving an email request about a feature of a product from a co-worker who had authority over her in the organisation's hierarchy. The email asked her to immediately give feedback to a proposal. The

Gardener felt the request was unreasonable and responded she would get to it soon as she could, but she did not make promises about when that would be. Since her response was written as an email, she used a polite and diplomatic tone but remained firm that she did not have the time to get to this specific request at the moment. Her thought about responding in this way was *'I didn't want to teach him that he could get me to react by communicating in that way'.*

Value 2: Learn About Teams and Organisations

A focus on learning about her team and organisation also proved important as a means for understanding how to navigate, engage, and lead as a member of her team. The audience of a communication is The Gardener's essential consideration in how she communicates as a leader. Supporting learning about the audience was her background as a user experience professional. She noted that learning about customers had always been a high priority for her, but more recently she had turned that training toward learning about the people on her team. For example, during one of our interviews, she noted that the timing of project work seemed more relaxed at this company than at other places she'd worked, which would require some adjustment for her.

Timing of work significantly mattered to The Gardener, and her efforts at learning about the organisation helped her think about ways to improve how her team approached project dependencies. She explained it in this way, *'I could really manage a lot more than I am right now, but I know I don't know everything I need to know to understand where the boundaries are. So, I'm kind of backseating a little bit just to see how things play out—to get a sense of the culture'.*

Examples of learning surfaced throughout the sampling period in many situations. In one, The Gardener overheard a group of people discussing a project team she knew something about, so she popped her head up from her cubicle to offer some information to the group. The group turned and looked at her as if they were surprised and did not say anything. She read their individual facial expressions and body language and sat back down feeling somewhat dejected. Her goal was to build rapport with the people in the group, but she learned from the interaction that even conversations in common spaces in this organisation could be somewhat exclusive.

Value 3: Communicate to Include

A clear leadership value of The Gardener was to communicate in ways that included people. In the previous sections we saw how she enacted inclusion by teaching effective collaboration, modelling behaviour, and prioritising learning about her team and their context to intentionally find areas where she could lead from within her team. She operationalised these motives to be inclusive of the people on her team and to find ways to make space for people to participate. She explained how her goal of inclusion played out in different kinds of communication events at work. For example, she once sent an email to her supervisor notifying him that she'd be off site at a training. The email was meant to be purely informational, but she also chose an email on purpose to protect her supervisor's time. She felt a more formal face-to-face discussion would have been disrespectful of her supervisor's time for such a simple notice.

In The Gardener's view, there were formal and informal methods she used to communicate to include others. She defined informal methods as strategies she individually developed and adopted and were perhaps less visible to people. She explained informal as pertaining to her individual practices, such as *'making sure that everybody has a say and can be heard as part of the collaboration process or our team meetings'*, or circling back to those she'd mistakenly interrupted *'so that it didn't feel like any one person was dominating the conversation or the design process'*. Meanwhile, formal strategies had been developed and adopted by the team (e.g., developing a communication plan or workflow) and as a result were more visible. She explained formal methods as *'really [m]aking an effort to communicate how I think that we should share ideas in terms of providing rationale and more detail around why we're making certain decisions throughout the design process'*.

Value 4: Be Responsible to the Team

As the examples so far have shown, The Gardener intuitively communicated and acted in ways that demonstrated a loyalty to her team over the project. This loyalty was rooted in the belief that effective teams lead to successful project work. Project work was high priority for The Gardener, but in the social spaces of work, she often prioritised the team over the project. When an individual would break from the team, The Gardener felt as though it violated some sort of unspoken rule that required explanation.

The emphasis on being responsible to the team was also about making sure people were contributing and collaborating in good faith. One example from a community project she'd worked on showed how The Gardener viewed the importance of celebrating individuals in the context of teams. The Gardener was part of a group of people who were working to resurrect a chapter of a local professional's association. To honour one of the senior people on the team, she advocated for creating an emeritus role to keep the person engaged and give them an opportunity to participate with the group.

Value 5: Empathise with People

Building from the previous examples, one of the most important leadership values for The Gardener was to empathise with people. She saw it both as a strength and a weakness of her leadership. At one point she explained, *'I probably practice a little too much empathy. I feel like I let people get away with things in a productivity sense a lot more than I should'*. Later, she further explained the importance of balance: *'There's a balance between empathizing with others and setting them up for success—however that plays out—and then balancing that with your own needs'*. She had been taken advantage of before because of her ability to empathise with people on her team. Empathy was important to The Gardener's leadership philosophy because she believed it helped put others into a position to succeed. One way this surfaced in her communicative activities was in the importance of withholding judgement in the face of uncertainty or ambiguity. She described moments where she had asked her team to try new or unfamiliar ways of working as a means for facilitating growth. In this way, she needed people on her team to empathise with her as well.

Introducing The Chef

Chefs purposefully assemble industry standards to consistently create a tasty mix of the resources and people needed to help a project succeed. Lammers and Tsvetkov (2008) discussed the 80/20 rule of project management, which broadly focuses on maximising return on investment.[*] They refer directly to the Project Management Institute as a 'cookbook' of industry standard practices. These practices are formalised into a body of knowledge that can be used in different organisations to deliver effective results. That is, a chef can bring their cooking skills in just about any kitchen. As well, chefs generally have training (The Chef in this excerpt is a certified Six Sigma Black Belt). In a cooking model, the project manager tends to emphasise the importance of the project over individuals. If gardeners tend to work from within the team, then chefs are the opposite, working more deliberately as a de facto team organiser (whether or not people follow is a separate issue). In other words, chefs deliberately work to develop and curate the management system teams use to stay organised, and some chefs will do that work with the team.

During the sampling period, The Chef was working as a consultant for an organisation that worked in health care. He was specifically brought in to help the organisation solve problems that had boiled over and had created a lot of tension across the team. He described the department he worked for in the organisation as experiencing a huge influx of work that they were struggling to manage. He explained it this way: *'They're trying to shift away from just reacting to all of the inflow of work that's coming in towards being prevention-oriented'*. His role was to help coach the team to become more productive and to simultaneously help them limit the amount of work going into their area. As he reflected on his role, he talked about how a lot of the work he'd done in health care was complex. Most of the complications arose from healthcare being view as a business, and The Chef believed too many companies would often write off work, instead of filing claims (and making money). In addition, The Chef was positioned as a contractor the organisation hired to help address business problems from a project management standpoint. He told me that the problems had been developing over several years and were neglected for a long time, and he identified the unfortunate result: the team had developed many bad habits that would have to be reversed.

When I asked The Chef about the kind of project management methodologies used by the organisation, he noted that it was elusive and did not really fit a traditional definition of waterfall, agile, or lean. He said that the issue for the project he was managing is that there was literally no system in place. He explained, *'Even the concept of waterfall and talking about flow just is not even part of the lexicon'*. The group had worked with the rest of the company to buy a project management technology solution to help centralise communication and create awareness of the intersection across all the different departments, but the adoption of that system was more about creating an improved customer experience across business units. He noted that his role was partially to help address this issue: *'This is me coming in after the fact and telling you my impression of it—a combination of company culture along with the product that they bought [. . .]'*. During the research, The Chef focused intently on the social aspects of communicating in a high-tension environment that was focused on making productive change. He worked to invite participation across several layers of the organisational network—from executive management to individuals on his team.

Leadership Values of The Chef

Given this context, the communication that I observed during the reporting period with The Chef focused on developing a system for managing project work. There were meetings with

---

[*] The 80/20 rule suggests project managers spend 20% of their time on project management activities that will lead to an 80% return on investment in the future.

individuals, teams, and at the executive level during which issues related to organisational and team culture clashed and made it challenging for him to do his work as their project manager. At the same time, there were clear tensions across project managers in other areas of the company as how to solve these problems (or even to agree on what the problems constituted). Working through these issues was challenging for The Chef because he felt that the organisational issues made it nearly impossible for him to do the job as he wanted to do it and believed it needed to be done, and it also clashed directly with how he understood the role of a project manager. The Chef wanted to develop a system with the team that would be useful for them moving forward, and he encouraged senior leadership to participate in that process by outlining clear goals and outcomes to support his efforts.

Value 1: Keep People on Task

An important value for The Chef was to keep people on task, particularly during meetings. To support this motive, he frequently acted in ways that would help make each meeting as productive as possible. He devoted a great deal of time preparing for meetings and learning from previous mistakes. Too often he felt blindsided by people's reaction to information he had prepared and presented. At one point, he told a story about a past experience where this happened with a vice president. In preparation for that meeting, he asked around how meetings with this person tend to go. He asked what kinds of reports the vice president wanted to see. The Chef explained this approach as, *'I try to come up with a sort of hypothesis of what's driving them, and then I actually test it during interactions'*. He noted a variety of strategies he used to keep people productive, most of them driven by reflecting about people's personalities and about his own mistakes working with teams in the past. He called this approach 'loss avoidance', in which you avoid losing productivity or harming a relationship because of a preparation error. In this way, The Chef put a lot of pressure on his own personal performance to deliver successful projects.

Value 2: Assign Roles to Individuals and Teams

The Chef also believed in the importance of everyone playing their role on the team, which included him as project manager. Of his role, he said, *'I am exactly in the middle of everything because I own nothing except the progress of the project'*. He would use several communication practices to show people that sticking to their assigned role was important to the success of the project. For example, he would arrange meetings, send follow-up emails, and embrace serendipitous check-ins to make sure people were aligned with the project. In these moments, The Chef would remind his team of the importance of roles in terms of the goal for the project. In reflecting on this during one of our interviews, he noted encouraging executive leadership to give a clearer charge to the team, as it would make implementing a system a far more productive process.

Value 3: Communicate to Clarify the Goal

In addition to keeping people on task and assigning roles, The Chef communicated in ways that would clarify project-related issues. For The Chef, clarifying information was as much about productivity as it was about not surprising people or catching someone off guard. In moments where there were communication bottlenecks, The Chef moved quickly to remove the road-block to get people back to work on the project. Sometimes these issues were interpersonal in nature, and at other times it had to do with clarifying the goal of the project for people on the team. He believed that in this particular organisation, a lack of clarity about the team's role was a deeply embedded issue that he continually needed to overcome to help the team be successful.

Value 4: Be Responsible to the Project

One of the major values motivating The Chef was to continue productivity toward the goal of a project in his actions and interactions with people. He would spend time investigating and learning about the existing project as a system to discover any issues that could easily be fixed. His training in Six Sigma certainly helped in this respect, and he noted the importance of process improvement during our interviews. And, since The Chef was also trained in user experience, he had a strong sense of how touchpoints in a management system could influence how people participated in project work. To get a view of these touchpoints, he would engage with people across different units to learn how information was coordinated. His goal for doing this work was to make sure people were honouring deadlines and understanding the dependencies of project work. He explained of his co-workers in different departments and of his teams, *'You need them to understand for the business to do things, a deadline has to be a deadline—as in the line that you are dead if you do not cross'.*

Value 5: Empathise to Motivate Action

The Chef confessed he had a very difficult time with the concept of empathy—not intellectually, but ethically. He felt that since his application of empathy was to make progress and motivate action—that because it was goal oriented—it somehow was less genuine. That said, The Chef did employ empathy as a leadership value, but his aim was to make progress on the project. He seemed to believe any emotional output that did not lead to productivity was bad for the project—and anything bad for the project was bad for the team. He also felt discussing emotions and people at work was dangerous. He would almost always rather discuss the system of managing work and would tolerate discussing feelings only if it led to action. The system, in his view, was safe to talk about. In regard to empathy, he concluded that, *'If you want my opinion, you've got to put an action on it'.* This view makes sense given The Chef's interest in evaluating productivity and metrics in general. The importance of measuring success directly correlated with his training in Six Sigma.

Comparing Communication Values of The Gardener and The Chef

So far, we've seen how The Gardener and The Chef embody two different leadership identities in the context of project management. Their values are important to acknowledge because they demonstrate how being a gardener or a chef influences project management communication and how they each perceive making space for people to participate. The Gardener focuses on her audience first and the project second, whereas The Chef focuses on the project first and

Table 2.1 Comparing Value of The Gardener and The Chef

The Gardener's Values	The Chef's Values
Teach methods of effective collaboration.	Keep people on task.
Learn about individuals and organisations.	Assign roles to individuals and teams.
Communicate to include.	Communicate to clarify the goal.
Be responsible to the team.	Be responsible to the project.
Practice empathy.	Empathise to motivate action.

then the audience. Both believe in encouraging participation, but The Gardener is positioned to cultivate it from within her team by communicating her values to people. Meanwhile, The Chef took a different role of making space by focusing on creating and iterating a management system for the project to succeed, which would ultimately benefit the team and the business.

Table 2.1 is a comparison of the values discovered across the two leadership profiles in this excerpt. I present these values not to position one approach against the other as more or less desirable, but to demonstrate how values influence how leaders communicate. I placed each of the elements in relation to each other to make comparisons easier to make.

The unique positionalities of The Gardener and The Chef also demonstrate an important aspect of their leadership values and agency as project managers. That is, The Gardener also acted in specific ways because of her role on the team. The situation and context helped to determine how she perceived this role. At the same time, The Chef was brought in as a consultant because of his training and experience. His role was to act *as a chef.*

From what we've learned from The Gardener and The Chef, leadership communication can be understood as a rhetorical performance that builds from the project manager's positionality and is refined through interactions with the team and extensions of the team. Leadership values are linked to the rhetorical context and situation. Furthermore, a leader's identity is not fixed, but it is value centric. Identity is constantly shifting. The Gardener and The Chef show how leadership identity is formed and reformed through rhetorical performance. In other words, leadership identity can be formed through interaction and participation, but an individual's values are far more reliant on other factors, such as training, education, and other professional experiences. These values are sense-making guideposts for The Gardener and The Chef and help them shape approaches to communication.

Leadership Identity as Rhetorical Performance

If the communication practices of project managers under a participatory paradigm focus on making space for people, then what we learn from The Gardener and The Chef is that leadership philosophy influences how space is or is not being made through communication. Leadership as a practice is rhetorical because, to be effective, it requires consideration of context, situation, and positionality before acting.

We can also understand these considerations by extending the concept of *terministic screens.* Herrick (2009) described terministic screens as *'any set of terms used to describe an object, event, or person simultaneously directs attention* toward *some factors and* away *from others'* (p. 228). For example, the language The Gardener and The Chef used to describe communication events were key in revealing how they perceived the event. For example, The Gardener described the 'pain' she felt for someone else as she worked to access the scheduling system. Using the term *pain* signalled her value of empathising with people on the team.

Meanwhile, The Chef described a meeting as 'running rampant', demonstrating his value of keeping teams on task. Leadership values, in essence, also help illustrate the philosophies underlying choices made about communicating. Both The Gardener and The Chef hope to extend invitations to participate, but their values help to determine what sort of participation they find productive.

However, just as development methodologies should not be applied as a template over people, leadership values are not implemented devoid of situation and context. The language used to describe the communication events can only help to illuminate what someone is paying attention to at a given moment—what they perceive in that moment as most important. For example, let's turn to back to an example with The Gardener. She noted that a new co-worker instant messaged her about accessing the team's scheduling system.

The Gardener stopped what she was doing and saw an opportunity to model the kind of interaction she wanted to see occur more often across the team. The Chef, we can speculate, might have identified that there was a problem with the system and tried to work with this person to isolate the problem to improve it. The Gardener and The Chef may have experienced the same moment but turned their attention to different aspects of that situation, producing different outcomes. The reason that leadership approach matters so much at the project level is because it produces different kinds of outcomes. As Drucker (2009) said, *'Leadership is a means. Leadership to what ends is the crucial question'* (p. 268).

Suffice to say, the communication events discussed in this excerpt also suggest that a project manager's leadership philosophy seems shaped quite a bit by their positionality in the group. These factors appear far more implicit. That is, what is charismatic in one context appears brutish or crude in another. Prescriptive leadership approaches decline to acknowledge the role of the social in enacting leadership at the project level.

While the cases in this excerpt suggest an alignment across individual personalities, beliefs, and values, they also emphasise the rhetorically responsive nature of leadership as informed by situation and embedded in context. Simply put, The Gardener inhabited the role of a gardener on her team because she was hired in that role. In addition, her personality tended toward sowing seeds and helping them grow. The same goes for The Chef. He was contracted by an organisation to come in and cook. So that is what he did.

In the context of this excerpt, the production of identities and social relations is important because it helps to further illustrate the effects of a paradigm shift from efficiency to participation. That is, the identities, or knowledge, of individuals and teams are not fixed. As such, communicating for participation also means making space for growth, what Biesecker calls 'radical possibility'. Project teams that approach communication events as identity-forming can still focus on exigence, such as discussing a disagreement about a new feature of a mobile application. However, what Biesecker's argument suggests is that leadership is socially coordinated through and by participation of the team.

Communication on teams is transformative. So much of the knowledge work today focuses on individual and collective learning, either through structures unique to a project, such as a project retrospective, or through professional development activities, such as certification or training. When leadership works as a means of facilitating this participation, project managers have to make space for people. The values of leadership can give space to certain ideas while, perhaps unknowingly, limiting space for others because of what a project manager perceives to be most important about a given communication event. In this way, leadership values at the project level can also be a constraining construct, giving presence to certain concerns and behaviours while diminishing or potentially silencing others.

References and Further Reading

Amidon, S., and Blythe, S. (2008). Wrestling with Proteus: Tales of communication managers in a changing economy. *Journal of Business and Technical Communication, 22*(1), 5–37. doi: 10.1177/1050651907307698

Asghar, R. (2014). *Leadership Is Hell: How to Manage Well—And Escape with Your Soul.* Los Angeles, CA: Figueroa Press.

Biesecker, B. A. (1989). Rethinking the rhetorical situation from within the thematic of 'différance'. *Philosophy and Rhetoric, 22*(2), 110–130.

Bolger, N., and Laurenceau, J. (2013). *Intensive Longitudinal Methods: An Introduction to Diary and Experience Sampling.* New York, NY: Guilford Press.

Demarco, T., and Lister T. (1999). *Peopleware* (2nd Ed.). New York, NY: Dorset House Publishing Company, Inc.

Drucker, P. F. (2009). *The Essential Drucker: The Best of Sixty Years of Peter Drucker's Essential Writing on Management* [Kindle version]. Retrieved from Amazon.com

Fairhurst, G. T., and Sarr, R. A. (1996). *The Art of Framing: Managing the Language of Leadership.* San Francisco, CA: Jossey-Bass Inc.

Grabill, J. T., and Pigg, S. (2012). Messy rhetoric: Identity performance as rhetorical agency in online public forums. *Rhetoric Society Quarterly, 42*(2), 99–119. doi:10.1080/02773945.2012.660369

Hart-Davidson, W. (2007). Researching the activity of writing: Time-use diaries, mobile technologies, and video screen capture. Studying the mediated action of composing with time–use diaries. In: H. McKee and D. DeVoss (Eds.). *Digital Writing Research: Technologies, Methodologies, and Ethical Issues,* 153–169. Cresskill, NJ: Hampton Press.

Hart-Davidson, W. (2001). On writing, technical communication, and information technology: The core competencies of technical communication. *Technical Communication, 48*(2), 145–155.

Herrick, J. A. (2009). *The History and Theory of Rhetoric: An Introduction.* Boston, MA: Pearson.

Higgs, M. (2003). How can we make sense of leadership in the 21st century? *Leadership and Organization Development Journal, 24*(5), 273–284. doi: 10.1108/01437730310485798

Kouzes, J. M., and Posner, B. Z. (2017). *The Leadership Challenge* (6th Ed.). Hoboken, NJ: John Wiley & Sons.

Lammers, M., and Tsvetkov, N. (2008, July). More with less: The 80/20 rule of PM. *TC World.* Retrieved from http://www.tcworld.info/e-magazine/content-strategies/article/more-with-less-the-8020-rule-of-pm/

Lauren, B. (2018). *Communicating Project Management: A Participatory Rhetoric for Development Teams.* New York, NY: Routledge.

Maxwell, J. C. (2007). *The 21 Irrefutable Laws of Leadership Workbook: Follow Them and People Will Follow You* (Rev. and update 10th Anniv. Ed.). Nashville, TN [u.a.]: Thomas Nelson.

Moskowitz, D. S., and Sadikaj, G. (2012). Event-contingent recording. In: M. R. Mehl and T. S. Conner (Eds.). *Handbook of Research Methods for Studying Daily Life*, 160–175. New York, NY: The Guilford Press.

Northouse, P. G. (2015). *Leadership: Theory and Practice* (7th Ed.). Thousand Oaks, CA: SAGE Publications.

Chapter 3

Teams

From Teams and Teamwork to Teaming

Darren Dalcher

One of the distinctions of project work is that it is done by dedicated teams of people, often acting outside the normal organisational structures associated with 'regular' work. Projects can thus be said to bring together collections of individuals who are focused on the achievement of specific objectives and targets. Teams can thus be viewed as the main way through which work gets done and value is delivered to organisations and societies. Such teams are often formed for the duration of the project and disbanded following the delivery of the objectives.

Yet the terminology we use to describe such collections of individuals is frequently problematic and laden with different meanings; indeed, the common interpretation of terms such as teams and groups can often be confusing.

The *Oxford English Dictionary* defines a *team* as *'two or more people working together'*. It further elaborates that to *team up* is to *'come together as a team to achieve a common goal'*. The *Cambridge Dictionary* describes the verb *team* as *'to act together to achieve something'*. The definitions chime with the view of US industrialist Henry Ford, who asserted that *'coming together is a beginning; keeping together is progress; working together is success'.*[*]

In contrast, *Oxford* views a *group* as *'a number of people or things that are located, gathered or classed together'*. *Cambridge* views a group as *'a number of people or things that are put together or considered as a unit'*. The *Collins English Dictionary* offers a much wider set of definitions, including: *'a number of people or things which are together in one place at one time; a set of people who have the same interests or aims . . . who organize themselves to work or act together; or a set of people, organizations, or things which are considered together because they have something in common'*. Confusingly, it also designates the verb form of *grouping together* as *'a number of things or people . . . that are together in one place or within one organization or system'*.

Merriam-Webster offers a more comprehensive definition of a group as encompassing *'two or more figures forming a complete unit of composition; a number of individuals assembled together or having some unifying relationship; an assemblage of related organisms—often used to avoid taxonomic connotation when the kind of degree of relationship is not clearly defined'*.

The terms *team* and *group* are often used interchangeably. So, are the terms really exchangeable, or is there a fundamental distinction between them?

---

[*] https://quotepark.com/quotes/16464-henry-ford-coming-together-is-a-beginning-staying-together-i/

The Difference Between Groups and Teams

In reality there are some subtle, as well as many clear, distinctions. In a nutshell, individuals in groups work independently, addressing their own agendas and priorities, whilst teams tend to collaborate on a single purpose or overarching goal. Groups may coordinate the individual efforts, whilst teams collaborate on achieving their common purpose, often displaying mutual commitment. Teams bring together a range of expertise and capabilities needed to combine and deliver meaningful results and often extend beyond organisational silos or functional structures. Teams are also more likely to be employed on temporary endeavours, providing a focused and cross-functional orientation supplemented by closer relationships and a sense of community. The result can be viewed as the ability to emphasise communal performance rather than celebrate individual achievements (Dalcher, 2016a: 2).

Teams often develop a collective identity and a greater responsibility for one another whilst supporting the wider group. Members are interdependent, acting out of collective interest and maximising the greater good by focusing on the main goal and key objectives. Team members develop a deeper mutual understanding that enables them to maximise the interest of the collective, with high-performing teams benefitting from the synergistic impacts of the assembled team.

Scottish American philanthropist and industrialist Andrew Carnegie determined that *'Teamwork is the ability to work together toward a common vision. The ability to direct individual accomplishments toward organizational objectives. It is the fuel that allows common people to attain uncommon results'.**

Katzenbach and Smith (2015) conclude that teams should be the basic unit of organisation for most businesses to enable them to achieve their highest levels of performance, especially as teamwork integrates performance and learning. In their bestseller, which has sold over half a million copies, Katzenbach and Smith further confirm that commitment to performance goals and common purpose is more important to team success than team building and establish that real teams are the most important spearheads of change at all levels.

Teams take time to form and learn to perform together. As each team is made of a collection of individuals, it is subject to their relationships, internal dynamics and willingness to cooperate and collaborate. Katzenbach and Smith (2015) note that all teams must shape their own purpose, performance goals and approach. Groups don't become teams just because that is what someone calls them. The best teams invest a large amount of time in shaping their own purpose that they can own and translate that purpose into specific performance goals so that members can become accountable with and to their own teammates (Katzenbach and Smith, 2008).

The Dynamic Dysfunctions of Teams

In the book *The Five Dysfunctions of a Team*, which has sold over two million copies, Lencioni (2006) highlights the root causes of politics, inability to deliver and dysfunctions of teams as the key problems plaguing teams that underperform—slightly paraphrased below—as:

---

* https://quotepark.com/search/?h=Andrew+Carnegie+%E2%80%98Teamwork+is+the+ability+to+work +together+toward+a+common+vision

Absence of trust. The fear of vulnerability in front of other team members prevents the building of trust within the team.

Fear of conflict. Productive conflict is avoided in order to preserve an artificial harmony.

Lack of commitment. The absence of buy-in from the team, or the lack of clarity about objectives, prevents team members from making crucial decisions needed to support and deliver the mission.

Avoidance of accountability. In order to avoid interpersonal discomfort, team members do not hold each other accountable.

Inattention to results. The pursuit of individual goals, agendas and personal status erodes the focus on collective and ultimate success.

Teamwork has the potential to become a sustainable competitive advantage that organisations can control. Indeed, overcoming the dysfunctions is possible. Teams are designed to achieve the results they set out to achieve. Improving team performance requires attention and effort to address the key dysfunctions. Teams that perform well display a more advanced set of teamwork characteristics. In particular, Lencioni (2005: 7) notes the following (summarised and slightly paraphrased) aspects:

- Team members trust one another and are comfortable being vulnerable with each other about their weaknesses, mistakes, fears, concerns and behaviours; they are also happy to tap into each other's skills, expertise and experience.
- Because they trust each other, team members can engage in passionate dialogue around critical issues and decisions.
- By being open and engaging in dialogue, they are able to achieve genuine buy-in, even following initial disagreements.
- As they commit to making decisions, team members are comfortable holding each other accountable, instead of relying on the team leader as the main source of accountability.
- They are therefore more likely to set aside their individual agendas and needs and focus instead on doing what is needed to secure team success.

Lencioni suggests that the first key question to ask is, *'Are we really a team?'*

Sometimes a team improvement effort is doomed from the start because the group going through it isn't really a team at all . . . You see a team is a relatively small number of people that shares common goals as well as rewards and responsibilities for achieving them. Team members readily set aside their individual or personal needs for the greater good of the group (Lencioni, 2005: 9).

The second question is, *'Are we ready for the heavy lifting?'*

Teams have great advantages, but they can only be attained through commitment and investment from the individual members.

In subsequent work, Lencioni (2016) concludes that the ideal team player has three major traits or virtues that impact the team's success: humility, hunger and people smarts. This combination of traits distinguishes individuals capable of contributing to a team effort and accelerates the process of building high-performing teams.

The Return of Trust

From the early cave dwellers and hunter-gatherers, humans have long understood the value of collaboration. Collaboration emphasises the purposeful nature of a partnership where all parties strategically elect to cooperate in order to attain a mutually desirable outcome or a particular benefit (Dalcher, 2016b: 1). However, the design of the ideal, or the perfect team, requires deeper consideration of the qualities of participants.

Improving the performance of teams is a life-long mission for many organisations. Google®, for instance, has invested a small fortune in trying to optimise their internal teams and improve their performance as a result. Their working assumption was that creating the best teams would require bringing together the best individuals, and somehow matching their skills and interests would create dream teams. In 2012 Google launched Project Aristotle, a study concerned with transforming productivity by building the perfect team and investigating why some teams succeed whilst others flounder. Previous studies at Google focused on what makes good managers, but it was also noted that employees interviewed in surveys consistently mentioned the importance of their teams. The study's aim was to bring together organisational researchers, psychologists, sociologists and statisticians, as well as researchers, all searching for the patterns of excellence in teams.

Over the years, many schemes, frameworks and models have been devised to measure the performance of teams and create optimal high-performing teams. The researchers began by reviewing over half a century of academic research on how teams worked. Google measures most aspects of their employees' lives, so they assumed the data would be rich enough to identify discernible patterns. The data included insights into team composition, skills, capabilities, background and common interests. Meanwhile, the rest of the research squad interviewed hundreds of individuals working in 180 teams across the organisation. Despite recording 250 different types of attributes representing individual traits, skills and team habits, the results did not yield any insights regarding the perfect mix required to underpin the best teams.

No matter how researchers arranged the data, though, it was almost impossible to find patterns—or any evidence that the composition of a team made any difference. '"We looked at 180 teams from all over the company," Dubey said. "We had lots of data, but there was nothing showing that a mix of specific personality types or skills or backgrounds made any difference. The 'who' part of the equation didn't seem to matter"' (Duhigg, 2016: 27).

Having discovered no discernible patterns, the group turned to group norms—the traditions, behavioural standards, gender balance and unspoken rules that were used by teams. Yet even the group norms seemed inconsistent across the different teams, offering multiple and often contradictory leads. The researchers continued to stumble in the dark, until they stumbled upon the concept of *psychological safety*, promoted through the work of Professor Amy Edmondson from Harvard Business School.

Psychological safety refers to the shared belief that the team provides a safe environment for interpersonal risk taking (Edmondson, 1999; Baer & Frese, 2003); a team climate or norm characterised by interpersonal trust and mutual respect in which team members feel empowered to speak, question decisions and participate without fear of being judged, rejected or punished (Kahn, 1990; Tucker & Edmondson, 2003; Edmondson et al., 2004; Carmeli, 2007; Edmondson & Lei, 2014; Newman et al., 2017).

Psychological safety, as a feature of the workplace, allows team members to share personal insights as well as feelings, thoughts and concerns in an attempt to improve performance (Schein & Bennis, 1965; Kahn, 1990; Edmondson, 2018). Psychological safety thus relies on trust amongst team members as the most fundamental ingredient in collective endeavours (Edmondson, 2002; Dalcher, 2017), enabling a greater focus on achieving shared goals (Schein, 1992).

The concept of psychological safety reminded the researchers that some team members talked about a safe space to take risks, while others bemoaned the tendency of their leaders to panic and grab control, depriving the team of opportunities for experimentation and development . . . This was the Eureka moment for the research effort (Duhigg, 2016). Upon revisiting the data, the researchers established that their best teams provided a safe space for members to talk to each other, listen and share. Above all, they enabled full and proper participation in the team.

Google now identifies psychological safety as the most important factor in building a successful team. It is less to do with how the team is put together, or the identity of the members, and more with how the members interact with and relate to one another and is consequently being viewed as making the greatest difference to team dynamics.

The five key dynamics identified as essential to team performance by the Google research team are described below (Rozovsky, 2015):

Psychological safety. Team members feel safe to take risks and be vulnerable in front of each other.
Dependability. Team members can count on each other to get thing done.
Structure and clarity. Team members have well defined goals, clear roles and specific execution plans.
Meaning of work. The work is personally important for team members.
Impact of work. Team members believe their work is significant and creates meaningful and useful change.

While all factors are viewed as important, psychological safety is recognised as underpinning the other four and is therefore essential in enabling the team to perform effectively and succeed.

A team is not a group of people who work together. A team is a group of people who trust each other. [*]
                                                                    — Simon Sinek

Robbins and Finley (2000: 156) used the metaphor of blood to represent the critical importance of trust in teams: *'Trust is the blood of teams. The river that carries it along, that pulses with life, that brings thought and power to everything the team attempts'.*

The deliberations of the Google research team appear to indicate that many of the detailed measurements employed in assessing team composition offer a poor prediction of actual team performance, at least in the context of the projects undertaken by Google.

The findings of Project Aristotle can perhaps be re-positioned as a simple behavioural checklist related to the team dynamics and the strength of the team environment, starting with the fundamental safety question (see Table 3.1).

The table sets out fundamental questions, starting with the individual level, that can be extended to the team environment to determine the ability of the team to work effectively and establish the norms and beliefs regarding the levels of safety and mutual trust underpinning the potential for enduring achievement within the team.

Who Is Packing Your Parachute?

Trust is essential to developing, growing and sustaining teams. Reflecting on his experience as the commander of the US forces in Afghanistan in the mid-2000s, General Stanley McChrystal

---

[*] https://quotefancy.com/quote/1415610/Simon-Sinek-A-team-is-not-a-group-of-people-that-work-together-A-team-is-a-group-of

**Table 3.1 Team Dynamics Checklist Inspired by
Project Aristotle Findings**

Area	Key question
Psychological safety	Am I safe? Or more specifically: Is it safe to be vulnerable and take risks in front of each other?
Dependability	Can I trust you? Perhaps rephrased as: Can we rely on each other to deliver high-quality work, as required?
Structure and clarity	What are we doing? Made more pertinent by asking: Do we know where we are headed and how to get there? (i.e., Do we have well-defined goals, clear roles and specific execution plans?)
Meaning of work	Do I really care? Slightly re-positioned as: Are we working on something that is personally important and relevant to all team members?
Impact of work	Will it make a difference? Do we believe that work is significant and purposeful and will likely create meaningful and useful change? (i.e.: Can what we are doing positively impact the greater good?)

devised the notion of Team of Teams (McChrystal et al., 2015). McChrystal discovered himself facing an enemy organised in flat networks that enabled it to regularly change, adapt and reconfigure itself. To combat the enemy, McChrystal investigated the ideas of complex systems and thereby recognised the need to transit from a fixed and cumbersome traditional military hierarchy towards a set of dynamic teams operating as high-performance teams.

McChrystal synthesised his (slightly paraphrased below) principles for creating high-preforming adaptive teams as having:

- A clear and common purpose
- The freedom to speak your mind
- The ability and trust to make decisions
- A shared consciousness around value and what 'good' looks like
- Trust in the capabilities, knowledge and intentions of other members
- Leading like a gardener by focusing on the creation of a nurturing and supportive environment in which good work can take place, without the need to task-manage (note the focus on cultivation and nurturing, which chimes with the Gardener narrative introduced in the previous chapter in the context of communication and support)

The power of teams is also reflected in having the ability of different members of the team to deal responsibly with all the required aspects and prepare for the normal contingencies of any situation. Joseph Charles Plumb was a US Navy jet pilot during the Vietnam War who successfully completed 75 combat missions (Plumb & DeWerff, 1973). On his next mission, he managed to bail out just before his plane was hit by a surface-to-air missile. He parachuted into enemy territory and was captured and held in a prisoner of war camp for over six years.

Years later he was dining in the US with his wife when a man seated at another table came over and said *'You're Plumb! You flew jet fighters in Vietnam from the aircraft carrier Kitty Hawk. You were shot down!'*

Plumb was intrigued and asked, *'How in the world, did you know that?'*

'I packed your parachute', the stranger replied.

Plumb jumped up in surprise and hugged the man.

*'I guess it work*ed*',* the stranger continued.

Plumb was quick to reassure him: *'It sure did. If your chute hadn't worked, I wouldn't be here today'.*

Plumb spent the next sleepless night reflecting on the stranger who saved his life. As a fighter pilot, he would have ignored the mere sailor in a white uniform. The sailor must have spent many hours in the bowels of the ship folding the silk parachutes over wooden desks. Yet, Plumb was grateful for his dedication and ability to carry out his duties in a professional manner. Plumb also recognised that he needed many different parachutes to get through his ordeal—his physical parachute, his mental parachute, his emotional parachute and his spiritual parachute.

We all have team members and indeed other support teams who provide specialist services acting for the greater good. We often take their presence and good will on trust. We never hear about them precisely because things often work out as intended. If we get to know them, or hear about them, it is probably because something went wrong. Their success criteria may well be to 'never make the news' (i.e., always deliver a service that does not draw attention to itself through failure or absence).

We could look around us and try to reflect on all the teams and unsung heroes that silently provide uninterrupted and perfectly reliable parachute services. Indeed, it is a sobering thought to ask yourself periodically, 'Who is packing my parachute?'

Creative Teams

What about the success of teams?

The work context is becoming increasingly more challenging as professionals and teams encounter a faster changing world replete with seemingly unprecedented levels of uncertainty, turbulence, novelty and ambiguity. Moreover, the complexity of many undertakings is also on the increase, requiring faster learning, skilful adaptation and well-considered experimentation. The implication is that to operate successfully, teams will require greater flexibility, an expanding diversity of potential responses and amplified agility and resilience skills that underpin their abilities to explore, make sense of, respond to and benefit from variations, change and opportunities.

A recent article in the *Harvard Business Review* reasons that cognitive diversity in a team leads to speedier problem solving. Reynolds and Lewis (2017) have studied how well executive teams could complete a strategic execution task under time pressure. Their conclusion is that diversity in age, ethnicity and gender has little, if any, impact on a team's ability to navigate complex or novel situations. However, the cognitive diversity, which they define as the *'differences in perspective or information processing style'* (Ibid: 2) is critical to dictating how successful a given team would be at solving a problem.

The early results from the 12-year study indicate that diverse teams involving a mix of thinking styles outperformed mentally homogenous teams. Indeed, some of the teams in which all members had the same thinking style never finished the task. Reynolds and Lewis conclude that 'tackling new challenges requires a balance between applying what we know and discovering what we don't know that may be useful. It also requires individual application of specialised expertise and the ability to step back and look at the bigger picture' (Ibid.: 4).

Homogenous teams will tend to apply similar logic and fail to identify and utilise alternative resolution approaches and diverse perspectives, which could be limiting, particularly in challenging contexts and novel situations. A high degree of cognitive diversity allows exploration of alternative routes and methods and the introduction of alternative perspectives and considerations whilst also generating accelerated learning and improved performance.

Peter Cook, our guest author in this chapter, is also concerned about the new dimensions of change in modern contexts. His contribution is developed from his book *Brain Based Enterprises: Harmonising the Head, Heart and Soul of Business*, published by Routledge. Cook draws upon his unique expertise as a leader of Human Dynamics, a creativity and innovation consultancy; his research career as the leader of global medical research teams; and the creator of the Academy of Rock, fusing business leadership with music. With his unique background and reputation as an innovator and deep thinker, Cook is both an agent provocateur, constantly challenging the status quo, and the epitome of cognitive diversity enabled through the blending of different approaches and perspectives for viewing the world.

In an increasingly demanding world, Cook views intelligence, ideas and innovation as the three core currencies of sustainable progress which can be harnessed to encourage improvement. He identifies an unprecedented level of convergence between humanity and technology, introducing a new level of man-machine dynamic. The convergence requires a rethinking of the relationships and adjustments to the practices we apply in the real world. His approach is to emphasise the role of brainy people, brainy teams and brainy enterprises, and his current contribution is focused on the role and impact of brainy teams. The distinction also allows Cook to address different levels of capability, which he positions as personal intelligence, collective intelligence and global intelligence. He thus offers a new level of diversity alongside a sensitivity to the abilities of people in teams and enterprises and a keen interest in augmenting and fusing capabilities with new technologies.

Cook addresses some of the key topics in teams, including levels of connectedness, team diversity, team chemistry and team transparency, often re-focusing attention around collaboration in innovative activities and novel contexts. Teams can make themselves more intelligent (and increase their diversity) through networking and leveraging their knowledge, expertise, connections and experiences. Leading teams in the age of intelligence requires new skills of facilitation, engagement and influencing (Cook, 2018: xiv). At the enterprise level there is also a greater need for improvisation, agility and responsiveness—and the liberation of the head, heart and soul, inspired by ideas from the art world.

Not surprisingly, Cook agitates for a more responsible agenda, both in terms of our interactions with machines and technology and of the social and sustainable dimensions of our actions. As part of his wider agenda, he advocates the replacement of Michael Porter's notion of *competitive advantage* with the idea of *sustainable coopetive advantage* through the incorporation of aspects of cooperative behaviour and sustainability considerations. The idea of intelligent teams can thus be offered as a new foundation for considering the power and success of teams through encouraging a new emphasis on cooperation, collaboration, sharing and increased knowledge assets, perspectives and capabilities available for teams to utilise. The result may well be the creation and development of more effective and better-informed teams capable of delivering in and responding to our rapidly changing world.

Teaming for Success

Harvard Business School professor Amy Edmondson maintains that organisational success and failure is dependent on a team's ability to 'team'—to learn and adapt to the environment and each other. She offers the example of the Water Cube, the magnificent 340,000 square foot box framed in steel and covered with semi-transparent, eco-efficient blue bubbles, hosting the swimming and diving events at the Beijing 2012 Olympic Games. The Water Cube won prestigious engineering and design awards and cost an estimated 10.2 billion Yuan.

> The goal was clear: Build an iconic structure to reflect Chinese culture, integrate with the site, and minimize energy consumption—on time and within budget. But how to do it all was less clear (Edmondson, 2012: 72–74).

Increasingly demanding challenges call for new approaches and new levels of engagement. Tristram Carfrae,[*] an Arup structural engineer based in Sydney, brought together a team of experts from 20 disciplines and four countries to deliver the special building. However, the undertaking required new approaches to managing projects and teams.

> Success depended on bridging dramatically different national, organizational and occupational cultures to collaborate in fluid groupings that emerged and dissolved in response to needs that were identified as the work progressed (p. 74).

Instead of using established teams, the strategy called for *teaming*—gathering experts in temporary groups as needed to solve problems as and when they emerge. The leader's job under such circumstances is not to manage or support the team, but to inspire and enable teaming in the right configurations needed to progress the joint purpose. Teaming can therefore emerge and evolve as members, specialists and stakeholders pull together and respond to what arises from the targeted pursuit of the intended purpose.

Teaming is not a noun but a new way of life, a continuous effort to undertake and complete a bigger and more complex undertaking that can only be understood as the details emerge and the opportunities are explored. Teaming implies a constantly shifting membership, albeit with a diversity of perspectives as necessitated by the conditions uncovered and the ideas being pursued.

Edmondson advocates a move from teams to 'teaming', replacing stable project teams with a flexible form of teamwork, by gathering diverse experts from different domains and specialisms into temporary groups to address emerging progress, problems and opportunities and enable a form of learning as we progress.

> Teaming helps individuals acquire knowledge, skills and networks. And it lets companies accelerate the delivery of current products and services while responding quickly to new opportunities. Teaming is a way to get work done while figuring out how to do it better; it's executing and learning at the same time (Ibid.: 74).

Teaming is ideal for complex, uncertain, novel and turbulent settings, where immense levels of learning and sense making are needed. It fosters diversity of perspectives and approaches by considering ideas from multiple domains and areas and enables better informed and more inclusive and intelligent solutions to be proposed, trialled and implemented.

---

[*]   https://www.arup.com/our-firm/tristram-carfrae-rdi

The key challenges in teaming (paraphrased from Edmondson, 2012: 78) are:

- Multiple functions must work together, so conflict may arise.
- People are geographically dispersed, so communication difficulties and time-zone differences present logistical difficulties.
- Relationships are temporary, so there is little time to build trust and mutual understanding.
- No two projects are alike, so no precedents exist.
- The work can be uncertain and chaotic, so fluid situations are in need of constant communication and coordination.

Nonetheless, the potential benefits are also enormous and include (Ibid.):

- Innovation from combined skills and perspectives
- Boundary-spanning solutions
- Developing an understanding of other disciplines
- Broader perspective
- Greater alignment across divisions
- Extensive networks of collaborations
- Ability to meet changing customer needs
- Flexibility and agility
- Ability to import ideas from other contexts
- Ability to manage unexpected events
- Experimentation

The key principles required for successful teaming would be quite familiar (adapted from Edmondson, 2012: 80–81):

Emphasising purpose. By articulating what is at stake, particularly for diverse and wide-ranging teaming arrangements.
Building psychological safety. Required to enable rapid sharing and trust building.
Embracing failure. Novelty courts failures as well as new learning opportunities.
Putting conflict to work. Diversity will foster differences, and conflict can be used to tease out new ideas and perspectives.

TEAM = Together Everyone Achieves More

The value of teams and their key contributions can be summarised through a two quotes:

We talk a lot about hope, helping, and teamwork. Our whole message is that we are more powerful together.[*]
—Victoria Osteen

Reflecting a greater responsibility towards wider society is becoming an essential part of contemporary thinking:

Cooperation is the thorough conviction that nobody can get there unless everybody gets there.[†]
—Virginia Burden

---

[*] https://www.brainyquote.com/quotes/victoria_osteen_708266
[†] https://quozio.com/quote/b3062b23/1025/cooperation-is-the-thorough-conviction-that-nobody-can-get

Looking back may enable us to develop a more enlightened and reliable path to a less certain future . . .

Teams have played a key part in enabling human achievement and collective development over our entire history. Ultimately, *teaming* may provide the next step by offering a more intelligent and informed approach for drawing from a vastly superior pool of knowledge and perspectives, responding to opportunities and maximising the sustainable value of our engagements, and developing a more responsible and inclusive basis for making decisions, addressing concerns and driving our future endeavours, and thereby enabling sustainable and enduring progress.

References

Baer, M., and Frese, M. (2003). Innovation is not enough: Climates for initiative and psychological safety, process innovations, and firm performance. *Journal of Organizational Behavior: The International Journal of Industrial, Occupational and Organizational Psychology and Behavior, 24*(1), 45–68.

Carmeli, A. (2007). Social capital, psychological safety and learning behaviours from failure in organisations. *Long Range Planning, 40*(1), 30–44.

Cook, P. (2018). *Brain Based Enterprises: Harmonising the Head, Heart and Soul of Business.* Abingdon, UK: Routledge.

Dalcher, D. (2016a). Thinking teams, performing teams and sustaining teams: Beginning the dialogue about working together. *PM World Journal, 5*(8), 1–6.

Dalcher, D. (2016b). The essence of collaboration: Extending our reach and potential. *PM World Journal, 5*(10), 1–5.

Dalcher, D. (2017). It starts with trust: People, perspectives and relationships as the building blocks for sustainable success. *PM World Journal, 6*(3), 1–7.

Duhigg, C. (2016). What Google learned from its quest to build the perfect team. *The New York Times Magazine, 26*, February 25. https://www.nytimes.com/2016/02/28/magazine/what -google-learned-from-its-quest-to-build-the-perfect-team.html

Edmondson, A. C. (1999). Psychological safety and learning behavior in work teams. *Administrative Science Quarterly, 44*(2), 350–383.

Edmondson, A. C. (2002). *Managing the risk of learning: Psychological safety in work teams,* 255–275. Cambridge, MA: Division of Research, Harvard Business School.

Edmondson, A. C. (2012). Teamwork on the fly. *Harvard Business Review, 90*(4), 72–80.

Edmondson, A. C. (2018). *The Fearless Organization: Creating Psychological Safety in the Workplace for Learning, Innovation, and Growth.* Hoboken, NJ: John Wiley & Sons.

Edmondson, A. C., Kramer, R. M., and Cook, K. S. (2004). Psychological safety, trust, and learning in organizations: A group-level lens. In: R. M. Kramer and K. S. Cook (Eds.). *Trust and Distrust in Organizations: Dilemmas and Approaches,* 239–272. New York, NY: Russell Sage Foundation.

Edmondson, A. C., and Lei, Z. (2014). Psychological safety: The history, renaissance, and future of an interpersonal construct. *Annual Review of Organizational Psychology and Organizational Behavior, 1*(1), 23–43.

Kahn, W. A. (1990). Psychological conditions of personal engagement and disengagement at work. *Academy of Management Journal, 33*(4), 692–724.

Katzenbach, J. R., and Smith, D. K. (2008). *The Discipline of Teams*. Waltham, MA: Harvard Business Press.

Katzenbach, J. R., and Smith, D. K. (2015). *The Wisdom of Teams: Creating the High-Performance Organization*. Waltham, MA: Harvard Business Review Press.

Lencioni, P. (2005). *Overcoming the Five Dysfunctions of a Team: A Field Guide for Leaders, Managers, and Facilitators*. San Francisco, CA: John Wiley & Sons.

Lencioni, P. (2006). *The Five Dysfunctions of a Team*. San Francisco, CA: Jossey-Bass.

Lencioni, P. (2016). *The Ideal Team Player: How to Recognize and Cultivate the Three Essential Virtues*. Hoboken, NJ: John Wiley & Sons.

McChrystal, G. S., Collins, T., Silverman, D., and Fussell, C. (2015). *Team of Teams: New Rules of Engagement for a Complex World*. New York, NY: Portfolio Penguin.

Newman, A., Donohue, R., and Eva, N. (2017). Psychological safety: A systematic review of the literature. *Human Resource Management Review, 27*(3), 521–535.

Plumb, C., and DeWerff, G. (1973). *I'm No Hero: A POW Story as Told to Glen DeWerff*. Westlake Village, CA: Captain J. Charles Plumb.

Reynolds, A., and Lewis, D. (2017). Teams solve problems faster when they're more cognitively diverse. *Harvard Business Review, 93*(3), 1–8.

Robbins, H., and Finley, M. (2000). *The New Why Teams Don't Work: What Goes Wrong and How to Make It Right*. Oakland, CA: Berrett-Koehler Publishers.

Schein, E. H. (1992). How can organizations learn faster? The problem of entering the Green Room. *Sloan Management Review, 34*(2): 85–93.

Schein, E. H., and Bennis, W. G. (1965). *Personal and organizational change through group methods: The laboratory approach*. New York, NY: John Wiley & Sons.

Scoro (2017). Infographic: Why your teamwork isn't working, https://www.scoro.com/blog/teamwork-infographic/

Rozovsky, J. (2015). The five keys to a successful Google team. Re: Work. https://rework.withgoogle.com/blog/five-keys-to-a-successful-google-team/

Tucker, A. L., and Edmondson, A. C. (2003). Why hospitals don't learn from failures: Organizational and psychological dynamics that inhibit system change. *California Management Review, 45*(2), 55–72.

Leading Brainy Teams

Peter Cook

Imagine a world where we work 15 hours a week with greater access to leisure, pleasure, and intellectual and social stimulation. We've been promised this for decades, but the advent of computers has hermetically attached us to our iPods, iPads and office pods. Artificial intelligence offers us a one-time opportunity to break free of our addiction to working on the chain gang, although it is as yet unclear as to whether our merger with artificial intelligence will lead to a 'War of the Worlds' or a harmonious fusion of man, woman, project and machine.

Brain Based Enterprises: Harmonising the Head, Heart and Soul of Business (Cook, 2018) explores the role that innovation and creativity will play to help us survive and thrive in the 4th Industrial Revolution. This is not the stone age, the steam age or the industrial age, but the information revolution, where value is created primarily through the intelligent combination of knowledge and wisdom. How shall we cope in a world where it has variously been predicted that up to 50 percent of our jobs will disappear in the next few decades? What does that mean for education, where the half-life of knowledge is in free-fall? What will become of money in such a world? How shall we fall in love? In a business sense, what will teams look like? How shall we project manage teams of diverse people? In this extract from the book, I begin by outlining the various scenarios that will inform our lives as we merge with machines and, later on, look at some implications for teams and teamwork.

Brain Based Enterprises

It's 07.05 AM on 05 January 2030 . . . The day begins for Julie:

Julie wakes up at exactly the optimum time to maximise her sleep, wellbeing and energy, to a vibration in her neck from her embedded wellbeing monitor. Some ambient music bathes the room, bathed in soft purple swirling lighting. The smell of freshly brewed coffee percolates upwards from the kitchen. These are things she chose in her psychological contract with Rover. In a few minutes, coffee, water and fruit slices are brought to her by Rover, her personal robotic assistant. It's time for Julie's early morning wellbeing session, led by her ever-faithful 24/7 digital guide, who has already ironed her underwear, run a bath, organised her bag for the day, checked her travel schedule, confirmed her appointments and so on.

Rover also monitored Julie's vital signs and adjusted her personal exercise routine around her expected physical activity during the day, to maximise her balance of mind, body and soul. Rover is, of course, a robot and makes rational decisions based on an aggregation of big data about what's best for Julie's work, life and play. However, Rover has also integrated humanity by taking on board Julie's own personal values within the decision-making algorithms that Rover uses . . .

We are seeing the earliest signs and signifiers of a world in which man and machine have switched roles with driverless trains, 3D printing, self-service shops, smart cities, smart homes, smartphones and drones. We can already measure our vital signs to improve our vitality and receive live updates on life-threatening conditions to help us live long and prosper. However, the transformation towards our love affair with machines is not exactly new. We perhaps began to notice the difference as long ago as 1822, with Charles Babbage's invention of the difference engine. Since that time, we have had the enigma machine, the Casio FX77 and many more devices that have enabled us to do ever more complex things.

Many more things are still to come in our enigmatic relationship with machines via the Internet of Things, which promises to have 50 billion devices connected to the internet by 2020. Innovation consultancy Arthur D. Little (2017) report that any technology innovations that enhance people's time to spend on higher-level Maslow[*] needs and that reduce or remove the need to focus on the lower-level needs is a good innovation. We will increasingly have the ability to separate the things that satisfy us from the things that we have to do. It is entirely feasible that we will have time to enjoy those things in life that we do purely for their intrinsic value, such as arts and crafts. Perhaps, like Julie's example in 2030, we'll use machines to clear the space and time for us to enjoy such things. From coal mining to data mining, we can envisage four potential future scenarios in our love/indifference/hate affair with man, woman, machines, robotics, artificial intelligence and official stupidity, as shown in Figure 3.1 (on next page) and described below:

War of the Worlds. In this dystopian view, humans battle it out with machines, and all lose the value of each others' contributions. Like the film of the same name, it is a zero-sum game for all concerned, with dramatic consequences for humanity, humility and technology alike. Despite this being a lose-lose game for all concerned, we humans love a little drama in our lives, so War of the Worlds is not a completely unlikely scenario, especially in some business sectors, where it may be seen as a battle for supremacy that will at least appeal to some alpha males and females.

Planet of the Apes. Humans decide to work without machines. This is an impoverished retro world in which humanity slides backwards overall, an 'ignorance is bliss' strategy. Although it sounds unlikely as a scenario, we already see attempts to ignore the march of automation in terms of the arguments about driverless trains in the UK and to a lesser degree road transport. Railways have the advantage of having rails, so the destination and journey is already pre-set to some degree. There are also already examples of driverless trains over the world. As I write, we have experienced a series of lengthy strikes by rail staff in the UK over the gradual erosion of human presence on their trains. The argument revolved around whether the trains would continue to have an onboard member of staff.

We have seen a less belligerent form of Planet of the Apes in the returns to various crafts, where human ingenuity and the personal touch are seen as more valuable/authentic than machine efficiency. Such nostalgia can co-exist with the efficiencies that can come from machines, where people are prepared to pay a premium price for handmade products and services, from craft beer to craft work.

Attack of the Clones. Machines not only augment human function, they mainly replace it, but without the human systems in place for us to enjoy the leisure time that this creates. We

---

[*] https://www.simplypsychology.org/maslow.html

Figure 3.1 War of the Worlds (*Source: Cook, P. [2018]. Brain Based Enterprises: Harmonising the Head, Heart and Soul of Business. Abingdon, UK Routledge.*)

live easy yet unfulfilled lives as a result. Some observers have predicted that the technological singularity will signal the end of the human era around 2040, as superintelligence advances at exponential rates. We have not exactly been attacked by clones up till this point except in the movies, but just notice the quiet revolutions in areas that we take for granted. Your switchboard operator is digital, your lift operator is electric, and some receptionists are now electronic.

The Attack of the Clones scenario seems fairly unlikely, yet we already see how automation can de-skill jobs, such as car manufacture and agriculture, if the people doing them do not step up to new levels to profit from augmentation. The choice is in our hands. All that needs to happen for this to become reality is for humans to decide to recline in their sofas and watch the world go by.

The Man (Woman) Machine. We work in an integrated way with machines, using them for what they do best and deploying human skills when they are of greatest advantage. As a result, we live easier, more fulfilled lives. This is a one-all draw in football terms, a win-win or 'cobotic' approach. This approach is already established in use within certain high-tech professions such as surgery, electronics, pharmaceuticals and opticians, so it is not a work of science fiction. It would appear to be the 'win-win' position if we are prepared to adapt ourselves to realise the benefits but will require systems-wide changes.

Brain-based enterprises take the view that the 'man-machine' scenario is the best one for humanity, although it will require each and every one of us to adjust our approach to work, learning and play to make the most of what automation and machines have to offer us. It will be the realisation of what synth pop futurist Gary Numan* offered us in his classic song 'Are Friends Electric?'

In the book, we explore impacts for individuals, teams and whole enterprises. Here we tease out some of the implications for teams, project leaders and leadership in general.

Leading Brainy Teams

Views of leadership have changed over the ages, from ideas about war propounded by Sun Tzu (1964) and Machiavelli's treatment via *The Prince* (1981), which focused on questions of influence and manipulation, through to the beginnings of a psychological approach around 100 years ago. It could be said that leadership thinking has mirrored the age in which the ideas were put forward. At the height of the Industrial Age, Frederick Taylor (1911) put forward the idea of scientific management, which focused on the organisation of work in the best way to gain output from workers. Henry Ford was a great advocate of Taylorism and believed that his factories could be organised along the lines of scientific management and detailed work study.

Later on in the 20th century, 'Fordism' and 'Taylorism' were superseded by socio-cultural ideas about leadership and notions that the leader was the most important variable and could flex and bend their style to fit the situation. This eventually produced theories and models of Situational Leadership and the desirable notion of being a 9:9 leader. After all, who would want to be a 5:7 leader or worse? Desirable though it may seem that we can be all things to all people, more recently the issue of authenticity has begun to take hold as a major idea in modern leadership thinking.

In the last 20 or so years, the task of leadership has also shifted focus towards the management of complexity, uncertainty and the unknowable through the seminal work of Ralph Stacey (1992) and Dave Snowden's Cynefin framework (2002), which offered five domains to help business leaders decide on the best approach to make sense of their own behaviour and that of others: simple, complicated, complex, chaotic and disorder. Team leadership must undoubtedly mirror the expectations and complexities of the age. Some of the considerations that leaders must face are explored here.

Team Chemistry

To move from brainy atoms (individuals) to brainy molecules (teams) needs the skills of team chemistry, otherwise known as facilitation, sometimes by someone within the team, sometimes by an external agent (catalyst), if the degree of personal involvement or complexity of the issue demands it. A great team facilitator will adopt a range of styles that are consistent with the need, shifting shapes in response to the evolving needs across the entire spectrum of behavioural styles available to them. John Heron's model of intervention styles (1999) is a useful way of thinking about facilitation, since he covers interventions across the spectrum from directive to non-directive and flags the many roles that a great facilitator must cover:

---

* https://en.wikipedia.org/wiki/Gary_Numan

Prescribing (directive). Essentially a 'tell' style. For example: *'Take these pills, and you'll feel better'.* Prescribing is probably the quickest way to get someone to do something. However, the quickest way is not always the most effective way. We know full well that we don't always take the doctor's advice if it does not accord with our own wants, whims and fancies as articulated by the Dunning-Kruger effect, according to which people of low ability tend to assess their own cognitive abilities as being superior to experts and vice versa (Kruger & Dunning, 1999). It is perhaps for this reason that the other styles exist, since we are not that great at taking direct advice if it is dissonant with our prevailing paradigm.

Informing (directive). Neutrally passing on information, ideas and knowledge. For example: *'I can tell you that your team scored minus 25 on risk taking'.* This gives people the chance to make their own minds up without feeling pressurised or manipulated. Informing does not draw a conclusion. It simply provides neutral information, leaving the recipient to draw their own conclusions and formulate actions.

However, one then needs a lot of time for team members to process the information provided to them and come up with options and actions to address the need. There is of course always a risk that the information will be processed but no action, or possibly the 'wrong' course of action, will result. Whilst informing may be more effective in the long term, it requires more time and processing power than prescribing.

Confronting (directive). Involves challenging viewpoints and requires the examination of motives. For example: *'You said that you wanted to devise a creative strategy, but I've noticed that every time we try to do this, you want to talk about what the company is doing about the Christmas meal'.* Confronting should not be confused with aggression—it can be done with a soft pillow as well as a hard edge.

Confronting is, however, one of the more difficult interventions that a facilitator can undertake, as it usually results in some level of cognitive dissonance, where people are held to account or get 'found out'. Done with skill, it can be very effective and relatively quick, but once again the Dunning-Kruger effect applies, and people can become actively defensive or, worse still, passively so, which is harder to spot. Non-directive interventions usually take longer than directive ones. After all they are literally less 'direct'. However, they may be very effective in more troublesome situations. They also require greater levels of skill and sleight-of-hand techniques to make them work.

Cathartic (facilitative). Interventions that enable people to 'get things off their chests'. For example: *'Can we spend some time exploring what it feels like for you to lead this project?'* Catharsis can be extremely powerful as a means of allowing people to relive tension about things that are hard to express in more direct terms.

One example of this is the use of extended metaphor, where the facilitator asks the team to describe the issue under discussion in metaphorical terms. Sometimes this level of detachment allows people to say things that are hard to say or unsayable.

Catalytic (facilitative). Providing a sounding board and helping others to come up with their own solutions. For example: *'Would you like to explain more about the opportunities for business improvement?'* Catalytic interventions build on the idea of catalysis in chemistry. A catalyst is used in small doses to promote a reaction but is itself not involved in the actual reaction and remains unchanged at the end of that reaction. It is once again a detached position to take for the facilitator, giving others space to reflect, consider novel ideas and rethink old approaches.

Supporting (facilitative). Feedback to staff in which they are actively listened to and encouraged in what they are doing. For example: *'I can understand why you would feel that the company* *is benefitting from your strategy to encourage innovation from what you have told me'.* Supporting is often of great value when using the more challenging interventions in the facilitator's toolkit.

It provides the essential positive assets in the 'bank balance' between the facilitator and the team to draw on when dealing with more challenging elements of the team's agenda. In general, it is always wise to use plenty of pull strategies if you are also pushing for change, and a sensible ratio is at least 2:1 pull:push. It is also important to consider the 'rhythm' of your interventions. After all, facilitation is like a dance at some level, and keeping in step with those you are attempting to engage in the dance of change is important if you are to maintain a high conversion ratio of thoughts into actions.

Great team leaders are both well-prepared and also great improvisers to follow lines of enquiry, balancing the need for direction with the need to facilitate thinking and action within teams. In general, a move towards more engaging styles of leadership will be needed to facilitate diverse teams.

Team Diversity

Gone are the days when a lone individual could envision and develop all the ideas to conceptualise and execute an innovative product or service. Innovation is now a team game, one where cross-disciplinary thinking and working are essential (Cook, 2016). In pharmaceuticals, we combine apps with traditional treatments as 'Healthware'. Remote medicine has become a burgeoning reality during the Covid-19 pandemic. In financial services, Fintech* may replace traditional banks that have always been interested in automating functions to reduce costs, provide better audit control and improve customer access. Even the United Nations can no longer recruit weapons inspectors who are PhD physicists or chemists alone. They must be skilled in computing, biotechnology, physics and so on to function effectively and work as an effective team to face the complexity inherent in modern weapons and warfare. How then shall we combine team intelligences for SCA (Sustainable Coopetive Advantage)?

Should diversity be distributed across the whole enterprise or concentrated in areas such as the research and development division? This is a hard question to answer with certainty, as it is highly situational and culture dependent. However, a mathematical comparison gives some clues. A study was made on the innovation structures at Apple® and Google and some differences observed:

In 10 years, Apple produced 10,975 patents from a team of 5,232 inventors. Google did 12,386 from a team of 8,888. However, Apple's core shows a group of highly connected super inventors at the centre. Google's structure is more dispersed, empowered and networked. The researcher Bernegger points out that there is more connectivity and collaboration at Apple, with the average number of inventors listed on a patent as 4.2 as compared with 2.8 at Google (reported in Wilson, 2017).

This translates into a ROI (Return On Innovation) of 9 at Apple compared with 4 at Google. It is probably a mistake to draw a broad generalisation out from this, as many organisational factors go towards success, but it is nonetheless an interesting study. Leaders must help teams collaborate in the Age of Intelligence, and structure as well as culture matter. *Brain Based Enterprises* explores both issues. As part of my work with world-class musicians, I have interviewed a number of music giants from Roberta Flack to John Mayall and members of Prince, Ozzy Osbourne and Meatloaf's entourage. These provide valuable insights into the day-to-day management of diversity, and more information can be found at *The Music of Business* (Cook, 2015).

---

* Software and other technologies that provide automated financial services.

Team Transparency

The Johari window is a classic model that helps us understand ourselves in concert with others. As such it can usefully be adapted to the world of data, information, knowledge and wisdom. Devised by psychologists Joseph Luft and Harrington Ingham in 1955 (Luft & Ingham, 1955), the Johari window took its name from their first two names, Joe and Harry. Here we apply the model to the question of sharing knowledge within and between teams.

As always, nobody does it better than Professor Charles Handy (2000), who offers us an eminently simple way of understanding the Johari window as a house with four rooms. The first room is our open source, the things that we and others know about ourselves—for example, our height, approximate age, LinkedIn profile and so on. The second is our hidden area, the things we know about ourselves but others do not—for example, medical history, relationships etc. The third area is our blind area, things that others know about us but we are unaware of—for example, at a trivial level, whether someone has placed a sticker on our back, whether someone has said something bad about us to them in private and so on. Finally, our unknown or unconscious area, the things that neither we, nor others know about us—for example, our futures.

Julie is able to communicate her thinking directly to others via an interface in her brain that allows people to access her thinking as and when needed. Access is on several levels: an open source region for work associates; a private region for friends and family and a personal region which contains Julie's thoughts on love, life etc. only accessible with express permission. She has a closed region of her mind, which is totally restricted even to her, although she may ask the interface questions about this area for the purposes of self-discovery and personal development.

The hallmark of intelligent teams will be that the open-source area will be maximised for maximum shared value. We have become progressively used to people knowing personal details about us through social media. However, work is normally different, as our professional knowledge is sometimes at the heart of our salary. Yet innovation arises from shared knowledge and wisdom. We must therefore find ways to encourage a gainsharing approach to team collaboration if we are to realise the open-source dream. Leaders must manage the transparent sharing of information and knowledge for everyone's advantage.

Summary

1. A harmonious fusion of man, woman and machine offers the best way forward for the age of intelligence. Reaching it will be challenging and it is likely that some industries will resist the onward march of technology. Ultimately Darwin will win, and it is a case of adapt or die.
2. Leading intelligent individuals in teams requires a style of leadership that is more directive in terms of setting a direction and rather more facilitative in terms of engaging the team on that journey. Brain based leaders also respect and celebrate the diversity within the team.
3. When facilitating intelligent teams, leaders need the full range of facilitation styles from directive to non-directive. The Brain Based Leader masters facilitation to get the best out of the diverse people they lead in teams.
4. In the internet age, team members expect transparency from leaders. At the same time knowledge sharing will be essential to create world-class products and services. This again is a function of good leadership.

References

Arthur D. Little. (2017). *Personal communication.*

Cook, P. (2015). *The Music of Business.* Faversham, UK: Cultured Llama.

Cook, P. (2016). *Leading Innovation, Creativity and Enterprise.* London, UK: Bloomsbury.

Cook, P. (2018). *Brain Based Enterprises: Harmonising the Head, Heart and Soul of Business.* Abingdon, UK: Routledge.

Handy, C. (2000). *21 Ideas for Managers.* San Francisco, CA: Jossey-Bass.

Heron, J. (1999). *The Complete Facilitator's Handbook.* London, UK: Kogan Page.

Kruger, J., and Dunning, D. (1999). Unskilled and unaware of it: How difficulties in recognizing one's own incompetence lead to inflated self-assessments. *Journal of Personality and Social Psychology,* 77(6): 1121–1134. American Psychological Association.

Luft, J., and Ingham, H. (1955). The Johari window, a graphic model of interpersonal awareness. *Proceedings of the Western Training Laboratory in Group Development.* Los Angeles, CA: UCLA.

Machiavelli, N. (1947). *The Prince.* New York, NY: F. S. Crofts & Co. (Appleton-Century-Crofts).

Snowden, D. (May 2002). Complex acts of knowing: Paradox and descriptive self awareness. *Journal of Knowledge Management,* 6(2), 100–111.

Stacey, R. (1992). *Managing the Unknowable: The Strategic Boundaries Between Order and Chaos.* San Francisco, CA: Jossey-Bass.

Sun-tzu and Griffith, S. B. (1964). *The Art of War* (15th Ed.). Oxford, UK: Clarendon Press.

Taylor, F. W. (1911). *The Principles of Scientific Management.* New York, NY: Harper & Brothers.

Wilson, M. (2017). The Real difference between Apple and Google. *Fast Company* 02.24.2017. https://www.fastcompany.com/3068474/the-real-difference-between-google-and-apple

Chapter 4

Leadership

The Followership Advantage: Reconfiguring Leadership for Success

Darren Dalcher

Many conversations about improvement, enhancement, governance, progress and the future inevitably resort to addressing leadership issues. Leadership is increasingly viewed as an essential life skill, a practical ability to guide other individuals, a team, an organisation, or even a country, towards a better future, an improved position or a defined outcome.

But where do we find examples of great leaders?

Traditionally, archetypal samples would emerge from either the political or the business arena, but in recent years both have been found wanting. Yet, as we face ever more complex and uncertain dilemmas and increasingly vexing, wicked problems, there appears to be a greater need to identify and follow strong and powerful leaders.

What Worked Before?

Great leadership is sometimes measured in terms of the followers that it engenders. This may well be a dangerous idea. Former US Speaker of the House, Ohio Congressman John Boehner asserted back in 2014 (Boehner, 2014) that *'a leader without followers is simply a man taking a walk'*. General George S. Patton* had an even more direct approach in mind when he proclaimed, *'Lead me, follow me, or get out of my way'*.

Ironically, despite the plethora of publications exploring effective leadership, relatively little has been written about the role of effective followership. In a private conversation with a leading architect and chief executive of the infrastructure and construction part of the London 2012 Olympic Games, he expressed an exasperation that we teach leadership and tell people what they ought to be doing, but we hardly ever 'teach' followership, as we implicitly assume that following is easy or well understood. According to Robert Kelley (1992), only 20 percent of the success of organisations is traced to the leader, while in practice 80 percent of the credit should be going to followers.

Kellerman (2008: *xix*) defines followers as *'subordinates who have less power, authority, and influence than do their superiors and who therefore usually, but not invariably, fall into line'*. Yet, followers are neither homogenous nor uniform. Kellerman offers a fluid typology, which can be positioned along a spectrum, indicating the rank or level of engagement by followers, encompassing five main types:

---

* https://www.azquotes.com/quote/520700

- **Isolates.** Utterly detached and disinterested individuals who keep a low profile, rarely respond to leaders, resent interferences from above, and reinforce the status quo by default.
- **Bystanders.** Observers who follow passively and let events unfold with little participation, while accepting control from above.
- **Participants.** Engaged individuals who typically care about their organisation and support their leader with their effort or time when they agree with their vision and views.
- **Activists.** Eager, energetic and deeply engaged individuals working for the cause and the leader.
- **Die-hards.** Individuals displaying the highest levels of engagement with the organisation or their cause; all-consuming supporters exhibiting total and absolute engagement.

Good followers therefore actively support effective and ethical leaders. It is thus expected that 'good followers' would also respond appropriately to bad leaders in the interest of the greater cause and the wider organisation. Kellerman's chief concern is about mindless or unquestioning followers and their impact. Based on historical events, die-hards may agitate and activists may follow blindly and encourage participants to take part, while bystanders may simply allow events, however painful or harrowing, to take place, whilst others choose to ignore the entire scene. Historical precedents offer some credibility to the notion of mapping the level of engagement and participation (Kellerman, 2004). They also seem to suggest that bystanders and other participants may tolerate, or even embrace, harmful actions with little, if any, questioning (see, for example, Dalcher, 2016, for a summary, or Zimbardo, 2007, for more detail). The direct implication is that followership needs to be taken more seriously; it also needs to encompass some sober responsibilities.

Beyond Toxic Leadership

Equating leaders with 'traditional' leadership theory, as we often do, is only seeing a limited part of the picture. The notion of leaders who can do no wrong has been tarnished by less than responsible business and political leaders and a series of environmental and business crises. Toxic or destructive leadership seems to thrive on three essential ingredients: destructive leaders, susceptible followers and conducive environments (Padilla, Hogan & Kaiser, 2007). Recent evidence suggests that leaders can no longer assume unwavering loyalty and trust. Nor can leaders take it for granted that followers will continue to exhibit unquestioning behaviours.

Nonetheless, hierarchical structures continue to imply that wisdom and insights always descend from above, reflecting Plato's preference for larger-than-life philosopher-kings endowed with charm, vision and forcefulness as rulers. Modern society affords a greater belief in the power of groups and in the ability of collections of individuals to get together, participate, engage, identify new concerns and propose alternative courses of action (Dalcher, 2015). But what is their remit? And what is their scope for doing right?

Keith Grint (2000) offers a panoramic view of multiple successful leaders, encompassing profiles of political and military figures such as Horatio Nelson, business tycoons such as Richard Branson and Henry Ford and other well-recognised historical figures including Florence Nightingale and Martin Luther King. While the book may well celebrate their successes, Grint opts instead to feature their propensity to fail and make mistakes. What appears to distinguish those we regard as successful leaders is their cadre of followers who support and cover up for them. Grint therefore concludes that *'the trick of the leader is to develop followers who privately resolve the problems leaders have caused or cannot resolve, but publicly deny their intervention'* (Grint, 2000: 420).

In subsequent work, Grint (2010) invokes Karl Popper as a proponent of an alternative and counterintuitive approach that focuses on the inherent weakness of leaders and the need to inhibit, restrain and accommodate such deficits:

> *Karl Popper provides a firmer foundation for this in his assumption that, just as we can only disprove rather than prove scientific theories, so we should adopt mechanisms that inhibit leaders rather than surrender ourselves to them* (p. 101).

Interpreting the writing with a contemporary lens implies an intellectual revolution in the way we view and react to leaders and leadership. It calls for moral and responsible judgement, thereby transforming the more transactional nature of the association between superior and subjects into an ethically and morally meaningful relationship.

Popper is thus cognisant of the potential risk of not deploying fully engaged, forever questioning and scrupulously uncompromising followers:

> *Otherwise, although omniscient leaders are a figment of irresponsible followers' minds and utopian recruiters' fervid imaginations, when subordinates question their leader's direction or skill these (in)subordinates are usually replaced by those 'more aligned with the current strategic thinking'—otherwise known as yes people. In turn, such subordinates become transformed into irresponsible followers whose advice to their leader is often limited to destructive consent: they may know that their leader is wrong, but there are all kinds of reasons not to say as much, hence they consent to the destruction of their own leader and possibly their own organisation too* (pp. 101–102).

Popper consequently holds followers responsible for their actions, and not least for not exercising their ability to inhibit the shortcomings and errors of their leaders. In an about face reversal of the hierarchical assumption of a free license to simply follow orders from leaders, he thereby engenders groups and individuals with responsibility to correct the course of leaders as constructive dissenters. This position offers an informed participative role, as surely therein lie the true roots of effective followership embedded within an implicit social and moral contract between the leaders and their true followers.

Rejecting the typical question of who should rule as the fundamental basis of political theory, Popper advances the alternative position of *'How can we so organise political institutions that bad or incompetent rulers can be prevented from doing too much damage?'* (Popper, 1945: 121).

This simple reframing places followers in a much more critical position, emphasising their role in securing and maintaining the enduring success of their mission, team, kingdom or empire. Drawing on Popper's proposition, good followership can thus be redefined around the ability to correct, steer and guide the leader towards securing improved outcomes, better alignment and more informed consent through the creative power of the wider group or community. This could perhaps be done by invoking the principles of teaming (for further information, see Chapter 3) by resorting to building greater trust (Dalcher, 2017) or through the use of social media, which seems to be creating a shift in the balance of power between leaders and followers (Kellerman, 2012).

Empowering Followers

Similar sentiment can be found elsewhere within the discipline with Warren Bennis ruefully proclaiming, *'If I had to reduce the responsibilities of a good follower to a single rule, it would be to speak truth to power'* (Bennis, in Riggio et al., 2008: *xxv*).

Ira Chaleff (2009) concludes from his extensive research that many significant failures, disasters and mishaps could have been avoided, prevented or mitigated if those lower in the hierarchy were successful at communicating the risks they were seeing in the system to their leaders. The *courageous follower* is his model that endeavours to make followers active partners who continuously scan and monitor the environment, and their leader, whilst feeling empowered to speak to and influence the hierarchy. The new aspects proposed through the work suggest a multitude of courageous actions at the root of the interaction of leader–follower dynamics, including:

- *The courage to assume responsibility* for themselves and the organisation, and to discover or create opportunities to fulfil their potential and maximise their value to the organisation in accordance with the common purpose and needs
- *The courage to serve* their leader and the organisation and pursue the common purpose
- *The courage to challenge* and stand up and give voice to discomfort
- *The courage to participate in transformation* and champion the need for change
- *The courage to take moral action*
- *The courage to speak to the hierarchy*

Leaders, in turn, are encouraged to engage in a more dynamic relationship and develop:

- *The courage to listen to followers*

In a similar vein, Kelley (1992) reasons that organisations require *star followers*, who display active involvement, critical thinking, independence and a positive disposition to achieve their organisation's vision. They are often referred to as the 'go-to person' or the 'right-hand person', thereby enabling positive followership. The special characteristics of *star followers* are:

- They leverage their strengths to complement weaknesses that their leaders may have.
- They approach everything with a critical mindset and make forthright statements that may challenge or criticise the leaders' decision if it clashes with wider beliefs or organisational goals.
- They subscribe to the organisation's goal and voluntarily cooperate and join in activities that support that cause, even if they are not directly responsible for the execution.
- They have a challenging spirit, constantly seeking new improvements, taking on new challenges with ideas and providing insights to leaders.

In many ways great followership is harder than leadership. It has more dangers and fewer rewards, and it must routinely be exercised with much more subtlety. But great followership has never been more important, if only because of the seriousness of the global problems we face, and the fact that they must be solved collaboratively, not by leaders alone but by leaders working in tandem with able and dedicated followers (Bennis, in Riggio et al., 2008: *xxvi*).

However, not many systems are designed with truly meaningful and responsible followership principles in mind . . .

Asking the Impossible

Traditional systems often emphasise old-fashioned ways of thinking enshrined in habits, traditions and well-established and rehearsed practices. Additional protocols are often applied to maintain and sustain such systems and ensure that the habits persist and endure.

Armies have long provided a fresh source of 'model leaders' ready to be adored, analysed, or debated. The introduction to Chapter 3 tells the story of a military leader forced to *'transit from a fixed and cumbersome traditional military hierarchy towards a set of dynamic teams operating as high-performance teams'*, in order to counter evolving enemy capability. In this chapter, yet another senior commander is forced to reflect and review their processes and overarching philosophy and devise a novel approach to leadership in a very traditional and highly demanding environment.

David Marquet was an experienced US Navy officer when he was appointed captain of a nuclear-powered submarine, the USS *Santa Fe* in 1999. The *Santa Fe* is a *Los Angeles* class nuclear-powered fast-attack submarine, also known as the 688 class after the hull number of the lead vessel, the USS *Los Angeles*.

At the time of his appointment, Marquet was well steeped in old-fashioned leader–follower dogma, navy tradition and its highly hierarchical management structures. The structures stress accountability and technical competence and concentrate power, authority and control at the top. Moreover, the confined and stifling environment of a submarine offers a perfect setting for reinforcing a strict *leader–follower* protocols (Marquet, 2012).

Marquet readily concedes that when he took command, the *Santa Fe* was recognised as being at the bottom of the fleet technically, operationally and emotionally, scoring extremely poorly in most measures of performance. Retention offers a good example: in 1998, the ship reenlisted a mere three crewmembers—a sure sign that trouble was afoot.

Dogged by poor morale, poor performance and the worst retention record in the fleet, Marquet took the first few weeks to get to know people and their jobs. His open-ended question to crew members upon meeting them for the first time was, *'What do you do on board?'* The answer most typical of the hierarchy and the state of vessel was, *'whatever they tell me to do'*, which implies reticent acceptance of the structure and the inability to do much about it. It also indicates that initiative and good will had gradually vanished through the protocols of repressive top-down control.

Perhaps the most telling and significant incident occurred during an early engineering drill, when Marquet unknowingly gave a technically impossible order to increase to a non-existent speed. His most senior and highly experienced officer, who knew it was not possible, nonetheless still relayed the order. Noticing that the helmsman had not reached over to make any alterations, Marquet interrogated him and was informed that this class submarine did not have that particular setting.

Marquet proceeded to question his leading officer, who acknowledged that he also knew the setting did not exist. When asked why he carried through with the order, the officer retorted, *'because you told me to'*.

This was the moment Marquet recognised that in a top-down command and control mode when the leader makes a decision which is not challenged by subordinates who know better, the entire unit fails. Perhaps it is even more sobering when the whole experience occurs inside a giant metallic tube with no real means of escape.

Marquet's internal response to the episode was to vow to henceforth never again give an order!

Marquet acknowledged that they were all in danger unless they fundamentally altered the way they did things. He did not want to continue operating with a herd of followers: he wanted his unit to be allowed to perform to their best ability. He therefore decided to take matters into his own hands and overhaul the prevailing culture in order to facilitate a more responsible, less hierarchical and better-informed structure.

Turn the Ship Around

Grint (2010: 19) asserts that there are three forms of authority: command, management and leadership. While this offers a more simplistic heuristic rather than a situational assessment tool, it makes it possible to appraise a given scenario, especially in terms of how decisions are made and what action gets implemented. Broadly, command structures emphasise the answers coming from above, management is concerned with organising processes, while leadership is largely focused on asking questions. This depiction generally matches Etzioni's (1961) typology of compliance, which distinguishes between coercive, utilitarian (calculative) and normative compliance.

What Marquet witnessed was a typical command setting, where the orders and the knowledge flow from top down on a need-to-know basis. Indeed, when questioned about his decision to still carry out the order, the senior officer protested that the order may have contained 'secret or privileged' knowledge only available to the commanding officers (Marquet, 2012: 81).

Moving to a system of shared values and pushing for leadership at all levels would entail fundamental shifts in culture, approach and structure. Noting a thirst to do better (especially when you have earned the reputation of worst in class) and an eagerness to improve and change, Marquet embarked on a push to turn his system into a *leader–leader* model, where actors are able to take responsibility for their actions and make their own decisions from a more well-informed position. Marquest's notion of a *leader–leader* relationship aims to build a resilient organisation, in which every individual is both a leader and a true participant.

Obtaining buy-in from his team, Marquet proceeded to implement his new system. The situation was totally transformed within a single year. The vessel went from worst to best in most measures of performance, including the ability to retain sailors and officers. The *Santa Fe* also started winning awards as the best ship in its class and became the envy of the fleet. Moreover, management author and guru Stephen Covey, who visited the submarine in 2000, acknowledged that it was the most empowered organisation that he had ever visited (Covey, 2013).

The ingredients for successfully implementing the *leader–leader* culture were simple and involved three main pillars:

Give control. Push authority down the ranks, including to all functional areas, where the real experts are based.

Increase competence. Introduce assurances of competency and knowledge in that process to ensure that decisions are fully thought through.

Improve organisational clarity. Establish an assurance around clarity, so that all crew are clear of the bigger picture when making those decisions.

The three pillars enable local decisions to be made, whilst continuing to be informed by operational necessities and strategic goals. With the strategic insights shared with the different functions, they are able to make decisions, prioritise and identify key trade-offs that work for the global best. Statements such as *'Our mission requires we submerge now before reaching the Oman waters to avoid detection'* can be utilised to frame all priorities and other decisions. After all, while getting the strategic goals wrong can affect the bottom line in most organisations, on a submarine at the bottom of the ocean, the implications could be far more dire, as people may die and the entire unit and vessel may be destroyed.

The Way Forward: I Intend to . . .

Marquet acknowledged the need for individuals to make decisions. Rather than have the entire crew wait on him to reach a consensus, he decided to step back and give people the space to reflect and deliberate. The idea was for people to make the best decision they could and to indicate their intent.

He recognised the value of the phrase *'I intend to . . .'* as a powerful mechanism for control, as it shifts the ownership of the plan to the proposer. *I intend to* is an empowered phrase emphasising intent and understanding of what needs to be done. Rather than seek permission or ask a question, it offers a viable and reasoned way forward, complete with a rationale and a synopsis of what measures and considerations have been included. For instance, an intent statement provides the following information and indicates that the intent has been well thought out and rigorously planned:

> *Captain, I intend to submerge the ship. We are in water we own, water depth has been checked and is four hundred feet, all men are below, the ship is rigged for a dive, and I've certified my watch team* (Marquet, 2012: 82).

The approach enacted by Marquet has become better known as *intent-based leadership,* which enables followers and team members to assume responsibility, consider the range of potential actions and options, make a preferred choice and act according to their authority. Intent-based leadership puts the onus on individuals to consider actions, implications and mitigating steps. Over time, participants are able to take control by considering what information would be useful for the leader in order to formally acknowledge the intent. This is done initially by trying to guess the potential questions and making sure everything is ready. In due course, actors progress to thinking what information they would need in the captain's place and what checks and controls they would like to see employed, which they then duly proceed to exercise, thereby further improving the quality of the information and the checks and procedures applied to it.

Marquet's ideas brought about radical change to the design of a very traditional, regimented, highly controlled and change-resistant organisation. His approach tries to develop everyone to become a responsible and valued leader. The leader–leader perspective elevates subordinates to the level of full participants with valued insights and empowers them to enhance, improve and grow.

Letting go is one of the most difficult things in life, whether in the workplace, or with children. But giving people, and indeed children, scope to improve makes them stay longer and even return. Marquet's colleagues became very reluctant to transfer from his command. But his methods also created many excellent officers and leaders who continued to share the philosophy and approach with their new subordinates, making new generations of leaders.

A key feature of the new approach was not to move the information to authority, but instead to shift the authority to the information. The impacts of the change were quite pronounced, and included:

- Alleviating the pressure on leaders to know all the answers

- Employing the real experts in judging and deliberating
- Encouraging individuals to take responsibility and accountability for their work
- Engaging the wider team
- Avoiding misinformed verdicts coming from the top down
- Preventing people from following bad orders
- Promoting mentorship, development and growth
- Enabling the entire organisation to become more responsive and resilient
- Developing pride in the work
- Strengthening accountability and responsibility

Ultimately, the captain still determines where the ship should go, but he or she can do so with the help of an informed and supportive crew, and hopefully with the knowledge that the team of experts are better deployed to make strategic decisions and correct any misapprehensions and shortcomings to deliver continued and exceptional performance.

The New Management: Human-Centred Systems

Some old leadership ideas no longer seem to apply. Robert Heller makes a forceful case for change by blaming CEOs for clinging to outmoded 'boss'-centred hierarchies. His message is simple: Reinvent management or perish (Heller, 1995).

The original notion of followers as passive recipients of leadership from powerful and influential bosses clearly needs replacing. A people-focused approach might engender a softer perception of followers as moderators of leadership who recognise the leader's role but are able to respond in a more transactional fashion by influencing the relationship through their own characteristics; however, this notion fails to recognise the constructive role of followers.

The transformation achieved by Marquet aboard the *Santa Fe* re-establishes the need to focus on the people at the core of change. Achieving and delivering require bringing people along. New management ideas and concepts would therefore need to take account of the role of people and the wider context within which they operate.

By positioning all individual followers as empowered potential leaders, Marquet was able to achieve a wider organisational transformation, resulting in significantly increased effectiveness levels. Leadership thus became a shared occupation through engaged and empowered followership. Over time, individuals were able to respond to new opportunities, grow and develop through a co-production of emerging leadership.

However, developing more nuanced and distributed leadership capable of variation, new insights and creativity requires a new type of brave and inspired leader who is able to embrace new ways of thinking and operating and happy is to share some of the spoils and glories of leadership.

Peter Drucker wryly observed that, '*We know almost nothing about management, that is why we write so many books on the subject*'. The section by Roland Bardy is developed from his book *Rethinking Leadership: A Human Centered Approach to Management Ethics*, published by Routledge. In it he offers a tangible contribution that aims to increase our knowledge and understanding of management and leadership. Indeed, his contribution is wide ranging and may yet play a part in integrating and improving what we know on a meta level and hence directly addressing Drucker's concern.

Bardy's work endeavours to connect the domains of leadership, corporate social responsibility and business ethics/management ethics with the human-centred paradigm that is so essential for management. Bardy (2018) responds to the lack of adequate research on the impact of leadership on people and society and the reciprocities therein and aims to bridge this gap in knowledge. His interest in how people-to-people relationships is governed by leadership within and beyond organisational boundaries impacts many pertinent aspects of managing projects, ranging from stakeholder engagement and business ethics, to change, teamwork and the consideration of how knowledge is built and managed.

Bardy is equally comfortable across both the academic and practitioner domains, and he is keen to explore the philosophical underpinning of ideas to better determine their impacts and influences. He therefore invites practitioners to explore the philosophical roots of concepts in an effort to improve the efficacy and impacts of their actions.

Bardy advocates a human-centric position, facilitating leadership in a manner that respects the rights and dignity of others. Given the social power exercised by leaders and managers, it is only appropriate to consider the ethical and human implications of our actions. Moreover, given the position of managers and the educational and developmental role they hold, it is even more critical that they employ ethical leadership and conduct in their dealings with colleagues.

A key contribution of Bardy's work is offered through his presentation of the four perspectives of human-centred management and their systemic integration into a framework for thinking about management. His approach encompasses the ethical, the social, the economic and the institutional, thereby offering a new window and perspective into the complex dynamics at play. The multiple perspectives explain some of the dilemmas and paradoxes invoked within management work as the different frames that we may utilise impact and play a part in the complex dynamics of relationships and connections. It is all too easy to simplify and focus on a singular perspective, but Bardy is concerned with presenting the emergent overall picture in a systemic way.

The complexity that emerges from Bardy's approach facilitates a deeper understanding of the multi-stakeholder dialogues required to make sense of complex environments. Project managers encounter conflicting concerns and multiple stakeholder communities; the framework on offer can herald a new way of making sense of such contexts. More crucially, however, it also provides an important interface for preparing and conducting multi-stakeholder dialogues, an increasing necessity in complex mega projects and large change initiatives, or indeed most social endeavours. It can also be used to underpin and enable complex trade-offs and decision-making when there is a need to incorporate a diversity of perspectives and interests. Ultimately, Bardy is keen to ensure that managers employ new perspectives and approach situations with new insights and tools, and he does a convincing job in offering connections and integrated perspectives that support such a vision and enable leaders to address the multiple concerns and aspects that they increasingly face.

Postheroic Leadership Is Here

The age of heroic leaders may be over. The case of the *Santa Fe* seems to affirm that 'traditional' leadership (coupled with tight control structures and strict environments) with an emphasis on a powerful figurehead with absolute authority and final decision-making powers can wreak havoc and embed and engender entrenched, unthinking followership within the rest of the organisation. And yet, Kellerman (2018) observes that leadership education, training and development still fall far short, failing to recognise new trends and respond to emerging opportunities, and are therefore in need of a major overhaul. One of the reasons for the apparent lack of progress is the use of the word 'leadership' and the general inability to define or understand it (p. 3).

Leadership as position (Grint, 2010) is generally in decline, especially as power, control and authority become less pertinent. Position may come from vertical hierarchy, privilege or birth, but modern societies tend to challenge such entitlements. Fletcher (2004) confirms that traditional 'power over' models are gradually being replaced by 'power with', emphasising relationships and collaborations.

The fundamental assumption of the 'few controlling the many' underpinning dated leadership models also seems to have passed its sell-by date. Marc and Samantha Hurwitz (2015) point out that leadership is only half the story, especially as the majority of the actual value within corporations is generated by teams, and they therefore make a case for rethinking the relationship between leadership, followership and collaboration. No individual is smarter and more knowledgeable than everyone within a connected community, and hence new modes and models of collaboration are essential to securing continued engagement and future success.

In the postheroic age, everyone does leadership; it is not a top-down construct. Instead, leaders rise to address specific aspects they are concerned with. Followers are essential to the success of organisations. In a team or a wider organisational setting, establishing decent followership that can support, curtail deviations, reduce inefficiencies and improve leadership is essential to the ability to sustain delivery, align with strategy and improve decision-making capability. Moving forward, the relationship between leaders and followers is recognised as mutually beneficial and continuous as people may alter positions.

Indeed, Joseph Raelin proposes that *'In the twenty-first century organisation, we need to establish communities where everyone shares the experience of serving as a leader, not sequentially, but concurrently and collectively'* (Raelin, 2003: *xi*).

The key characteristics of postheroic leadership (adapted from Fletcher, 2004) can be summarised as follows:

- **Leadership as practice.** Leadership can be viewed as shared practices that are enacted by people at all levels; the practices are distributed throughout the organisation
- **Leadership as social process.** Leadership is a dynamic, multidirectional, collective activity, with human interactions at its core
- **Leadership as learning.** The social interactions embedded in leadership result in learning and growth for the organisation as well as the individuals involved; the outcomes of interaction include mutual learning, greater collective understanding and the resulting positive action

Repositioning Leadership and Followership

Old-style leadership thinking ascribes leaders with recognition and glory for success whilst ignoring the role and contributions of followers. Postheroic leadership is also about learning to celebrate the contributions of all participants. Yet, success is not just about glory. The success enjoyed by Marquet aboard the *Santa Fe* may stem from his ability to anticipate and propagate the conditions and expectations of the postheroic leadership epoch. It is worth pulling out and emphasising three key factors:

- **People.** The approach to developing the leader–leader model accentuates the personal, human and people-centric nature of management and leadership; it also relies on building relationships, setting expectations, communicating, developing and mentoring.
- **Emancipation.** The approach enables individuals to operate and specialise according to their expectations; rather than simply empower, it liberates and emancipates experts and novices alike, creating a transformed set of meaningful relationships.
- **Development.** The approach to developing individuals and enabling them to carry out their enhanced duties allows space for growth and development; it also fosters the *psychological safety* needed to encourage the team to share personal insights, feelings, thoughts and concerns—a key factor recognised by Google® as essential to forming effective teams (see Chapter 3).

These factors change our perception of leadership, hinting at the need for a new definition embracing the development of followers and the role of social meaningful relationships. Marquet himself proposes that leadership should be defined as *'embedding the capacity for greatness in the people and practices of an organisation and decoupling it from the personality of the leader'*.

Leadership is not about the personality, identity, or even the position of the leader. As a people-centric approach, it is focused on the development of supportive (occasionally in the critical sense) and supported followers.

In his introduction to Marquet's book, Stephen Covey summarises leadership as follows: *'Leadership is communicating to people their worth and potential so clearly that they are inspired to see it in themselves'*.

This again emphasises the developmental role of a good leader. However, we must not forget that the leader is also human and thus requires help, development and support to continue to achieve his/her own potential.

Maybe US President John F. Kennedy got it right when he observed, 'Leadership and learning are indispensable to each other'.

Good leaders learn by doing. We are still not clear on how best to develop leaders. Perhaps leadership really comes to the fore when we don't know all of the answers and we need to learn and make sense of new circumstances. Yet, we persist in asking our leaders to guide us through unprecedented and more demanding contexts, with wider implications and dependencies. It certainly appears to be the case that in order to cope better, leaders need to learn to become leaders in situ, and they will continue to learn from their followers, who they empower to support them, and as they grow together and become a wider learning community, they can improve, develop and flourish progressively and symbiotically.

References

Bardy, R. (2018). *Rethinking Leadership: A Human Centered Approach to Management Ethics*. Abingdon, UK: Routledge.

Boehner, J. (2021). *On the House: A Washington Memoir*. New York, NY: St. Martin's Press.

Chaleff, I. (2009). *The Courageous Follower: Standing Up to & for Our Leaders*. San Francisco, CA: Berrett-Koehler Publishers.

Covey, S. R. (2013). *The 8th Habit: From Effectiveness to Greatness*. London, UK: Simon & Schuster.

Dalcher, D. (2015). Here comes everybody: Reframing the stakeholder concept when just about everyone can become your stakeholder. *PM World Journal, 4*(10), October, 1–6.

Dalcher, D. (2016). On the importance of context: Why situational awareness remains an essential focus. *PM World Journal, 5*(12), December, 1–6.

Dalcher, D. (2017). It starts with trust: People, perspectives and relationships as the building blocks for sustainable success. *PM World Journal, 6*(3), March, 1–7.

Etzioni, A. (1961). *A Comparative Study of Complex Organisations*. New York, NY: The Free Press.

Fletcher, J. K. (2004). The paradox of postheroic leadership: An essay on gender, power, and trans-formational change. *The Leadership Quarterly, 15*(5), 647–661.

Grint, K. (2000). *The Arts of Leadership*. Oxford, UK: Oxford University Press.

Grint, K. (2010). *Leadership: A Very Short Introduction* (Vol. 237). Oxford, UK: Oxford University Press.

Goodpaster, K. E., and Matthews, J. B. (1982). Can a corporation have a conscience? *Harvard Business Review, 60*, 132–141.

Heller, R. (1995). *The Leadership Imperative: What Innovative Business Leaders Are Doing Today to Create the Successful Companies of Tomorrow*. New York, NY: Truman Talley Books/Dutton.

Hurwitz, M., and Hurwitz, S. (2015). *Leadership Is Half the Story: A Fresh Look at Followership, Leadership, and Collaboration*. Toronto, CA: University of Toronto Press.

Kellerman, B. (2004). *Bad Leadership: What It Is, How It Happens, Why It Matters*. Boston, MA: Harvard Business Press.

Kellerman, B. (2008). *Followership: How Followers Are Creating Change and Changing Leaders*. Boston, MA: Harvard Business School Press.

Kellerman, B. (2012). *The End of Leadership*. New York, NY: Harper Business.

Kellerman, B. (2018). *Professionalising Leadership*. New York, NY: Oxford University Press.

Kelley, R. E. (1992). *The Power of Followership: How to Create Leaders People Want to Follow, and Followers Who Lead Themselves*. New York, NY: Broadway Business.

Marquet, L. D. (2012). *Turn the Ship Around! How to Create Leadership at Every Level*. New York, NY: Portfolio Penguin.

Padilla, A., Hogan, R., and Kaiser, R. B. (2007). The toxic triangle: Destructive leaders, susceptible followers, and conducive environments. *The Leadership Quarterly, 18*(3), 176–194.

Popper, K. R. (1945). *The Open Society and Its Enemies* (Vol. 1) (4th Ed.). Princeton, NJ: Princeton University Press.

Raelin, J. A. (2003). *Creating Leaderful Organisations: How to Bring Out Leadership in Everyone*. San Francisco, CA: Berrett-Koehler Publishers.

Riggio, R. E., Chaleff, I., and Lipman-Blumen, J. (Eds.). (2008). *The Art of Followership: How Great Followers Create Great Leaders and Organisations* (Vol. 146). San Francisco, CA: Jossey-Bass.

Zimbardo, P. (2007) *The Lucifer Effect: How Good People Turn Evil*. London, UK: Random House.

Human-Centred Management: A Systemic Interrelation

Roland Bardy

Management and leadership have been defined in terms of objectives, tasks, traits, behaviour, motivation, interaction patterns, role relationships or occupation of an administrative position. Most definitions reflect the assumption that it involves a process whereby intentional influence is exerted over people to guide, structure and facilitate activities and relations in a group or organisation. The eminent management scholar Gary Yukl has said that true leadership only occurs when people are motivated to do what is ethical and beneficial for an organisation—but he admits that leaders will more often than not attempt to merely gain personal benefits at the expense of their followers, and that, despite good intentions, the actions of a leader are sometimes more detrimental than beneficial for the followers (Yukl, 2010: 23).

This raises the question of whether there is a divisive difference between leadership and management—with the obvious conclusion that there is an overlap between the two. The overlap will be wider or narrower depending on the person who executes the position. One definition which shows this best is by viewing *management* as an *authority relationship* directed at delivering a specific routine, with *leadership* being a *multidirectional influence* with the mutual purpose of accomplishing real change (Rost, 1991).

But, as has been pointed out by Bowie and Werhane (2004), there is an additional issue that comes into view when looking at who manages a manager. A manager typically works for another, and even top managers serve as *agents* for the stockholders of a business or for the elected officers in a public administration entity. This interrelation has a systemic aspect, as it is not just those connections that are intertwined, but there is a definite intertwinement as well between the various perspectives that integrate management—and, since it is all about the nexus between humans, we should talk about human-centred management.

The ideas explored in this section are based on the book *Rethinking Leadership: A Human-Centred Approach to Management Ethics* (Bardy, 2018), which lays a foundation for what may be called a *framework* for delineating human-centred management. The book proposes that human-centred management is determined by a systemic connection between various perspectives. Intertwining management and the human-centred paradigm is much more than just a two-way relationship. It is a systemic approach that combines ethics, social relations, economic effects, and institutional conceptions. It is necessary then to embrace all these interrelations in order to validate the analysis. Systemic interconnectedness is an entity in itself, and it is to be studied on its own (Jiliberto, 2004). So, in order to attain a characterisation of human-centred management, the systemic view combines the ethical, social, economic, and institutional perspectives.

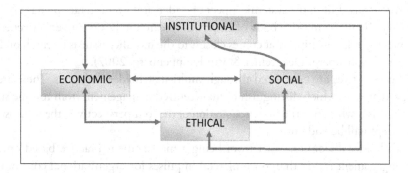

Figure 4.1   Interrelations Between the Ethical, the Social, the Economic, and the Institutional

The four perspectives influence each other within a systemic interrelation, as illustrated in Figure 4.1, and this sequence of mutual effects and feedbacks is a system of its own.

This portrait of interconnectedness presents multiple impacts: Ethical reasoning motivates social relations; it has an effect on the economic outcomes of any decision made by a leader or a manager, and it shapes the way the institutions work in a society—be they educational, legislative, or judicial bodies. Conversely, institutions may inspire the ethical reasoning of decision-makers; they may frame the structure of economic activities and of societal organisation. The mutual impacts continue with the interlacing of social and economic occurrences and of social and institutional arrangements.

With this construct of combined perspectives, the framework differs from other setups of management ethics, which follow a pure stakeholder approach (like Bowie and Werhane, 2004) or a moral principles framework (like Schumann, 2001). Both moral principles and stakeholder relations are integrative parts of the multi-perspective framework as well, but the systemic dimension treats them as parts of a larger holistic entity.

The Four Perspectives

The combination of ethical, social, economic, and institutional perspectives within the topic of human-centred management makes this a complex phenomenon. Complexity is inherent in ethics issues, as they tend to be represented by different viewpoints of different people, and they are often conflictive and prone to ending up in dilemmas (Krebs, Denton & Wark, 1997; see also Poliner, Shapiro & Stefkovich, 2016, who present dilemma situations faced by educators).

This makes the phenomenon of human-centred management attractive for systems theory and systems thinking. It sounds logical that the perspectives would be regarded as elements of the *system* of human-centred management, influencing one another within this entity and exerting a combined effect on other systems (an organisation, a group of stakeholders, groups of a society, etc.). But while social interaction in general has long been the subject of systems thinking, with, for example, the work of Niklas Luhmann in Germany (see Luhmann, 1995) and of Talcott Parsons in the US (see Parsons, 1980), the systemic aspect of leader–follower interaction has not been dealt with extensively. There is a massive body of empirical research in leadership effectiveness, but it is based on a one-way relationship; what comes closest to the morality issue is research on fairness in leadership (van Knippenberg, De Cremer & van Knippenberg, 2007).

The four perspectives are connected through multi-stakeholder dialogues. There are multiple facets in these dialogues which distinguish human-centred management from routine stakeholder management. This is why, after the first presentation of the four perspectives, the multi-stakeholder dialogues concept will be laid out.

Multi-stakeholder dialogues, apart from being a management practice based on reciprocal stakeholder engagement rather than on unilateral impulses for organisational control (Heugens, van Den Bosch & van Riel, 2002), have also been employed to evaluate scientific/technological advances for social/ethical and ecological risks and benefits. They promote collective learning as they uncover shared meanings and relational responsibilities. By engaging in dialogue, it is argued by Burchell and Cook (2008), ethical obligations and responsibilities are being co-constructed. The process of dialoguing with multiple partners, as it entails ethics and socio-economic considerations, requires a moral foundation as will be shown below.

The Ethical Perspective

Leaders who acknowledge that there are universal principles that govern human behaviour beyond written rules and codes act morally by nature. They abide by ethical principles in all the decisions they make, even though the outcomes of the actions they take may not always be uniform. Strict uniformity would concur with what is called *universalistic ethics,* meaning that an action is morally right or wrong under similar circumstances, irrespective of place, time, and sociocultural context. However, *universal* does not mean *absolute*, because there may be justifiable exceptions. This is often criticised as a casuistic position. For the casuist, the yardstick by which to measure the morality of an action is the circumstances[*] surrounding the person committing the action at the time that it is committed. When circumstances, place, and time vary, one should not refrain from applying a different judgement. This casuistic stance turns its attention to individual cases and to debating the relative merits of choosing a solution to a specific problem from among a number of alternatives. Leaders often find themselves in situations like this, as their moral judgement usually has to incorporate economic and social considerations.

One outstanding management scholar who recognised this interrelation early on was Peter F. Drucker. While his casuist view on ethics earned him a number of negative critics (Schwartz, 1998; Klein, 2000), it was from the cognition of multiple perspectives that Drucker took business ethics very seriously and developed a clear position on business morality. The social perspective in business morality was one of his foremost concerns.

---

[*] Often, these circumstances are deemed to be culture, ethnicity or geographical location. This relativism, or relativistic ethics, argues that different groups of people ought to have different ethical standards in their respective societies. The question is whether a norm can properly be described as 'ethical' unless it is understood as having cross-cultural validity. Within the purpose of this book, a further discussion on relativism and universalism is not needed. In praxis, moral reasoning and decision-making are always context specific, and it does not make a difference if it occurs in, let us say, the US, the UK or China.

The Social Perspective

All decisions made by a leader eventually have a social consequence; therefore, the impact of human-centred management on society is about benefitting and advancing the condition of people. The impact of business leaders on society at large has gained increasing prominence, both in management literature, which analyses, interprets and also reinvents this relationship, and in practice, with many individual cases of exemplary performance.

Also, a considerable number of academic and professional associations that pursue real life dissemination have been set up, such as Business in Society LLC (http://businessinsociety.net), the Academy of Business in Society (http://www.abis-global.org) and the Caux Round Table (http://www.cauxroundtable.org), to name just a few. All are connected to and some of them are co-founders of the Principles for Responsible Management Education (PRME) Initiative, which is the first organised relationship between the United Nations and business schools, with the PRME Secretariat housed in the UN Global Compact Office (http://www.unprme.org). This development has created a new range of concepts attempting to redefine and broaden business's responsibilities with respect to society and introducing the idea of corporate citisenship as a core metaphor (Smit, 2013). Citisenship, nowadays, needs institutions in order to fully develop, which is why the fourth perspective of conjoining leadership and morality is about institutions. Markets are the foremost institutions that are relevant for businesses, so the economic perspective is presented here before the institutional.

The Economic Perspective

There are two aspects to this perspective: One is the reverberation of moral behaviour in a leader's environment, which for business leaders means the markets and the moral market axiom (Boatright, 1999). This relates to the question of whether the economic model of capitalism promotes moral behaviour or not. The most common definitions of capitalism include private ownership of the means of production, voluntary exchange of labour and goods, and competitive markets (e.g., Heilbroner, 2008). But the moral feature of voluntary exchange (or free markets) and competition is human freedom. There are three contingent features (Homann, 2006):

1. Markets are built on a systematic feedback mechanism where buyers determine preferences through purchasing patterns.
2. Responsibility is clearly set in open markets. When a product or service is not acceptable to consumers, the producer has to adapt it to meet the needs of buyers.
3. Competition ensures innovation of goods and services as the imperative for providing effective solutions to problems and ensuring that they are rapidly disseminated.

Human freedom is a determinant, thus, for being able to choose between alternatives. This is a precedent for morality: morality is unattainable unless human beings have the freedom to choose between alternative actions or products without external coercion. Therefore, capitalism, which is free ownership in a market where labour and goods are exchanged freely and prices are defined by supply and demand, is inextricably a system that maximises human freedom.

The system cannot *guarantee* that all members of society behave morally. But as capitalism is conducive to free will, it naturally *promotes* moral behaviour to the greatest extent possible, in contrast to an economic system where the decision-making power is concentrated in one central entity that also defines what is good or evil.

When the people of a community or country can exert their decision-making power, they will eventually opt for a capitalistic system, and it is this system that can easily adapt to the many diverse cultures of the world (Meltzer, 2012).

As an additional note on freedom of choice, it should be emphasised that in order to make a moral decision (i.e., one that aims at doing good), people/leaders need to have the mental capacity to discriminate. The German philosopher Immanuel Kant (1724–1804) called this attribute *reason*. One of the criteria he gave for assessing morality was that an act is performed not for a particular outcome but for the sake of *goodness itself*. What would this mean in business life? Yukl (2010: 334) gives an excellent example to illustrate *goodness itself*:

> In the 1970s river blindness was one of the world's most dreaded diseases, that had long frustrated scientists trying to stop its spread in developing countries. A potential cure for the disease was discovered by researchers at Merck. The new drug Mectisan would cost over $200 million to develop. And it was needed only by people who could not afford to pay for it. When Roy Vagelos, the CEO of Merck, was unsuccessful to get governments of developing nations to pay for the drug, it became obvious that Mectisan would never make any profit for Merck. Nevertheless, Vagelos decided to distribute Mectisan for free to the people whose lives depended on it. Many people in the company said the decision was a costly mistake that violated the responsibility of the CEO to stockholders. However, Vagelos believed that the decision was consistent with Merck's guiding mission to preserve and improve human life. The development of Mectisan was a medical triumph and it helped to nearly eradicate river blindness. This humanitarian decision enhanced the company's reputation and attracted some of the best scientific researchers in the world to work for Merck (Useem 1998, cited in Yukl, 2010).

Vagelos followed what George W. Merck had enunciated 25 years earlier: '*We must never forget that medicine is for people. It is not for the profits. Profits follow, and if we have remembered that they never fail to appear*' (Gibson, 2007: 39). Now, if *reason*, according to Kant, leads to performing an action not to attain a particular outcome but for the sake of goodness itself, this implies that an additional outcome (the 'profits that follow' as stated by George W. Merck) is accepted as *reasonable*.

R. E. Freeman further developed Kant's profit theory, coining the term *Kantian Capitalism* and relating Kant's ideas on who has to benefit from an action to stakeholder theory (Evan & Freeman, 1988). This directly connects Kant's reasoning about goodness with the modern theory of the firm embedded on value creation as the highest business objective, with profits not an end but an effective result (Laffont, 1975).

The Institutional Perspective

This perspective is based on two aspects: One is the influence that moral leaders *exert* on institutions (with business associations being closest to business leaders although business leaders might also have an effect on other organisations—e.g., political institutions) and, conversely, the motivation a leader *receives from* institutions. The other aspect is that institutions are agencies with the power to deploy moral norms across organisations. This concept has been called *ethics of institutions*, and its basis is that a competitive market economy founded on capitalist principles and practices is sustainable with a carefully devised institutional system enabling everyone to pursue individual interests (Lütge, 2005).

Institutional ethics distinguishes between actions and conditions of actions. This distinction was initially made by Adam Smith, who, besides being the 'father' of free market economics, was a moral philosopher by training. In his first writings (e.g., *The Theory of Moral Sentiments*, published in 1759), he introduced a systematic differentiation between actions and conditions of actions, pioneering the idea of a link between competition and morality. His argument is that morality, which incorporates the idea of the solidarity of all, is the essential element in the conditions or the *rules* by which markets work; the members of the market act in a way that respects the actions of others. Only under these pre-conditions can competition be effective and foster productivity. Adequate conditions for the actor's direct competition to an optimal level of advantages and benefits for all people. As the rules are the same for everybody, no one can exploit a situation where another behaves morally—everybody is induced to behave morally.

The institutional perspective is directly related to issues of corporate social responsibility (CSR), maintaining that a corporation is an institution within society that has to deploy moral behaviour towards other members of that society.

There are numerous organisations worldwide that offer recommendations on fostering CSR. Many of them are member-driven organisations where committed leaders work together on principles for moral governance. One example is the International Chamber of Commerce's *Nine Steps to Responsible Business Conduct,* which are directed to companies of all sises including small and medium-sised companies.* And leaders who understand what human-centred management is will, conversely, shape the outcome of those organisations.

In that context, it is worth paying attention to developments in China, where institutional ethics constitute a central focus of political philosophy. This raises questions such as, 'What is a good institution?' 'What should a good institution be like?' 'How is such an institution possible?' and 'What is the value of a good institution?' Typically, what Chinese ethicists ask for is to uphold the historicist mode of thought—i.e., traditional philosophies such as Confucianism and the standpoint of the unity of substance and form (Zhaoming, 2007).

The Four Perspectives and the Human-Centred Paradigm

All four perspectives of the human-centred management paradigm focus on human beings. The *ethics perspective* is a humanistic concept, where the term *humanism* stands for both an emphasis on the value of human beings *(people-centred or human-centred)* and on critical thinking over acceptance of dogma (reason-centred rationalism and empiricism). The *social perspective* deals with relations between human beings and between individuals and society. The *economic perspective* is about activities that are designed and delivered to meet and serve human needs, and the *institutional perspective* considers agencies that are set up to promote well-ordered human coexistence.

Relations between human beings in a society are at the core of ethics. The focus of ancient philosophies was always on the role of a person in society and his or her contribution to the improvement of the community. The leading examples are Plato, son of powerful politicians in ancient Athens, who laid down his central theses in his work *Republic,* and Aristotle, the educator of the Macedonian prince who was to be Alexander the Great, with his treatise entitled *Politics.*

---

* http://www.iccwbo.org/products-and-services/trade-facilitation/9-steps-to-responsible-business-conduct

So, from its beginnings in ancient times, ethical reasoning has always connected the individual and society.

Institutions arose in modern societies whose structures are much more complex and pluralist than those of ancient Greece. They need agencies that ensure that all members of a society, and especially the less fortunate, partake in progress and prosperity. Institutions exist to serve humans. And this also applies to any economic undertaking. Human beings pursue economic goals as a matter of survival, so human activity is embedded in business activity, which should make it self-evident that the economy and all businesses serve human needs.

While this has been a canon of philosophers and economists for centuries, there have also been conspicuous examples to the contrary—of greed, maltreatment and manipulation of human beings, corruption, and misuse of power. And all this happens in spite of remarkable writing about business morality by eminent academicians and practitioners and severe punishment by law for transgressions. However, many successful attempts have been made to reduce the chances for fraudsters to get away unpunished—e.g., through the US Securities and Exchange Commission (SEC). The SEC created a pertinent website which it even named after Bernie Madoff, who was sentenced to 150 years in prison for deceiving hundreds of investors.[*] And German lawmakers substantially expanded the scope of what was considered commercial bribery in German criminal law in the aftermath of the Siemens scandal (Primbs & Wang, 2016).

But an important question is still, why people do act immorally, even though most are aware of their guilt in harming other people, and even though they probably know that they will be found out in the end? In the long run, ethical, social, economic, and institutional norms will prevail, as this work intends to show. Prevalence of the 'good' requires perseverance in dialogue between stakeholders, who then all benefit from the correlation between the ethical, social, economic, and institutional perspectives of human-centred management.

Interrelating the Four Perspectives Through Multi-Stakeholder Dialogues

There is more to systemic thinking[†] than merely determining interrelations. In organisational development theory, which has made extensive use of systems thinking, organisations are viewed as open systems that interact with their environment. Katz and Kahn (1978) have set up a model that interprets organisational interrelations in terms of input, throughput/transformation and output (see Figure 4.2).

The model factorises the environment of the organisation: The elements, both tangible and intangible, of the external environment are input into the organisation, and the results of the output into the environment are fed back into the organisation. This contributes to the functioning of the system, and a boundary is created that goes beyond the organisation.

---

[*] https://www.sec.gov/spotlight/secpostmadoffreforms.htm
[†] The author has refrained from using the term 'systemic morality' because this has been applied to a totally different concept by Goodpaster and Matthews (1982). They employ the term to denote that a pure capitalist approach to business ethics places morality, responsibility, and conscience in the role of the invisible hand of the free market system.

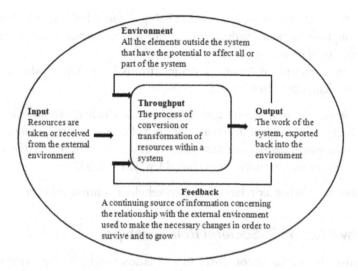

Figure 4.2   Katz and Kahn Open System Model. (*Source:* Katz, D., and Kahn, R. L. [1978]. *The Social Psychology of Organisations* [2nd Ed.], 78. New York, NY: John Wiley & Sons. Used with permission.)

We can draw an effective parallel from this model to the combination of the four perspectives that conjoin leadership and morality. The ethics perspective could be expressed as an input into the *throughput* of moral behaviour and moral decisions that consider human and societal concerns in parallel with what is needed to achieve political or business objectives. Output is the impact on society, with the economy and institutions as the *environment* that helps to develop ethical reasoning shaped by exemplary leadership based on moral behaviour.

This mutual influence works through intensive communication. Effective communication is essential to enhance the results of a leader's actions and to promote how institutions can inspire ethical reasoning of decision-makers. Effective communication is a necessary condition for optimising transmission of knowledge.

The stakeholder relation theme is distinctly engrained in the human-centred paradigm. In the definition by Carroll (1996: 74), who was one of the first to relate stakeholder relations to ethics, a stakeholder may be thought to be '*any individual or group who can affect or is affected by the actions, decisions, policies, practices, or goals of the organisation*'. But human beings need not be conceived as '*isolatable, individual entities . . . who have separate wills and desires which are constantly colliding*' (Buchholz & Rosenthal, 2005: 138, 141). If the community of stakeholders and business is seen as nothing more than the sum of its parts, the end will be irreconcilable tension. We need to find a different way that would lead to unity.

Effective unity between people—stakeholders in our context—arises in a form of action and thinking that does not fragment the whole and proclaims *implicate order* (Bohm, 1980). The term was coined by Bohm in the field of quantum theory; in the context of organisations, the argument is that nothing binds individuals and institutions together except self-interest, so the solution starts by making all parties aware that taking account simultaneously of economic performance and its social aspects will serve common as well as individual interests. This philosophical stance has been called 'American pragmatism'. It rejects the view of individuals as atomic, separable, isolated units and sees the individual as inherently social. It builds a bridge from the Greek philosophers' notion of ανθρώπος ξώον πολιτικόν ('man is a political being'),* and it holds that individuals consider others in the development of their conduct, and, in this way, a common content is developed that provides a community of meaning.

A prominent representative of American pragmatism is John Dewey, who wrote extensively about morality and democracy. In his words,

> [T]o learn to be human is to develop through the give-and-take of communication an effective sense of being an individual distinctive member of a community; one who understands and appreciates its beliefs, desires, and methods, and who contributes to a further conversion of organic powers into human resources and values (Dewey, 1984: 332).

This closely relates to stakeholder relations and stakeholder communication.

Communicative Action in Societal Relationships

The first prerequisite is to achieve consensus in a situation in which all participants are free to have their say, which is the epitome of Habermas's *discourse ethics* (Brand, 1990). Habermas's philosophical paradigm recognises that knowledge is fundamentally dependent on relations between subjects. Knowledge is by definition a *construct* to be agreed on by the parties involved, based on mutual understanding, which leads to 'shared sensing' (Hannerz, 1992). And it is only after the creation of mutual understanding that action can be undertaken.

Habermas argues that most people and organisations tend to engage in *strategic action*, based on egoistic achievement of specific outcomes and where success is judged by *'the efficiency of influencing the decisions of rational opponents'* (Habermas, 1982). This hypothesis contrasts with communicative action that is oriented towards shared understanding, where partners in an interaction set out, and manage, to influence each other, so that their action is based on *motivation through reason* (Brand, 1990).

Effective communicative action needs to include Seyla Benhabib's (1993) call for an extension to Habermas' paradigm. Benhabib adds another purpose of moral discourse: she calls it *achieving a reflective position of reversibility*. This is an empathetic ability to put oneself in another's shoes, which is necessary to achieve a moral point of view (Daboub & Calton, 2002b). Benhabib shifts attention away from procedures for achieving purely rational agreement and towards the need to create and sustain practices in which reasoned agreement becomes *a way of life*. She maintains (see Benhabib, 1993: 337) that there are just two principles by which moral claims of dependent stakeholders receive legitimisation, which are:

- The principle of universal moral respect: recognising the right of all human beings capable of speech and action to be participants in a moral conversation.
- The principle of egalitarian reciprocity: within such conversations, each person has the same symmetrical rights to various speech acts, to initiate new topics, and to ask for reflection about the presuppositions of the conversation.

This approach enables decision-making in a pluralist context among a diversity of stakeholders without giving priority to any when they endorse different or even conflicting cultural and moral frameworks (Doorn, 2009). This is the context that is regularly found when leaders, especially in

---

* Clarifying the basic ideas of Greek philosophy on morality lays outside the scope of this introduction. The reader is referred to pertinent literature.

business, explore the impacts of their decisions on the community and institutional environments of their firms and on society in general.

Furthermore, effective communications leading to the achievement of moral objectives need to consider that all relationships are subject to three critical issues: agreement, congruency, and accuracy. Grunig and Hunt (1984) give a definition of these terms along the following lines:

- *Agreement* refers to the extent to which organisations and stakeholders are able to identify a common situation and recognise the validity of the other party's concerns.
- *Congruency* represents a status in which the perception of one party is influenced by the mental model of the other party. Full and open exchange of information is impossible unless the other party's values, knowledge, and interests are acknowledged, accepted, and 'assumed'.
- *Accuracy* derives from the perception that congruency may or may not be a fair reflection of the stakeholders' true values and beliefs. The accuracy relation indicates the veracity of the organisation's perception of the interests of the stakeholders. To the extent that the organisation's perception closely correlates with the stakeholders', the organisation has a more solid base for developing an effective communications strategy. Less congruent and less accurate perceptions lead to less effective communications.

Effective relationships, whatever their type, require operational learning and communication skills, including reflection, inquiry, and advocacy (Isaacs, 1999), wherein (see Simcic, Brønn & Brønn, 2003):

- The objective of *reflection* is to become increasingly aware of the thinking and reasoning processes that distinguish between actual 'data' and abstractions.
- *Inquiry* engages the communicating parties in a joint process of understanding the thinking and reasoning of each other, from where statements and conclusions can be advanced.
- *Advocacy* is the process of communicating one's own thinking and reasoning in a manner that makes them visible to others.

A prudent facilitator of a dialogue seeks a proper balance between inquiry and advocacy, avoiding one-way communication as much as feedback-overflow. What should be achieved here is 'organisational listening competency' (Burnside-Lawry, 2010).

Organisational listening competency is another element of success in conducting multi-stakeholder dialogues. When encounters of stakeholders are prone to produce conflicts and misunderstandings, mastery of listening skills ranks ahead of negotiation skills (Gable & Shireman, 2005). This brings us to the building blocks for knowledge-based multi-stakeholder dialogues that leaders use to reach common understanding on moral issues related to their decision-making. Since most societal relationships have an economic underpinning—although one may very well uphold the ethical position that our lives are not measured in dollars (Allaway, 2005)—stakeholder dialoguing is exemplified here in the business environment.

The Building Blocks for Multi-Stakeholder Dialogues

Any stakeholder engagement and all communication processes need to be prudently and carefully prepared. It is not enough merely to request a dialogue between societal groups and institutions. Outcomes that meet moral standards will only be produced when it is known who the relevant stakeholders are and whether their claims are legitimate, how to talk to them, and how such dialogues are to be organised in a democratic way (Belal, 2002).

A variety of *engagement mechanisms* has been described in the literature (Friedman & Miles, 2004; Kaptein & van Tulder, 2003). Some scholars have even proposed generic strategies for stakeholder management (Savage et al., 1991) and general communication models for talking to different constituencies (Crane & Matten, 2004). But rarely do we find this linked to Habermas's discourse ethics, whose outlines were exposed above. Habermas's model should be taught in management courses, at least in principle, as it lays down a textbook recipe for executing proper stakeholder dialogues.

Stakeholder engagement is not just an effort to synchronise the relationships between a business organisation—or any other institution—and its constituencies and where the communication process can be managed as one way (Andriof, 2001; Foster & Jonker, 2005). A more effective approach is to build a framework that gives stakeholders a role where they feel that it is *they* who allot the firm a *social license to operate*. For this, the firm must build two-way relationships in which the interests and concerns of all parties are taken into consideration and decisions are made in the light of those—often conflicting—interests and concerns (Bendell, 2000).

The conceptual approach, methods, and responsibilities entailed in a genuine stakeholder communication must be prepared and promulgated through a collective effort by the management team that will execute the business purpose, the representatives of all stakeholders, and the facilitators of the stakeholder dialogue.

A critical success factor is a clear-cut philosophical concept that combines ethical, economic, and social considerations. This holds true especially for multi-stakeholder dialogues, where aggravating effects have to be taken into account. For example, cultural differences may have such an effect, as they often pose a noticeable barrier to common understanding and arriving at a consensus. It is crucial to move away from a narrow definition of *ethics* that covers only the obligations the institution owes to stakeholders and the obligations that stakeholders owe to the institution. The ethics that govern stakeholder dialogues must strive to balance the full variety of stakeholders' values. This requires a format of *organisational learning* where the organisation comprises all participants in the dialogue (Payne & Calton, 2002; Daboub & Calton, 2002a), with the overall objective of securing trust and a *level playing field*.

The building blocks of the knowledge base to be developed are based on:

1. Ethical leadership and governance, trust building, social responsibility, effective articulation of ethics and economics
2. Morality, self-interest, and the markets
3. Entrepreneurship, development and collaboration: fostering the spirit of business
4. Foundations of sustainable development
5. Social interaction: acts and modes of cooperation and the rule-finding discourse
6. Combining multi-stakeholder dialogues with other standardised ethics initiatives, such as predefined codes, norms and procedures; organisational approaches to social and/or environmental issues
7. Fundamental learning and communication skills in conflictive environments: reflection, inquiry, and advocacy
8. This list could also be pertinent to the curriculum of a business school or business course because its building blocks refer to universally accepted subjects. Unfortunately, many still assume that subjects such as ethics and communication can be learned by *osmosis* (Carnevale, 2000; Rao & Sylvester, 2000).

All the items of the list have their base in a proper understanding of communicative action in societal relationships and could demonstrate what may be regarded as success factors for fruitful multi-stakeholder dialogues. But many business school materials, even those in schools that focus on organisational behaviour and culture and value, tend to be theoretical and not action oriented (Ashkansay, Wilderrom & Peterson, 2000). On the other hand, books on the topic of general cultural consulting only offer a random path (e.g., Reeves-Ellington, 2004).

A *level playing field* puts each stakeholder into the same position while accepting that not all stakeholders have the same level of importance. Ranking this importance was developed by Mitchell, Agle and Wood (1997), who categorise stakeholders by three attributes:

1. Power, which refers to the ability to get others to do what they otherwise would not do (along the lines of Max Weber, 1947).
2. Legitimacy, which refers to the mandate of the stakeholder—its right to exercise its powers in relation to the claim on the firm.
3. Urgency of a stakeholder claim, which refers to the need to expedite the process of stakeholder interaction.

By combining these attributes in various ways, four types of stakeholders can be distinguished (see Wartick & Wood, 1999: 113):

- Long-term core stakeholders who share the attributes of legitimacy and power, but not urgency (e.g., shareholders).
- Stakeholders who share the attributes of power and urgency, but not legitimacy, and tend to become violent or coercive radical-action groups.
- Dependent stakeholders whose claims are legitimate and urgent, but who lack power (e.g., secondary stakeholders).
- The immediate core stakeholder group which combines all three attributes, thereby making it mandatory for managers to properly manage the stakeholder relationship with this group as first priority.

Frameworks for Preparing and Conducting Multi-Stakeholder Dialogues

Stakeholder participation and involvement have been recognised for several years as a crucial factor in the context of sustainable development issues (see, for example, van Tulder & van der Zwart, 2006), and multi-stakeholder standards have emerged for these issues with considerable potential for effective consensus building, knowledge sharing, and interest representation (Fransen & Kolk, 2007). Yet the literature is recognising that currently there is a lack of specificity of the multi-stakeholder concept, and it suggests refinement of multi-stakeholder standards (Ibid.).

There is no general *toolkit* for addressing multi-stakeholder dialogues, even in the advanced discussions on environmental issues, and much less when dialogues take place in a foreign environment unfamiliar to firms who go international. Specific formats have been promoted only for high-level dialogues—for example, by the Secretariat of the United Nations in creating the NGO Coalition on Sustainable Development in 1997, through various initiatives at other UN organisations, and with the 2011 UN Department of Public Information publication *NGO Conference on Sustainable Societies—Responsive Citisens* (UN DPI, 2011).

Another example is Rupert Brown's 2001 textbook, *Group Processes: Dynamics Within and Between Groups*, which does not address communicative and ethical issues. Likewise the *Consensus Guiding Principles* of the Canadian National Roundtable on the Environment and the Economy (NRTEE), first published in 1993, and the United Nations Environment and Development Forum (UNED) *Methodological Framework on Multi-Stakeholder Processes*, by Minu Hemmati (2001), are primarily directed at instrumental procedures.

More recently, the WHO *National e-Health Strategy Toolkit* lists recommendations for stakeholder engagement which also encompass ongoing monitoring and evaluation (WHO & ITU, 2012).

For a framework to be generally applicable, it should comprise the following steps (see Benson & Dodds, 2010):

- **Process initiation.** Scoping, identifying a core coordinating group, locating the issues to be addressed, identifying a clear timeline and milestones.
- **Mapping key issues and actors.** Connecting topics and actors, establishing a system by which stakeholder groups can select or elect representatives, choosing the language and terminology used for the dialogue, approaching possible facilitators, examining potential confrontations, etc.
- **Preparing the dialogue.** Producing position papers based on stakeholders' input developing sharing information rules, agreeing on principles to guide the facilitators' work.
- **Conducting the dialogue.** Ensuring a comfortable physical atmosphere, assigning experienced rapporteurs to document the session, deciding on the admission of observers.
- **Follow-Up.** Establishing expected outputs, such as a facilitator's summary, an agreement report or a set of recommendations to keep records, ensuring that the final document is accepted by all stakeholders and communicated to their constituencies in de-briefing, and agreement on media coverage.

Benson and Dodds' catalogue reads like a text from a project management course. It is undeniably important to have good command of state-of-the-art techniques in this field. It is more effectively applied when the stakeholder community is clearly identified, and all members understand and accept the general objectives and the 'rules of the game'. Nonetheless, a different approach is necessary to address the challenges that leaders face in effective communication, where an initial consensus cannot be expected and where the communicative potential for including the majority of possible stakeholders has yet to be developed.

While primary stakeholders (the transactional stakeholders in the definition by Wartick & Wood, 1999) are the main responsibility of the firm (Clarkson, 1995), support must also be sought from secondary, non-transactional stakeholders in the community that interfaces with the organisation.

Local communities are commonly regarded as secondary stakeholders who do not directly influence the economic activities of a firm but indirectly have influence on or are influenced by the firm. Secondary stakeholders, apart from local communities, may also include local media, trade unions, competitors, analysts, environmental activists, and supervisory bodies set up by coalitions of non-profit organisations.

The importance of specific government institutions and supervisors may shift, depending on the process of stakeholder involvement, and, likewise, the importance of local communities may increase or decrease. Other external stakeholders are the 'natural environment' and 'future generations', which may come into play when groupings are formed that represent the interests of the biosphere and of the generations to come.

To exert a moral impact on an institution or any other stakeholder, a business leader must not only have excellent communicative skills and outstanding arguments, but he or she must also be personally committed to the ethical foundation of leadership behaviour and business behaviour. What that foundation should convey to all stakeholders is that businesses (especially large international or multi-national businesses) have to assume responsibility to halt or diminish any potentially negative economic, social, and environmental impacts of their business activity.

The discussion about corporate social responsibility has placed businesses at the centre of an often hot and spirited debate about what 'rights' businesses can expect to enjoy in society and what 'duties' society can reasonably expect businesses to perform. But what needs to be emphasised are the ethical underpinnings. If business leaders actively partake in the CSR discussion and in deliberations about what ethics are and how they are practiced and deployed in the organisation, then they must engage in understanding its philosophical attributes. It has been said that *'concepts, which are the bread and butter of management',* have direct, but often ignored, philosophical foundations (Joullié, 2014: 198; see also Joullié, 2016; De Borchgrave, 2006; Small, 2004).

References

Allaway, J. (2005). Our lives are not measured in dollars. The Alaska Native Claims Settlement Act Unrealised. *Journal of Land, Resources & Environmental Law, 25,* 139–147.

Andriof, J. (2001). Patterns of stakeholder partnership building. In: J. Andriof and M. McIntosh (Eds.). *Perspectives on Corporate Citisenship,* 215–238. Sheffield, UK: Greenleaf.

Ashkansay, N. M., Wilderrom, C. P. M., and Peterson M. F. (2000). *Handbook of Organisational Culture and Climate.* Thousand Oaks, CA: SAGE Publishing.

Bardy, R. (2018). *Rethinking Leadership: A Human Centered Approach to Management Ethics.* Abingdon, UK: Routledge.

Belal, A. R. (2002). Stakeholder accountability or stakeholder management. A review of UK firms' social and ethical accounting, auditing, and reporting practices. *Corporate Social Responsibility and Environmental Management, 9*(1), 8–25.

Benhabib, S. (1993). *Situating the Self: Gender, Community and Postmodernism in Contemporary Ethics.* New York, NY: Psychology Press.

Bendell, J., Ed. (2000). *Terms for Endearment: Business, NGOs and Sustainable Development.* Sheffield, UK: Greenleaf.

Benson, E., and Dodds, F. (2010). *The Stakeholder Empowerment Project.* Geneva and New York, NY: Stakeholder Forum.

Boatright, J. R. (1999). Does business ethics rest on a mistake? *Business Ethics Quarterly, 9*(4), 583–591.

Bohm, D. (1980). *Wholeness and the Implicate Order.* London, UK: Routledge & Kegan Paul.

Bowie, N. E., and Werhane, P. H. (2004). *Management Ethics.* Malden, MA; Oxford, UK; Carlton, Australia: Wiley-Blackwell.

Brand, A. (1990). *The Force of Reason: An Introduction to Habermas' Theory of Communicative Action.* Sydney, AU: Unwin Hyman.

Brown, R. (2001). *Group Processes: Dynamics Within and Between Groups.* Malden, MA; Oxford, UK; Carlton, AU: Wiley-Blackwell.

Buchholz, R. A., and Rosenthal, S. B. (2005). The spirit of entrepreneurship and the qualities of moral decision making: Toward a contemporary conceptual framework for stakeholder theory. *Journal of Business Ethics, 58*(1–3), 137–148.

Burchell, J., and Cook, J. (2008). Stakeholder dialogue and organisational learning: Changing relationships between companies and NGOs. *Business Ethics: A European Review, 17*(1), 35–46.

Burnside-Lawry, J. (2010). *Participatory Communication and Listening: An Exploratory Study of Organisational Listening Competency.* PhD Thesis. RMIT University, Melbourne, AU. http://researchbank.rmit.edu.au/eserv/rmit:4933/Burnside_Lawry.pdf.

Carnevale, A. P. (2000). *Community Colleges and Career Qualifications.* Washington, DC: American Association for Community Colleges.

Carroll, A. B. (1996). *Business and Society: Ethics and Stakeholder Management* (3rd Ed.). Cincinnati, OH: Southwestern Publishing.

Clarkson, M. B. A. (1995), A stakeholder framework for analyzing and evaluating corporate social performance. *Academy of Management Review, 20*(1), 92–117.

Crane, A., and Matten, D. (2004). Questioning the domain of the business ethics curriculum. *Journal of Business Ethics, 54*(4), 357–369.

Daboub, A. L., and Calton, J. M. (2002a). Stakeholder learning dialogues: How to preserve ethical responsibility in networks. *Journal of Business Ethics, 41*(1), 85–98.

Daboub, A. L., and Calton, J. M. (2002b). World trade and anti-globalisation: Ethical implications. *Proceedings of the Seventh Annual Conference, Free Trade in the Western Hemisphere: The Challenges and The Future.* Laredo, Texas, April 11–12, 2002.

De Borchgrave, R. (2006). *Le philosophe et le manager.* Bruxelles, BE: De Boeck Université.

Dewey, J. (1984). The public and its problems. In: J. A. Boydston (Ed.). *The Later Works* (Vol. 2). Carbondale and Edwardsville, IL: Southern Illinois University Press.

Doorn, N. (2009). Applying Rawlsian approaches to resolve ethical issues: Inventory and setting of a research agenda. *Journal of Business Ethics, 91*(1), 127–143.

Evan, W. M., and Freeman, R. E. (1988). A stakeholder theory of the modern corporation: Kantian capitalism. In: T. Beauchamp, and N. Bowie (Eds.). *Ethical Theory and Business.* (2nd Ed.), pp. 75–93. Englewood Cliffs, NJ: Prentice Hall.

Foster, D., and Jonker, J. (2005). Stakeholder relationships: The dialogue of engagement. *Corporate Governance, 5*(5), 51–57.

Fransen, L. W., and Kolk, A. (2007). Global rule-setting for business. Critical analysis of multi-stakeholder standards. *Organisation, 14*(5), 667–684.

Friedman, A. L., and Miles, S. (2004). Stakeholder theory and communication practice. *Journal of Communication Management, 9*(1), 89–97.

Gable, C., and Shireman, B. (2005). Stakeholder engagement: A three-phase methodology: Learning to manage your relationships with stakeholders. *Environmental Quality Management, 14*(3), 9–24.

Gibson, K. (2007). *Ethics and Business: An Introduction.* Cambridge, UK: Cambridge University Press.

Grunig, J., and Hunt, T. (1984). *Managing Public Relations.* Orlando, FL: Cengage Learning.

Habermas, J. (1982). Reply to my critics. In: J. B. Thompson and D. Held (Eds.), pp. 219–283. *Habermas: Critical Debates.* Cambridge, MA: MIT Press.

Hannerz, U. (1992) *Cultural Complexity.* New York, NY: Colombia University Press.

Heilbroner, R. L. (2008). Capitalism. In: S. N. Durlauf and L. N. Blume, L. N. (Eds.). *The New Palgrave Dictionary of Economics* (2nd Ed.). Palgrave Macmillan Publishing Company.

Hemmati, M. (2001). United Nations Environment and Development Forum (UNED). *Report on Multi-Stakeholder Processes—A Methodological Framework*. London, UK: United Nations.

Heugens, P. P., Van Den Bosch, F. A., and Van Riel, C. B. (2002). Stakeholder integration: Building mutually enforcing relationships. *Business & Society, 41*(1), 36–60.

Homann, K. (2006). *The sense and limits of the economic method in business ethics.* Wittenberg Center for Global Ethics Discussion Paper Nr. 2006-5. Available at: http://www.wcge.org/download/DP_2006-5_Homann_-_The_Sense_and_Limits_of_the_Economic_Method_in_Business_Ethics_o.pdf; accessed May 16, 2016.

Isaacs, W. (1999). *Dialogue and the Art of Thinking Together: A Pioneering Approach to Communicating in Business and in Life.* New York, NY: Doubleday.

Jiliberto, H. R. (2004). A holarchical model for regional sustainability assessment. *Journal of Environmental Assessment Policy and Management, 6*(4), 511–538.

Joullié, J.-E. (2014) The philosopher and the manager. *International Journal of Management Concepts and Philosophy, 8*(4), 197–208.

Joullié, J.-E. (2016). The philosophical foundations of management thought. *Academy of Management Learning & Education, 15*(1), 157–179.

Kaptein, M., and van Tulder, R. (2003). Toward effective stakeholder dialogue. *Business and Society Review, 108*(2), 203–224.

Katz, D., and Kahn, R. L. (1978). *The Social Psychology of Organisations* (2nd Ed.). New York, NY: John Wiley & Sons.

Klein, S. (2000). Drucker as business moralist. *Journal of Business Ethics, 28*(2), 121–128.

Krebs, D. L., Denton, K., and Wark, G. (1997). The forms and functions of real-life moral decision-making. *Journal of Moral Education, 26,* 131–146.

Laffont, J. J. (1975). Macroeconomic constraints, economic efficiency and ethics: An introduction to Kantian economics. *Economica, 42*(168), 430–437.

Lütge, C. (2005). Economic ethics, business ethics and the idea of mutual advantages, *Business Ethics: A European Review, 14*(2), 108–118.

Luhmann, N. (1995). *Social Systems.* Stanford, CA: Stanford University Press.

Meltzer, A. H. (2012). *Why Capitalism?* Oxford, UK: Oxford University Press.

Mitchell, R. K., Agle, B. R., and Wood, D. (1997). Toward a theory of stakeholder identification and salience. *Academy of Management Review, 22*(4), 853–886.

NRTEE of Canada. (1993). *Consensus Guiding Principles.* Quebec, CA: NRTEE (National Roundtable on the Environment and the Economy).

Parsons, T. (1980). *Social Systems and the Evolution of Action Theory.* New York, NY: The Free Press.

Payne, S. L., and Calton, J. M. (2002). Towards a managerial practice of stakeholder engagement: Developing multi-stakeholder learning dialogues. *The Journal of Corporate Citisenship, 2*(6), 37–53.

Poliner Shapiro, J., and Stefkovich J. A. (2016). *Ethical Leadership and Decision Making in Education: Applying Theoretical Perspectives to Complex Dilemmas* (4th Ed.). Abingdon-on-Thames, UK: Routledge.

Primbs, M., and Wang, C. (2016). *Notable Governance Failures: Enron, Siemens and Beyond.* University of Pennsylvania Law School Seminar Paper Spring 2016. Penn Law: Legal Scholarship Repository.

Rao, M., and Sylvester, S. (2000). Business and education in transition. *AAHE* (American Association for Higher Education) *Bulletin*, *52*(8), 1–13.

Reeves-Ellington, R. (2004). What is missing from business education? Meeting the needs of emerging market business education. In: I. Alon and J. R. McIntyre (Eds.). *Business Education and Emerging Market Economies. Perspectives and Best Practices*, pp. 27–48. Norwell, MA: Springer US.

Rost, J. C. (1991). *Leadership for the Twenty-first Century.* New York, NY: Prager.

Savage, G. T., Nix, T. W., Whitehead, C. J., and Blair, J. D. (1991). Strategies for assessing and managing organisational stakeholders. *Academy of Management Executive, 5*(2), 61–75.

Schumann, P. L. (2001). A moral principles framework for human resource management ethics. *Human Resource Management Review, 11*(1), 93–111.

Schwartz, M. (1998). Peter Drucker and the denial of business ethics. *Journal of Business Ethics, 17*(15), 1685–1692.

Simcic, Brønn, P., and Brønn, C. (2003). A reflective stakeholder approach: Co-orientation as a basis for communication and learning. *Journal of Communication Management, 7*(4), 291–303.

Small, M. W. (2004). Philosophy in management: A new trend in management development. *Journal of Management Development, 23*, 183–196.

Smit, A. (2013). Responsible leadership development through management education: A business ethics perspective. *African Journal of Business Ethics, 7*(2), 45–58.

UN DPI (United Nations Department of Public Information). (2011). Sustainable societies— responsive citisens. *Declaration of the 64th Annual UN DPI/NGO Conference.* Bonn, DE: United Nations.

Useem, M. (1998). *The Leadership Moment: Nine Stories of Triumph and Disaster and Their Lessons for Us All.* New York, NY: Times Business/Random House.

van Knippenberg, D., De Cremer, D., and van Knippenberg, B. (2007). Leadership and fairness: The state of the art. *Europ. J. of Work and Organisational Psychology, 16*(2), 113–140.

van Tulder, R., and van der Zwart, A. (2006). *International Business—Society Management: Linking Corporate Responsibility and Globalisation.* London, UK, and New York, NY: Routledge.

Wartick, S., and Wood, D. (1999). *International Business and Society.* Oxford, UK: Oxford University Press.

Weber, M. (1947). *The Theory of Social and Economic Organisation.* Translated by A. M. Henderson and T. Parsons. New York, NY: Oxford University Press.

WHO (World Health Organisation) and ITU (International Telecommunication Union). (2012). *National eHealth Strategy Toolkit.* Geneva, CH: WHO Press, World Health Organisation.

Yukl, G. A. (2010). *Leadership in Organisations* (7th Ed.). Upper Saddle River, NJ: Prentice Hall.

Zhaoming, G. (2007). Institutional ethics and institutional good. *Social Sciences in China, 6*, 4.

Chapter 5

Life Cycle

Organising for Project Work: Thinking Beyond Project Delivery

Darren Dalcher

Life cycles are fundamental to the management of project work. Indeed, Professor Peter Morris, reflecting on the prevailing state of the profession, affirms that *'the one thing that distinguishes projects from non-projects is their life cycle'* (Morris, 2013: 150).

The notion of the project life cycle has become a ubiquitous part of the theory and practice of project management to the extent that it often defines and delineates the process, flow, rhythm, dynamics and boundaries of projects. In doing so, it also shapes the discipline and the way we think about projects, organising work and temporary structures.

Why Life Cycles?

The life cycle concept, as we know it, serves many purposes. The life cycle represents a path from the origin to the completion of a venture. Division into phases enables managers to control and direct the activities in a disciplined, orderly and methodical way that can be responsive to change. Phases group together directly related sequences and types of activities to facilitate visibility and control, thus enabling the successful completion of the venture.

The project life cycle acts as an important management tool focusing on the allocation of resources, the availability of key individuals, the integration of activities, the support of timely decision-making, the reduction of risk and the provision of control and governance mechanisms.

The additional benefits associated with using a life cycle approach include (see Dalcher, 2002):

- Attaining visibility
- Breaking work into manageable chunks
- Identifying the tasks
- Providing a framework for coordinating and managing
- Controlling project finance
- Identifying and obtaining correct resource profiles
- Encouraging systematic evaluation of options and opportunities
- Addressing the need for stakeholder review
- Providing a problem-solving perspective
- Verifying ongoing viability on a progressive basis
- Encouraging continuous monitoring
- Managing uncertainty
- Providing a common and shared vocabulary

Control is attained through the division into phases and the breaking up of work into identifiable and significant milestones and meaningful deliverables (products delivered at certain times). Partitioning activities into phases gives the impression of a natural order of thought and action. The spacing of activities along a time axis suggests the mutual exclusivity of stages and the primarily unidirectional flow of activities.

Each phase has specific content and management approaches with clearly identified decision points between them. Matching the content requires the application of an ever-changing mix of resources—skills, tools, expertise, money and time. Introducing phases with formal interface points encourages the opening of a communication path and the transfer of project information through formal handover or technology transfer between life cycle phases.

Rethinking Project Management

As highlighted above, the project life cycle has dominated and shaped project management thinking. The resulting instrumental rationality is often interpreted as how projects ought to be performed in the real-life environment of project work (Dalcher, 2016). Some of the ideas implied through this type of thinking have been challenged by the UK Government-funded Rethinking Project Management Network (Winter & Smith, 2006; Winter et al., 2006). Over the course of two years, the Network brought together senior practitioners and leading researchers *'to develop a research agenda aimed at extending and enriching project management ideas in relation to developing practice'* (Winter & Smith, 2006). Overall, the network found a strong need for new thinking to inform and guide practitioners beyond the current conceptual base (Winter et al., 2006: 640).

The main outcome of the network was the development of a new agenda for research presented in the form of five directions identified by the participants as critical to the management of projects. Each direction is represented as a move from a current way of thinking, represented on the left, towards a more promising perspective—as described on the right (see Table 5.1 and Winter et al., 2006; Dalcher, 2016).

The propositions related to the current position put forward (and re-stated on the left-hand side of Table 5.1) reflect a growing dissatisfaction with the life cycle-dominated position recognising multiple shortfalls. The first direction acknowledges the limitation of a simplistic life cycle as a dominant influence within the discipline, further recognising the unchallenged assumptions it harbours. The second challenges the instrumentality of the life cycle image implying a temporary apolitical production process replete with codified and understood knowledge. The third direction addresses the fixation with delivering a product or artefact, while the fourth bemoans the narrow conceptualisation and the assumption of a clearly identified single objective that is fully known at the start. The last direction tackles procedural adherence and unchallenging approach and perspectives with which the principles and approaches are applied, so we shall return to this point towards the end of the section.

The Rethinking Project Management Network published its findings in 2006. Reflecting on the progress made a decade later, Dalcher comments that *'At first glance, it would appear that the practice of project management has not been transformed in the way the original researchers and Network participants were advocating. Research still plays a very limited part in refreshing, informing or supporting the content of the bodies of knowledge'* (Dalcher, 2016: 813).

Table 5.1 Rethinking Project Management, Proposed Directions for Future Research

The Life Cycle Model of Projects and PM	Theories of the Complexity of Projects and PM
From: The simple life cycle-based models of projects, as the dominant model of projects and project management. **From**: The (often unexamined) assumption that the life cycle model is the actual terrain.	**Towards**: The development of new models and theories which recognise and illuminate the complexity of projects and project management. **Towards**: New models and theories which are explicitly presented as only partial theories of the complex terrain.
Projects as Instrumental Processes	**Projects as Social Processes**
From: The instrumental life cycle image of projects as a linear sequence of tasks to be performed on an objective entity 'out there', using codified knowledge, procedures and techniques, and based on an image of projects as temporary apolitical production processes.	**Towards**: Concepts and images which focus on social interaction among people, illuminating the flux of events and human action and the framing of projects (and the profession) within an array of social agenda, practices, stakeholder relations, politics and power.
Product Creation as the Prime Focus	**Value Creation as the Prime Focus**
From: Concepts and methodologies which focus on product creation—the temporary production, development or improvement of a physical product, system, facility etc.—and monitored and controlled against specification (quality), cost and time.	**Towards**: Concepts and frameworks which focus on *value creation* as the prime focus of projects, programmes and portfolios.
Narrow Conceptualisation of Projects	**Broader Conceptualisation of Projects**
From: Concepts and methodologies which are based on the narrow conceptualisation that projects start from a well-defined objective 'given' at the start and are named and framed around single disciplines—e.g., IT projects, construction projects, HR projects etc.	**Towards**: Concepts and approaches which facilitate broader and ongoing conceptualisation of projects as being multidisciplinary, having multiple purposes, not always predefined, but permeable, contestable and open to renegotiation throughout.
Practitioners as Trained Technicians	**Practitioners as Reflective Practitioners**
From: Training and development which produces practitioners who can follow detailed procedures and techniques, prescribed by project management methods and tools, which embody some or all of the ideas and assumptions of the 'from' parts above.	**Towards**: Learning and development which facilitates the development of reflective practitioners who can learn, operate and adapt effectively in complex project environments, through experience, intuition and the pragmatic application of theory in practice.

Evidence regarding the theoretical basis of project management remains elusive. However, to an extent, the argument about the theoretical basis of project management misses the point. Project management is a portmanteau activity that brings together a whole range of established business, organisational and social scientific theories about working collaboratively, communicating, making decisions, managing resource and so on, that are already documented in other contexts. Given the tendency to import what works from other areas, does project management need an exclusively theoretical basis of its own or rather just a link to each of the established forms of activity associated with managing projects involving people in social and societal contexts? (Ibid.: 815).

Reflecting on the Shape, Efficacy, and Purpose of Life Cycles

The fifth direction proposed by the Rethinking Project Management Network encourages reflection and questioning in and of practice. Dalcher (2016) observes a greater need to develop deliberative and reflective professionals capable of dealing with permeable boundaries and unstructured situations characterised by increasing levels of volatility, complexity, uncertainty and ambiguity. This implies the development of new skills, capabilities and habits.

> *Ultimately, the shift in practitioner development seems to be from relying on fixed expectations, standards and models in pre-understood and pre-defined contexts towards a more dynamic and reflective approach informed by the relevant context and situational needs and therefore capable of coping with the inherent complexity and uncertainty* (Dalcher, 2016: 802–803).

The network has questioned the dominance of life-cycle thinking within existing practice. The departure point for the remainder of this section is to take a further step back and to question the efficacy and rationale of the life-cycle concept itself. Indeed, if the life cycle concept was adopted from other disciplines, does it even work there as purported when it was borrowed, appropriated and imported into project management thinking, lore and habits?

The reflection will take the form of six largely open questions related to the nature and purpose of life cycles, before returning to address its appropriation from other disciplines and the unquestioning mode of its application within the project management community.

1. **Where is the cycle in the (project management) life cycle?** While there are multiple variations on the theme of the life cycles of projects in terms of the number of steps and their names, most follow a similar essential flow of activities, beginning with a relatively well-defined concept and ending with the delivery of a result, deliverable, artefact or product. Indeed, the typical manifestation is of a short and typically limited sequence of activities, which is not repeated and contains no iterative elements. There is no cycle in the prevailing models as applied within project management—so why don't we rename it as the project life sequence?

2. **Life means alive?** Life cycles often represent the different stages of the idealised life that a live subject may go through. Does something need to be alive to have a life cycle? For that matter, is the project management life cycle really concerned with the 'life' of project management?

3. **Life surely implies start to finish?** If life implies full life, the traditional project life cycle is a misnomer, as it does not encompass the full life of a project.
   » Life cycles are typically applied in biology—for example, to capture the stages of life of a frog through a number of distinct phases:
   » Egg mass → tadpole → froglet → adult frog (who is now able to initiate the next cycle . . .)
   » This allows life cycles to reflect change over time. Yet, project management life cycles often seem to assume a fully defined concept, which is transitioned into a working product, result or artefact, where we seem to lose interest. That is a rather restricted focus of interest and could be viewed as the equivalent of zooming in to a limited segment concerned with the development of a tadpole into a formed froglet (with no consideration of the purpose of the froglet or the ultimate shape of the chain of development).

4. **Life cycle as transforming?** For a life cycle to be meaningful it must represent a set of transformations that occur over the life of the subject or the lifespan of an object.
   » Given the limited gaze encompassed by project management thinking, it is perhaps better to acknowledge that the simplistic life cycle utilised in project management thinking encompasses more of a simplistic system transformation model where we are concerned with the input and output of a single transformation activity.

» The minimal concern shown in the future beyond the transformation does imply an interest in a single transformation with the following format: input → process → output

» Subsidiary interests may encompass the knowledge, constrains and guidance that direct the transformation (in addition to the available resources, which may be counted as the input), but ultimately, this is both a limited and limiting view of process.

5. **Is the life cycle encompassing birth to death span?** Span is absolutely crucial to adopting a life cycle perspective. If life cycles capture the full life span, shouldn't project management life cycles reflect the same desire?

» Other life cycles encompass the birth and death of the subject. The narrow conceptualisation captured within the project management life cycles ignores most aspects of life (and says nothing about death).

» In product development there is an increasing emphasis on 'cradle to grave' coverage, encompassing the full life cycle of a product. While we may not need to reflect on the potential for resurrection or redeployment of a product in a new guise, some projects do exactly that. The London 2012 Summer Olympic Games allowed part of the stadium to be dismantled and delivered to a new location to start life as an enhancement to a different stadium expansion project. Innovation and new product development often extend the scope of 'cradle to grave' thinking to encourage re-purposing and reuse of materials, thus engendering 'cradle to cradle' thinking. This would imply a significant extension to the scope of interest in the life of a product or project, rather than the traditionally limited zooming in.

» At the other end, the early stages play a key part in defining, constraining and shaping the project, and yet our life cycles pay little attention to early decisions and their impacts. In life cycle equivalents, if we could gain a better understanding of the influences on egg mass (and tadpole) creation, we would have a far richer insight into the ecology of frogs and their environmental relationships with their habitat than if we limited our gaze to fully formed frogs and wondered why they are afflicted with certain symptoms, conditions or manifestations.

6. **Whose life cycle is it anyway?** In project management we often refer to project life cycles (Dalcher, 2015), but in the great scheme of things, are we talking about project life cycles, project management life cycles, product life cycles, product management life cycles, or project spans?

» Do we always relate to the same thing? Do we all consider life cycles in the same way?

» Should we instead formulate clearer definitions of what we mean—and develop a better understanding of which aspects need to be described, detailed and depicted in our conversations.

Ultimately, are we correct to talk about, focus on and structure our project work around the idea a life cycle?

The Problem with Shared Practice

We will return to explore the implications of the above questions later in the section. However, for now it is useful to question the persistence of performance shortfall. Given that projects are essential to enabling, embedding and driving improved performance, one would expect blind spots to be addressed and obstacles to be removed in the perennial search for improved efficiency. In an age of austerity, one might also expect deeper assumptions to be questioned and challenged as organisations continue to seek to achieve more with less. And yet, organisational errors, failed projects and poor performance persist in many settings.

The Rethinking Project Management Network identified a major problem with the life cycle as the way of thinking about projects and project management. They identified multiple concerns around the perspective and context; however, ten years later, many of the concerns were still receiving little attention.

> *While project management is often introduced as a practice, the majority of the literature still conveys an instrumental rationality associated with a prescriptive model that assumes universal applicability in all contexts* (Dalcher, 2016: 817).

Organisations, training courses and the professional bodies in general seem reluctant to address some of the major concerns and resist the temptation to rethink the fundamental tenets of the profession.

> *In summary, it might prove simpler to refer to the instrumental rationalistic nature of classical project management knowledge observed by the Network and remark that it retains its hold on certain parts of the profession. Challenging the hegemony of professional body infused knowledge may require a considerable investment in time and momentum to engender the more significant and far reaching rethink advocated by the Network* (Ibid.: 815).

The Death of Common Sense?

Gary Klein, a leading organisational psychologist, has investigated the organisational inability to improve through the lens of insight. He notes that organisations inadvertently suppress the insights of their workers in ways that are ingrained and invisible, resulting in stifled innovation and sub-optimal performance.

> *Organizations stifle insights because of forces locked deep inside their DNA: they value predictability, they recoil from surprises, they crave perfection, the absence of errors. Surprises and errors can play havoc with plans and with smooth operations. In their zeal to reduce uncertainty and minimise errors, organizations fall into the predictability trap and the perfection trap* (Klein, 2014: 151).

The predictability trap asserts that managers prioritise predictability in order to minimise ambiguity and uncertainty for their executives, who abhor surprises. Such abhorrence results in the development of meticulously developed, yet unrealistically precise, plans that do not allow for surprises. They further eschew uncertainty by applying stricter controls and creating new forms and further levels of governance mechanisms to reinforce the pursuit of certainty.

The perfection trap refers to the organisational pursuit of devising perfect processes, procedures and systems through a concern with eliminating waste, reducing errors and becoming lean. Errors and imperfections are easy to define, measure, manage and eliminate. Becoming preoccupied with their elimination assumes that the best processes are already installed.

The quest for perfection, for mistake-free performance, can be thought of as a war on Error. It is right up there with the quest for predictability. These are both inherent in running an organization that depends on managing people and projects. In well-ordered situations, with clear goals and standards and stable conditions, the pursuit of perfection makes sense. But not when we face complex and chaotic conditions, with standards that keep evolving (Klein, 2014: 155).

When the two traps combine, it is all too simple, and much safer, to eliminate shortfalls rather than begin a search for improvement, creativity and development. It also makes it easy to follow a recipe for success or a prescribed life cycle . . .

Cutting down on errors seems pretty straightforward. You list the steps needed to perform a task, or define the standards for each step, and then check if the workers are following the steps and adhering to the standards. You are on the lookout for deviations so that you can bring workers back into compliance (Klein, 2014: 155–156).

Turning Knowledge into Action

While individuals may have privately identified and lodged their frustrations with the status quo in terms of existing methods and aspects that do not work, organisations as collectives can often remain resistant to new knowledge and insights and avoid the necessity to make use of new knowledge. Indeed, US Professors Jeffrey Pfeffer and Robert I. Sutton (2000) observe that many organisations fail to take the vital step of transforming knowledge into action, which they refer to as the *knowing–doing gap*. Pfeffer and Sutton conclude that an organisation's culture plays an important part in sustaining or exacerbating the gap. Their message is that executives must use plans, analysis, meetings and presentations to inspire deeds rather than allowing them to act as substitutes for action.

A key reason for the continuing gap revolves around the lack of accessible, reliable content that can be considered. Even when there is access to such new content—for example, through academic journals—practitioners may feel unable or unwilling to implement it because they may consider the contribution to be too theoretical or devoid of any practical potential impact.

It appears that the reluctance to adopt new practices comes down to the accessibility of the content and the perceived reliability as well as the practicality and value associated with its potential implementation in a practical setting. This chapter offers the potential to bridge that gap and encourage a new level of thinking around project life cycles and frameworks. The section by Robert Buttrick is derived from the fifth edition of his book *The Project Workout: The Ultimate Guide to Directing and Managing Business-Led Projects,* published by Routledge (Buttrick, 2019). Robert's work makes a valiant effort to address the knowing–doing gap by offering an accessible framework that has been tried and tested in practice and can offer a new perspective on the successful deployment of projects. Indeed, Buttrick's work begins with a deep analysis of lessons from the best and most successful organisations, which attempts to distil key lessons that have worked well and utilise them as a basis for developing an informed framework.

The framework expands thinking around projects to incorporate the needs and concerns of the project sponsor and make sure that projects are driven by benefits which support the organisational strategy. The shift in perspective beyond the project manager's gaze enables projects to be considered as vehicles for change. The dual focus on directing and managing projects is an important development in life cycle thinking and is able to address some of the concerns related to the complex domains of projects, involving multiple stakeholders, benefits, priorities and concerns.

As project management becomes a profession in its own right, it is important to update our thinking on projects and endeavour to make sense of an increasingly complex context for project work. Rising to the challenge, Robert offers a practical and pragmatic perspective for regaining control of life cycles. His framework enables practitioners and organisations to rise beyond the predictability and perfection traps to consider new and applicable improvements that have been shown to work and contribute to project success. His framework also offers a way of making sense of the confusing claims and counter claims by various communities related to projects and the best methods for delivering value.

Reflection Reprised: Looking at Impacts

It is particularly encouraging to see an extended version of the life cycle that considers the wider implications and ramifications of project work. This section concludes by expanding the earlier reflections to consider the practical implications of life cycles through the articulation of a set of principles before trying to predict what they might mean for the life cycles of the future:

1. **Beyond linearity.** Project sequences offer a way of organising and structuring work; however, many projects entail some iterative elements that require making sense of the context, discovering new knowledge, sharing insights with stakeholders, prototyping, and exploring new opportunities and proposals for addressing them.
2. **A hybrid world.** Project work need not exist within a particular camp or adhere to a particular approach or methodology simply due to the predictability trap or the perfection trap. Given that every project is different, it is important that the context is acknowledged and the specific needs and requirements are addressed. In practice, most project managers are pragmatic, and many projects display hybrid characteristics as we fuse, mix, adapt and match ideas that can support project work. A philosophy- or method-agnostic perspective is able to benefit from devising and tailoring life-cycle approaches that match the specific context of the project or programme.
3. **Spectrum of positions. Between and around opposites.** While we live in a society that increasingly demonises a particular position or approach and preaches and advocates for its opposite, it is useful *not* to fall into the trap of identifying a binary contradiction and committing ourselves to a particular camp. Habit is a dangerous surrogate for predictability and perfection. . . . Given our acceptance that most projects pragmatically mix elements from different perspectives, we can afford greater freedom of positioning. In a hybrid world, there is no need to anchor ourselves to a particular position or stance.
4. **Learning enables.** If projects deliver change, and we are allowed to respond to opportunities rather than pursue pre-approved plans, we would be able to adapt, embrace innovation, and be in a better position to respond to the increasing turbulence, uncertainty, ambiguity and novelty of life. Continuous learning may require multiple iterations, but it also harbours the potential for greater innovation and an improved fit with an ever-changing context, emerging new technologies and shifting priorities.
5. **Design overlaps with realisation.** Any attempt to solve a problem and impose a solution leads to new insights. Imposing a strict management structure in the form of a life

cycle may stifle innovation, but more crucially, it may not allow us to respond to learning, discovery, prototyping and opportunities that emerge. Utilising hybrid models may enable managers to explore different options and possibilities before proceeding down a particular path. (A similar case could be made for the intertwining of requirements, or problem definitions, with design as a form of engaging with proposed solutions. Indeed, a problem–solution separation can be overly simplistic, compartmentalised and counterproductive.)

6. **Social element.** Projects involve people, so that perfect plans can never hold: iteration and prototyping allow greater exploration of needs, expectations, requirements, design options, and their cumulative impacts. It also enables buy-in and validation and facilitates improvement possibilities.

7. **Focus on value.** If projects are designed to deliver beneficial change, which will be measured by the organisation, the realisation of benefits is a crucial part and a major emphasis of project work. The direct implication is that projects must consider the expected value so what is deployed is able to be utilised to deliver the benefits. Managers must (at least) be aware of the implications of the required benefit and deploy the project in ways that will not exclude such realisation.

8. **Adoption precedes use, which precedes benefit realisation.** In order for a project to deliver the benefits identified in the business case, it is important to ensure that users will be able to utilise the results in order to enable and facilitate the benefits. In this way, the actual value can begin to accrue following deployment.

9. **Think benefits.** Extending the tail end of the life cycle to include the realisation of benefits is insufficient. It must be matched by suitable upfront planning. If we expect to harvest benefits, we need to plan for their capture and ensure that they progress from the business case in order to inform the project design. Increasingly, more projects include some element of benefits capture, and this needs to be reflected in the planning.

10. **Cradle to grave.** Decommissioning and disposal need to encompass upfront preparation during the definition phase. This is likely to include the development of a set of disposal requirements and to ensure that subsequent decisions do not impact, curtail or block future disposal options.

11. **Our actions matter.** Consideration of future decommissioning and disposal are part of a product life cycle that considers the full economic costs of developing and utilising a product over time. Once again, this requires upfront planning. Adopting a whole life cycle or a full product life cycle perspective enables executives and managers to responsibly engage with the long-term future implications of their project-related actions and guarantees that project managers are informed of such future options to ensure that current actions do not jeopardise future intentions.

12. **Responsible project stewardship.** Responsible project management increasingly looks at the social and environmental impacts of projects alongside the economic and administrative concerns. Meanwhile, society is increasingly concerned with extended producer responsibility involving everyone benefitting financially from a product or system. Executives within organisations have an increasingly emerging responsibility for proper end-of-life disposal of systems and assets in a responsible, affordable and effective manner. Such issues of stewardships are likely to require additional planning and consideration throughout the fully extended life cycle required to justify, support and enable project work.

The Demise of Project Delivery

However, the most significant and profound implication of reflecting on project life cycles relates back to our inability to look beyond our very own predictability trap and perfection trap and to conceive the life cycle in its proper context.

National governments and other organisations have been emphasising the importance of the project delivery profession. An alternative label is *solution professionals.* The problem with such a definition is that it zooms in on the predictable and definable aspects of projects, typified through the limited life cycles that launched this discussion.

The final reflection is therefore concerned with developing an informed attitude that recognises the limitation of focusing on the notion of delivery as a pre-occupation. The management of projects is much bigger and more expansive than project delivery and should not be brought down to its lowest common denominator.

The five directions identified by the Rethinking Project Management Network in 2006 point to the fundamental problems in pursuing such a position. The six reflections detailed and explored above indicate why such a position is not sustainable, while the 12 considerations enumerated directly above pinpoint the need to move forward and the type of concerns that need to be addressed.

To become influential, project management needs to consider the ability to integrate, extend and develop strategically in order to address wider organisational and societal concerns (Dalcher, 2017). To shrink the focus of interest would be an unforgivable error.

The fifth direction identified by the Rethinking Project Management Network encourages reflective practice and the questioning of assumptions, underpinning knowledge, and the expectations and practices that become embedded due to the limited ability to challenge the status quo and question the underpinning logic of prevailing practice.

Now is the time to progress our understanding of what it takes to be successful in project work and to define the basis for responsible project management and informed project stewardship. Any other position would simply continue to underpin the enduring dissatisfaction with the ability to deliver beneficial change through effective projects.

In order to continue to improve and reposition the discipline, we need to deliver the final proposition that builds on the earlier principles:

13. **Progress from a culture of delivery to an ethos of value.** Projects enable significant beneficial change; however, they should be considered, developed, deployed and utilised for the right purpose.

The profession is ready for a step change in how projects are described and positioned. In order to bridge the knowing–doing gap, we now need to remove relics of old thinking patterns and abolish redundant or lazy terminology. The notion of project delivery must go!

To accept a trivialised role as project delivery professionals is to eschew professionalism, reflection and responsibility and ignore the potential impacts and responsibilities of the profession.

Projects are part of a bigger landscape of enabling change, strategy and value. It is only when the capability, output or outcome of project work is used as a result of a comprehensive change programme that benefits can be realised, resulting in meaningful value. Benefits-driven projects and programmes support the investment cycle, with portfolios and governance structures utilised to monitor the results and question the continuing alignment with strategy and the realisation of expected and emerging benefits.

In this way, the management of projects can demand a seat at the top table, rather than relinquishing its position to become a subservient and trivialised service discipline.

References

Buttrick, R. (2019). *The Project Workout: The Ultimate Guide to Directing and Managing Business-Led Projects* (5th Ed.). Abingdon, UK: Routledge.

Dalcher, D. (2002). Life cycle design and management. *Project Management Pathways.* Princes Risborough, UK: Association for Project Management.

Dalcher, D. (2015). Whose success is it anyway? Rethinking the role of suppliers in projects. *PM World Journal, 4*(5), 1–5.

Dalcher, D. (2016). Rethinking project practice: Emerging insights from a series of books for practitioners. *International Journal of Managing Projects in Business, 9*(4), 798–821.

Dalcher, D. (2017). Commercial management and projects, a long overdue match? *PM World Journal, 6*(10), 1–6.

Klein, G. (2014). *Seeing What Others Don't: The Remarkable Ways We Gain Insights.* London, UK: Nicholas Brealey.

Morris, P. W. (2013). *Reconstructing Project Management.* Chichester, UK: John Wiley & Sons.

Pfeffer, J., and Sutton, R. I. (2000). *The Knowing-Doing Gap: How Smart Companies Turn Knowledge into Action.* Boston, MA: Harvard Business Press.

Winter, M., and Smith, C. (2006). *Rethinking Project Management, Final Report* (May). Manchester, UK: EPSRC Network.

Winter, M., Smith, C., Morris, P., and Cicmil, S. (2006). Directions for future research in project management: The main findings of a UK government-funded research network. *International Journal of Project Management, 24*(8), 638–649.

The Project Framework: Understanding Gates and Stages

Robert Buttrick

Projects as Vehicles of Change

Ignore the reborn discipline of enterprise-wide project management at your peril! No longer the preserve of the engineering and IT sectors, project management is fast becoming a core competence which many organisations require of their employees and an activity every executive and manager should be familiar with. Projects, in the modern sense, are strategic management tools, and this section, based on a chapter from the latest edition of *The Project Workout* (Buttrick, 2019), shows how they can be used as vehicles of change.

Most organisations are never short of suggestions for improvement, and your own is probably no exception. Ideas can come from anywhere within the organisation or even outside it: from competitors, customers, or suppliers. Actually deciding which initiatives the business leaders should spend time and money on is more difficult. Care needs to be taken in choosing which projects to do, as:

- There is probably not enough money, manpower, or management energy to pursue all the ideas.
- Undertaking projects which do not align to the organisation's strategy will, almost certainly, create internal conflicts between senior managers, confuse the direction of the business and ultimately, reduce the return on the company's investment.

Business leaders should consider for selection only those projects which:

- Have a firm root in the organisation's strategy
- Meet defined business needs
- Will realise real benefits
- Are derived from gaps identified in business plans
- Are achievable

Having created a shortlist of 'possible projects', it is important to work on them in the right order, recognising interdependencies, taking account of scarce skills and resources and bringing the benefits forward whenever possible.

Figure 5.1 illustrates how selecting the right projects will help to achieve the business objectives by realising benefits to support the business strategy. Two key roles are associated with projects:

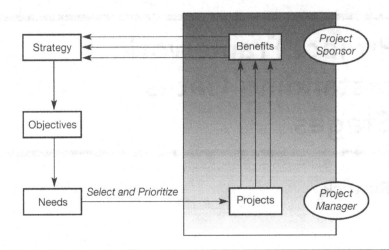

Figure 5.1 Select the Right Projects to Support Your Strategy. Selecting the right projects will help you achieve your objectives by realising benefits which support your strategy. (Copyright © PA Consulting Group, London. Adapted with permission.)

- The **project sponsor**, who wants the benefits the project will provide
- The **project manager**, who manages the project on a day-to-day basis, ensuring its deliverables are presented on time, at the right quality and to budget

To illustrate these key project roles, imagine you want to build an extension to your house for a home office. To gain the benefits this will bring, you accept the price and the inconvenience of building works. The architect's role is to design an appropriate solution to meet your needs. As project manager, the benefits he receives for carrying out the work is his fee, but he must, however, understand your needs fully to deliver an appropriate solution. In a good partnership, sponsorship and management are mutually compatible. Thus:

- The **project sponsor** is primarily 'outcome and benefits focussed'; he or she **directs** the project.
- The **project manager** is primarily 'action focused' towards the achievement of the outcomes and benefits the sponsor needs. He or she **manages** the project on a day-to-day basis.

The framework for managing business-led projects is aimed at making the results of projects more predictable by:

- Being outcome and benefits focussed
- Building in quality
- Managing risks and exposure
- Exploiting the skill base of the entire organisation

As a project progresses, the amount of money invested increases. If none of this money is spent on reducing the risks associated with the project, then it is poorly spent. Your objective, as a business leader, project sponsor or project manager, is to ensure that risks are driven down as the project moves from being an idea to becoming a reality.

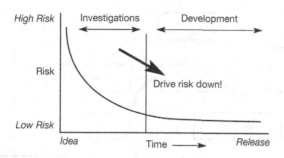

Figure 5.2 Managing the Risk. The investigative stages are crucial, and you should hold back any development work until your investigations show you know what you are doing and have proved that the risks are acceptable.

Figure 5.2 demonstrates this. The investigative stages are crucial, and you should hold back significant development work until your investigations show you know what you are doing and have proved that the risks are acceptable. This is achieved through a staged approach, where each stage serves as a launch pad for the subsequent stage. In this section, I have used five stages, but other models are acceptable if they suit the environment and culture of your organisation.

Gates and Stages

Stages

A stage is a specific time period during which work on the project takes place; information is collected, outputs created and outcomes recognised.

For each stage of the project, you should carry out the full range of work, covering all functions needed to meet the requirements (see Figure 5.3). The people from each function should not work on the project in isolation but as a cross-functional team, with members in continuous

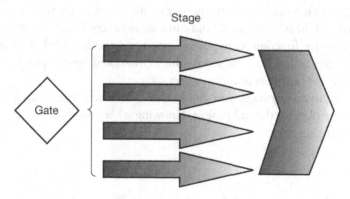

Figure 5.3 Address All Aspects of the Project in Parallel. For each stage in the project, you should carry out the full range of work covering the entire scope of functional inputs required. In this way your knowledge develops and increases on all fronts at a similar pace and solutions are designed, built and tested in an integrated way.

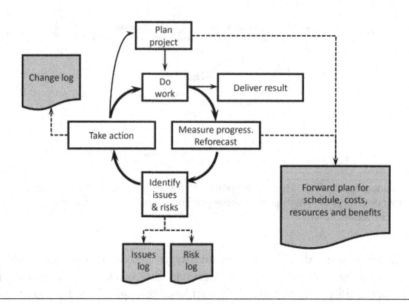

Figure 5.4   A Typical Stage. A stage can be represented by the project control cycle, together with the plan and key control tools needed to manage it.

dialogue to enable the development of the best overall solution. In this way, knowledge develops on all fronts at a similar pace and solutions are designed, built and tested in an integrated way. No one area of work should advance ahead of the others. The solution should not be what is optimal for one function alone but a pragmatic solution which is best for the whole organisation. This has the benefits of shortcutting the functional hierarchies as it forces people with different perspectives to work together, rather than in their organisational siloes, enabling the flat, lean structures we all seek to attain to work in practice. Further, work on any one stage should be limited to what is needed at the next gate: there is little point in spending effort and money until necessary.

During each stage, it is essential for the project manager to forecast and reforecast the benefits likely to be gained and the time, resources and costs needed to complete the project. He/she should always keep the relevant function managers informed and check, on behalf of the sponsor, that the project still makes sound business sense. This is illustrated by the 'project control cycle' in Figure 5.4, which is the heartbeat of every project stage.

Before work begins on any stage, you should have a detailed project plan for at least the next stage and an outline plan for the full project. Knowing what you are going to do next increases confidence and decreases risks.

Gates

Gates are the decision points preceding every stage. Unless specific criteria have been met, as evidenced by certain approved deliverables, the subsequent stage should not be started. Being a decision 'point', gates are special milestones on the project. Gates serve as points to:

- Check the project is still required and the risks are acceptable.
- Confirm its priority relative to other projects.

- Agree the plans for the remainder of the project.
- Make a go/no go decision regarding continuing the project.

Do not regard gates as 'end-of-term exams', but rather as the culmination of a period of continual assessment, with the gates acting as formal review and decision points.

Gate criteria are often reinforced at consecutive gates to ensure the same strands of the project are followed through as the project progresses. The further into the project you move, the more confidence you should have in the responses to the criteria and in achieving your overall objectives.

At each gate, you will need to answer three distinct questions (Figure 5.5):

- Is the project viable in its own right?
- What is its priority relative to other projects?
- Do you have the funding to continue the project?

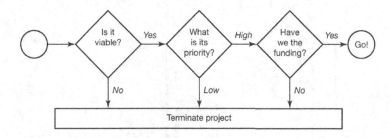

Figure 5.5   The Three Decisions Required at Each Gate. Is there a real need for this project, and is it viable in its own right? What is its priority relative to other projects? Do you have the funding to continue the project?

It is expedient to think in terms of these questions because, in many organisations, different people or groups are required to address each of them.

The first question (viability) concerns the viability of the project, assuming no other constraints. Does it align to your strategy? Does it make business sense? Are the risks acceptable? Have you the resources to undertake the work and operate its outputs?

The second question (priority) concerns the project in its context. It might be a worthy project *but* how does it measure against other projects you want to do or are currently doing? Are there more worthwhile projects for the organisation to spend time and money on? Is it 'a risk too far', bearing in mind what you are already committed to?

The third question involves funding. Traditionally, businesses have formal rules concerning the allocation of funds, which are generally managed by a finance function. You might have a viable project; it might be the best of those proposed, BUT have you the working capital to finance it?

Gates—An End or a Beginning?

Gates have traditionally been defined as end-points to the preceding stage. The logic is that the work in the stage culminates in a review (end-of-stage assessment) where a check is done to ensure everything is complete before starting the next stage. This viewpoint has come about

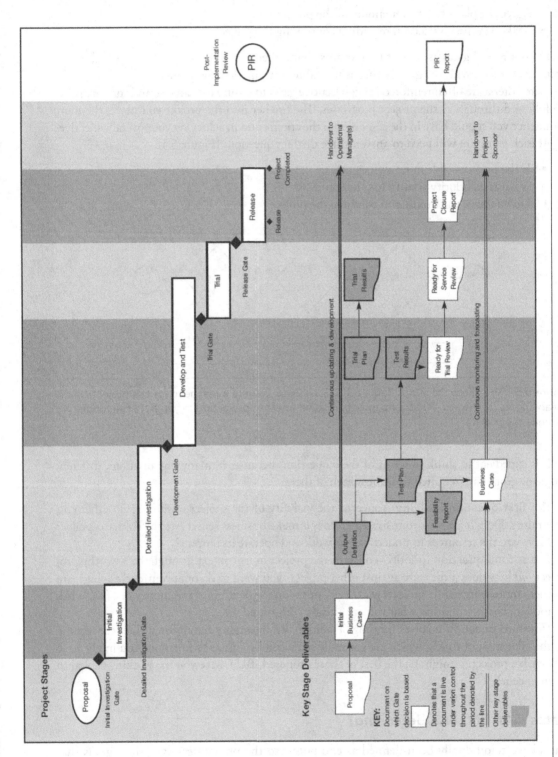

Figure 5.6 The Project Framework as a Bar Chart. The project framework is shown here in bar chart format at the top, with the document deliverables for each stage shown below.

because people have confused system or software development **processes** with project **life cycles**. An IT development process rightly concentrates on quality, and hence the need for 'completeness' before moving on. Project management, however, is based on business risk. Due to time pressures, it is often necessary to start the next stage before everything in the previous stage has been completed. For example, the typical project framework in Figure 5.6 shows it could be sensible to undertake a trial operation of any new output before the process, training and communication work is completed.

What is essential is to have sufficient work done to start the next stage with confidence. So, if you treat a gate as the end of a stage, this gives rise to the difficulty of having a 'rule' that common sense encourages us to break.

The solution to this dilemma is to treat gates as entry points to the next stage. In this way, the next stage can begin as soon as the pre-defined criteria have been met, regardless of whether the full work scope of the previous stage has been completed. You simply need to ensure the risks are acceptable and you have the resources and time built into your plan to complete the unfinished work. In this way, stages can overlap, reducing timescales without increasing the risk associated with the project. If you want certain deliverables in the preceding stage to be 100 percent complete before you move on, ensure that need is added to the gate criteria. You are in charge, not some blanket, often arbitrary rule.

This approach also opens another powerful characteristic of the staged framework—namely, gates are compulsory, stages are not. In other words, provided you have done the work needed to pass into a stage, how you arrived there is immaterial. This allows you to follow the strict principles of the staged framework, even if a stage is omitted. In this way, you can accommodate the concept of 'simple' projects.

If you still aren't convinced, think of this from a senior executive's point of view. How many executives like to make decisions on what has already happened? Senior executives make decisions about what they are going to do next; this fits in with the 'entry gate' approach perfectly. They like to announce they are investing untold millions over the next six months into the company's development. Personally, I have never met an executive who led by looking backwards.

The Project Framework

As we have learned, projects draw on many resources from a wide range of functions within an organisation. Ensuring these are focused on achieving specific, identified benefits for the organisation is your key management challenge. You can increase the likelihood of success for your projects, and hence of the business as a whole, by following a project framework (also called a project life cycle) which:

- Is benefit driven
- Is user and customer focussed
- Capitalises on the skills and resources in the organisation
- Builds 'quality' into the project deliverables
- Helps manage risk
- Allows many activities to proceed in parallel (hence greater velocity)

Most modern approaches to tackling projects achieve these objectives by breaking each project into series of generic stages and gates, forming a framework (or life cycle) within which every project in the organisation can be referenced.

If business leaders were to take such an approach, it would enable them to gain control of two key aspects of their business:

1. The knowledge that each project is being undertaken in a rational way with the correct level of checks and balances at key points in its life cycle.
2. The entire portfolio of projects can be viewed at a summary level and, by using the generic stage descriptions, show where each project is and the implication this has on risk and commitment.

The project framework is shown in Figure 5.6 as a bar chart and in Figure 5.7 as a diagrammatic overview.

The stages are:

Identify the need—Proposal. A need is first formally recognised by describing it (i.e., say *why* you want to initiate a project in terms of the business outcome you need/want to achieve). If known, you should also describe what you believe the project will produce (i.e., its output but don't jump to conclusions too soon).

Have a quick look—Initial Investigation Stage. The first stage in the project—a quick study of the proposal to outline the scope and make a rough assessment of the possible ways of meeting the need, benefits, resources and costs necessary to complete it. At the end of this stage, you should be sure of why you are doing it. You may also know what you are doing, although this may comprise a range of defined options. You should know how to go about at least the next stage, even if not the full project.

Have a closer look—Detailed Investigation Stage. A feasibility study, definition and full investment appraisal culminating in a decision to proceed with development work. At the end of this stage, you will have high confidence in all aspects of the project and, if authorised at the next gate, 'What you *want* to do' becomes 'What you *are going* to do!'

Do it!—Develop and Test Stage. The actual development and implementation work.

Try it—Trial Stage. A trial of all aspects of the development in the users' or customers' operational and working environment. What has been created may work very well under 'test conditions', but does it work under normal operational conditions?

Use it—Release Stage. The last stage in the project, when you unleash your creation on the world! This is when products are launched, new computer systems used, new manufacturing plant goes into production, new organisation units start operating, new processes are invoked, acquisitions sealed and disposals shed. The ongoing operational aspects are embedded in the organisation to ensure the required business changes have been absorbed and, finally, the project is formally recognised as complete.

About three to six months after completion, a check, known as a *Post-Implementation Review,* is done to see if the project is achieving its business objectives, the business changes have been absorbed into usual practice and the outputs are performing to the standards expected.

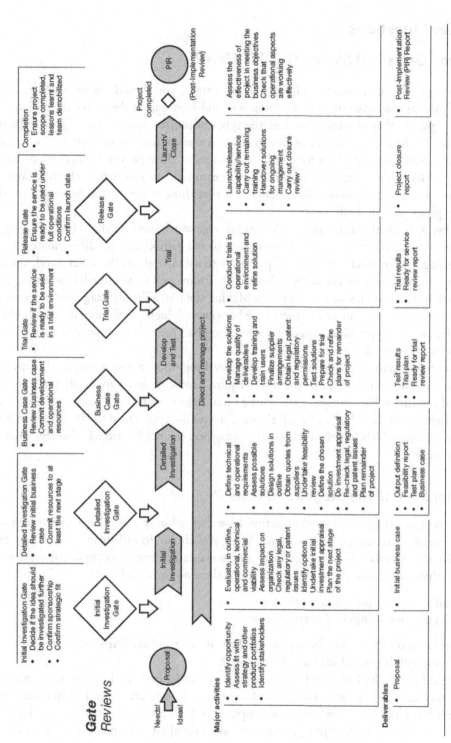

Figure 5.7 The Project Framework in Diagrammatic Form. The project framework is shown here in a format which clearly distinguishes between the gates and the stages. It also shows the activities and deliverables which relate to each stage.

Some Key Questions

How Many Gates and Stages Should I Have?

Notably, as a gate is the decision point for starting a stage, you should always have the same number of gates as you have stages, plus a 'project completion' gate at the end of the project. To decide the right number of stages, consider the types of project undertaken in your organisation. Do they fit the generic stages described earlier? Are there some modifications you would like to make? Some organisations have only four stages in their projects, others six or more. Generally, the fewer the better, but they must be meaningful to you, reflect the risks and fit every project you are likely to do. My experience is that three stages are too few and five will fit most purposes, so if in doubt try five.

Of the five stages used in this section, it is the trial stage which is often either left out or merged with the develop and test stage. I prefer to have the trial as a distinct stage to differentiate it from testing. Testing is very much an internal, 'private' activity. A trial, on the other hand, can be 'public', involving real users and customers. You are therefore open to poor media comment or to hostile reactions from employees and suppliers. Making the trial a distinct stage forces people to focus on whether they really are ready. There have been enough high-profile cases of failure of beta tests on software and of premium automobiles receiving bad press due to a poor state of market readiness to act as a warning to us all.

You may find instances of organisations with anything up to a dozen stages. This usually happens because the industry and project type require a more granular approach. For example, in regulated industries, like aerospace, the gating often reflects mandatory regulatory approvals. In the rail industry in the UK, Network Rail has a project life cycle called GRIP (Guide to Rail Investment Process) which has eight stages; like aerospace, the rail industry is also regulated as safety is paramount.

What Should I Call the Stages and Gates?

The stage and gate names used in this section have evolved over a number of years and are based on experience in several organisations. What you choose to call them is up to you, but that decision is not trivial. Words are emotive and hence can be both very powerful movers for change or inhibitors of change. In all organisations there are words which:

- Mean something particular to everyone
- Mean different things to different people

You can build on the former by exploiting them in your project framework, provided the meaning is compatible with what you wish to convey.

You should avoid the latter and choose different words, even making up new words if the dictionary cannot help you. For example, working in one company I found the word 'concept' problematic. 'Concept' to some people, is a high-level statement of an idea (the meaning I wanted to convey), but to others it means a detailed assessment of what has been decided should be done (this was not what I wanted). Rather than try to re-educate people in their everyday language, a different word (proposal) was used which had no connotations in that organisation.

There can be similar problems with the word 'implement': it has so many preconceived meanings, it is better not to use it at all! Implement to some people means carry out the 'meaty part' of the project plan, whilst to others it means put whatever you created into beneficial use.

'Execute' is another interesting word; to some people it is more associated with capital punishment than undertaking projects! For this reason, the International Standards Organisation's committee on project management avoids the use of the word and its derivatives, despite many 'hard-nosed' business people liberally using it to show how effective they are.

If you look at the list of possible names in Table 5.1 (on page 116), you will notice that certain words appear in more than one place. This is a sure sign that they might be misunderstood, but not necessarily in your organisation.

The same issues apply to naming the gates. For these, however, it is better to name each one according to the stage it precedes. This emphasises the 'gate as an entry point' concept. An alternative approach is to name the gate after the document which is used as the control on the gate. In Table 5.2, I have mixed these. Again, this is your choice, but make sure the same terminology applies across the whole organisation.

I do, however, strongly advise you not to refer to the stages and gates by a number or letter. It will cause difficulties later (including significant cost) if you need to revise your framework. You will not believe the number of times a 'Gate 0' or 'Stage 0' has had to be added to the front of a framework. Using proper names is simpler, more obvious and will not box you in for the future if you do not get it right at the start or there are real pressures to change.

Table 5.2 A List of Alternative Gate Names

Gate Names Used in This Chapter	Possible Alternatives	
Initial investigation gate	Concept gate Initiation gate	Proposal gate
Detailed investigation gate	Feasibility gate Evaluation gate	Design gate
Development gate	Business case gate Authorisation gate	Implementation gate Execution gate
Trial gate	Beta gate Validation gate	Commissioning gate
Release gate	Ready for service gate Operation gate	Implementation gate Handover gate
Project completed	Closure gate Project end gate	

How Do I Decide What Work Is Done in the Investigative Stages?

The investigative stages exist to reduce risk (see Figure 5.2, on page 127) and everything you do should have that aim. If any proposed activity does not reduce risk, you should consider postponing it to a later stage.

What Is the Best Way to Depict a Project Framework?

If your project framework is to be understood, you need to communicate it in an unambiguous way, making sure it is clear that stages and gates serve different purposes. In *The Project Workout* and in Figure 5.7 (on page 133), I use circle, arrow and diamond icons:

- A circle depicts activities which happen before a project starts or after it is completed.
- A diamond represents a gate.
- An arrow represents a stage.

This approach has been used in several diverse organisations and is now incorporated in the British Standard on project management (BS6079 Part 1) and the UK Government's project delivery standard. Gates are shown and labelled separately from stages. The gates are described with the key questions which should be asked by the decision makers. The stages are described by the activities undertaken during the stage with a list of deliverables generated within the stage.

Where Do People Go Wrong?

In designing their project frameworks, I have found people make mistakes in two key areas: at the very start and at the end. All too often, I see frameworks with minimal start-up activity, immediately followed by the Develop and Test Stage. They have, in effect, gone from 'idea' to 'do it' in one small step. In all but the simplest projects, such a leap is naïve and might account for why so many projects are ill-defined and doomed to failure or rampant cost escalation and time slippage. By all means, make it easy to start the project (i.e., pass through the initial investigation gate), but do ensure there is rigour in the actual investigations. A business-driven project comprises both investigation and implementation stages.

At the end of the project, people often confuse Project Closure with the Post-Implementation Review. The former looks at project efficiency and delivery, whilst the latter looks at benefits realisation and operational effectiveness. These two views cannot be combined, as the measurement points are separated by time. Also, note that Proposal and Post-Implementation Review are not stages of the project—they are activities which happen *before* and *after* the project, respectively; that is why they are shown as a circle and not an arrow in Figures 5.6 and 5.7, earlier.

Isn't This Just a 'Stage Gate'?

Have you come across people using the term 'stage gate'? Often, I find people use as the term as yet another piece of management jargon without really understanding what they are saying. When I come across it, I wonder if they really understand what they are talking about. Do they understand what this term means and where it comes from? It derives from R. G. Cooper's Stage Gate® approach to product development and is used to describe his whole process, not any particular feature (Cooper, 1990). As we have seen earlier, 'gates' and 'stages' are related but different, and you need to be unambiguous in how you name, describe and depict them. Figure 5.8 shows some real-life examples of how people depict their project life cycles, muddling 'stage' with 'gate', hence confusing their readers.

Example A starts well, in that there are a number of stages depicted. Unfortunately, it does not show where the decision points are. Where does the project start or end?

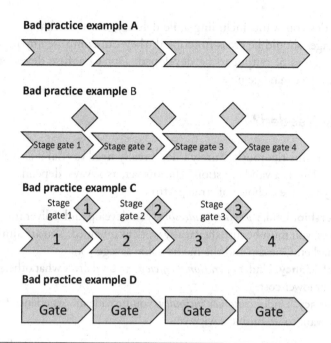

Figure 5.8 Bad Practice Depictions of Project Frameworks. How you depict the project framework is crucial if you want it to be understood. This figure shows four examples of badly defined project life cycles where it is not at all clear what the author's intentions are. None of the examples make it clear when a project starts or finishes nor the nature of the gates themselves (entry or exit?).

Example B has the same issues as example A. Although a number of decision points have been added, it doesn't clarify matters much—for example, is 'stage gate 1' the first stage of the project or the activity before the project starts?

Example C has all the issues raised in examples A and B, except in this case it seems the decision points (gates) are labelled as 'stage gates'. I wonder what the stages are called—gate stages? Notice the numbering, which implies that the 'gates' are decisions at the end of a stage, rather than decisions to start a new stage.

Example D shows the gates as if they were periods of time, with no clue as to what happens between them.

If you are designing a project life cycle, don't fall into the real-life traps highlighted in the bad examples above. Make sure you understand the difference between a gate and a stage; avoid using the term 'stage gate' and make sure your depiction of the project life cycle is clear and unambiguous. For any project life cycle, it must be clear when the project starts, each stage starts and when the project ends.

Isn't This 'Waterfall'?

No. A project framework or life cycle is not the same as waterfall development, although you can, if you want to, design a project framework to specifically mirror a waterfall method (see Table 5.3 on page 116). A stage within a project can comprise whichever development methods or activities you want, including agile delivery, business change and benefits realisation. In fact, as stages should be cross-functional, they can comprise any number of methods, depending on the types of output to be developed. Don't confuse development or delivery approaches with project management.

Is a Trial Really Needed?

'I have already tested this rigorously. Surely I don't really need to trial it as well? Won't this just delay the benefits?' This is a valid question. The answer, as always, depends on the context. For example, assume you have a choice of strategy from:

> **Product leadership.** Under *product leadership,* you develop and deliver innovative, new products and services; you must be sure they really work as intended. You are aiming to be first and best in your market. One slip and the media could savage you.
> **Operational efficiency.** Under *operational efficiency,* you deliver what others deliver but more efficiently and at lower cost.
> **Customer intimacy.** Under *customer intimacy,* you provide an experience for your customers such that they want to do business with you.

Thus, if your strategy is to have any practical meaning, you must be sure that nothing in your organisation compromises it, including how you run your projects. The choice of 'to trial or not to trial' comes down to risk. What is the likely impact on your business if this goes wrong? How confident are you that it won't go wrong? With this in mind, you might choose to subject certain aspects to a trial more rigorously than others—balancing reducing your time to market (and hence realising benefits) with the risks.

Always assume you need a trial. Omit it only if you have proved to yourself and your stakeholders that it will not add any value to your project. Never skip the trial because you are in a hurry!

If in doubt, try it out!

How Can I Apply the Framework?

The staged approach to directing and managing projects is the framework for the management of any type of project, for any purpose. It is not concerned with the technicalities of how specialist deliverables are created. As such, its flexibility provides project managers with the opportunity to tailor it to suit the requirements of their individual projects. This ensures an optimum path through the generic project framework, rather than one tied up in bureaucracy.

Particular types of project require their own methods and steps, but provided you know how they match the overall high-level framework, they can be used with confidence and in an environment where the business also knows what is happening. A common project framework in an organisation will ensure alignment between different parts of the organisation with clearer communication and understanding. Table 5.3 (below) shows a range of different project types and how their key activities could fit into a standard framework.

If in doubt, try it out!

The invasion starts

Launch
the boats!

Britain →

GLUG!

Meanwhile, back at the boat yard where the new Mark IV self draining assault boat is built

We haven't had time to try it out. But I'm sure it will work.

Table 5.3 How the Different Project and Activities Fit the Project Framework

	Initial Investigation Stage	Detailed Investigation Stage	Develop and Test Stage	Trial Stage	Release Stage
Product development	Concept	Alternatives and feasibility	Develop and test	Market validation	Market launch
Product withdrawal	Initial investigation	Detailed investigation	Develop and test	Pilot withdrawal	Close operations
Information systems	Analysis	Logical and outline physical design	Detailed design, build and test	Pilot	Cutover
Bid or tender	Receive request and evaluate	Prepare detailed tender	Develop, build, internal test	Commissioning trials	Handover
Construction (customer viewpoint)	Inception study	Feasibility study, tender design	Detailed design and construction	Commissioning trials	Handover
Publishing	Proposal	Prepare manuscript	Edit, typeset	Final proof	Launch
IT waterfall	Requirements review	Analysis and design	Build	Beta test	Cutover
DSDM/agile	Feasibility	Foundation	Evolutionary development (releases and sprints)	Deployment	Deployment

Summary

Projects are now vehicles for driving change in pursuit of your organisation's objectives, and, when used in the right context and environment, they can form a sound basis for competitive advantage. Fundamental to the effective management of projects is the project framework, based around the project life cycle, which seeks to manage risk through incremental progression, in stages, from business requirement to benefits realisation.

1. Projects should align to strategy, meet defined business needs, realise benefits and be achievable.
2. Manage risk on your projects by taking a staged approach.
3. Stages are periods of time when work is undertaken.
4. Gates are decision points prior to starting the next stage.
5. Define the 'Go' criteria for each gate.
6. At each gate ask, *'Is this project viable on its own; what's its priority relative to other work and initiatives, and have I the funds to do complete it?'*
7. Design your standard project framework to suit what your organisation does and the words it uses.
8. Tailor the project framework to suit the circumstances and level of risk of your particular project.
9. Work in cross-functional project teams to develop the right solution for the organisation, rather than one which is convenient for the dominant function.

This section is adapted from *The Project Workout* (Buttrick, 2019), which provides practical advice and techniques to direct and manage a project. Aimed at both project sponsors and project managers, it seeks to work through the life cycle of a project from initial idea to successful result with the aid of 'Workouts': exercises, techniques and checklists to help you put the advice and insights into practice.

References

Buttrick, R. (2019). *The Project Workout: The Ultimate Guide to Directing and Managing Business-Led Projects* (5th Ed.). Abingdon, UK: Routledge.

Cooper, R. (1990). Stage-gate systems: A new tool for managing new products. *Business Horizons, 33*(44–54). 10.1016/0007-6813(90)90040-I

Chapter 6

Portfolios

Organising for Success in Project Portfolios, Initiatives and Strategies

Darren Dalcher

Project portfolios offer an established way of organising and prioritising projects, programmes and investment opportunities for both private and public sector organizations. Project portfolios also enable the governance and management arrangements required to underpin effective strategy execution. Yet, project portfolios differ greatly in the assumptions they embody and the way they are set up and utilised. This chapter explores the diversity of different types and settings of project portfolios and their role in supporting execution, innovation and strategic alignment of initiatives before turning attention to the success of different portfolio arrangements.

Portfolios: Definitions and Strategies

While the term *portfolio management* can mean different things to different people, the basic idea of organising investments, or projects, into a planned structure that allows the full range of investments to be scrutinised is relatively straightforward. The 7th edition of the *APM Body of Knowledge* reasons that *'portfolios are used to select, prioritise and control an organisation's programmes and projects in line with its strategic objectives and capacity to deliver'* (APM, 2019: 13). The aim of such an arrangement is to enable an organization to make the most of its existing resources, select the most appropriate investments against the emerging context and strategic intent, and maximise throughput and value to the organization.

The management of portfolios enables organizations to focus on investments and the potential value that they deliver, especially in terms of proposed change initiatives, product ranges and/or agreed activities and address multifaceted and complex concerns. This is often achieved by balancing project and change initiatives and business as usual, while optimising value, or return on investment.

While portfolios have been successfully utilised in traditional financial portfolio theory, some of the ideas and concepts are not directly transferable to the project arena. Traditional financial portfolios are typically managed in bottom-up fashion so that the selection of investments maximises a return for a given risk limit or minimises the risk for a desired return.

This is predicated on the assumption that all potential investment opportunities have been valued independently to determine the potential value they can add to the portfolio (Lockett et al., 2008: 79). Yet, in the project context, there is no exhaustive collection of all possible projects. Moreover, projects can be created and performed in a multitude of ways (Ibid.) and may be reshaped during execution. Consequently, a simplistic evaluation of risk and return offers limited insights. Furthermore, given the multitude of interdependencies between projects, the specific contextual factors, and the need to consider organizational capability and strategic importance, a top-down shaping and influencing of the portfolio of projects, informed by perceived strategic value, appears more likely.

Note however, that the increasing appeal and application of agile and lean development and management methods enables organizations to defer some of the portfolio allocation and selection decisions, experiment with limited results, and adopt a more bottom-up and real-time opportunistic approach to portfolio prioritization, as upfront decisions can be partially deferred while new knowledge and insights are bought, and heightened understanding and alignment can improve and enhance (or overturn) earlier decisions.

Indeed, agile approaches allow for changes of course and direction further downstream, thereby offering a new balance between intention, strategy and results through a combination of top-down and bottom-up organization.

Portfolio management offers a range of benefits (Jenner & Killford, 2011), as it:

- Helps achieve the best return from the total investment in change programmes and projects
- Ensures successful delivery
- Realises the full benefits in terms of efficiency savings and contribution to strategic objectives across all sectors
- Provides the tools and techniques to identify and prioritise overall investment

However, it is important to acknowledge that portfolios are initiated for a variety of reasons. Pellegrinelli (1997) makes a reference to a portfolio programme configuration, which enables the grouping of relatively autonomous projects with a common theme. The existence of a theme enables the performance of the individual projects to be improved through coordination, of either common resources or a common technology. Artto (2001: 8) likewise emphasises the need to share similar strategic objectives and shared resources amongst projects in a portfolio, which are subject to similar sponsorship and management arrangements.

Other early work in the area (Combe & Githens, 1999) recognised a wider variety of rationales for adopting a portfolio approach and therefore proposed the three general types of: value creating, operational, or compliance portfolios. The types are further elaborated as follows:

- **Value-creating portfolios.** Encompass enterprise projects concerned with improving the organization's bottom line, which are viewed to be of strategic importance.
- **Operational portfolios.** Comprise functional projects which make the organisation more efficient or improve organisational performance.
- **Compliance portfolios.** Include essential projects, which are required to meet legal, environmental, health and safety, or other regulatory compliance purposes. *Note:* Similar setups may be required to respond to compelling market forces or dominant new technologies.

It is worth pointing out that the typology put forward by Combe and Githens appears to reflect the general distinction between vision-led programmes, emergent programmes and compliance programmes identified in *Managing Successful Programmes* (MSP, 2011) and emphasised previously through Mintzberg's distinction between deliberate and emergent strategies (see, for example, Mintzberg, 1978; Mintzberg & Waters, 1985). Generally, vision-led programmes (MSP, 2011) are derived in a top-down fashion (Rayner & Reiss, 2013) from a clearly defined strategy (Thiry, 2015), representing a *deliberate* attempt to shape the required activities to align with organisational strategy and match the strategic objectives. In contrast, *emergent* programmes (MSP, 2011) roll together existing activities that emerge in ad hoc (Thiry, 2015) yet bottom-up fashion (Rayner & Reiss, 2013) and are better managed in a coordinated fashion (Thiry, 2015), as also identified by Pellegrinelli (1997). Compliance activities can fit into either the strategic, vision-led, or the emergent, ad hoc type of activities, depending on the perceived level of urgency and the perceived strategic value (see also Thiry, 2015: 51).

Portfolios: Why and Where?

Portfolio management systems allow organisations to make the most of their investments and projects, especially in comparison with the expected returns. Portfolios are particularly concerned with the interdependence between projects and programmes, in terms of:

- Scarce or limited resources
- Balance within the portfolio (e.g., between risks and returns)
- Alignment with the strategic intent and main priorities
- Timing
- Capacity bottlenecks (APM, 2019: 13)

Durbin and Doerscher (2010) estimate that well over a million people in more than 170 countries make use of some aspect of portfolio management to make informed business decisions. Indeed, given that the demand for project work is greater than the capability to deliver such projects, portfolio management plays a crucial role in determining which aspects of the work are feasible, desirable and achievable and identifying their wider contributions to the organisation.

An unpublished report by the UK's Cabinet Office (2008) identified that organisations adopting a portfolio management approach realise benefits through the following factors:

- More of the 'right' programmes and projects being undertaken
- Removal of redundant and duplicated projects
- More effective implementation of programmes and projects
- More efficient resource utilisation
- Greater benefits realisation
- Improved transparency, accountability and organisational governance
- Improved engagement and communication between senior management

'Our experience over the years has shown us that it is reasonable to expect increases of 15 to 35 per cent in the ability of the organization to accomplish work by implementing portfolio management depending on your current culture, tools and processes' (Durbin & Doerscher, 2010: 349).

In an increasingly volatile environment, long-term success depends on the accomplishments of the range of initiatives undertaken by the organisation. Success also requires a more intimate understanding of the complexities and interactions of such initiatives. Meanwhile, the external environment appears to be ever more demanding, while technology continues to introduce new competitors, stakeholders and participants. Organisations find themselves tightly bound into supply chains, with little margin for variation or error. In an effort to develop greater effectiveness, many adopt portfolio management in order to make sure that they are doing the right things as they seek to innovate, improve, grow and take advantage of an increasingly complex environment and setting. Portfolio management thus provides a governance opportunity to control, guide and influence the direction of the initiatives within the portfolio whilst enabling better informed and more connected decision-making.

Cooper, Edgett and Kleinschmidt (1997) summarise a set of detailed interviews conducted in 35 leading organisations. Their study identifies the three main goals of portfolio management as:

- Maximising the value of the portfolio against an objective, such as profitability.
- (Finding) balance in the portfolio—portfolios can be balanced in many dimensions, with the most popular being risk versus reward, ease versus attractiveness and breakdown by project type, market and product line.
- (Providing the) link to strategy—looking for strategic fit and resource allocation.

The three main goals observed in the initial research—value maximisation, balanced decision framework and strategic alignment—also chime with Bridges' (1999) proposed paradigm of focusing on fit (identification of opportunities and assessment), utility (analysis of the usefulness and value) and balance (development and selection of balance) as the three core concerns of portfolio management.

However, the discipline of project portfolio management is becoming more proactive and responsible and therefore more focused on governance, assurance and wider impact assessments related to both trade-offs and investments. Subsequent updates by Cooper and Edgett (2010) redefine the third goal as *business strategic alignment,* to ensure that the portfolio continues to reflect the business strategy and that the investment across the portfolio aligns with the organisation's strategic priorities. They also add two further goals of portfolio management:

- **Pipeline balance,** to ensure the resources and focus are not spread too thinly and obtain the ideal number of projects required to achieve the balance between pipeline resource demands and available resources.
- **Sufficiency,** to ensure that the financial goals are achievable through the projects selected in the portfolio.

Small enterprises may typically employ a single, company-wide project portfolio management system (Rayner & Reiss, 2013) to address the full range of concerns; however, the majority of larger organisations are likely to define more than one portfolio to account for the product line, geographic, political or technological divisions of the organisation, sector, industry, market or multi-party collaboration.

In the context of the UK Government, a portfolio is often used as an umbrella term encompassing the total collection of projects, programmes and initiatives currently being undertaken, thereby providing a perspective on the total investment. Indeed, the UK's Office of Government Commerce (OGC) detailed guidance on the *Management of Portfolios* (Jenner & Kilford, 2011) defines the portfolio as *'the totality of the organisation's investment in the changes required to achieve its strategic objectives'.* Portfolio management is the *'coordinated collection of strategic processes and decisions that together enable the most effective balance of organisational change and business as usual'.* The methodology for managing the portfolio, developed by the OGC (Ibid.) consists of two management cycles—one dedicated to portfolio definition and the other to portfolio delivery—five principles and twelve portfolios management practices.

In more general terms, portfolio management is used as the continual process of creating, delivering and evaluating the set of initiatives, activities and projects at the enterprise level, as they go through the repeated cycles of fit, utility and balance considerations. The approach allows the enterprise to manage the full portfolio and the results in tandem with the evolution of the business strategy, in an effort to optimise and maximise the value of business investments whilst exploring new and emerging business opportunities.

One Portfolio, or More?

While portfolios have traditionally been viewed in terms of a central enterprise resource, they can also be adopted within functional areas, domains or departments. Indeed, the 7th edition of the *APM Body of Knowledge* clarifies that portfolios are used to structure investments and can be managed at an organisational or functional level to optimise strategic benefits or operational efficiency. Portfolios address three major questions:

- Are these the projects and programmes needed to deliver the strategic objectives, subject to risk, resource constraints and affordability?
- Is the organisation delivering them effectively and efficiently?
- Are the full potential benefits from the organisation's investment being realised? (APM, 2019: 13).

There is no one-size-fits-all, ideal arrangement for allocating projects or devising portfolios. Martinsuo (2013) notes the contextual nature of portfolio decisions and setups.

Portfolios are initiated for a variety of reasons. Rather than simply having one major project portfolio within each organisation, many businesses would choose to have multiple portfolios. For example, Moore (2009) maintains that projects targeted at innovation and those concerned with improvement should be managed separately. The reason is that the *metrics* for success and the *expectations* for success are quite different. Moreover, the timing for returns on innovation will differ significantly. An extremely innovative project may yield nothing in the first five years before experiencing dramatic growth thereafter, whereas a maintenance project will yield a steady single-digit return.

Managing innovative and process improvement projects in a similar manner, or even in the same category of portfolio, *'is likely to lead to mismanagement of either the innovative or the incremental projects, and most likely it is the innovative that will be curtailed. In the worst case, grouping together different types of projects could even cause both to be mismanaged'* (Ibid.: 27). Different management styles are needed for different project portfolio types. For conventional project portfolios, the power of management rests primarily in the veto; innovation projects, in contrast, will need to bring ideas together and let them coalesce into workable solutions.

Kliem and Verzuh (2016: 453) are similarly mindful that projects fulfil multiple purposes within organisations and therefore recognise a mix of categories within a portfolio. Portfolio categories may include:

- Mandatory growth projects, which generate new revenue
- Cost-cutting projects, which make operations more efficient
- Sustaining projects, such as preventive maintenance

While it may seem efficient to run a single project portfolio, and while it may simplify optimisation, in practice it is important to ensure that innovation is managed appropriately and allowed to develop over time. From a purely pragmatic perspective, there may be a single portfolio utilised to monitor where resources are allocated, but the different treatment of innovation, improvement and sustaining projects would justify the division by type of activity, with different work flow and selection criteria applied in different parts of the organisation.

Pennypacker and Retna (2009) acknowledge that most companies do not attempt to run all their projects at the enterprise level, therefore making a case for tiered portfolios, where standalone portfolios may exist at a business unit or organisational level as well as at the wider enterprise level. In practice, some organisations define specific tiers of portfolios to reflect prioritisation, project size, criticality or location within the enterprise. Such schemes can become complicated with multiple tiers and levels. One organisation has even developed 27 recognised levels of portfolios, resulting in a complex and multi-tiered architecture.

Other portfolio configurations may reflect geographical necessities: Unger et al. (2014: 39) report that at Siemens AG, the German multinational engineering and electronic conglomerate company, project portfolios are handled by either an individual national unit, such as an IT customer-oriented project portfolio of their business unit in South Korea, or managed as a sector-based portfolio encompassing projects set in individual countries or those that span national boundaries and involve multiple operations.

Portfolios can be established for other oversight purposes: Some organisations identify a distinction between strategic portfolios and annualised programmes, which are also referred to as 'delivery portfolios'. Delivery portfolios can be organised by spending cycle, function or delivery type and offer a specific focus on the full range of initiatives targeting delivery in a particular financial year or accounting period.

Different sectors create their own functional portfolios. IT is particularly recognisable as having distinct structures and portfolios, often accompanied with their own approaches, methodologies, theories and a more comprehensive approach to encourage strategic alignment, portfolio flexibility, project pipelines, architecture, asset and resource management, and portfolio prioritisation (see, for example, Bardhan et al., 2004; Bonham, 2005; Daniel et al., 2014; Jagroep et al., 2014; Krebs, 2009; and Rothman, 2016).

Many organisations have dedicated R&D or innovation portfolios that focus on new product development, new discoveries or even underground oil and gas exploration projects. New products are vital to the success of pharmaceutical, aerospace, and heavy engineering constructors and therefore merit their own dedicated portfolios. Portfolios may feature product lines related to a particular compound or drug or focus on a particular disease, such as dementia or Parkinson's disease, allowing for parallel, multiple options and approaches for tackling a particular condition. Portfolio review groups, in consultation with executive and company boards, will often decide on which compounds, drugs, or solutions merit further investment, and therefore will determine which should be prioritised and which could be delayed or cancelled. Such decisions are crucial, as they shape the future of the company, their priorities and their market position. The decisions also determine the product pipeline, which may shape projects and initiatives for the next decade or beyond, given the long lead times experienced in R&D and product development.

Entrepreneurial organisations can also use portfolios as the basis for prioritising lines, areas or types of activities that will shape the future endeavours of the corporation. Cooper et al. (2001: 3) recognise portfolio management in R&D as a dynamic decision process in which the active list of new product (and R&D) projects is constantly updated and revised as new projects are evaluated, selected and prioritised, and existing projects and products are accelerated, killed or deprioritised and resources are allocated, diverted and reallocated to reflect the uncertain and changing nature of available information, the emergence of dynamic opportunities, the resolution of divergent goals and the multiplicity of decision makers and players.

Organisations are faced with different settings and hence need to match the complexity of their decisions with adequately sourced management and decision-making structures, often regarded as different strategic buckets. Exxon Mobil Chemical, for example, uses six categories of projects to identify the right balance for investment between:

1. Cost reductions and process improvements
2. Product improvements, product modification and customer satisfaction
3. New products
4. New platform projects and fundamental/breakthrough research projects
5. Plant support
6. Technical support for customers

Senior management review the spending split amongst the different categories before considering the target breakdown of the ideal split against the current reality and making judgements based on future priorities and intentions.

Successful operation requires a balance between the different types of activities needed for sustainable and effective performance. Christensen et al. (2012) assert that executives and investors might finance three different types of innovations with their capital, managing each as a portfolio. The economy, they argue, requires all three types to occur regularly. The current economy has been overly focused on efficiency innovations, missing opportunities for new markets and empowering innovations, which all need to be managed in distinct portfolios. The three portfolio types are defined as follows:

Empowering innovations portfolios. Transforming expensive products into affordable ones that many more people can buy. These are innovations that create new jobs, because they require more and more people who can build, distribute, sell and service these products. Empowering investments also use capital to expand capacity and to finance receivables and inventory. Such innovation requires many millions of new jobs that go unfilled because people don't yet have the skills to fulfil them.

Sustaining innovations portfolios. Replacing old products with newer models. They keep the economy vibrant, and in dollars they account for the most innovation. But they have a neutral effect on economic activity and on capital.

Efficiency innovations portfolios. Reducing the cost of making and distributing existing products and services. A natural part of the economic cycle, but these are the innovations that streamline process and actually reduce the net number of available jobs. They also preserve many of the remaining jobs because, without them, entire companies and industries would disappear in competition against companies from abroad that have already innovated to become more efficient.

Ultimately, it appears that there are at least three different ways of setting up portfolio management boundaries:

- The boundaries of specific organisational units, functions or strategic business units (SBUs)
- The enterprise level
- A specific project or innovation type

However, additional arrangements may be needed to deal with specific types of initiatives concerned with satisfying the particular strategy required for the wider organisation.

The Case for Strategic Initiatives

Robert Kaplan and David Norton followed their pioneering work on balanced scorecards, strategy maps and strategy-focused organisations by zooming in on the need to link strategy to operations in order to develop and maintain a competitive advantage. Their book *The Execution Premium* (Kaplan & Norton, 2008) focuses on the implementation of formal systems for the successful implementation of strategy. In the book, the authors describe the need to translate a strategy into strategic themes, objectives, measures and targets that represent *what* the organisation wants to accomplish. However, execution requires bridging the execution gap, and therefore strategic initiatives are utilised to represent the *how*.

> 'Strategic initiatives are the collections of finite durations discretionary projects and programs, outside the organization's day-to-day operational activities, that are designed to help the organisation achieve its targeted performance' (p. 103).

While the need for an explicit link between long-term strategy and immediate actions may appear obvious, they point out that their own survey reveals that 50 percent of organisations fail to link strategy to short-term plans and budgets (p. 4).

> 'A senior executive summarized many executives' frustration with the lack of alignment between strategy and action plans when he said, "half my initiatives achieve strategic goals. I just don't know which half"' (p. 103).

Reading Between the Lines:
So Why Do Strategic Initiatives Fail?

Kaplan and Norton propose an initiative management process model encompassing three distinct core activities required to align action with priorities:

1. **Choose strategic initiatives.** Identify what action programmes are needed for executing the strategy.
2. **Fund the strategy.** Identify a source of funding that is separated from the operational budget.
3. **Establish accountability.** Determine who will lead the execution.

However, in reading the discourse related to the specific steps, it would appear that the true insights into the nature of the execution gap reside in the limitations and barriers associated with each of the steps.

Strategic plans require coordinated action that often extends beyond organisational boundaries, functions and business units. Kaplan and Norton reflect that in their original conception of scorecards, they encouraged companies to select initiatives independently for each strategic objective. However, they subsequently concede that selecting initiatives independently ignores the integrated and cumulative impact of multiple related strategic initiatives (Ibid.: 104). Those following only the earlier writing of the authors may thus miss the opportunity for integrating, choosing instead to optimise around individual activities and initiatives.

The new advice is that initiatives should not be selected in isolation, as the achievement of a strategic objective *'generally requires multiple and complementary initiatives from various parts of the organization. . . . We continue to recommend that each nonfinancial objective have at least one initiative to drive its achievement but also that the initiatives be bundled for each strategic theme and considered as an integrated portfolio'* (Ibid.: 104–105).

In other words, in order to achieve the associated performance objectives of a strategic theme, it will often be required that the entire collection of initiatives, or the full portfolio of actions, is implemented. Successful execution with regard to organisational strategy thus requires a synergistic perspective rather than localised optimisation at an initiative or unit level.

There are a number of additional barriers to the successful execution of strategic initiatives, which require a unified enterprise response:

- **Integrated justification.** Strategic initiatives may be justified on a standalone basis in different parts of the organisation, leading to strategic drift over the duration of the initiative.
- **Integrated funding.** Cross-business portfolio funding is not common. However, the risk is that only parts of the initiative will be supported in different areas, leading to patchy, or partial, execution. Budgets typically focus on local accountability and responsibility centres or functional departments. However, strategic initiatives require uniform funding to bridge existing silos and secure delivery across the different business units and areas.
- **Integrated resources.** A similar logic applies to the availability of people and project resources. To avoid local interpretation and prioritisation, strategic initiatives need to be resourced and justified centrally.
- **Integrated governance.** Responsibility and accountability for the wider initiative need to rest with executive team members who can manage across teams, units and silos.

Strategic initiatives will often have a compelling business case that specifies the proposed benefits and the expected value proposition, and these can be used as the basis for leading and delivering successful strategic initiatives across the wider enterprise.

Durbin and Doerscher (2010: 8) propose that organisations operate in a continual cycle of change, where each cycle begins by understanding current operations and the value derived from them. Change events cause a shift in the operational basis, thereby driving a series of change management stages that move the organisation towards a new and improved future state. The cycle of change is in turn managed through the use of three types of portfolios reflecting the shifting position of the organisation in the change delivery cycle that enable the organisation to balance demand and capacity. The cycle emphasises:

- **Strategic portfolios.** Facilitate operational planning to guide the future direction of the organisation; organise strategies and evaluate ideas and opportunities used to analyse and redistribute human and financial capacities to support new organisational goals and objectives, offering the basis for high-level trade-off decisions.
- **Investment portfolios.** Organise the investment alternatives and make investment decisions; make comparisons between competing ways to implement the plan by considering factors such as strategic balance and alignment, timing, effort, risk, cost and benefit.

- **Execution portfolios.** Direct projects, programmes, services and work activities and facilitate tactical resource management; allow managers to strike a balance between the competing demands of different tasks and confirm the value delivered.

Durbin and Doerscher offer a portfolio ecosystem that cycles through the three different types of portfolios that, in turn, enable organisations to determine the potential for the delivery of value, manage the commitment of funding and resources, and assign the resources to ensure that things get done. The proposed ecosystem uses the different portfolio types to deliver meaningful and relevant change and appears to chime with the findings of Kock et al. (2015; 2016) and Heising (2012) that ideation portfolio management, or the detailed consideration of options at the front end of the portfolio, leads to better results for both individual projects and the integrated portfolios. They also address the need to reflect structural alignment with the needs of portfolio management in order to enable effective strategy implementation (Kaiser et al., 2015). The ecosystem therefore appears to offer a natural candidate to be extended and implemented within a strategic initiative portfolio, thus becoming a dedicated portfolio system intended to successfully realise the strategic themes of the organisation and to optimise decisions around the key principles that are considered to be of strategic importance.

Potential Principles for Collecting Projects and Programmes Into a Portfolio

This section has already identified multiple reasons for assembling projects and programmes into distinct portfolios. The principles and reasons for collecting and prioritising initiatives within a portfolio include:

- Implement strategic ambition
- Maximise value
- Balance different needs (or types of innovation)
- Manage common resources
- Share common technology
- Share or link risks
- Share sponsorship and management arrangements
- Allocate budget
- Justify investments
- Achieve enterprise visibility
- Prioritise initiatives
- Reduce/enhance risk profile
- Enhance a particular product line
- Match to a particular risk/investment appetite
- Increase the flow of value through a pipeline
- Create a particular funnel for a product or type of project
- Respond to opportunities
- Foster diversification
- Coordinate the delivery of benefits
- Utilise as a framework and focus for organisational ambidexterity

- Justify compliance work
- Address sustainability, product stewardship and social considerations

Portfolios often endeavour to achieve multiple objectives by offering a link between the execution of initiatives and the wider enterprise strategy and hence may pack together multiple aspects and rationales.

Agile portfolio management, a burgeoning new area of interest, endeavours to distil the key principles of portfolio management by focusing on the rapid creation of value. However, it is important to align value realisation with the relevant strategy and rationale. By identifying the general rationale and balance needed in a portfolio, it becomes possible to refine the key principles driving the leading choices and decisions and begin to determine the dimensions, rules and guidelines for measuring and determining success in setting up the portfolio.

Rethinking Project Portfolio Success

The track record of project portfolios can sometimes be a little challenging to decipher. Jonas (2010) notes that it remains difficult to determine the overall success or failure of a portfolio, especially as it needs to be realised at different points during the lifespan of a portfolio. Martinsuo and Lehtonen (2007) observe that the performance of a portfolio should not be examined on a single dimension, advocating instead that achievement should be measured at the single project, the portfolio and the organisational levels. Müller et al. (2008: 38) define portfolio success as a combination of 'achieving desired portfolio results, and achieving project and program purpose for the overall portfolio'. Marenwick (2015) summarises the main portfolio success criteria, in accordance with research completed by Beringer et al. (2013) and Mekskendahl (2010), as a combination of:

1. **Economic success.** Maximisation of the financial value of the portfolio
2. **Strategic fit.** Linking the portfolio to the organisational strategy
3. **Portfolio balance.** Balancing the projects within the portfolio whilst taking into account the organisation's capacities
4. **Average project success.** The average success rate of a project within the portfolio

Agile portfolio management would encourage a wider focus on value, extending beyond the financial aspects. Indeed, benefits realisation based on utilisation and achievement of intended impacts and outcomes may offer a more valuable utilisation measure. The success of specific projects may also need to be considered in the context of the wider portfolio and the delivery of the intended benefits, expected usefulness, promised impacts and the overall value that is captured.

Project-oriented organisations rely on their portfolio management and governance systems. Projects may be accelerated, killed or deprioritised, and resources are allocated and deallocated as deemed expedient (Cooper et al., 2001). 'Killing' a specific project may be justified at the enterprise portfolio level (Unger et al., 2012), where there might be better ways of utilising resources, or perhaps other related projects or initiatives which may deliver all or some of the benefits. Indeed, some projects may conflict with other initiatives, and hence it would make more sense if they were delayed or cancelled. Yet, at the strategic initiative level, specific initiatives should be terminated if, and only if, they do not jeopardise the wider strategic theme. Clearly, some strategic themes may only be achieved if and when the entire collection of initiatives, which underpins them, is realised.

Furthermore, Kock and Gemünden (2019) recognise the role of longitudinal interdependencies, where new opportunities emerge from existing exploratory projects, and subsequent projects are needed to ensure that such strategic options are duly exploited. Consideration of any specific part of the portfolio can only be determined through understanding the synergy and role that it plays within the wider portfolio and the relationships that exist between different undertakings and the usage points, opportunities that become available, and benefits that are likely to be delivered to the enterprise.

Success is a difficult concept. In some R&D contexts, the marketability of particular compounds, solutions or drugs, and how they are perceived by the wider population, may enforce a particular spin on the value or perceived acceptability of proposed solutions. In other setups, such as the oil and gas and other energy exploration endeavours, particular locations, or working with specific regimes and communities, may likewise colour and influence the perceived success of particular initiatives, or even the way the entire company is portrayed. In such settings, the ability to innovate and diversify and the need to explore alternative options, often in parallel, informs and feeds into the direct value derived from the portfolio arrangements.

Even within the confines of project-centric portfolios, different definitions abound. Kopmann (2014) advocates that project portfolio success embraces three dimensions: the strategic aspect, the exploitation aspect, and the stakeholder aspect. Corresponding management activities would thus require features of strategic control, stakeholder involvement and governance for portfolio exploitation. The following section of this chapter written by John Wyzalek expands on the dynamic relationships amongst the different aspects, especially in turbulent and fast-changing settings, building on his earlier work on the connection amongst portfolios, strategic goals and stakeholder management.

The overall success of a portfolio would inevitably extend beyond the initial definition phase of the portfolio and may also include an element of preparing for the future, as proposed by Meskendahl (2010). Wyzalek's approach in the next section adds a continuous alignment dimension that takes into account factors such as turbulence, opportunity, change and the pursuit of evolving strategic organisational goals that emerge and change over time. His perspective and approach elevate portfolio management to a strategic discipline embedded within and supportive of organisational targets, aims, ambitions, strategic stakeholder engagement and continuous achievement through alignment.

Kopmann et al. (2017) show that portfolios can be used to support both deliberate and emergent strategies. They also demonstrate that 'strategic control activities not only foster the implementation of intended strategies, but also disclose strategic opportunities by unveiling emerging patterns' (p. 557). Turning their findings around would imply that portfolios may be utilised to develop and explore emergent strategies. Under such conditions, the success criteria would surely also need to reflect the exploration value and the enabled flexibility that come from the emergent strategy. Indeed, Hoffmann et al. (2020) advocate adding agility as an important design goal for portfolios to allow for rapid adaptations, flexible reprioritisation and dynamic adjustments in response to changing strategic trajectories and emerging opportunities.

Given the diversity observed in the types of portfolio setups, the key criteria applied in establishing the portfolio and the subtleties of determining success and failure at multiple levels and perspectives (Dalcher, 1994; 2014a; 2014b), it should be clear that the key criteria applied in determining success need to be context specific (Korhonen et al., 2014, Martinsuo & Geraldi, 2020). Reflecting Engwall's (2003) observation that 'no project is an island', Unger et al. (2014:

38) similarly note that project portfolios as collections of projects are parts and products of their organisations and hence are embedded within their context and culture. Indeed, Martinsuo (2013: 798) re-affirms that *'recent studies show evidence that the success of portfolio management is highly dependent on the context'*.

Undeniably, what appears clear is that we must talk about and measure success in different ways. Success is a complex and multi-layered concept (Dalcher, 2012; 2014a), especially in the context of portfolios. The principles for collecting projects into a portfolio must play a key part: the multiple bases, arrangements and rationales for portfolios, as highlighted above, demarcate a starting point in the conversation about success in portfolio settings. If there are different reasons for establishing a portfolio, different purposes for grouping key investments together and different approaches for governing and making decisions, then they must also form the basis for defining what is important and whether the intention and purpose have been achieved.

An interesting omission from the accepted criteria appears to relate to one of the original objectives of applying portfolios—to optimise the deployment of resources across projects. The common theme amongst projects grouped together offers an added synergy and the potential for the sharing of common resources, common technology, or common sponsorship, management and governance structures. While the case for commonly sharing technology, resources and arrangements offers the potential for both savings and synergies, there appears to be little effort to quantify or justify such savings.

The literature on portfolio success does not directly address the value that comes from the sharing, other than in applicability to organisational strategy. Yet, common resourcing, the sharing of expertise, or even the justification of a new technology split across multiple projects can make a compelling case for success. One potential exception is the area of agile portfolio management, which takes into account portfolio blending, or the bringing together of initiatives that provide economies of scale, alongside the more traditional prioritising and balancing (see, for example, ABC, 2017). Agile portfolio management thus suggests that at every portfolio event-driven retrospective or regular stand-up, the performance of the portfolio is evaluated. Such evaluation enables adjustments to the prioritisation, blending and balancing in order to improve the performance of the overall portfolio. While the focus in agile portfolio management may be on the near term, the explicit recognition of blending places it at the core of performance review and assessment. Other parts of the portfolio management community are yet to explicitly acknowledge the importance of common grouping to determine the overall value and success of a portfolio.

The discussion around portfolio success in the extant literature is relatively sparse. Generally accepted criteria appear to offer little pragmatic value or guidance. Moreover, the different needs and requirements of specific setups, such as strategic initiatives, imply that specific criteria need to be applied and tailored to each context individually. The mode of execution of the portfolio and the increasing tendency to set up agile portfolios will also require more refined ways of determining success and doing so more rapidly and frequently. The balance between the different components and interests should also be taken into account. The completion of a small part of a portfolio can be significantly less critical than the successful completion of a strategic initiative. Indeed, in a strategic context, specific actions and their completion may seem irrelevant against major strategic imperatives.

Achieving the right balance between establishing the variety of projects and initiatives and the selection of appropriate ones is crucial to the success of the portfolio. In a world that increasingly demands doing more with less, the abilities to develop enterprise portfolio capability and

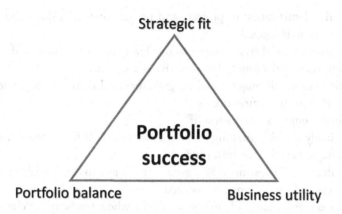

Figure 6.1   Project Portfolio Success Triangle

to consider projects and initiatives globally are of paramount importance. While portfolio objectives emphasise strategic alignment, or fit, value maximisation and portfolio balance, the exact dimensions of each, and the values that underpin the selections for the portfolio will also need to feature in the assessment of attainment, especially as organisations endeavour to balance the need to efficiently exploit the known and innovatively explore new opportunities. Identifying the right mix of options and supporting the strategic choice of the options that maximise the enterprise's intentions is critical to success.

While it seems tempting to propose a performance triangle based on fit, utility and balance of the portfolio as an initial way of mapping success (see Figure 6.1), it is also important to recognise that such a scheme would underplay the complexities inherent in portfolio decision-making. Such a triangle would miss the value of common deployment of expertise, skills, tools, and other resources across multiple projects. It would also miss out on contextual issues, such as the balance between exploration and exploitation and the specific types of innovation required, and will not necessarily address the implied critical importance of strategic initiatives and strategic alignment.

Overall, therefore, the specific scenario for success needs to be tailored to the specific initiatives and activities that are invoked, and their relative importance to the overall sustained performance of the enterprise should play the key part in planning for and in gauging the achievement of the intended performance, measured in terms of the fit, utility and balance of the actual portfolio. However, this should be done with the caveat that portfolio success is situated within the direct context of the organisation and the specific benefits sought, including the common sharing of expertise, resources and tools, and should therefore play a critical part in shaping and influencing any meaningful assessment of portfolio performance against appetite, expectations and emerging opportunities and challenges.

Perhaps a more sensible approach to defining portfolio success should focus on what we are trying to achieve through the creation and structuring of the portfolio and the competing and overlapping constraints and priorities. According to the Association for Project Management's Portfolio Management Specific Interest Group (APM, 2020) there are multiple values, added benefits and improved outcomes when portfolio management is implemented and executed properly. Portfolio management can therefore offer the following contributions to business success (p. 3):

- Ensures early identification of projects and programmes that don't add value/benefit, so they are not started/stopped
- Ensures management of risk at the collective level, increasing success of the 'right' projects and programmes, and a link to business risk management
- Ensures visibility of all projects and programmes and their interdependence and enables tracking and focus to ensure success
- Provides better engagement with staff
- Supports timely decision-making and re-orientation of inflight projects and programmes so that strategic benefits are optimised
- Supports effective and optimised allocation of resources to better enable the highest-priority 'right' projects and programmes to succeed
- Provides robust governance of change across the whole landscape of change/projects

The list of benefits can be further augmented by additional contributions to the organisation and the business, such as focusing on and optimising the use of scarce resources, emphasising beneficial impact on customers and stakeholders, and encouraging innovation and exploration of new opportunities.

Ultimately, success is contextual and deeply situated. The most pertinent set of contributions that apply to any specific organisation and portfolio setup should therefore form the basis for evaluating and assessing the success of that specific arrangement. Delivering successful portfolios can thus be informed by and tailored to match the real needs, opportunities and expectations that relate to a given situation.

References

ABC (2017). *Agile Portfolio Management.* Regus Ashford, UK: Agile Business Consortium.

APM (2019). R. Murray-Webster and D. Dalcher (Eds.), *APM Body of Knowledge* (7th Ed.). Princes Risborough, UK: Association for Project Management.

APM (2020). *Portfolio Management: A Practical Guide.* Princes Risborough, UK: APM Portfolio Management Specific Interest Group, Association for Project Management.

Artto, K. A. (2001). Management of project-oriented organization—A conceptual analysis. In: K. A. Artto, M. Martinsuo, and T. Aalto (Eds.). *Project Portfolio Management: Strategic Management Through Projects.* Helsinki, FI: Project Management Association Finland.

Bardhan, I., Sougstad, R., and Sougstad, R. (2004). Prioritizing a portfolio of information technology investment projects. *Journal of Management Information Systems, 21*(2), 33–60.

Beringer, C., Jonas, D., and Kock, A. (2013). Behavior of internal stakeholders in project portfolio management and its impact on success. *International Journal of Project Management, 31*(6), 830–846.

Bonham, S. S. (2005). *IT Project Portfolio Management.* Boston, MA: Artech House.

Bridges, D. N. (1999). Project portfolio management: Ideas and practices. In: L. D. Dye and J. S. Pennypacker (Eds.). *Project Portfolio Management: Selecting and Prioritizing Projects for Competitive Advantage*, 45–54. West Chester, PA: Center for Business Practices.

Cabinet Office (2008). *Benchmarking Reliable Delivery*, unpublished. London, UK: Cabinet Office.

Christensen, C. M., Allworth, J., and Dillon, K. (2012). *How Will You Measure Your Life?* New York, NY: Harper Business.

Combe, M. W., and Githens, G. D. (1999). Managing popcorn priorities: How portfolios and programs align projects with strategies. *Proceedings of the PMI 1999 Seminars & Symposium*, Philadelphia, PA. Newtown Square, PA: Project Management Institute.

Cooper, R. G., Edgett, S. J., and Kleinschmidt, E. J. (1997). Portfolio management in new product development: Lessons from the leaders, II. *Research-Technology Management, 40*(6), 43–52.

Cooper, R. G., Edgett, S. J., and Kleinschmidt, E. J. (2001). *Portfolio Management for New Products*. New York, NY: Basic Books.

Cooper, R. G., and Edgett, S. J. (2010). Portfolio management. *The Innovation Times*.

Dalcher, D. (1994). Falling down is part of growing up: The study of failure and the software engineering community. In: J. L. Diaz-Herrera (Ed.). *Software Engineering Education*, 489–496. Berlin/Heidelberg, DE: Springer.

Dalcher, D. (2012). The nature of project management: A reflection on the anatomy of major projects by Morris and Hough. *International Journal of Managing Projects in Business, 5*(4), 643–660.

Dalcher, D. (2014a). Rethinking success in software projects: Looking beyond the failure factors. In: G. Ruhe and C. Wohlin (Eds.). *Software Project Management in a Changing World*, 27–49. Berlin/Heidelberg, DE: Springer.

Dalcher, D. (2014b). What can project success, or failure, tell us about project management theory. In: S. Rietiker and R. Wagner (Eds.). *Theory Meets Practice in Projects*. Nuremberg, DE: GPM.

Daniel, E. M., Ward, J. M., and Franken, A. (2014). A dynamic capabilities perspective of IS project portfolio management. *The Journal of Strategic Information Systems, 23*(2), 95–111.

Durbin, P., and Doerscher, T. (2010). *Taming Change with Portfolio Management: Unify Your Organization, Sharpen Your Strategy and Create Measurable Value*. Austin, TX: Greenleaf Book Group Press/Routledge.

Dye, L. D., and Pennypacker, J. S. (Eds.) (1999). *Project Portfolio Management: Selecting and Prioritizing Projects for Competitive Advantage*, 45–54. West Chester, PA: Center for Business Practices.

Engwall, M. (2003). No project is an island: Linking projects to history and context. *Research Policy, 32*(5), 789–808.

Heising, W. (2012). The integration of ideation and project portfolio management—A key factor for sustainable success. *International Journal of Project Management, 30*(5), 582–595.

Hoffmann, D., Ahlemann, F., and Reining, S. (2020). Reconciling alignment, efficiency, and agility in IT project portfolio management: Recommendations based on a revelatory case study. *International Journal of Project Management, 38*(2), 124–136.

Jagroep, E., van de Weerd, I., Brinkkemper, S., and Dobbe, T. (2014). Framework for implementing product portfolio management in software business. In: G. Ruhe and C. Wohlin (Eds.). *Software Project Management in a Changing World*, 193–221. Berlin/Heidelberg, DE: Springer.

Jenner, S., and Kilford, C. (2011). *Management of Portfolios*. London, UK: The Stationery Office.

Jonas, D. (2010). Empowering project portfolio managers: How management involvement impacts project portfolio management performance. *International Journal of Project Management, 28*(8), 818–831.

Kaiser, M. G., El Arbi, F., and Ahlemann, F. (2015). Successful project portfolio management beyond project selection techniques: Understanding the role of structural alignment. *International Journal of Project Management, 33*(1), 126–139.

Kaplan, R. S., and Norton, D. P. (2008). *The Execution Premium: Linking Strategy to Operations for Competitive Advantage*. Boston, MA: Harvard Business Press.

Kliem, R., and Verzuh, E. (2016). Project portfolio management: Align project resources with business strategy. In: E. Verzuh (Ed.). *The Fast Forward MBA in Project Management*. Hoboken, NJ: John Wiley & Sons.

Kock, A., Heising, W., and Gemünden, H. G. (2015). How ideation portfolio management influences front-end success. *Journal of Product Innovation Management, 32*(4), 539–555.

Kock, A., Heising, W., and Gemünden, H. G. (2016). A contingency approach on the impact of front-end success on project portfolio success. *Project Management Journal, 47*(2), 115–129.

Kock, A., and Gemünden, H. G. (2019). Project lineage management and project portfolio success. *Project Management Journal, 50*(5), 587–601.

Kopmann, J. (2014). Refining project portfolio success and its antecedents. *Project Management Institute Research and Education Conference Proceedings,* Phoenix, AZ. Newtown Square, PA: Project Management Institute.

Kopmann, J., Kock, A., Killen, C. P., and Gemünden, H. G. (2017). The role of project portfolio management in fostering both deliberate and emergent strategy. *International Journal of Project Management, 35*(4), 557–570.

Korhonen, T., Laine, T., and Martinsuo, M. (2014). Management control of project portfolio uncertainty: A managerial role perspective. *Project Management Journal, 45*(1), 21–37.

Krebs, J. (2009). *Agile Portfolio Management*. Redmond, WA: Microsoft Press.

Lockett, M., De Reyck, B., and Sloper, A. (2008). Managing project portfolios. *Business Strategy Review, 19*(2), 77–83.

Marnewick, C. (2015). Portfolio management success. In: G. Levin and J. P. Wyzalek (Eds.). *Portfolio Management: A Strategic Approach*. Boca Raton, FL: CRC Press.

Martinsuo, M. (2013). Project portfolio management in practice and in context. *International Journal of Project Management, 31*(6), 794–803.

Martinsuo, M., and Geraldi, J. (2020). Management of project portfolios: Relationships of project portfolios with their contexts. *International Journal of Project Management, 38*(7), 441–453.

Martinsuo, M., and Lehtonen, P. (2007). Role of single-project management in achieving portfolio management efficiency. *International Journal of Project Management, 25*(1), 56–65.

Meskendahl, S. (2010). The influence of business strategy on project portfolio management and its success—A conceptual framework. *International Journal of Project Management, 28*(8), 807–817.

Mintzberg, H. (1978). Patterns in strategy formation. *Management Science, 24*(9), 934–948.

Mintzberg, H., and Waters, J. A. (1985). Of strategies, deliberate and emergent. *Strategic Management Journal, 6*(3), 257–272.

Moore, S. (2009). *Strategic Project Portfolio Management: Enabling a Productive Organization* (Vol. 16). New York, NY: John Wiley & Sons.

MSP (2011). *Managing Successful Programmes*. Office of Government Commerce. London, UK: The Stationery Office.

Müller, R., Martinsuo, M., and Blomquist, T. (2008). Project portfolio control and portfolio management performance in different contexts. *Project Management Journal, 39*(3), 28–42.

Pellegrinelli, S. (1997). Programme management: Organising project-based change. *International Journal of Project Management, 15*(3), 141–149.

Pennypacker, J., and Retna, S. (2009). Project portfolio management: A view from the management trenches. Hoboken, NJ: John Wiley & Sons.

Rayner, P., and Reiss, G., (2013). *Portfolio and Programme Management Demystified: Managing Multiple Projects Successfully*. Abingdon, UK: Routledge.

Rothman, J. (2016). *Manage Your Project Portfolio: Increase Your Capacity and Finish More Projects.* Raleigh, NC: Pragmatic Bookshelf.

Thiry, M. (2015). *Program Management.* Farnham, UK: Gower Publishing Limited.

Unger, B. N., Kock, A., Gemünden, H. G., and Jonas, D. (2012). Enforcing strategic fit of project portfolios by project termination: An empirical study on senior management involvement. *International Journal of Project Management, 30*(6), 675–685.

Unger, B. N., Rank, J., and Gemünden, H. G. (2014). Corporate innovation culture and dimensions of project portfolio success: The moderating role of national culture. *Project Management Journal, 45*(6), 38–57.

Strategic Goal Alignment and Portfolio Stakeholder Management

John Wyzalek

Project portfolios are associated with goals and strategy. A group of projects is considered a portfolio only when its deliverables aid an organisation in achieving goals considered to be strategic (Dietrich & Lehtonen, 2005). As organisational goals and strategy change, the projects forming the portfolio change. A project portfolio can be considered to be a likeness of the organisation, and the challenges that face organisational managers also face project portfolio managers.

This does not mean that project portfolio managers are executives managing an organisation, but it does mean the project portfolio managers must be aware of how an organisation is managed in the present and for growth. Growth occurs over an expanded timeframe, and so does a portfolio. Unlike a project whose end is planned the moment a project is conceived, a project portfolio is open-ended because its end is never planned—only its next change is planned.

Modern portfolio management came into force with theories developed by Markowitz (1952) and Roy (1952), who proposed that a unique portfolio of investments can maximize resources by providing the highest yield for the minimum of risk. Their work left open the problems of how a portfolio is structured and how its structure changes in response to strategic changes. The theory was applied to organisational management as the problem of finding an optimal use of resources to yield a portfolio of products and services that enable an organisation to realize strategic goals. When applied to project management, the theory was translated into the optimal use of resources to support projects that realize organisational goals.

Structuring a portfolio by finding the optimal use of project resources is a complex problem related to scheduling and planning, at which project management excels. Changing portfolio structure is related to strategic management, which increasingly has influenced how effective project management is accomplished.

Portfolios may change in response to a change in the portfolio organisation's *internal* environment, such as a change in strategy by executive management, availability of resources, or policies and procedures. They may also have to change in response to changes in the *external* environment, such as a change in the market, technology, regulations, or economy.

Stakeholder management can help a portfolio manager become aware of internal and external factors that may change a portfolio. It can also help a portfolio manager deal with the changes caused by new strategic goals set by management. Finally, it can help a portfolio manager grow a portfolio by establishing long-term relationships with stakeholders who support the portfolio.

An Example and Some Definitions

A stakeholder has been defined as any individual who has influence over an organisation (Freeman, [1984] 2010), and stakeholder management as managing that influence such that the organisation's aims and goals are met. A portfolio stakeholder can influence how a portfolio is resourced and structured, as well as how its strategic goals are set. Stakeholders exist inside and outside a portfolio and a portfolio's organisation.

For example, a manufacturer is adding to a line of products and is relying on a long-term partner to supply a natural resource, which is key to manufacturing these products. To procure the needed quantity of this resource locally, the partner would have to use protected lands, which requires a waiver from the state government. Environmental groups, local communities, local businesses, and local governments have learned of this development and oppose the waiver. This opposition has been broadcasted by the media, and consumers are rallying to save the protected land by boycotting the manufacturer's products. There has been a slight decrease in sales revenue, which threatens the new product development, and a larger decrease could threaten the manufacturer's existence.

Executive managers at the manufacturer are considering options that include weathering the negative publicity and boycott to pursue their current goal as is, ways to reformulate production so it uses other resources, or cancelling the new product launch and developing a different line of products. The executives are split into two groups: one favours sustainable manufacturing and the other favours traditional manufacturing.

Through its ability to supply key resources, the long-term partner is a stakeholder to the portfolio. The state government is a stakeholder because it could grant a waiver so the protected land can be used to obtain resources needed for the new production. Like the long-term partner, consumers are stakeholders whose purchases of the company's products provide financial resources. Executive managers are stakeholders who establish goals for the portfolio, establish its resource levels, and approve its structure.

One group of executive managers is opting to secure the needed resources by lobbying government officials to gain the waiver and move forward with production despite the negative publicity. This group of managers exhibits what it is known as "instrumental" stakeholder management (Donaldson & Preston, 1995), in which stakeholders are viewed as a means to an end. The other group of executive managers are looking for a compromise or to stop production in order to preserve protected lands as well as win the support of environmental organisations and the public at large. This group exhibits "normative" stakeholder management, in which stakeholders are viewed as having intrinsic rights that must be respected (Ibid.).

Stakeholder management is related to a fundamental conception of what is an organisation, whether the organisation is a company, a portfolio, or a project. This conception has its origin in the work of Barnard ([1938] 1968), who viewed an organisation in its most basic form as a relationship between individuals and in its more advanced forms as a system of cooperation. When an organisation is viewed as a system of relationships among individuals, the importance of managing relationships with stakeholders is clear. This view can also guide a portfolio manager in relationships at various levels—individual, project, portfolio, and organisation.

The portfolio manager in the example could rely on his relationships with the executive team members to see whether the portfolio is keeping its current goal or may be restructured as new production is modified or halted. No matter which strategic direction is taken, the organisation and the portfolio are experiencing turbulence. The portfolio manager should be engaging team members to steady them through the turbulence. Any relationships with the partnering organisation should also be managed so they stay strong through this difficult time.

Strategic Goal Alignment for Managing a Portfolio and Its Stakeholders

Projects whose deliverables help an organisation realize its goals and form a portfolio are considered to be in strategic alignment. Ensuring project goals align with those of the portfolio is a key activity in portfolio management (Cooper, Edgett & Kleinschmidt, 1997). Portfolio managers have to be experts at resourcing and structuring portfolios so they have strategic alignment. They can apply this expertise to managing stakeholders. Goal alignment is a principal that portfolio management can use in managing stakeholders and can provide benefits beyond attaining goals. By aligning stakeholder goals with those of their portfolios, executive and portfolio managers can develop lasting relationships that can benefit a portfolio long term.

When managers engage stakeholders to learn about their goals and aims, the managers are practicing normative stakeholder management in several ways. The managers are acknowledging that the stakeholders have goals and are implicitly affirming the stakeholders' rights to have these goals. When managers communicate to stakeholders the portfolio's goals, they are acting in a transparent way as well as helping to ensure support for the goals. By showing transparency and respect for stakeholder goals, managers are signalling their trustworthiness to stakeholders. Trust is key to any relationship in business, and it helps to foster long-term relationships.

Communication feeds a relationship, and it can help feed a portfolio. A stable relationship with stakeholders who are suppliers can help stabilize an organisation's supply chain to provide long-term resourcing for portfolio-related activities. Communication with multiple external stakeholders can help managers to learn about new trends in the marketplace, competitors, and changing regulations. It enables managers to sense changes in an organisation's environment and set new strategic direction. The trust developed by open communications can help managers earn support for new strategic initiatives, taking the organization into new markets.

When a portfolios' goals align with those of external stakeholders, it not only helps the portfolio to attain goals, it also helps to ensure that stakeholders can aid a portfolio over the long term. When stakeholders are able to attain their goals, they are aided in their pursuit of strategic growth and long-term survival. They are able to provide the portfolio organization with resources, which enable a portfolio to attain goals, and information, which may guide senior managers in determining strategy and the portfolio's goal.

As portfolio managers communicate goals and guide their portfolios to their attainment, they are sending an important message to all stakeholders that portfolio goals take precedence. Individuals can hold multiple goals at the same time. For example, executive managers are often conflicted between the goal of short-term cost cutting to boost their organizations' stock prices, which may boost their own compenzation as well as benefitting shareholders, over long-term growth strategy that may be costly in the short-term. Or portfolio team members may place their own career or personal objectives over the needs of the portfolio. Foss and Lindenberg (2013) have studied this problem and theorize that by working to attain goals that benefit an organization, a manager is sending the signal that organizational goals are most important and are the goals that all in the organization should be working to attain. This is known as the *Theory of Joint-Production Motivation* and focuses on the actions of individual managers. An individual's normative actions that place the collective's goals above the individuals can influence other individuals to take similarly normative actions.

When placed in the context of portfolio management, portfolio managers who demonstrate actions that prioritize portfolio goals can influence other portfolio stakeholders to act to attain portfolio goals. When these actions also align with stakeholder goals, they not only reinforce attaining portfolio goals, they also reinforce the relationships with stakeholders and help ensure these relationships benefit both the portfolio and the stakeholders.

In the case of the manufacturer that is being confronted with a possible boycott, there could be multiple solutions. By considering which stakeholders' goals align, or could be made to align, with the organization's, executive management may be able to determine a solution that benefits the organization as well as stakeholders. Perhaps the supplier does not want the negative press, supports environmental protections, or is looking to expand operations in new locations where alternative resources can be had at lower cost. By deciding to use different resourcing to develop the new product, executive management could satisfy its goal for new product development, satisfying its supplier's goals as well as strengthening the relationship with the supplier.

Perhaps the political climate favours protecting public lands, and a prominent politician on the regulating board is seeking higher office. Reformulation would satisfy the goals of groups interested in saving the land as well as build a relationship with the politician, who may be the next governor or federal representative. A new set of goals would also give consumers the impression that the organization listens to its customers and is responsive, which could increase product sales. Or there could be a coalition of developers and suppliers who want to exploit the protected lands, because the marketing department does not believe the negative press would affect the new product's sales, and keeping the original goals and establishing relationships with members of the coalition are more beneficial.

If the portfolio manager in this organization has strong relationships with stakeholders, the manager can at a minimum anticipate changes to the portfolio. The manager could also use those relationships to provide information that could influence the managers who decide whether to set new goals. This information can be about the costs and risks of restructuring the portfolio. It could include market intelligence gathered from the supplier and other strategic portfolio partners. The portfolio manager should not be an advocate for a particular solution but should provide needed information. The information should relate to goals and the risks associated with them to enhance signals that the portfolio benefits the organization.

Conclusion

Portfolio managers are experts at strategic alignment, which ensures that resources are used only on those projects that help to attain organizational goals. To aid them in becoming experts at strategic stakeholder management, they can apply the principal of strategic alignment with their portfolio's stakeholders. To do so requires open communication about those goals with stakeholders and dialogue to see how these goals align with those of stakeholders. When possible, portfolio managers may seek compromise with stakeholders for more fit between portfolio and stakeholder goals. By focusing on strategic goal attainment and taking actions to realize it, portfolio managers signal behaviour that can influence stakeholders to act towards goal attainment. They are signalling transparency and a normative stance that help to establish the trust needed for durable relationships. All these actions to align goals between stakeholders and portfolios aid portfolios as they execute strategy and adapt to change in the external environment. Stakeholders who have an established relationship with an organization, the portfolio, and portfolio manager can supply resources needed to sustain the portfolio in the present and information about market trends, regulations, and other important stakeholders such as competitors needed to grow the portfolio in the future.

References

Barnard, C. I. (1968). *The Functions of the Executive* (30th Anniv. Ed.). Cambridge, MA: Harvard University Press. (Original work published 1938.)

Cooper, R. G., Edgett, S., and Kleinschmidt, E. (1997). Portfolio management in new product development: Lessons from the leaders, I. *Research Technology Management 40*(5), 16–28.

Dietrich, P., and Lehtonen, P. (2005). Successful management of strategic intentions through multiple projects—Reflections from empirical study. *International Journal of Project Management, 23*(5), 386–391.

Donaldson, T., and Preston, L. E. (1995). The stakeholder theory of the corporation: Concepts, evidence and implications. *Academy of Management Review, 20*(1), 65–91.

Foss, N. J., and Lindenberg, S. (2013). Microfoundations for strategy: A goal-framing perspective on the drivers of value creation. *Academy of Management Perspectives, 27*(2), 85–102.

Freeman, R. E. (2010). *Strategic management: A stakeholder approach*. Cambridge, UK: Cambridge University Press. (Original work published 1984.)

Markowitz, H. (1952). Portfolio selection. *The Journal of Finance, 7*(1), 77–91.

Roy, A. D. (1952). Safety first and the holding of assets. *Econometric, 20*(3), 431–449.

Chapter 7

Entrepreneurship

The Entrepreneurship Turn: Repositioning Projects as Successful Ventures

Darren Dalcher

It is often said that we live in the age of entrepreneurship. The Global Entrepreneurship Monitor estimates that there are more than 582 million people in the world in the process of starting or running their own businesses (GEM, 2018). According to Bygrave (2010: 1), more than a thousand new businesses are born every hour of every working day in the United States, and the majority of new jobs are created by such emerging new businesses. However, entrepreneurship encompasses much more than venture formation and can occur in many different ways . . .

The notion of entrepreneurship has attracted considerable interest within the management and business communities since its first appearance in 1437 (Westhead & Wright, 2013: 4). The common use of the term in French implies a go-between or a middleman able to make connections and direct the resources provided by the various connections. In 1734 Richard Cantillon offered a distinction between the three types of agents in the economy: the landowners, who provide the primary resource; the entrepreneurs, including farmers and merchants, who organise resources and accept risks by buying at a certain price and selling at an uncertain one; and the hirelings who rent out their services (Stokes & Wilson, 2017: 35). Jean-Baptiste Say (1803) popularised the use of the term through his pioneering writing, which distinguished between the profits of those who provided capital and those entrepreneurs who utilised it for economic activity.

Stokes and Wilson (2017) observe that in the Middle Ages, entrepreneurs managed large projects such as castles and cathedrals on behalf of wealthy landowners or the Church. Yet, while entrepreneurship to this day seems to imply novel projects and undertakings in challenging new contexts, it is seldom invoked in project management dialogue. One might have expected the relative proximity between the disciplines to have resulted in greater commonalities and sharing; however, in reality, the project management community has remained somewhat oblivious to advances in entrepreneurship and to the potential for interdisciplinary collaboration.

What Is This Thing Called Entrepreneurship?

There is no single, simple and agreed upon definition of entrepreneurship. Entrepreneurs, perhaps the most recognisable face of entrepreneurship, have proved to be a popular topic of study, but they also appear to be difficult to characterise, leading Bannock (2004: 89) to conclude that entrepreneurs, much like elephants, are easier to recognise than to define. Say (1803) refers to entrepreneurs as the individuals who consciously move economic resources from an area of lower productivity into an area of higher productivity and greater yield. Over 200 years later, making resources more productive still chimes with a budding interest in creating and enhancing value for individuals and for society at large. Entrepreneurship is often associated with new ventures—the starting and running of new businesses. Westhead and Wright (2013: 1) suggest that entrepreneurs can be *'vital agents of innovative change whose actions lead to the creation of new firms. They can also transform existing firms to exploit economic and socially beneficial opportunities'*.

Entrepreneurship has been associated with the creation of something new or different, including new enterprise (Lumpkin & Dess, 1996), new organisations (Low & Macmillan, 1988), as well as new ventures, new markets, and new opportunities (Read et al., 2017), or a new business, where one did not exist before (Aulet, 2013: 6). Bygrave (2010: 3) defines an entrepreneur as *'someone who perceived an opportunity and creates an organisation to pursue it'*, while Shane and Venkataraman identify entrepreneurship as *'the scholarly examination of how, by whom, and with what effects opportunities to create future goods and services are discovered, evaluated, and exploited'* (2000: 218).

Entrepreneurs are often associated with promoting and creating new economic development and social well-being. However, whilst entrepreneurs are linked to 'generating' new sources of competitive advantage, their actions can also play a part in 'destroying' or replacing older firms, traditions, occupations and jobs, as implied by Joseph Schumpeter's (1934) ideas about the entrepreneur as a destabilising force. Indeed, Davidsson (2004) positions entrepreneurship as 'new entry' through the launching of product, service or business model innovation, as well as 'imitative entry', where a new competitor appears on the scene, giving buyers expanded choice opportunities, and thus threatening established firms. Entrepreneurs can thereby have a wider impact on surrounding systems and environments as they seek to create and enhance value:

> *Entrepreneurship can disrupt most industrial sectors, forcing significant changes in product and service offerings, new logistics processes, and new business models* (GEM, 2018: 16).

Drucker (1986) positions the entrepreneur as a change agent—someone who is always searching for change, responding to it and exploiting it as an opportunity. Entrepreneurship thus combines both the individual and the societal and organisational context within which they are operating. Stevenson offers a neat description capturing the core essence, which has become known as the Harvard Business School definition: *'Entrepreneurship is the pursuit of opportunity beyond the resources you currently control'* (see, for example, Stevenson, 1983; Stevenson & Gumpert, 1985; Stevenson & Jarillo-Mossi, 1990).

Stokes et al. (2010) propose a wider perspective encompassing three dimensions of entrepreneurship focused on:

- The outcomes of entrepreneurship
- The processes taken by entrepreneurs
- The behaviours required by entrepreneurs

Entrepreneurship can therefore be perceived as a synthesis of the three dimensions—for example, by observing the behaviours undertaken within and alongside the processes of discovery, development, creation and exploitation related to new ventures, with a focus on value and outcomes.

Entrepreneurship is thus concerned with emergent phenomena (Stokes et al., 2010: 34), as responding to opportunities is translated into value realisation. Hisrich and Peters perhaps best capture the inherent complexity in terms that will chime with the experiences of many project managers:

Entrepreneurship is the process of creating something new with value by devoting the necessary time and effort, assuming the accompanying financial, psychic, and social risks, and receiving the resulting rewards of monetary and personal satisfaction and independence (Hisrich & Peters, 2002: 8).

How Project Management Lost Its Way

In the wake of the Second World War, project management was entrusted with a significant range of intricate and demanding undertakings, often requiring the integration of complex components, sub-systems, systems, projects, programmes and specialisms (Dalcher, 2015: 1). Many of the new initiatives were ambitious, unprecedented, and extremely innovative, requiring an entrepreneurial mindset and a systemic approach to match the rising ambition and complexity levels.

Klein and Meckling (1958: 352) note an increasingly significant focus on efficiency inherent within operations management thinking. The allure of greater efficiency, they contend, can also be stretched beyond existing operations to guide future development efforts. Invoking two illustrative characters, the optimiser and the sceptic (introduced as 'Mr Optimiser' and 'Mr Skeptic' in the original), they further highlight the growing gulf between the different positions. Both characters are given a sum of money and a fixed time to develop a desired military solution (p. 355).

The optimiser sets off by endeavouring to exhaustively and systematically analyse and compare all the different alternative final systems. Meticulous estimates and plans are drawn to determine optimal timing for the release and consider the integration of sub-systems and components. Careful matching and precise estimates allow the optimiser to design the most efficient end product. Once all the decisions have been made, the optimiser is able to re-focus on the optimal allocation of resources, ensuring optimal apportionment against a fixed plan. The wish to control costs will often eliminate the possibility of parallel experimentation and duplicate components resulting in linear, planned progression (pp. 355–356).

The sceptic, on the other hand, prefers to delay commitment to a particular solution, concentrating instead on developing a strategy that is consistent with a wide range of potential final systems, recognising that full detail of an operational environment 10 years in the future enables one to eschew the need for binding detailed estimates.

The immediate concern is with getting some development going (p. 356) as a way of buying information about the emerging needs and the context. Performance factors can be given as a wide range of potential characteristics, which will be gradually refined throughout the process. This means that specific commitment is deferred until more information is available following further experimentation, testing, mock-ups and prototyping. The resulting development effort is kept flexible (p. 357), enabling informed decisions to emerge from the iterations and the ensuing learning. Resources are committed by stage, so that the range of alternative options is progressively narrowed as development proceeds on the basis of the information acquired in practice.

Klein and Meckling assert that potential users are likely to prefer, and actually choose the product of the sceptic (p. 358). They reason that the general method for development assumed by the sceptic is more efficient. The authors caution that optimising estimates are unlikely to remain relevant over the course of development, suggesting that the optimised cost estimates would often require revision by a factor of 2 or 3 (p. 358). Evidence from a number of military fighter aircraft cases is duly provided to support the assertion.

Premature optimisation as advocated by the optimiser has two key disadvantages: It prevents designers and planners from finding out more about the nature of the alternatives, whilst also making it difficult to incorporate new information into existing initiatives. Instead, *"final" commitments do not have to be made on the basis of low confidence estimates'* (p. 361), allowing for greater flexibility, exploration and learning.

Other disciplines appear to have engendered similar thinking: Koen (1985) sounds a note of caution about attempting to optimise solutions from an engineering perspective, especially given that engineers do not model reality, but rather a version of society's perception of reality (p. 12), and that different positions would emphasise different solutions from the point of view of a specific engineer (p. 11). Optimum is thus based on a subjective notion of best, at a given point in time, from a given perspective of a particular engineer and their specific interpretation. Hirschman (1967) advocates for an adaptive form of model for development that supports voyages of discovery (p. 78), through multiple and parallel approaches to collecting sufficient information, and experimental prototypes before committing to any particular course of action (p. 82).

More broadly, pre-eminent management thinker Peter Drucker recognises that entrepreneurship must be consciously striven for, requiring a constant effort (2001: 103). Indeed, he maintains that entrepreneurship must be treated as a duty and organisations must therefore become disciplined about entrepreneurship by working at it and by continually practicing it. Nonetheless, finding a room for entrepreneurship alongside other modes of operation can be the real challenge:

> It is not size that is an impediment to entrepreneurship and innovation; it is the existing operation itself, and especially the existing **successful** operation (p. 103).

Drucker reasons that the new, the entrepreneurial, has to be organised separately from the old and existing (p. 104), warning that existing units always fail as carriers of entrepreneurial projects. The existing is chiefly concerned with efficiency, with little appetite for experimentation, and it is therefore likely to postpone or defer action on anything new, innovative or entrepreneurial:

> No matter what has been tried—and we have now been trying every conceivable mechanism for thirty or forty years—existing units have been found to be capable mainly of extending, modifying and adapting what already is in existence. The new belongs elsewhere (p. 104).

Wherever we look for answers beyond the realm of regular operations and the optimisation that comes with efficient familiarity, we need new modes of inventing, creating and resolving. Drucker makes a case for a special locus for the new venture, whilst advocating nurturing and support to enable initiatives to grow and develop:

> The best, and perhaps the only, way to avoid killing off the new by sheer neglect is to set up the innovative project from the start as a separate business (p. 105).

Whilst optimisers can exist within regular business, creating new opportunities through experimentation and exploration requires nurturing and support and the application of an entrepreneurial approach to projects, opportunities, uncertainty and achievement that emphasises the new and innovative exploratory thinking identified by Klein and Meckling.

Reflecting on the Loss of Direction

Klein and Meckling's paper was published over 60 years ago, and it has since been identified as a classic and recognised as making an important contribution to the discipline of project management (Brady et al., 2012; Davies et al., 2018). Since its publication, according to a Google® Scholar search, the paper has been cited by around 150 other articles and papers. The citations represent a range of disciplines and interests, encompassing economics, innovation, operations research, project management, development, management theory, decision theory, decision-making, uncertainty and complexity, quality management, procurement, contracting, defence studies, public administration, and design theory. More crucially, the citations appear to be spread over the entire 60-year span, perhaps indicating the continued relevance of the topic.

The number of citations is relatively modest. However, the journals in which these articles appear include many well-established and esteemed publications, such as *Administrative Science Quarterly, The Journal of Business, Management Science, IEEE Transactions on Engineering Management, IEEE Transactions on Systems Science and Cybernetics, California Management Review, Public Administration Review, Research Policy, Communications of the ACM, Behavioural Science, World Politics, The Eastern Economic Journal* and *The Annals of the American Academy of Political and Social Science*, representing the wider relevance of the topic. Given the breadth of interests, both in terms of citing disciplines and the range of publications, it is surprising that the total count of citations is not higher. It appears that while striking a chord, the paper remains in the margins of multiple interacting concerns.

In many ways, Klein and Meckling's paper is central to the theme and issue of cost overruns and more widely to project cost estimation, project procurement and project failure. Shaping projects and programmes through early decisions makes a major difference to how initiatives are organised and how they are positioned for success. This is an area that continues to be of major interest to the project management community. Nonetheless, it is notable that the original paper was situated as an operations research contribution, where the chief interest often revolves around efficiency of operation, rather than focusing on the setting of project work and the impact that such early decisions can have on the unfolding dynamics, as well as the ultimate success of projects and the benefits that accrue over time. The project management community may have remained oblivious to the paper due to the explicit link to operations management and the fact that the paper has not been immediately visible or signposted from within the main sources revered by the community.

And yet, more recent work within project management continues to support similar conclusions: Shenhar and Dvir (2007) note that project management is based on a simplistic and largely rational model, decoupled from the external environment and the business need and ignorant of the emergent nature of projects and the need to shape the project.

> Projects exhibit high failure rates due to senior managers and project teams underestimating, up front, the extent of uncertainty and complexity involved in their projects and failing to adapt their management style to the situation (Brady et al., 2012: 719).

Willman (2014) notes that the 19th and early 20th centuries were characterised by two features relevant to the design of business: the first was the belief in technological progress, and the second was an inclination towards optimisation (pp. 39–40). The assumption is that thinking systematically and rationally about a business problem could improve the chosen dependent variable—be it efficiency, productivity, profit etc. (p. 40). This is related to the application of scientific and engineering principles to the management of firms, often in the guise of scientific management or as part of a search for improvement in efficiency and productivity (Dalcher, 2017b). Willman (2014: 41) cautions that the tendency towards optimisation carries several common characteristics:

- Such endeavours are obsessed with efficiency as an outcome variable.
- They believe in general rather than specific solutions, and hence search for universal applicability and the promotion of one best way of doing things.
- They select simplifying points or principles to simplify and generalise their means and methods.
- Since it is often carried out by engineers, they see the world in antiquated engineering terms, thus ignoring human agency.

Willman summarises the approach as devising the one best way to complete a task, and then ensuring that the workers closely follow the rules and prescriptions (Ibid.). Consequentially, value creation is not considered, as divergent objectives are frowned upon and collectives are assumed to aggregate human interests, as the resolution efforts overly focus on managerial measures for monitoring and incentives (p. 46). The obsession with a single factor, such as efficiency, can often obscure other relevant perspectives and stifle further development (Dalcher, 2017b: 8). From a project management viewpoint, the resulting standardisation is overly simplistic and carries the potential to trivialise the task at hand as well as the means needed to achieve it, thereby delivering solutions that consistently fail to address the full complexity of the problems and the interests of participants.

In their landmark study, Lenfle and Loch (2010: 32) take issue with the ideology of standardised project management *'which takes the project mission and goals as given and adopted a phased 'stage-gate' approach as the professional standard'*. They lament the adoption of a control-based perspective with phased stage-gates over novelty and flexibility. They note that the characterisation of project management represents a certain irony, as the Manhattan Project and the first ballistic missile projects, which are said to be the origin of contemporary project management, fundamentally violated the phased life cycle approach and the emphasis on control. Early projects, they contend, *'applied a combination of trial-and-error and parallel trials in order to 'push the envelope' and achieve outcomes considered as impossible at the outset'* (p. 32).

The need to operate in uncertain and unpredictable environments requires gradual sense making of the environment as planners and designers endeavor to utilise emerging insights and new knowledge.

> *The discipline seems to have lost its roots of enabling 'push the envelope' initiatives, de facto focusing on controllable run-of-the-mill projects instead. We argue that this matters a great deal: it has prevented the project management discipline from taking center stage in the increasingly important efforts of organizations to carry out strategic change and innovation. PM has an opportunity [to] regain the central place it should never have lost in the management of strategic initiatives, innovation, and change, but this will require adding more flexible methods to the available toolkit* (p. 33).

Leading-edge projects still require innovative solutions and development approaches. While parallelism, concurrency, iteration and experimentation may be making a comeback in other domains, the fixation with instrumental rationality and control has robbed project management of its ability to fully engage with pathbreaking innovation. Indeed, if project management continues to ignore its creative roots, other disciplines are likely to step up and offer similar concepts packaged under different guises, such as systems engineering, business analysis or enterprise systems (Dalcher, 2015; 2017a), leaving project management to grapple with simpler, less demanding and more trivial undertakings.

Lenfle and Loch identify two critical limitations resulting from the loss of roots:

- The focus on project management as an execution discipline
- The assumption that uncertainty control and elimination are feasible (p. 48)

In doing so, the discipline fails to address the need to embrace uncertainty as a source of innovation, choosing instead to seek the elimination of uncertainty, thereby limiting the potential for flexibility, innovation and creativity. More critically, it misses out on the creative essence of projects. Such positioning removes the discipline from key core areas of management, including strategy making and innovation (p. 48), and thus excludes the possibility for strategic flexibility, resilience and diversity (Dalcher, 2018). It also trivialises the discipline and dilutes the power of project management, thereby opening the door to other approaches and perspectives that are able to bridge the gap and incorporate innovation and strategic thinking with flexible deployment (as highlighted in the introductory part to Chapter 5).

The self-restriction may have originated from a set of historical accidents (Lenfle & Loch, 2010), but their combined impact continues to bound and limit the discipline and its ability to manage meaningful change. To address the gap, Lenfle and Loch challenge the community to reposition projects as a strategy-making tool, thereby broadening the traditional mission of projects, as well as to reinvigorate and expand the process to accommodate novel and innovative projects replete with uncertainty. Focusing on uncertainty would enable new managerial approaches and governance structures that would once again support parallel thinking, experimentation and information finding and enable project management to resume a position as a creative and responsive discipline.

And How We Can Find It Again—Repositioning Projects Alongside Entrepreneurship

Entrenching entrepreneurship culture and behaviours are essential to regaining the competence to embrace uncertain opportunities. Peter Drucker's most important caveat to those seeking to embed entrepreneurship in business is to not mix managerial and entrepreneurial concerns (2001: 106). Entrepreneurship requires its own climate and approach, which diverges from optimising concerns. To succeed and prosper in times of rapid change, there is a need to adopt entrepreneurial thinking alongside embedding policies that create the desire to innovate and the habits of entrepreneurship and innovation (p. 107), so that enterprising thinking, practices and conventions can flourish.

Project management is still searching for that severed connection with innovation and creativity. The close bond between innovation and project management, evident in the early studies, has weakened as the two disciplines drifted apart, following *'largely distinct and diverging intellectual and practical trajectories, while addressing similar questions'* (Davies et al., 2018: 969).

Earlier work identified within the discipline calls attention to the need to reposition and focus on innovative projects as well as uncertainty and its wider role. A rather neglected avenue with enormous untapped potential is thus offered by looking at the discipline of entrepreneurship. The following section, 'Effectual Project Management: Thinking Like an Expert Entrepreneur', is written by Laura Mathiaszyk, Christine Volkmann and Stuart Read. The contribution builds upon the second edition of the book *Effectual Entrepreneurship* by Stuart Read, Saras Sarasvathy, Nick Dew and Robert Wiltbank (2016), published by Routledge. The ideas explored by the authors are underpinned by the notion of effectuation, offering specific insights dedicated to the context of project management.

Effectuation is associated with the pioneering work of Saras Sarasawathy (2001) and colleagues who advocate a fundamental distinction between causation approaches to opportunity identification and exploitation on one hand, and effectuation on the other. Causation implies a search and discovery of opportunities—akin to achieving a specific pre-determined external goal though exploitation of a specific set of given means. This implies the identification and detailed analysis of the most promising opportunity, perhaps in keeping with the style of Klein and Meckling's optimiser.

Effectuation recognises that opportunities are created. New partnerships bring new funds and new directions. Entrepreneurs can thus utilise evolving means to derive and attain new and emergent goals. Much in common with Klein and Meckling's sceptic (or Skeptic) model, the approach is better suited to complex decisions in uncertain contexts wherein solutions and options adapt and evolve over time through learning and interaction with the domain. Effectuation recognises a plurality of possible new ends, given a set of available means.

Sarasvathy and Venkataraman (2011: 113) contend that there exists an 'entrepreneurial method', analogous to the scientific method, offering a valid, yet alternative approach to interpreting, and even creating, the world that we encounter. The implication is that the entrepreneurial approach provides an alternative to the scientific approach, which aims to unleash human potential rather than harness it, and to engender new ends as well as to achieve old ones (p. 115). The notion chimes with the development of design principles emphasising contingency, transformation and action, with a dominant logic which replaces experimentation with effectuation (Ibid.).

Reformulating entrepreneurship as a method of human action offers a powerful alternative way of tackling large problems by keeping goals flexible and utilising means-based action and available resources. Effectuation thus affords a process through which opportunities can be created and enacted upon by identifying and actioning the next best step. Sarasvathy (2012) boldly asserts that the entrepreneur plays a key part in worldmaking, intimating that making new worlds should be no less mystifying than finding out about existing ones:

> One of the main insights we have gained over the last decade of research into effectuation can simply be put as follows: Analogous to the scientific method, there exists an entrepreneurial method. Moreover, the scale of possibilities the entrepreneurial method opens up for us is more potent than that offered by the scientific method. . . . Simply put, what the scientific method has afforded us in terms of understanding the actual world we live in, the entrepreneurial method enables us in terms of making new ones (Sarasvathy, 2012: 2).

Effectuation can be viewed as a logic of thinking used by expert entrepreneurs to create successful ventures and reinvigorate the underpinning approach needed for thriving in uncertain contexts. The comprehensive work of Read and his colleagues makes entrepreneurship and effectuation accessible, whilst offering essential insights into the nature of the enterprise and the dynamics required for success in uncertain and complex settings. Following through the set of pragmatic principles and perspectives offers an informed glimpse into the characteristics of the entrepreneurial mindset and the way expert entrepreneurs operate, especially when the creation of new opportunities is being pursued.

Entrepreneurs expand the problem space and increase returns as they work through emerging enterprise opportunities and the resources currently available. Read and his colleagues make important contributions to our understanding of risk, change and entrepreneurship as an unfolding route to development and growth. Their work implies situational sensitivity to context, including the stage of the project and the challenges and opportunities that emerge. It also enables us to reconsider the balance between planning-based and flexible or responsive modes of operation and develop a contingent approach that encourages pragmatic sensibility in matching and combining approaches, resources and partnerships.

Whilst entrepreneurship is a transformative activity, it is widely recognised that the vast majority of ventures end up doing something different to the notion they started up with. As projects increasingly seek to address opportunity and realise value under conditions of uncertainty, the writing of Read and his associates engenders a new path and process for engaging with entrepreneurship and renewing the long-lost connection between projects and meaningful achievement. Effectuation offers a way of revisiting the lost roots of projects and benefitting from established ideas that have been curated and nourished within a neighbouring discipline.

Predefined optimised routes offer only limited value and possibility in particularly constrained and well understood contexts. In less predictable settings, entrepreneurial approaches and effectuation offer an enticing prospect, as mistakes and missteps open the potential for new opportunities and entrepreneurs get to shape, direct and influence the future. Entrepreneurs are increasingly called upon to link and connect ideas, concepts and contacts, creating the potential for new arrangements of people, possibilities and partnerships. This is likely to intensify given that in the aftermath of economic and social crises, entrepreneurial activity triggers, drives and sustains economic recovery.

Challenging times call for a good dose of positive scepticism in order to defy tradition and overcome convention. As we increasingly look to create beneficial opportunities, operate in the face of uncertainty and engage with successful practice in a pragmatic and ambidextrous fashion, we must reinvigorate and cherish our ability to create new paths, learn and improve, and build on new insights and knowledge. Innovation and entrepreneurial activity may well hold the key to repositioning our projects as instruments for renewal, particularly in uncertain and unstructured societal contexts, as we continually engage with new ventures, markets, contexts, settings and opportunities.

References

Aulet, B. (2013). *Disciplined Entrepreneurship: 24 Steps to a Successful Startup*. Hoboken, NJ: John Wiley & Sons.

Bannock, G. (2004). *The Economics and Management of Small Business: An International Perspective*. London, UK: Routledge.

Brady, T., Davies, A., and Nightingale, P. (2012). Dealing with uncertainty in complex projects: Revisiting Klein and Meckling. *International Journal of Managing Projects in Business, 5*(4), 718–736.

Bygrave, W. D. (2010). The entrepreneurial process. In: W. D. Bygrave and A. Zacharakis (Eds.). *The Portable MBA in Entrepreneurship* (4th Ed.). Hoboken, NJ: John Wiley & Sons.

Dalcher, D. (2015). Complexity, projects and systems: Just going around in circles? *PM World Journal*, *4*(12), December, 1–6.

Dalcher, D. (2017a). Commercial management and projects, a long overdue match. *PM World Journal*, *6*(10), October, 1–6.

Dalcher, D. (2017b). What has Taylor ever done for us? *PM World Journal*, *6*(4), 1–11.

Dalcher, D. (2018). Strategy as learning to discover the way forward. *PM World Journal*, *7*(2), February, 1–12.

Davidsson, P. (2004). *Researching Entrepreneurship*. New York, NY: Springer.

Davies, A., Manning, S., and Söderlund, J. (2018). When neighboring disciplines fail to learn from each other: The case of innovation and project management research. *Research Policy*, *47*(5), 965–979.

Drucker, P. F. (1986). *Innovation and Entrepreneurship*. London, UK: Routledge.

Drucker, P. F. (2001). *The Essential Drucker*. Oxford, UK: Butterworth-Heinemann.

GEM (2018). *Global Entrepreneurship Monitor 2017–18*. London, UK: Global Entrepreneurship Research Association.

Hirschman, A. O. (1967). *Development Projects Observed*. Washington, DC: The Brookings Institution.

Hisrisch, R. D., and Peters, M. P. (2002). *Entrepreneurship. Starting, Developing and Managing a New Enterprise*. Homewood, IL: Irwin.

Klein, B., and Meckling, W. (1958). Application of operations research to development decisions. *Operations Research*, *6*(3), 352–363.

Koen, B. V. (1985). *Definition of the Engineering Method*. Washington, DC: ASEE Publications.

Lenfle, S., and Loch, C. (2010). Lost roots: How project management came to emphasize control over flexibility and novelty. *California Management Review*, *53*(1), 32–55.

Low, M. B., and MacMillan, I. C. (1988). Entrepreneurship: Past research and future challenges. *Journal of Management*, *14*, 139–161.

Lumpkin, G. T., and Dess, G. G. (1996). Clarifying the entrepreneurial orientation construct and linking it to performance. *Academy of Management Review*, *21*(1), 135–172.

Read, S., Sarasvathy, S., Dew, N., and Wiltbank, R. (2017). *Effectual Entrepreneurship*. London, UK: Routledge.

Sarasvathy, S. (2012). Worldmaking. In: A. C. Corbett and J. A. Katz (Eds.). *Entrepreneurial Action. Advances in Entrepreneurship, Firm Emergence and Growth* (Vol. 14), 1–24. Bingley, UK: Emerald Group Publishing,

Sarasvathy, S. D. (2001). Causation and effectuation: Toward a theoretical shift from economic inevitability to entrepreneurial contingency. *Academy of Management Review*, *26*(2), 243–263.

Sarasvathy, S. D., and Venkataraman, S. (2011). Entrepreneurship as method: Open questions for an entrepreneurial future. *Entrepreneurship Theory and Practice*, *35*(1), 113–135.

Say, J. B. (1803). *Traité d'économie politique: Ou simple exposition de la manière dont se forment, se distribuent et se consomment les richesses* (Vol. 9). Paris, FR: Guillaumin.

Schumpeter, J. A. (1934). *Theory of Economic Development*. Cambridge, MA: Harvard University Press.

Shane, S., and Venkataraman, S. (2000). The promise of entrepreneurship as a field of research. *Academy of Management Review*, *25*(1), 217–226.

Shenhar, A. J., and Dvir, D. (2007). *Reinventing Project Management: The Diamond Approach to Successful Growth and Innovation*. Boston, MA: Harvard Business Review Press.

Stevenson, H. H. (1983). *A Perspective on Entrepreneurship* (Vol. 13). Cambridge, MA: Harvard Business School.

Stevenson, H. H., and Gumpert, D. E. (1985). The heart of entrepreneurship. *Harvard Business Review, 85*(2), 85–94.

Stevenson, H., and Jarillo-Mossi, J. (1990). Preserving entrepreneurship as companies grow. In: R. Kuhn (Ed.). *Creativity and Strategy in Mid-Sized Firms.* Englewood Cliffs, NJ: Prentice Hall.

Stokes, D., and Mador, M. E. H. (2010). *Entrepreneurship.* London, UK: Cengage Learning EMEA.

Stokes, D., Wilson, N., and Wilson, N. (2017). *Small Business Management and Entrepreneurship* (7th Ed.). London, UK: Cengage Learning EMEA.

Westhead, P., and Wright, M. (2013). *Entrepreneurship: A Very Short Introduction.* Oxford, UK: Oxford University Press.

Willman, P. (2014). *Understanding Management: The Social Science Foundations.* Oxford, UK: Oxford University Press.

Effectual Project Management: Thinking Like an Expert Entrepreneur

Laura Mathiaszyk, Christine Volkmann and Stuart Read

The Most Complex of Them All?

Quick—think of a complicated project. Did implementing an ERP system in a large organisation come to mind? Maybe developing a next-generation high-technology product? How about starting a new venture? The new venture might not have been your first intuition. But take a step back and consider it. It represents the ultimate complicated project—all the complicated projects rolled up into one mega-complicated project. That new venture needs a new product or service. It needs an ERP system. It needs a strategy and a customer generation/retention process. It needs marketing and finance and human resources . . . and the list continues. Much work has sought to bring ideas and processes from project management to entrepreneurs, but surprisingly little has gone in the other direction.

In this section, we seek to expose a few things entrepreneurs, in many ways super-project managers, have learned from starting ventures, and translate them back into ideas for managing projects in larger organisations. As we do, it is important to appreciate one additional complexity borne by the entrepreneur: Aside from the broad aspiration of building a venture, the goals of the project (the venture) are uncertain at the start and can be subject to constant revision as the project unfolds. As such, the tools and approaches learned by expert entrepreneurs may be extremely valuable to project managers facing similar levels of uncertainty.

Corporate Projects and Entrepreneurial Projects

Useful tools help capture relevant information, enable managers to strategise and facilitate a plan that fits project target, context and surrounding conditions. Thereby, tools differ in various aspects. Projects that have a fixed goal or objective use tools to sequence the steps and follow the most efficient linear or causal logic (please see Figure 7.1: Traditional Waterfall). In situations of greater ambiguity, breaking a big project down into smaller 'sprints' enables manageable work increments and allows for project objectives to evolve after the project has begun by implementing agile or dynamic cycles (please see Figure 7.1: Agile or Scrum). But entrepreneurs face a far more open-ended problem. In addition to managing a different project

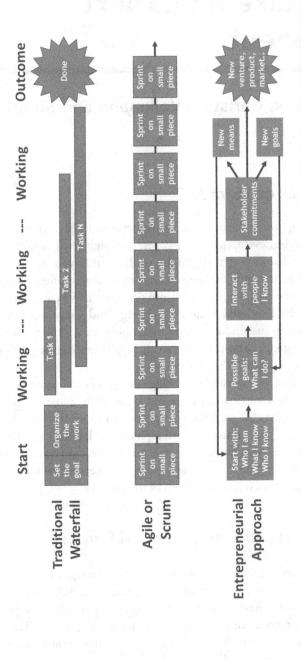

Figure 7.1 Contrast of Traditional Waterfall, Agile and Entrepreneurial Project Approaches

for each function in the organisation, it is unclear at the outset what the startup will end up doing. Certainly, the objective is to create a viable venture, but that is a very broad goal. More than 90 percent of new ventures end up doing something different than the idea they started with (Reynolds, Carter, Gartner, & Greene, 2004), so the notion that entrepreneurs write a business plan and execute it in a systematic and organised fashion is naïve. Instead, the entrepreneurial approach to a project starts with the resources readily available at hand, explicitly incorporates feedback loops into the process, and functions atop elements within the control of the entrepreneur (Sarasvathy & Dew, 2005). A stylised representation of the entrepreneurial approach is contrasted with the traditional and agile approaches to project management in the diagrams in Figure 7.1.

What Expert Entrepreneurs Learn

Within the entrepreneurship literature, scholars have been fascinated to understand how experts in the domain think. Effectuation (Sarasvathy, 2001; Read et al., 2016) offers a clear and well-researched foundation of entrepreneurial expertise that we develop and apply to project management. Effectuation was induced from a cognitive science study of 27 entrepreneur founders (started multiple ventures, taken at least one to $250M in sales, spent more than 15 years in the domain). The central finding in effectuation is that expert entrepreneurs focus on elements within their control 'to bring about effect'—i.e., shape, develop, initiate, and create beneficial outcomes. Effectuation contrasts with causal or linear processes that build on prediction, goal setting and forecasting. The general explanation for why expert entrepreneurs learn effectual heuristics is connected with their domain. New venture creation is an inherently uncertain activity, where (market) analyses are expensive and insufficient because of high complexity and unknown dynamics. In such a domain, predictions offer the entrepreneur limited meaningful input, so the entrepreneur adopts alternative heuristics. The entrepreneurial approach diagrammed in Figure 7.1 assumes the environment is constructible through the actions of the entrepreneur and their committed stakeholders and enables project goals to emerge as negotiated residuals of stakeholder commitments.

While it was developed in entrepreneurship, effectuation offers a more general behavioural scientific answer to the question of how individuals handle complexity and uncertainty. Effectuation has consequently attracted significant attention in corporate strategy (Faschingbauer, 2010; Ambrosch, 2010; Blekman, 2011). Davidsson (2005) was the first to suggest the relevance of effectuation to projects characterised by uncertainty, but until now little work has picked up and developed his observation.

Effectuation Principles

Within the process diagrammed in Figure 7.1, there are a series of specific heuristics expert entrepreneurs employ which help them take action in uncertain situations. In Table 7.1, we outline those heuristics and contrast each with a causal (predictive) alternative. The fundamental difference between effectual and causal heuristics is that causal heuristics assume the ability of the entrepreneur to apply prediction to goal setting and then take appropriate actions to achieve those goals. In contrast, each effectual heuristic enables the entrepreneur to act in uncertainty using a foundation of control instead of prediction.

Table 7.1 Effectuation and Causation Principles

Issue	Causation (Prediction-Based Heuristics)	Effectuation (Control-Based Heuristics)
Starting point	Goals: Goals determine the actions and thus the resources required for a project.	Means: Readily available means, resources and contacts define the starting point for a project.
Risk perception	Expected returns: Project should maximise return on invest/outcome.	Affordable loss: Project should not risk more resources than are affordable to lose.
Attitude toward outsiders	Competition: Protection of ideas is important, as a project is positioned in a competitive environment.	Partnership: Partnerships emerge as stakeholders and commit resources to the common project while influencing its development; collaborate.
Attitude toward surprise	Avoidance: Planning and focus on goals help to avoid surprises.	Leverage: Surprises provide the foundation for new opportunities.
View of the future	Forecast: Future environment is externally given, forecast provides insight.	Create: Prediction is not possible, since future environment depends on own actions.

Starting with their own readily available means of what they know, who they know and what they have, entrepreneurs begin taking action immediately without waiting for others to provide resources. Considering risk according to what they are willing to lose means the worst case is always within the control of the entrepreneur. Building goals together with self-selected stakeholders means entrepreneurs share the risk, gain access to partners' resources and prioritise goals through commitments—goals more likely to be valuable as they are tested with each new partner. Finally, treating unexpected events as the source of new opportunities means entrepreneurs don't fail when things don't go as expected, but rather take the opportunity to learn, iterate, and create something perhaps even more valuable moving ahead.

Effectual Decision-Making in Project Management

Effectuation is largely unknown in the project management world. But because effectuation is derived from research into entrepreneurial cognition, managers facing situations of uncertainty and complexity can benefit from what expert entrepreneurs have learned. Today's world changes fast. Volatile markets, intense competition, crises and growing complexity combine to present managers with a relentless demand for innovative technologies, new knowledge and strategy. Once these demands turn into projects, managers face complex performance requirements, regulations, vertical organisation layers, shifting customer demand and widespread coordination with external stakeholders (Morieux, 2011). Uncertainty is the norm (McKelvie, Haynie & Gustavsson, 2011) and managers have to make thoughtful project decisions without adequate predictive information (Busenitz & Barney, 2007).

As applied to project management, we expect that effectuation operates the same way expert entrepreneurs use it in starting new ventures. The starting point is the accessible means. The project team following effectual decision-making strategy works with resources at their disposal, including skills, competencies, contacts and social networks. Team members self-select into the project. Each new member brings new means, ideas and psychological ownership that enable the co-creation processes of the stakeholders to expand and advance the project (Read et al., 2009). The project output, therefore, arises from the interaction between the individuals involved in the project (Sarasvathy, 2001).

The commitments of project team members follow the affordable loss principle—how much they are willing to put at risk as part of engaging in a particular project. As a result, there is always a preference for alternatives that face small potential failure if they are unsuccessful and the potential to learn from those failures and iterate. Davidsson (2005) describes it as follows: *'It is more important to limit the damage if unsuccessful than to get the highest possible return if successful'* (p. 12).

The effectual approach to project management builds on partnerships and asks: *'With whom do I have to ally, in order to be able to take the [. . . project] one step further?'* (p. 12). To answer this question, effectual project management involves social networking, forming partnerships, and obtaining commitments from potential customers or suppliers. At the end of the effectual process, the project team may have created a 'crazy quilt', as Sarasvathy (2001) describes it, composed of diverse fabric swatches provided by each of the various partners. Commitments advance the cycle of resource transformation and converge the cycle toward constraints on project outcomes, as diagrammed in Figure 7.1. Throughout the process, effectual strategy is 'sensitive to what comes up along the road and prepare[s] to turn these contingencies into business strengths' (Davidsson, 2005: 12). Sarasvathy (2008) describes this form of leveraging contingencies with the proverbial phrase, *'When life gives you lemons, make lemonade'* (Ucbasaran, 2008: 226).

In the same way effectuation contrasts with causation when understanding the logics of expert entrepreneurs, an effectual approach to project management contrasts with a goal-oriented project management approach such as the waterfall.

Empirical Study of Effectuation in Project Management

In order to build a more complete understanding of the differences associated with an entrepreneurial project management approach compared with a goal-oriented waterfall approach, we designed and conducted an empirical study. The study examines managers' heuristics when facing project complexity and analyses success outcomes. Often discussed in the project management literature, complexity is integrally connected with the concept of uncertainty, the setting where effectuation originated (Sarasvathy, 2008). While uncertainty provides a characteristic of the external environment, complexity describes internal features of the project and how organisation is perceived by individuals involved (Müller, Geraldi & Turner, 2012). As such, the study is driven by two questions:

- Do project managers apply effectual or causal decision-making heuristics more intensely when they perceive their project environment as complex?
- What effects does the choice of effectual or causal decision-making have on project success?

We include both hard (financial and market) and soft (innovativeness and learning) success measures, as these two outcome categories may not be correlated. A project may achieve some level of near-term financial success but fail to build team knowledge or innovation which provides more sustainable growth for the organisation. Alternatively, a project might deliver novelty but fail to achieve the financial results necessary to sustain the organisation. Projects and project management must seek to address both.

Measures

Effectual and Causal Decision-Making

We measure strategy using the effectuation/causation scale originally developed by Brettel et al. (2012). Because the authors analysed strategy behaviour in R&D projects, some questions were revised to fit a more general project context. The scale was characterised by forced-choice items, indicating the degree of difference between effectual and causal heuristic in project strategy (Bradley, Wiklund & Shepherd, 2010). For example, one item pair consists of: New project findings influenced the project target vs. New project findings did not influence the project target. We validated the 23-item scale and found strong reliability, as indicated by a Cronbach's Alpha of 0.74.

Complexity

We measured project complexity as it is perceived by managers in practice using an existing scale (Geraldi & Albrecht, 2007; Jaafari, 2003; Maylor et al., 2008; Shenhar & Dvir, 2007; and Williams, 2005).

Hard Project Success

We measured general project success using nine dimensions established in prior research (Müller & Turner, 2006). The construct was operationalised using a five-point Likert scale ranging from 'very low' to 'very high'. In order to establish the dependent variable of hard project success, we took the mean of all nine items into an unweighted additive score. Using a Cronbach's Alpha of 0.78, we documented a high degree of internal consistency.

Soft Project Success

Soft project success was measured using a scale validated by Brettel et al. (2012). The items asked if the project met expectations in terms of (1) the learning and expertise that could be leveraged in other projects, (2) the generation of new ideas as a starting point of potential future projects, and (3) the enhancement of competencies and capabilities. We integrated the three items with Cronbach's Alpha of 0.68.

Sample

We sampled 395 public companies in over 42 countries. The companies had a turnover of at least USD $50 million with more than 500 employees, are on average 45 years old, and belong to different sectors including manufacturing, trade, and service activities. The survey addressed business owners (first- and second-level management, 43.7% of sample) as well as middle

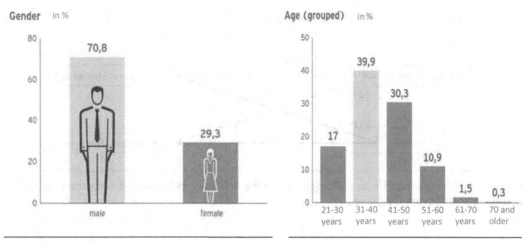

Figure 7.2   Gender of Sample

Figure 7.3   Age of Sample

management (56.3% of sample). Gender distribution was 70.8 percent male and 29.3 percent female (see Figure 7.2). Managers were on average 40 years old (see Figure 7.3), had 14 years of professional experience, and on average worked nine years in their present company.

Finding 1: Causal heuristics are positively associated with hard success outcomes, effectual are positively associated with soft success outcomes

Focusing on the main effect of relationships between decision-making heuristic and outcomes, we find causal decision-making strategy positively associated with hard success factors, while effectual decision-making is positively associated with soft success measures (see Figure 7.4). We interpret this result as a function of the differences in the processes underlying causal vs. effectual approaches. Causal strategy often starts with preset goals and runs along a tight project plan that—if nothing unexpected happens—leads to efficiently reaching that goal.

Effectual strategy, on the other hand, offers room for self-selected stakeholders to co-create different effects that in the end may lead to an innovative but unexpected outcome. Thus, while the effectual process is not as efficient at achieving one specific goal which results in a hard success outcome, it inherently grows breadth in experiences and competencies, as indicated by the soft success measures.

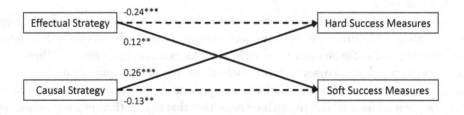

Figure 7.4   Main Effects of Effectuation/Causation and Hard/Soft Success Outcomes

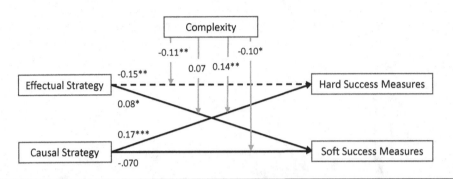

Figure 7.5   Moderating Effects of Complexity on the Relationship Between Effectuation/Causation and Hard/Soft Success Outcomes

Finding 2: Complexity weakens the relationships between effectuation and outcomes

The results of our moderated regression indicate that after accounting for the moderating impact of complexity, the main effects between effectuation and both hard and soft success outcomes weaken though remain significant (see Figure 7.5).

Finding 3: Complexity also weakens the connection between causal heuristics and soft outcomes

After including the moderating effect of complexity, the relationship between causal strategy and soft project success is not significant.

Finding 4: Managers rely on causal heuristics even as complexity grows

Overall, our findings indicate a managerial preference for causal strategy in complex situations. This result is surprising, as research has shown expert entrepreneurs prefer effectual decision-making in contexts of high uncertainty (Read et al., 2009). We infer that because companies encourage and train employees on causal tools and techniques (Frame, 2002), deeply embedding predictive heuristics (Staw & Epstein, 2000), managers continue to rely on causal heuristics even when complexity rises and effectuation may be more suitable.

Illustrating how this happens, managers in a traditional organisation get assigned a goal (e.g., from top management) and are tasked with reaching that goal in a preset time frame. Jeopardising the goal is out of a question. Managers then determine the steps to acquire resources, organise the workflow and assign tasks.

This causal approach is effective when clear objectives need to be reached in a fixed time frame. Starting with junior positions, project managers are taught methods that support the causal process, such as Sig Sigma, a set of techniques for process improvement. When they report results, they run failure analyses to further streamline the process and improve outcomes next time. Excellence initiatives honour solutions that optimise resources and reduce process cycle time. This inference is consistent with research on cognition that in situations of stress, when cognitive systems are taxed, people tend to apply well-known (decision-making) patterns.

Discussion

At first glance, our results might suggest a dichotomous choice in front of project managers. Adopt causal heuristics and achieve hard results. Or adopt effectual heuristics and achieve soft results. However, neither represents a sufficient solution, particularly as projects become more complex. The more detailed implication of our findings is that decision-making need not be dichotomous. Certain heuristics can be applied to certain situations. The practical implication of our results is an image of the ambidextrous project manager, selectively and situationally applying diverse sets of heuristics as a project progresses and different issues arise.

A Project Management Fairy Tale

Let us consider a hypothetical story of Sarah, a project manager at YumCo, a multinational firm in the fast-moving consumer products space. Sarah has been charged with bringing another innovative snack food to the market. Competition is strong, complexity is substantial, and expectations are high within her organisation. Seeking to deliver solid financial results and an innovative product while encouraging learning and collaboration in her team, Sarah intends to select and employ different heuristics, depending on the situation. As we narrate her story, we pay special attention to the underlying logic in her decisions.

Project Start (Effectual)

This is not the first time YumCo has created a new product. In fact, the organisation already offers successful product lines of energy bars, snack cookies and salty crackers. Sarah and her team worked on these and other prior YumCo product lines. To support these existing products, YumCo owns manufacturing plants and distribution warehouses in the many different countries in which it serves its distribution partners. Sarah's first step is to bring her team together to assess their means—the things they know, the assets available and the people they know. It is a long list, and certainly the team will not use every single resource. However, these resources are within the control of Sarah and her team. It is not necessary to commit large investments or find experts, as these resources are available and well understood. These will serve as the starting inputs for the project.

Transformations (Effectual)

Together with her team, Sarah begins to generate ideas: starting points; primitive product prototypes or descriptions that offer enough specificity to initiate conversations with possible partners. Because she encourages a diversity of ideas, suggestions range from a protein-fortified ice cream snack to breakfast muffins infused with caffeine for customers needing a little boost at the start of their work day. She is careful not to let any of these ideas go further than a simple description or drawing. These are only starting hypotheses which need to be tested, and it will be hard for her team to revise or reject them later if they invest too much time now.

Interactions (Effectual)

Almost immediately, Sarah sends her team out into the world. The hypotheses provide a starting point for conversations with distributors, retailers and end customers in every segment. To get those conversations going, Sarah points her team to the people they already know, either individually or through corporate relationships. The team is encouraged to let those conversations assume a different direction, as the person they are interacting with is willing to bring their own resources toward a new idea which is interesting to both her team and the partner.

Early Commitments (Scrum/Agile)

A big chain of supermarkets which features in-store cafés gets excited talking with one of the members of the team. The supermarket doesn't want another snack food on the shelf, but they do want innovative snacks to serve at their cafés. The idea of caffeine-infused snack cake treats is something their customers have been asking for. They offer space in 20 of their cafés and offer to pay the cost of manufacturing for a trial of caffeine-infused treats. Sarah shifts gears. The team moves into execution mode, focused on quick cycles necessary to bring a small selection of caffeine-infused treats as quickly as possible to 20 test cafés.

Dealing With the CFO (Causal, With an Effectual Option to Manage Downside)

As part of the experiment, Sarah has to execute an agreement between YumCo and the supermarket chain. The agreement goes to YumCo's CFO for financial review. While Sarah knows this experiment will likely be only the first of many before this project scales up a new product offering, she also knows the CFO deals in forecasts. So she completes two pieces of documentation regarding the experiment. The first is a projection of the possible size of the opportunity if the experiment is successful. And the second is a detailed expenditure plan for the experiment, detailing costs she will incur in the near term, regardless of whether the experiment in successful or not. She is also careful to ensure the budget for the whole project well exceeds the cost of this particular experiment, so her team will have room to learn and iterate if this experiment is not successful.

Experiment Failure (Effectual)

At the cafés, many customers purchased a cup of coffee and enthusiastically tried one of the experimental caffeine-infused snack cake treats. The comments were overwhelmingly positive, and initially trial units sold quickly. But repeat purchases were few. Customers discovered that consuming a caffeine-infused snack cake treat with a cup of coffee left them jittery, anxious, and unable to sleep in the evening. A month into the trial, the caffeine-infused snack cake treats sat largely overlooked on the shelves in the cafés. After the experiment concluded, members of the YumCo and supermarket teams conducted a debrief. One of the supermarket employees shared a note from a customer who was sorry to see the caffeine-infused snack cake treats go. The customer was an athlete and stopped at the café for water on his way home from the gym. The treats provided him with a little energy that let him keep working after having been physically exhausted by his exercise.

Pivot (Effectuation, Moving to Scrum/Agile)

Sarah and her team created a new prototype with healthier ingredients, a little protein and the same caffeine fortification that had been present in the snack cakes. They took it to gyms and started the conversations again. A national chain of gyms offered to pay in advance for a large order they would sell at their front desks to athletes on their way out of the gym. Sarah and her team shifted gears and initiated focused activity cycles to deliver this second experiment.

Rollout (Causal)

The initial order to the gym sold well. Based on the volume numbers from the initial order, the gym placed a second, larger order. Based on the success with one gym, YumCo began targeting other gyms for the new product. And based on all these data, Sarah and her team began to plan the sequence of most efficient steps to full rollout. The end of a workout would never be the same.

Implications for Practice

Though simplified, Sarah's story highlights the importance of having alternative heuristics to deal with different aspects of a project. For the uncertainty embedded in the creation processes, she focused on what was in her control (team knowledge, company means and external partnerships) and anticipated iterations as well as inexpensive failures. Not until she had a specific goal did Sarah shift into the traditional (causal) approach of project management, where she invested significant time and resources against a prediction.

To act according to project circumstances and context, managers need a variety of different heuristic tools. Once these are available, project managers confronted with different project problems, phases and challenges can apply heuristics appropriately and successfully. As project managers strive to make good decisions—even as complexity arises or context changes—we encourage project managers to consider the following:

1. Acknowledge not every heuristic is appropriate for every situation. Projects have many different tasks and problems. Project managers are best prepared if they work with a diverse set of strategies. Each of the project approaches diagrammed in Figure 7.1 (on page 180) has a time and place.
2. For your next assignment, choose a project or context that enables learning about a broad range of diverse decision-making heuristics. Reading and simulating the different decision-making heuristics—e.g., in workshops or similar settings—is a good starting point, but applying these heuristics over time in real-life project situations is necessary to build ambidexterity. Reflect from time to time and change perspectives regularly to positively influence the learning process.
3. Use the team to widen the portfolio of perspectives. Each individual will have had different experiences, and pausing at each step to invite project management approach suggestions will encourage options from the team. Not only does this strengthen the team relationship and commitment—it also widens the set of available heuristics and helps project managers select strategy that matches projects conditions.

From Experts to Experts

If you are an expert project manager in a large firm and the effectuation principles feel foreign to you, take heart. As difficult as it may be for you to imagine applying the heuristics of expert entrepreneurs in your job, expert entrepreneurs find it equally hard to plan, optimise surprise out of a project, and drive efficiently toward a single goal. It is why so many entrepreneur founders leave their ventures (or get thrown out) as their firms become successful and need more causal approaches. Bill Gates and Mark Zuckerberg are two of the few who have successfully embraced both effectual and causal heuristics, bringing an uncertain venture to a Fortune 100 firm. So though it's rare, you know it's possible to be an expert times two.

References

Ambrosch, M. (2010). *Effectuation—Unternehmergeist denkt anders!* Wien, DE: Echomedia-Verlag.

Blekman, T. (2011). *Corporate Effectuation: What Managers Should Learn from Entrepreneurs!* The Hague, NL: Sdu Publishers bv. Academic Service.

Bradley, S., Wiklund, J., and Shepherd, D. (2010). Swinging a double-edge sword: The effect of slack on entrepreneurial management and growth. *Journal of Business Venturing, 26*(5), 537–554.

Brettel, M., Mauer, R., Engelen, A., and Küpper, D. (2012). Corporate effectuation: Entrepreneurial action and its impact on R&D project performance. *Journal of Business Venturing, 27*(2), 167–184.

Busenitz, L., and Barney, J. (1997). Differences between entrepreneurs and managers in organizations: Biases and heuristics in strategic decision-making. *Journal of Business Venturing, 12*(1), 9–30.

Davidsson, P. (2005). The entrepreneurial process as a matching problem. *Academy of Management Conference,* Hawaii. Retrieved from: http://eprints.qut.edu.au/2064/

Faschingbauer, M. (2010). *Effectuation—Wie erfolgreiche Unternehmer denken, entscheiden und handeln.* Stuttgart, DE: Schäffer-Poeschel.

Frame, J. D. (2002). *The New Project Management: Tools for an Age of Rapid Change, Complexity, and Other Business Realities.* New York, NY: John Wiley & Sons.

Geraldi, J. G., and Albrecht, G. (2007). On faith, fact, and interaction in projects. *Project Management Journal, 38*(1), 32–43.

Jaafari, A. (2003). Project management in the age of complexity and change. *Project Management Journal, 34*(4), 47–58.

Maylor, H., Vidgen, R., and Carver, S. (2008). Managerial complexity in project-based operations: A grounded model and its implications for practice. *Project Management Journal, 39*(1: suppl.), S15–S26.

McKelvie, A., Haynie, J. M., and Gustavsson, V. (2011). Unpacking the uncertainty construct: Implications for entrepreneurial action. *Journal of Business Venturing, 26*(3), 273–292.

Morieux, Y. (2011). Smart rules: Six ways to get people to solve problems without you. *Harvard Business Review, 89*(9), 78–86.

Müller, R., and Turner, R. (2006). *Choosing Appropriate Project Managers: Matching Their Leadership Style to the Type of Project.* Newton Square, PA: Project Management Institute.

Müller, R., Geraldi, J., and Turner, J. R. (2012). Relationships between leadership and success in different types of project complexities. *IEEE Transactions on Engineering Management, 59*(1), 77–90.

Read, S., Dew, N., Sarasvathy, S. D., Song, M., and Wiltbank, R. (2009). Marketing under uncertainty: The logic of an effectual approach. *Journal of Marketing, 73*(3), 1–18.

Read, S., Sarasvathy, S., Dew, N., and Wiltbank, R. (2016). *Effectual Entrepreneurship.* London, UK: Routledge.

Reynolds, P. D., Carter, N. M., Gartner, W., and Greene, P. G. (2004). The prevalence of nascent entrepreneurs in the United States: Evidence from the panel study of entrepreneurial dynamics. *Small Business Economics, 23,* 263–284.

Sarasvathy, S. D. (2001). Causation and effectuation: Toward a theoretical shift from economic inevitability to entrepreneurial contingency. *Academy of Management Review, 26*(2), 243–263.

Sarasvathy, S. D. (2008). *Effectuation. Elements of Entrepreneurial Expertise.* Cheltenham, UK: Edward Elgar.

Sarasvathy, S. D., and Dew, N. (2005). New market creation through transformation. *Journal of Evolutionary Economics, 15*(5), 533–565.

Shenhar, A. J., and Dvir, D. (2007). Project management research—The challenge and opportunity. *Project Management Journal, 38*(2), 93–99.

Staw, B. M., and Epstein, L. D. (2000). What bandwagons bring: Effects of popular management techniques on corporate performance, reputation, and CEO pay. *Administrative Science Quarterly, 45*(3): 523–556.

Ucbasaran, D. (2008). The fine 'science' of entrepreneurial decision-making. *Journal of Management Studies, 45*(1), 221–237.

Williams, T. (2005). Assessing and moving on from the dominant project management discourse in the light of project overruns. *IEEE Transactions on Engineering Management, 52*(4), 497–508.

Chapter 8

People

Building from the Inside: The Power of Social Organising

Darren Dalcher

The previous chapter noted that effectuation recognises that opportunities are created and effectuation thus puts forward a 'new' entrepreneurial way of thinking about developing business. In particular, it was observed that effectuation recognises a plurality of possible new ends, given a set of available means. Entrepreneurs expand the available problem space as they work through emerging opportunities, utilising the resources and connections at their disposal. It is not surprising, therefore, that the vast majority of entrepreneurial ventures ultimately develop results that are significantly different to the initial concept they started with.

So, where do entrepreneurs find their inspiration, and what resources can they rely upon? Serial entrepreneur Sir Richard Branson puts it into context when he states that, *'Clients do not come first. Employees come first'.* The explanation is rather simple, as Branson quickly adds that, *'If you take care of your employees, they will take care of the clients'.* Branson's ideas do not appear to chime with post-industrial thinking that emphasises shareholder value. Indeed, they don't directly support a move towards stakeholder thinking either.

Putting Your People First

Conventional wisdom dictates that businesses put their customers first, and endeavour to satisfy or even delight them. The customer is always right, goes the thinking, and after all, we do need them to return and use our service that continues to delight them repeatedly.

This makes sense to the extent that business relies on customers to engage with the product or service so that the company can start collecting value from the new patterns of use. So, it would take a brave entrepreneur to turn things on their head and reverse the business model. But that's what successful entrepreneurs do.

HCL Technologies (HCLT) is an Indian multinational technology company headquartered in Noida, Uttar Pradesh, India. The company aims to deliver innovative technology solutions based around emerging ideas such as digital, the Internet of Things (IoT), cloud, automation, cybersecurity, analytics, infrastructure management and engineering. HCLT was originally formed as a research and development division of HCL and emerged as an independent company in 1991, when HCL ventured into the competitive software services business.

Vineet Nayar took over as the CEO of HCLT in 2005. Nayar (2010) candidly admits that when he took over, he did not have a grand plan for the business. Indeed, while Nayar managed to completely transform his business, the phases for the transformation became clear to him only after the transformation fog had started clearing.

When Nayar took over, HCLT was one of the five major IT services companies based in India, with a global workforce of thirty thousand employees, operations in 18 countries and a yearly revenue of $700 million (p. 3). Yet, Nayar quickly recognised that behind the impressive numbers, the company was moving more slowly than its rivals, whilst continually losing its marketshare, talentshare and mindshare. The company was dropping to the back of the pack (p. 4) and needed drastic action to keep up with the competition and reposition its own ambition. Following extensive deliberation, the company made the commitment to change and embarked on a difficult journey to re-establish itself and recover its market position.

The change they embarked upon was a constantly evolving reflective journey that was meant to reflect their newly devised value and overarching priority, which they defined as *'employees first, customers second'* (p. 7). Nayar acknowledges that while their thinking defied conventional wisdom, it offered a new way of viewing their role:

> *The conventional wisdom, of course, says that companies must always put the customer first. In any services business, however, the true value is created in the interface between the customer and the employee. So, by putting the employees first, you can bring about fundamental change in the way a company creates and delivers unique value for its customers and differentiates itself from its competitors. . . . Thus, when a company puts its employees first, the customer actually does ultimately come first and gains the greatest benefit, but in a far more transformative way than through traditional 'customer care' programs and the like (p. 7).*

As product and services become commodities, companies are increasingly expected to distinguish themselves by how such services are delivered. However, such a fundamental shift in the relationship with the market would necessitate a significant change in the way that companies are structured and managed.

A Journey to Change

Nayar and his team developed a four-phase transformation journey to engender the new structure and mindset needed to create the required change (paraphrased below):

- **Mirror mirror.** Creating the need for change—by confronting the truth through a series of frequent and open conversations and continually evaluating the current position, whilst also turning employees' eyes away from the past and towards a better possible future state.
- **Trust through transparency.** Creating a culture of change—transformation requires people to align themselves and work together towards a goal and ask questions of each other as they push the envelope of transparency in communication and information sharing.
- **Inverting the organisational pyramid.** Building a structure for change that supports people in the *value zone*—the place where value is really created, which happens to be the interface between the customer and the employee.
- **Recasting the role of the CEO.** Transferring the responsibility for change from the office of the CEO to the employees in the *value zone*—whilst transforming the company into a self-governing organisation.

Nayar notes that the *value zone*, where the power is created, is often buried inside the organisation, devoid of the authority required to increase the speed and quality of innovation and decision-making. Value creators are often accountable to line managers and hierarchies, who do not directly contribute to creating value. But because they hold the formal authority and the value creators are accountable to them, such 'superiors' occupy a *zone of power* (p. 12).

To address such concerns requires organisations to intentionally invert the pyramid so that blocking or value-limiting management and hierarchical structures that embed such inequalities can be removed or mitigated.

The shift makes formal management and managers, as well as enabling or supporting structures such as HR, finance or training, accountable to those who actually create value (p. 12). Without making such shifts, meaningful change is impossible. HCLT even created an electronic trouble ticketing system by which employees could open a trouble ticket on any of these functions, and management would have to resolve these issues within a certain period of time, especially given that the ticket would only be closed by the employees.

To engender beneficial change, leaders and managers must therefore stop thinking of themselves as the only source of change (p. 13). They must instead ask questions, *'seeing others as the source of change, and transferring ownership to the organisation's growth to the next generation of leaders who are closer to the value zone'* (Ibid.). The value of the change approach adopted by Nayar is in being able to unleash the power of the many and loosen the stranglehold of the few who are currently in senior positions.

Individuals can begin to question processes and explore methods for improvement. Experimentation is essential: many small catalysts are utilised to shift thinking and initiate the journey to create meaningful and sustainable change. This implies many small experiments with various practices in an effort to determine which ones make a difference.

> Only in this way can you begin to create a company that is self-run and self-governed, one in which employees feel like the owners, are excited by their work, and constantly focus on change and disruptive innovation at the very heart of the value zone (p. 13). . . . The role of the CEO is to enable people to excel, help them discover their own wisdom, engage themselves entirely in their work, and accept responsibility for making change (p. 164).

Nayar's change journey fired the imagination of both employees and customers and set HCLT on a journey of transformation that has made it one of the fastest growing and most successful and profitable global IT services companies and, according to *BusinessWeek*, one of the 20 most influential companies in the world (*BusinessWeek*, 2010). *Fortune Magazine* characterised HCLT's management as the world's most modern (Kirkpatrick, 2006), and Vineet Nayar himself was selected in the elite list of Thinkers Fifty (Trombley, 2006). The book chronicling the experience and the process has become a best seller, selling over 100,000 copies in seven languages.

The concept initiated by Nayar has continued to evolve within the company and has now transformed into a truly *employee-driven, management-embraced* paradigm. The approach allows micro innovations to gather greater momentum and become new employee-led business lines. With tens of thousands of employees participating in collaboration, sharing and online social innovation platforms, the company continues to embrace innovation in the digital space. The results are convincing: Revenue has tripled, with a 24 percent compound annual growth rate. The number of customers has also tripled over a five-year period and the future of the company, which is continuing on its innovation and improvement journey, appears to be promising.

Creating Positive Organisations

The successful transformation at HCLT repositions employees at the core of organisational innovation, achievement and success. Engagement is crucial, and the case clearly hints at the need to develop a deeper understanding of the social domain and its impact on performance, as well as on organisational and business success. The relationship between individuals and the wider organisation plays a major part in defining and determining the dynamics for success and requires a much deeper scrutiny. The authors in the following section are happy to rise to the occasion and explore such issues. The contribution was written by Ian Macdonald, Catherine Burke and Karl Stewart and draws on the second edition of their book *Systems Leadership: Creating Positive Organisations*, published by Routledge.

Macdonald, Burke and Stewart (2018) are concerned with how people come together to achieve a productive purpose. Their work emphasises the role of social systems and structures and offers an important contribution that helps to put the case in a wider context: People have a strong need to contribute and belong. The success of organisations may thus depend on their ability to form and sustain social organisations that satisfy and support such needs. The authors clarify that poor social organisation, which includes poor leadership, is a major driver of poor productivity, which is likely to lead people to give up or maintain a minimalist approach required to sustain their position.

Positive organisations can fulfil the needs of individuals and play an active part in building a worthwhile society, to which individuals and citizens would aspire to belong. Macdonald, Burke and Stewart pay particular attention to the relationships and divisions that form between the social, technical and commercial domains of work. The domains offer a useful distinction when thinking about framing issues of work, authority and interactions. Positive leadership offers the ability to integrate the different domains and perspectives in order to solve problems and devise more holistic and 'healthier' organisational designs. While the technical and commercial aspects may be well understood and well explored, the social domain merits more attention. Moreover, the interaction between the three different domains is particularly important to explore and build upon in an effort to improve organisations, their productivity, and the well-being of their employees.

Rather than offer a recipe, the authors encourage leaders to consider, analyse and predict the consequences of their decisions. To support such deliberations they develop the vocabulary, language, models and propositions needed to consider types of social organisations, domains of work and the nature and use of authority in social organisations. They thereby provide the means for considering the achievement of organisational purpose, the need for creative and purposeful working and the productive relationship between the organisation and its employees.

Creating positive organisations is an extremely appealing notion, and the use of systems leadership offers many advantages and fresh insights. Organisational design has been an extended area of interest, with many contributions. Nonetheless, the work of Macdonald, Burke and Stewart offers potential hope for greater productivity.

Positive organisations are essential to the development of a healthy and just society. Whilst there is no quick and easy solution, creating long-term, sustainable success depends on understanding the principles and ideas presented by the authors in a wider holistic perspective and endeavouring to position and design organisations that can help individuals to thrive within the social structures and arrangements that we devise.

The Power of Social Organisations

Stanford (2007) notes that the purpose of organisation design is to create high-performing and adaptable enterprises. However, she also concludes that in order to be successful, such design must involve much more than focusing on the organisation chart and reporting arrangement: Crucially, *'it needs to include the culture, group processes, leadership, measurement and stakeholder engagement if it is to result in an organisation that is aligned in a way that will achieve the organisation's strategic goals'* (Ibid.: front sleeve).

Attempts to decouple people from the technical aspects of work through scientific management (Dalcher, 2017) have failed to simplify the systemic complexity required in modern organisations. Indeed, connecting the technical aspect to the organisational and personal perspective (Mitroff & Linstone, 1993; Linstone & Mitroff, 1994) or to the social and commercial domains (Macdonald et al., 2018) emphasises the need to develop holistic understanding of the connections and interactions and explore the inevitable impacts on performance, productivity and the enduring success of the business.

People—individuals—play a crucial part in the success of organisations, and yet their role is often ignored as we endeavour periodically to create a new understanding based on the technical needs and priorities. If only life were that simple!

We live in an age of social and connected systems. As we increasingly endeavour to tackle new domains, undertaking and challenges through the use of new technologies, collaboration models and platforms, the role of humans in achieving enduring success is likely to become more pronounced and critical.

> *In economic terms we have gone from an Industrial Economy—where we hired hands—to a knowledge economy—where we hired heads—to what is now a Global Human Economy—where we hire hearts* (Seidman, 2015: 1).

The new challenges would require more entrepreneurs like Richard Branson to see and position our very own people in new ways. They would also require pioneers such as Vineet Nayar to be brave and creative in inverting structures and designs in order to empower the value creators within the value zones in our organisations to create new opportunities and relationships, whilst decoupling old structures and ways of thinking in order to enable them to innovate and effectuate. Only very few leaders would invert power structures in search of true achievement and innovation. The rest of us will need guidance, models and insights, such as the ones produced by Macdonald, Burke and Stewart, to open our eyes, analyse the different relationships across the different domains and create positive organisations that can endure in healthier and more supportive settings. People will continue to be central to our enduring success, and we must therefore create new ways of unshackling them from the past, allowing them the freedom of the future and enabling their transformation journey between the two.

References

BusinessWeek (2010). https://www.bloomberg.com/news/articles/2008-12-10/the-worlds-most-influential-companies

Dalcher, D. (2017). What has Taylor ever done for us? *PM World Journal*, 6(4).

Kirkpatrick, D. (2006). The world's most modern management—In India. *Fortune Magazine,* April 14. https://archive.fortune.com/2006/04/13/magazines/fortune/fastforward_fortune/index.htm

Linstone, H. A., and Mitroff, I. I. (1994). *The Challenge of the 21st Century: Managing Technology and Ourselves in a Shrinking World.* New York, NY: SUNY Press.

Macdonald, I., Burke, C., and Stewart, K. (2018). *Systems Leadership: Creating Positive Organisations* (2nd Ed.). London, UK: Routledge.

Mitroff, I. I., and Linstone, H. A. (1993). *The Unbounded Mind: Breaking the Chains of Traditional Business Thinking.* New York, NY: Oxford University Press.

Nayar, V. (2010). *Employees First, Customers Second: Turning Conventional Management Upside Down.* Boston, MA: Harvard Business Press.

Seidman, D. (2015). Surviving the thriving in the human economy. *Forbes,* June 25. https://www.forbes.com/sites/dovseidman/2015/06/25surviving-and-thriving-in-the-human-economy/#2fea5b222c18

Stanford, N. (2007). *Guide to Organisation Design: Creating High-Performing and Adaptable Enterprises.* London, UK: Economist Books.

Trombley, S. (2014). *Fifty Thinkers Who Shaped the Modern World* (Reprint Ed.). London, UK: Atlantic Books. ISBN: 978-1782390923.

Social Process for Project Leaders

Ian Macdonald, Catherine Burke and Karl Stewart

A project involves a group of people who are assigned to work on a special task instead of, or in addition to, their normal work load. A project is created to give concentrated attention to a task of limited and specific duration which may require interdisciplinary skills and experience or expertise from various organisational units or even different organisations.

Projects come in many different sizes and shapes. There are large construction projects that involve hundreds of people from a variety of trades. There are small group projects such as process improvement teams (PIT) which may have only three people with the authority to call on special expertise within the organisation when needed.

There are, of course, many sizes between the extremes, as there are differing times to completion, from a few months to several years. Despite their differences, they all have several things in common. To have a successful project, all three organisational domains—technical, commercial and social—must be taken into account. Most organisations are pretty good at the first two but leave a lot to be desired on the social processes in human interaction.

Ian Macdonald, Karl Stewart and Catherine Burke developed Systems Leadership Theory to provide a set of coherent models to assist in understanding the social domain, including the culture of and behaviour in organisations. It is a coherent and integrated theory of organisational behaviour based on over 50 years of worldwide research across many organisations and cultures. It has a clear leadership model that is also directly related to a theory of human capability that, in turn, is related to structure and systems. These ideas have been applied in a variety of organisations and projects in countries around the world and have led to successful project outcomes.

The entirety of the theory cannot be covered in one short section; for this we refer you to the book *Systems Leadership: Creating Positive Organisations*, 2nd ed. (Macdonald, Burke & Stewart, 2018). Briefly, the theory begins with a model of core shared values which are found in all human societies. These values of fairness, honesty, trust, respect for human dignity, courage and love are the values that hold human social groups together. Different individuals and groups have stories (we call them *mythologies* because these are stories that carry a fundamental truth even when the specifics are fanciful) that demonstrate what is fair or respectful or courageous. Groups that share common mythologies have what we define as a *common culture*.

One of the potential difficulties in project work is that members of the project team may have differing mythologies and therefore may view certain leadership behaviour as unfair or disrespectful, even if that is not the intent of the leader nor seen in the same way by others on the team. It may take some time, but the leader must learn the mythologies of each member of the team and be able to see the world from each team member's viewpoint if the project is to be successful.

There is also an essential need to recognise the complexity of the project in order to assign a leader who is capable of handling such complexity. The work of Brown (1960; 1971), Jaques (1976, 1989), Jaques (Ed.) (1978), Macdonald (1984), Stamp (1978) and Burke and Smith (1992) demonstrates the development of the ideas of levels of work, as does Chapter 9 in *Systems Leadership* (2018). We have found that most, but certainly not all, projects can be led at the third, fourth, or fifth level of complexity. A few, like the Manhattan Project to develop the atom bomb, may require at least the seventh and possibly the eighth level of capability in the leader.

When the leader is at too low a level, or the project is not well defined, many things can go wrong. The poet Robert Burns (1785) was not thinking of projects when he wrote, '*The best-laid schemes o' mice an' men gang aft a-gley, An' lea'e us nought but grief an' pain For promis'd joy,*' but, as shown in the example below, he anticipated what can happen to a project leader.

Tim's Story

'That was the worst experience I've ever had'. I was speaking with Tim, a young IT programmer, who was deemed ready for a managerial position which needed to be filled immediately. He had turned it down emphatically, and as an external consultant, I was asked to find out why and to perhaps learn what the organisation could do to persuade him to take the role.

We had a lengthy chat over tea in one of the company's cafeterias. The line quoted above was the last thing he said about the experience he had had with 'management'.

At the time I started working at this corporation, they had a policy of trying people out to see how well they would do as a manager by giving them a significant but short 'project', usually with a three- to nine-month deadline. In this way, it was believed, their managerial skills could be tested. The newly appointed 'project manager' was told what they were to accomplish but was given no explicit authorities or resources, although there was sometimes a suggestion that they could 'take' up to three co-workers to work on the project. Part of the test was to see if they could figure out the authorities and find the people to work on the project and also complete it on time.

According to Tim, the way this was done was to call on your friends, especially those whom you had helped on their 'projects'. To do this, his friends had to sneak time from their own work without telling their managers and try to get the work done, often after hours. Tim needed a person with special expertise, whom he knew by reputation, but who was not a close friend. The specialist was friendly but said he had no time to help, 'Sorry'. Tim felt had no authority to ask the specialist's manager to allow him to work on Tim's project. In addition, he had no authority to reward his 'staff', and he had no authority to assign them tasks. It all had to be negotiated on a you help me, and I'll help you, basis.

One of the big problems was Tim's inability to get things done through his friends, who were also busy with other work assigned by their managers. He didn't feel he could ask for help from these managers, so he rewarded his friends with pizzas and drinks when they were willing and able to stay late to work on the 'project'. Some would promise to have one part of the project done at a certain time but then failed to meet the promised deadline.

In the end, Tim worked very long hours with the help of one close friend and they completed the project. It lacked certain elements because the specialist's knowledge was not available to Tim, but it was deemed a good effort thanks to Tim's fine social process skills. At the end, Tim was exhausted, had lost a couple of friends who had abandoned him during the project, and swore NEVER to do something like this again—to NEVER become a manager.

Manager and Project Leader Roles

Now, testing for managerial skills, especially social process skills, by having someone manage a project is not a bad idea. When done properly, it can be a good opportunity to teach someone about what it is like to take accountability for the work performance of others; to assign tasks, to review and recognise performance (good and bad). To do this, however, it is necessary to be clear on exactly what a manager is and must do as well as how project management may differ from management in general.

To sort out Tim's problem and to inform the leadership of the corporation on better ways to prepare people for management, it was necessary to begin by clarifying terms, so we could all agree upon what we were talking about. For example, we defined a 'manager' as a person who is accountable for his or her own work and the work performance of people reporting to him or her over time. Using this definition, it becomes clear that a manager is, and must be, a leader of people. The manager will be either a good leader or a bad leader, but he or she will, inescapably, be a leader.

A managerial role is essentially an open-ended structural role with a particular position (one level of work higher than his or her direct reports) and a set of authorities and tasks. In order to lead people effectively and accept accountability for their work performance, it is necessary for a manager to have certain minimum authorities—the VAR3I authorities—which define the managerial role:

V: Veto appointment to the role. That is, no one should be appointed to the team against the wishes of the manager.
A: Assign tasks. The manager assigns work to members of the team, and anyone else who wishes to assign work must clear it with the manager.
R3: Review, recognise and reward. That is, the manager has the authority to review the work of team members and to give appropriate feedback, both positive and negative, (recognition) and make financial changes in the form of a salary and/or performance pay.
I: Initiate removal from role. Here the manager, after due process, can require the person to leave the current role and the team if necessary. This is not the same as dismiss, as the person may be suitable or acceptable for another role in the organisation, to be determined by the manager's manager (M+1).

We define authority as *'the exertion of will in the context of the mutual acceptance of agreed limits'*. As such, authority is never without limits. There are both external and internal constraints on the authority an organisation can grant to its managers, including law, regulations, organisational policies, boundaries of the role, etc. Some people may also exercise power defined as *'the exertion of will while breaking one or more limits of authority'*. Power-based systems alienate a large part of the work force and are counterproductive. Systems of authority show respect for human dignity, drive out unauthorised power networks and thus release tremendous energy for productive purposes.

No matter what the laws or policies state, however, no one has authority unless the leader's direct reports accept it. To be fully accepted as a leader requires a good understanding of the universal values, mythologies and cultures as demonstrated by his or her behaviour and systems.

A project leader role differs from that of a manager in that it is not open-ended—it ends at the completion of the project, when each individual returns to his or her regular position. A project may be part-time or full-time and involves leadership skills that require clear authorities and tasks but are not the same as an open-ended managerial role. It is time-limited and has specific authorities.

VP: Veto selection to project team. The project leader carries the authority to veto the selection of people to the project team.

A±: Assign tasks within agreed-upon limits. This authority is similar to that of the manager, but in this case the additional limits are imposed by the project leader's and team members' managers. The agreed limits apply for the duration of the assignment to the project team, although they may be renegotiated if demands of the work or the work environment require changed limits.

R2±: Recognise and review differentially within agreed-upon limits. Again, the authority to assign work and the authority to recognise differentially must be commensurate. As with the authority to assign tasks, the limits to the authority of the project leader to review and recognise differentially are set by the project team member's manager. The project leader may also have the authority to recommend financial reward to the team member's manager.

RP: Remove from the project team. The project leader has the authority to remove a project member from the team. The project team member returns to his or her previous role and organisational unit upon the exercise of this authority by the project leader

Project leader authorities apply in the relationship between a project team leader and a project team member who is not a subordinate of the project leader in the normal organisation structure but is specially assigned to the project team. The project team member remains the direct report of his regular manager. Project team members may work in the same work stratum as the project leader, or they may work one or more levels above or below the project leader. The project leader usually does not have the authority to alter salary, although his or her input on work performance may be important information to the project team member's actual manager. It is important that the project team member is informed of the limitations that apply to the project team leader's authority.

Whether a manager or project leader, the person will need additional authorities, which may include a right to spend money (budget), to have access to information, to allocate resources, to sign contracts, to have the facilities necessary to carry out the project, and perhaps other authorities specific to the project. The project leader needs to have the authority to speak with the managers of his project team members and to seek the assistance of his own manager if that is needed to deal with managers at that level or higher.

The authorities on any given project may be more complicated, as the leader may have two different authority regimes in relation to different members of the team. Some team members may be his or her direct reports, while others may be the direct reports of the other managers. In the first case, managerial authorities will apply; in the second, project leadership authorities will apply. These differences need to be understood by members of the team and require considerable social process skills from the project leader.

Getting It Right

So what went wrong in Tim's situation? A lot, you say; obviously this type of 'project manager' role is neither a managerial nor a project leader role. It is simply a mess, and no one who reads this book is likely to make so many mistakes. Nonetheless, we have known organisations which have created managerial roles almost as poorly structured as this example; they typically have high turnover. Back in the day, they found themselves discussed on 'f...ed company'* and may be driven out of business.

Because we have had to deal with human relationships from the time we are babies—getting Mom's attention when we are hungry, or the nappy is full—up through getting along with others in school and later on the job, we have our own ideas about human behaviour and relationships based on experience. Suggesting that some of these ideas may not foster good working relationships, or are simply wrong, can be quite threatening. Therefore, we have stressed the need for clear definition of terms, so we can agree about what it is we are discussing.

To begin. A project is like a task, and if it is to be carried out effectively, task (or project) assignment must include the following:

- **Context.** The situation in which the project will likely be performed, including the background, relationship to other tasks and/or projects, and any unusual factors to be taken into account. What might be the opportunities, risks and threats?
- **Purpose.** Why this project? What is to be achieved by accomplishing it?
- **Output.** What is to be produced stated in terms of quality and quantity?
- **Resources.** Defined in terms of cost or resource use. Other resources include people, authorities (including the authority to speak with and ask for resources from specific managers other than one's own), access to information, facilities and assets assigned to facilitate completion of the project.
- **Time.** The targeted completion time—a deadline indicating when the project is to be completed.

Poor Tim had none of this except the 'what'. He was told what was to be done, but without clear information on quality and quantity. The rest of the essential information he had to surmise, and of course he was provided no clear authorities or resources. When assigning a task or project, it is essential that it be a two-way conversation. This ensures there is no confusion about the key information, and it also allows the project leader to discuss any issues or questions with the manager when it is assigned and later as need arises. Tim had not felt he could do that, as it would have shown he did not know what he believed he should have known to get the opportunity.

In some cases, the manager may be clear on what is needed and why (the output and the purpose), but the selected project leader has expertise the manager lacks. In this case, the project may be assigned in two (or more) steps, the first step being to learn what would be needed to achieve the purpose, and then for the potential project leader to lay out a project plan, including whether the purpose can be achieved given the output desired. Such a plan could also estimate time to completion, the quantity and quality of output achievable in that time frame and the resources (including authorities) likely to be required to complete it. The manager and project leader can then discuss whether or not the plan is likely to meet the manager's purpose and if adjustments are needed. While the project leader may propose what is to be done, the decision to go ahead is up to the manager.

---

* https://www.businessinsider.com/wsj-is-the-new-f-ed-company-2009-8?r=US&IR=T

If the project task is clearly stated in terms of CPQ/QRT,* the outcome is more likely to be positive. The project leader will also be able to accept accountability for the outcome of the project and be able to answer the following questions:

- What did you do?
- How did you do it?
- Why did you do it that way?

Team Leadership and Team Membership

The project leader must have good social process skills—the ability to interact with others at work to produce a productive outcome. This is where Systems Leadership Theory, which focuses on human social processes and relationships, can help.

The importance of social process skills has been demonstrated in several studies of team success (or lack thereof). Woolley (2010: 686–688) led a team from MIT and Carnegie Mellon that found one of the key factors in team success was 'high average social sensitivity'. *'They were skilled at intuiting how others felt based on their tone of voice, their expressions and other nonverbal cues'* (Duhigg, 2016a).

Beginning in 2012, Google® began Project Aristotle, conducting extensive research to learn why some teams perform very well and others less so. They identified 'psychological safety' as key to team performance—people listen to each other and show sensitivity to each other's feelings and needs (Duhigg, 2016b). Research also indicates the importance of clear understanding of the purpose of the team and the impact of their work.

This research demonstrates the importance of social process skills in the success of teams. Of course, people are both social creatures who form groups to achieve together what we cannot achieve as individuals, yet remain individuals, with individual needs. There is, and always will be, potential tension between what is advantageous for an individual and what is advantageous for the group. The key to a good organisation is managing the social process so that individuals are encouraged and allowed to use their capability to achieve the overall purpose of the group, yet are also recognised for their contributions as individuals. The individual gains personal satisfaction and reward whilst achieving the common goal.

Of course, some project leaders will be better at this than others, but people who are qualified to be a project leader can learn to be more effective at leadership. While there is considerable literature around the issue of 'born' leaders, or the personality required to be a leader, in our experience it is at best pointless, and at worst dangerous, to ask people to change their personalities. You can, however, ask someone to state context and purpose and explain tasks clearly. These can be observed, recognised and improved.

A clear definition of a project is given at the beginning of this section. We have defined a team as a group of people, including a leader, with a common purpose, who must interact with each other in order to perform their individual tasks and thus achieve their common purpose. A project may be made up of one or more teams.

---

* Context, Purpose, Quality/Quantity—Quality/Quantity, Resources, Time

While there has been much hype regarding agile and Scrum, wherein there is no leader of a team, our work in countries all over the world suggests that all teams will have a leader, whether by appointment, election or simply bullying (exercising power rather than authority). We recommend that project leaders be appointed by their manager, who should be in the best position to know the level of work required and the skills needed by the project leader.

This does not mean the project leader is an authoritarian 'boss', as that is commonly understood. To have an effective project and social process, the relationship between a team leader and team members is mutual. The leadership role and the membership role complement each other. Each has contributions to make if the project is to be completed successfully. The subtleties of these relationships cannot be conveyed in a short section but are discussed more fully in Chapter 15 of *Systems Leadership* (Macdonald et al., 2018).

Remember in teamwork, you are part of the whole. It is only by active cooperation, however, that the whole will be greater than the sum of the parts. The steps and traps of a team leader and team members that are described below should be seen as authorities. Many organisations that have adopted this model require these steps from both leaders and members, whether in managerial or project-leader roles. They are part of work reviews and performance assessments.

This demonstrates that, even in an executive hierarchy, authority does not simply flow downwards. Team members have the authority to require the leader to be clear about context, purpose, tasks, etc., and can demand a review. There is a clear and proper flow of authority upwards. Also, team members have authority with regard to each other requiring collaboration, information and feedback. This approach confounds the simplistic assertion that hierarchy is, by its nature, 'authoritarian', and that teams must be wholly democratic. Good team leadership provides the order necessary for effective and efficient progress. A false democracy does not.

In brief, the steps needed to be taken by the project leaders and team members are enumerated in Table 8.1.

Some of these are self-explanatory, but others need a bit more fleshing out. Critical issues are those things that threaten the purpose of the project—potential significant problems that must be overcome for the project to be completed successfully. Most leaders need help in order to identify

Table 8.1 Complementary Authorities of Leaders and Team Members

Leader	Member
Explain context and purpose	Clarify context and purpose
Identify critical issues	Contribute to the 'how'
Encourage contributions	Listen
Make a decision about the plan	Accept decisions concerning which plan
Assign tasks	Clarify tasks, ask questions
Monitor progress	Cooperate
Coach	Accept coaching
Review	Demand review
Avoid traps	Avoid traps

critical issues and contributions to their solution. Not listening to others and therefore implying they have no contribution to make is almost always a mistake.

Identifying and resolving critical issues is best done in an orderly process in which a potential critical issue is put forward and members of the team as well as the leader take time to think about proposals for resolving it. Such thought processes may lead to a recognition that the issue identified is not critical, or if it is, various proposals may be put forward, and the leader must decide which if any have merit. This process continues with each critical issue as it is identified and solutions proposed.

Team members have work to do to put forward their thoughts about the problems and ways of solving them. Any member may identify what appears to be a trivial point that turns out to be crucial. It is for the leader to decide in the end what is relevant. It is not only the leader who pays attention to the social process. Timing is critical if you want to be heard. Be available and accessible within the leader's sight. Don't give up if not heard initially. However, do not continue to press a point if it has been recognised.

While it is important to make a contribution, it is equally important to listen to other points of view. It is difficult for the leader if all members are switched to send and none to receive. You may find this difficult especially if you think others are making apparently silly or trivial suggestions or ideas you had already thought of and dismissed. Listening is really hard work. It is not a passive process.

The project leader must take all this in and make a decision on what is to be done. Leadership is not a matter of democracy or consensus. In a leadership role, your position is based upon your perceived capability to make decisions, and your role is accorded the authority to do so. When team members have had a fair go, they must accept the leader's decisions and commit to the chosen path, even if one's worst enemy has had his or her suggestions accepted.

The project leader must assign tasks using the CPQ/QRT model. To back this up and embed this process in the team, team members must clarify their tasks if they are uncertain about what their tasks are and what to do next; if and how their tasks complement other people's tasks and how their tasks will help to achieve the purpose and overcome problems—*why* they are doing these tasks. Team members must work to complete their tasks and cooperate with others. For example, do not hide information or use it to exercise power.

As the project moves forward, the project leader must monitor progress along several dimensions (at once):

- **Technical** (the most obvious): Are the solutions working? Do they need to be modified? Will the methodology/plan actually solve the problem?
- **Social:** Is the team cohesive? Are people involved, using initiative, interacting, or are they forming sub-groups, fragmenting, only doing 'what is necessary'? Do they look interested? Engaged?
- **Temporal:** Is there a programme, a timetable/schedule? Is it being achieved?
- **Environmental:** The *leader* does the work of monitoring the environment, allowing team members to concentrate on the task at hand. What is happening around the team and what intervention is required to help overcome problems?

Ultimately, if any or all of the above are going wrong, what contingency plan does the leader have? Can he or she answer this *before* a problem arises, even if only in outline? Here the leader may have to revisit critical issues, stop the process and re-evaluate.

The project leader is also a coach, and team members are expected to accept some coaching. As team members work, they may need help to complete their tasks or improve their methods. Leaders are helpers. This is a very sensitive area, because the *way* in which a leader coaches will affect whether people will accept help. First, a leader must make it clear to the team member whether he or she is:

- **Giving an instruction.** Telling someone to do something differently and expecting them to do it.
- **Giving advice.** Suggesting a person think about using your ideas but leaving it up to them.
- **Teaching.** Showing/telling someone how to do something because they recognise that they don't know how. This area is critical to a leader, as few people like being told how to do something while they are in the middle of work unless they think they are having problems. Consequently, do not be afraid to ask.
- **Asking.** Gain information from members—for example, why do you do that? Do you want any help?

Although an important part of the leader's work is coaching, do not forget the leader may well learn from the team.

Finally, the process and outcome must be reviewed: what has been done to date in longer projects, and at the end of the project. The project leader and members must discuss whether the purpose has been achieved or not and the process with the team. This is the opportunity, when everything associated with the task is still fresh in people's minds to give recognition (positive and negative) to team members and to comment on the leader's perception of his or her leadership behaviour—in particular, those things that were not done as well as they might have been. If the project leader does not initiate the review, the project team members have the authority to demand such a review.

It is very important for a leader to draw out the views of team members—a process that will usually be easier if the team has been successful than it will be if the outcome was poor. It needs to be done, however, if all of the team is to learn from the experience.

The social process of these reviews will determine, to a large extent, how successful they are at engendering improved work performance. It is vitally important to recognise people's work and to encourage individuals and the team to learn from what they have done—what they can build on and what they need to change. We all benefit from knowing if we have achieved our purpose

Traps for Team Leaders

A leader can make many mistakes, and the majority of leaders will make some. The same is true for team members. The traps for leaders and for team members are not complementary, as in the steps. In our experience these are the most common traps for the team leader.

- **Not seeing the problem from the member's viewpoint.**
- **Getting over-involved in the action.** Taking over a team member's work not only annoys the member, it prevents the leader from doing his or her own work of monitoring and coaching.
- **Feeling you have to have the answer.** It is the leader's work to make sure the best solution is implemented. Not being able to generate the complete solution personally is not a failure—the leader is being paid for his or her judgement.

- **Being the technical expert.** Like the trap above, this one arises because the leader behaves as though he or she has to know more than anyone else in the team. Superior technical knowledge and expertise is often mistaken for leadership, when in fact it masks poor social process and, at times, questionable capability.
- **Ignoring social and programming issues.** Part of the culture that emphasises technical knowledge also downgrades the importance of or difficulty in the other areas of social process and programming. Programming includes checking progress against plan while at the same time monitoring how the team members are relating to each other.
- **Issue fixation.** Allowing a single problem to gain the most attention, blowing it up out of proportion. It is essential to note how this affects other areas and what impact its solution has on the rest of the problems.
- **Not willing to stand out in a crowd.** This is one of the most common and most damaging traps—when a leader is reluctant to appear to be a leader. This leads to an over-dependence on consensus, an attempt to achieve a 'collective accountability' when leadership behaviour is directed toward a merging with the group. The result is a rudderless slow approach that lacks direction and clear programming. Be reassured that teams *do* like the leader to be *decisive*.

Traps for Team Members

- **Keeping quiet.** This is where the team member does not ask questions or put forward ideas, behaving in a way that suggests that passive acceptance and blind obedience is what is required.
- **Not listening.** Allowing other people to speak does not equal listening. There is a difference between waiting for 'some idiot to finish' and actively listening. Women often note that when they put forward an idea, it is ignored; it is then repeated by a man in the team, and everyone reacts by saying it is a great idea. Women do not appreciate this, nor do minorities, who often confront the same issue.
- **Getting on with my job.** This involves ignoring the situation and the needs of others, with blinkers on, and continuing to do your own work whatever the circumstances.
- **Getting on with other people's jobs.** Team members may interfere with other people's tasks because they think they know better. Such behaviour can also be an attempt to exercise power, disguised as cooperation, but is very different from cooperating.
- **Wandering off.** We have seen team members wander off either mentally or physically, and often both, exploring possibilities without reporting back and in doing so missing vital information. Often it is with good intention, or due to boredom. However, it causes distraction.
- **Fragmenting the team.** This is a variation of wandering off and involves setting up ad hoc subgroups to rework the problems, changing the tasks and redefining the purpose, again without feedback. This is an exercise of power—setting up internal factions that polarise the team and undermine the leader.
- **'I knew I was right'.** Going along with a 'bad' plan while actually undermining it in order to prove it was bad and having the dubious satisfaction of seeing it fall apart.

- **Ignoring coaching.** Being overly sensitive to questions from others (especially the leader) as to why you are doing something in a certain way. This may mean that you miss ways to improve.
- **Fear of taking over.** Holding back because you worry you might take over the leadership inhibits your potential and the team's resources.

Conclusion

This approach to project leadership and project team membership provides a practical guide to improve social process skills for both leaders and team members. It is far from complete, as it omits a number of the subtleties that are discussed in *Systems Leadership*. Good teamwork is an essential social process skill within an effective organisation or project.

Using these approaches will also help the leader demonstrate the core values of honesty, trust, fairness, respect for human dignity, courage and love that are essential to team cohesion. Clear statements of context and purpose along with the required output in quantity and quality terms, resources available and targeted time to completion allow everyone to get on with the project without confusion and missteps.

These will not make a perfect world for the project leader, but they have proven in many settings to make things much better. Tim, by the way, had training in these materials and went on to take a project leadership role at Level III. Last we heard, he was quite successful in a managerial job at Level V.

References

Brown, W. (1960). *Exploration in Management*. London, UK: Heinemann.

Brown, W. (1971). *Organization*. London, UK: Heinemann.

Burke, C., and Smith, D. (1992). *Organizing Corporate Computing: A History of the Application of a Theory, Festschrift for Elliott Jaques*. Arlington, VA: Cason Hall & Co.

Burns, R. (1785). "To a mouse." *Poems and songs*. https://www.bartleby.com/6/76.html

Duhigg, C. (2016a). *Smarter Faster Better: The Secrets of Being Productive in Life and Business*. New York, NY: Random House.

Duhigg, C. (2016b). What Google learned from its quest to build the perfect team. *The New York Times Magazine*, February 25.

Jaques, E. (1976). *A General Theory of Bureaucracy*. London, UK: Heinemann.

Jaques, E. (1989). *Requisite Organization*. Falls Church, VA: Cason Hall & Company.

Jaques, E. (Ed.), with R. O. Gibson and D. J. Isaac (1978). *Levels of Abstraction in Logic and Human Action*. London, UK: Heinemann.

Macdonald, I. (1984). *Stratified Systems Theory: An Outline*. Uxbridge, UK: Individual and Organisational Capability Unit, BIOSS, Brunel University.

Macdonald, I., Burke, C., and Stewart, K. (2018). *Systems Leadership: Creating Positive Organisations* (2nd Ed). London, UK: Routledge.

Stamp, G. (1978). Assessment of individual capacity. In: Jaques, E. (Ed.), with R. O. Gibson and D. J. Isaac. *Levels of Abstraction in Logic and Human Action*. London, UK: Heinemann.

Woolley, A. W., Chabris, C. F., Pentland, A., and Hashmi, N. (2010). Evidence for a collective intelligence factor in the performance of human groups. *Science, 330*(6004), 686–688.

Chapter 9

Hacking

Hacking Innovation: Revisiting Teams, Productivity and Limits

Darren Dalcher

Earlier chapters have focused on entrepreneurship (alongside innovation and creativity) and on the need to reconnect with people at the core of management work. This chapter links the two areas while revisiting established writing in the domain of managing software projects and people, highlighting some of the pioneering thinking that has emerged from that domain before turning to explore new possibilities that can refresh some of the insights and renew some of the conversations.

The Mythical Man-Month: Mixing Effort and Progress

Re-reading old classics can prove to be a source of both immense pleasure and intense frustration. The pleasure comes from being reacquainted with an old friend after an extended absence. It is often enriched by the ability to make sense of and see afresh through some of the ideas and writing that appeared in the original source. The passage of time often allows for progress to be seen through an informed lens. But therein also lies the source of deep frustration, when 55 years after the fact, many of the lessons and insights remain equally relevant, yet still appear not to have been embraced or understood.

The Mythical Man-Month was written by Fred Brooks (1975) to recount his experience of managing a very large and rather complex project for IBM 10 years earlier. It contains a series of essays that enable the readers to join Brooks in making sense of his management journey. The book is the undisputed best seller in software engineering, selling over a million copies. Yet, its appeal extends well beyond the realms of the software engineering community, generating reviews, citations and correspondence from lawyers, doctors, psychologists and sociologists (Brooks, 1995: 254). If we look for the underlying reason for the enduring appeal of the book, it might well be that the focus on software engineering is simply the context utilised for a more intimate reflection on people, teams, interactions, communication and achievement in projects—areas that still merit attention and that may still defy full understanding.

Indeed, the challenges, constraints and tribulations recounted by Brooks reflect the experiences still encountered on many large projects. Brooks metaphorically locates large-system projects in the prehistoric tar pits, where *'many great and powerful beasts have thrashed violently . . . Most have met goals, schedules and budgets. Large and small, massive or wiry, (yet) team after team has become entangled in the tar'* (Brooks, 1995: 4).

To this day, the annals of failure are still filled with many a great behemoth mired in the metaphorical tar pits. Brooks notes that everyone seems to be surprised by the stickiness of the problem before asserting that more software projects have gone awry for lack of calendar time than for all other reasons combined (p. 14). He duly identifies a number of contributing causes (which are paraphrased below):

- **Estimation.** Techniques for estimating are poorly developed and reflect an unvoiced assumption that all will go well.
- **Techniques.** Estimation approaches tend to confuse effort with progress, fallaciously assuming that people and time are interchangeable.
- **Position.** The inherent uncertainty of the estimates allows managers to collapse schedules in order to respond to wishes and expectations.
- **Monitoring.** Schedule progress is poorly monitored.
- **Action.** The response to identified slippage is to add resource (manpower), which Brooks equates with dousing a fire with gasoline.

However, there are two additional, albeit linked, monumental issues that Brooks labels as fallacious thought modes:

- **Optimism.** Firstly, there is a false optimism that pervades thinking in computer systems and enables management decisions to anchor on simplistic and naïve assumptions about future progress (pp. 14–15). Thinking around the excessive optimism described by Brooks chimes with contemporary global discussions around strategic misrepresentation, wishful thinking, conspiracy of optimism and optimism bias (Ascher, 1993; Sharot et al., 2007; Flyvbjerg, 2008, 2009; Love et al., 2011; Sharot et al., 2011; Sharot et al., 2012; Dalcher, 2013).
- **Mythical effort.** Secondly, the basis of estimating and scheduling in software projects is erroneously derived. The unit of effort utilised in such calculations leads to significant miscalculations. Brooks takes issue with the mythical concept of man-month (a hypothetical representation of the work done by one person within one month), which underpins much of project thinking. When effort is represented utilising the currency of person-months, the cost inevitably depends on the product of the number of people employed and the number of months. Progress, on the other hand, does not!

Indeed, the relationship between effort and progress is far more difficult to determine and untangle. *'Hence the man-month as a unit for measuring the size of a job is a dangerous and deceptive myth. It implies that men and months are interchangeable'* (Brooks, 1995: 16).

In reality, people and months can only be regarded as interchangeable commodities when a task can be partitioned without the need for communication or coordination amongst the team members (i.e., when no interaction overheads need be considered).

This implies a labour-intensive task that can be carved into segments. When there is a need for dependence amongst individuals or a requirement for continuous communication, the simple measure no longer holds. More complex and more demanding interactions therefore defy the excessive simplicity implied by the 'mythical man-month' concept. Indeed, such confounding misunderstanding, and its significant impact on how projects are understood and managed, give the book its rather unique title.

Mind What You Wish For . . .

So, what happens when a project is behind schedule?

Conventional logic applying the mythical man-month formula would typically result in adding manpower to the project to recover the schedule.

Indeed, when asked to name their single magic solution by the mythical project genie, many project managers would request either more time or more money. Money is often used as a proxy for additional resources or manpower. Where time cannot be made, managers may resort to trying to achieve more over available time by resorting to the mythical man-month.

The logic is rather compelling. To make up for lost time, we add resource, thereby enabling faster progression and execution. Brooks refers to such naïve addition of manpower as *regenerative schedule disaster* (Ibid.: 21).

Brooks offers the example of a task estimated at 12 man-months, assigned to three people, for four months. If the work meant to be completed over the first month is only finished after two months have elapsed, what options would be available to the project manager?

The options are summarised, rebadged and repositioned as follows:

1. **Early obstacle.** If the task has to be completed on time, and the delay (or mis-estimate) only relates to the initial month of the work, nine person-months of effort still remain to be completed over two calendar months. The simple solution is to add two people to the three already assigned to the project.
2. **Systemic error.** If the task has to be completed on time, but the delay/mis-estimation applies to the rest of the work, then 18 months of effort remain to be completed over two calendar months, requiring nine team members. Hence, six people must be added to the three already assigned to the project.
3. **Reschedule.** Allow enough time to complete the work needed in the new schedule by taking account of the delay or mis-estimation.
4. **Trim the task.** Reduce some elements of functionality or scope, or eliminate some activities in order to allow a minimal task to complete on time.

Brooks maintains that the first two alternatives are disastrous due to the regenerative effects of such action. In the first case, the two new people, assuming they can be recruited and assigned immediately, without any further delay, would require training in the task by one of the experienced professionals. The training will have used up three person-months for work not appearing in the original estimate. Moreover, the addition of personnel would necessitate repartitioning of the work, further integration and testing and other overheads. By the end of the third month, substantially more than seven person-months remain, and only five trained people and one month are available. The remaining work thus becomes even more urgent. *'The temptation is very strong to repeat the cycle, adding yet more manpower. Therein lies madness'* (p. 25).

This is of course the simplest case. If Scenario 2 is more pertinent and the entire task has been miscalculated, a far more extreme injection of resources may be expected, with wider-ranging impacts and an even greater need for further resource consumption.

Whilst the numbers involved in the illustrative case are small, Brooks invites readers to imagine the regenerative impact of adding hundreds of people to a project running late, and doing so in multiple iterations, as progress is consistently being closely monitored. Drawing on his experience, Brooks concludes, with what has become known as Brooks' Law, that *'Adding manpower to a late software project, makes it later'* (p. 25).

Reflecting on the impact of adding manpower, Brooks notes that, while the programming work performed increases with direct proportion to the number of programmers (N), the resulting complexity of a project increases by the square of the number of programmers (N^2). Therefore, he asserts that it should follow that thousands of programmers working on a single project should become mired in a complex nightmare of human communication and version control.

Reimagining the Computer at IBM

Brooks' Law is derived from his experience of managing a significant project for IBM. Yet, while he explains the implication of the mythical man-month mindset, he does not frame it with the actual figures from his own project. It might therefore be useful to gain an appreciation of the source of his experience by looking at other material related to the project and its context.

Brooks was a manager concerned with developing the IBM System/360 computer family. People outside the industry may not immediately recognise the product, but System/360 introduced a fundamental innovative transformation in the computer industry, akin in significance to the launch of the Ford Model T, the release of Boeing's first jetliner, the 707, or the development of the incandescent light bulb.

In the 1960s IBM were the dominant computer manufacturer in the US. By 1961, they controlled two-thirds of the American market; however, they offered a fragmented range of incompatible machines from across six different product lines, which could not be upgraded, adapted or upscaled.

Computer hardware was application specific and typically divided into scientific (fixed-word length, binary arithmetic) and business (variable-word length, decimal arithmetic) ranges. The two types were developing and growing independently, so companies like IBM had many different lines of computers, which were developed separately, utilising different languages and different systems software. Developers had to have a total understanding of the hardware, the operational limitations and the operational requirements, as development was intimately tied to the host machine.

New computers were being introduced every year or two (Glass, 1997). The case for each new machine was compelling, yet each new computer was different from, faster and cheaper than its predecessor. Software people were therefore forced to re-write the programmes on a new computer platform whenever a new one appeared. And yet, software was free, as hardware vendors were only too keen to give away systems software (without which the hardware would not work).

To tackle the challenge, IBM established the SPREAD (Systems Programming Review Engineering and Development) task force in 1961 and based it in a secret facility hidden at a remote location. The bold recommendation of the task force was to replace all existing IBM machines with a new, unified product line that would support scientific as well as business computing. Moreover, from the smallest model, the range could share the same accessories—tapes, disks and printers—and run the same programmes (SPREAD, 1961).

Prior to the introduction of System/360, manufacturers built each new computer model from scratch, and so the operating system would also need to be built from scratch. The emergence of the general-purpose IBM 360 series signalled the beginning of a new era. Computers were becoming faster and cheaper. The 360 family offered a range of options and platforms to suit all needs whilst allowing for growth and increasing modularity.

System 360 would deliver a family of compatible computers that could fill every data processing or computation need, offering a range of cost and performance options. Customers could start with small computers and move up or just add components as their demands increased, taking their old software along with them. No longer was there a need to ditch the computer every other year and re-write all the existing code. The 360-range comprised anything from a small business machine to the largest scientific computer.

The proposed new concept represented a major corporate gamble that would make all existing IBM machines obsolete. The name System/360 reflects the proposed flexibility of the range and its ability to deal with any permutation of commercial and scientific information processing requirements. System 360 played a pivotal role in revolutionising IBM and, ultimately, transforming the entire industry. For the first time the company manufactured its own components. Engineering and manufacturing were standardised on a worldwide basis, as overseas plants and labs concentrated on producing one product line for both the domestic and foreign markets.

The development of a common architecture, as opposed to a specific implementation, enabled compatibility across the entire range. This gave customers the flexibility to change machines and still retain their code. In one stroke IBM had shifted the focus from a single, one-off machine (computer) to the notion of computer systems.

To announce the launch, on April 7th, 1964, IBM held a press conference in Poughkeepsie, New York, while simultaneous events were held in 165 other US cities and 14 other countries, engaging a total audience of 100,000 customers. IBM had even chartered a full train to deliver journalists from New York City to the main press conference. Speaking at the main event, Thomas Watson, Jr., President of IBM, announced that it was a sharp departure from previous computing concepts. *'The result will be more computer productivity at lower cost than ever before. This is the beginning of a new generation—not only of computers, but of their application in business, science and government'.*

Managing the Massive Project

Yet, the radical notion of compatible software for the entire product range was responsible for placing tremendous demands on the programmers. The concept of the 360 family nearly failed when software problems created significant delivery delays. Previously, IBM's annual spending on software had been around $10 million (Fishman, 1981: 97). The anticipated expenditure for the 360 family was a far more significant $125 million, representing by far the most advanced, most expensive and most challenging software project IBM had ever attempted (Ibid.). Lack of knowledge about testing software by the product test engineers and the unavailability of the hardware hampered the development [Ibid.]. More critical was the fact that software personnel were not involved in the early planning and subsequently managed the software effort separately (Ibid.: 101).

While Brooks (1995: 31) talks about the original 200-person team who started the project, Fishman (1981: 97) reports that at its peak the project involved 2,000 programmers who were attempting to complete the undertaking. In March 1966, Watson admitted to software problems and remarked that the programming costs would run nearly as high as the hardware development costs. The actual cost, according to insiders, was in the region of $500 million (p. 101)—four times the original estimate. Additional enhancements to the software would cost even more (Ibid.).

Cortada (2019) notes that the software development staff was described as being in 'disarray' as early as 1963. In response, IBM added 1,000 people to the operating system project, costing more for software in one year than had been planned for the entire development of System/360.

Reflecting on the cycle of the project, Brooks (1995: 20) notes that many of the tasks were sequential in nature, so that even when coding was apportioned to more programmers at the behest of management, there would be an essential need to test and debug the combined efforts of all individuals. Moreover, the more people that became involved, the greater the need to coordinate their efforts (p. 18). Programmers would thus waste as much time communicating as was saved by increasing the size of the team (p. 24).

> The promises the company had made for the software were too ambitious, because it had not measured which features were essential to the customer and which he could do without. Thus programming costs were grossly underestimated (Fishman, 1981: 101).

Engaging in such a transformational project had not been easy, as Watson later explained:

> The expense of the project was indeed staggering. We spent three-quarters of a billion dollars just on engineering. Then we invested another $4.5 billion on factories, equipment and the rental machines themselves. It was the biggest privately financed commercial project ever undertaken (Sparkes, 2016).

Indeed, the actual total cost was close to $6 billion; this equates to well over $40 billion in today's terms. In terms of total project costs in the 1960s, this was second only to the Apollo project. Nowadays, such a high price tag would also easily qualify the undertaking as a very significant megaproject.

Fortune Magazine branded IBM's System/360 as the '$5 billion gamble' (Wise, 1966). To put that number in context, IBM's total revenue in 1962 was $2.5 billion, so the investment of what turned out to be $6 billion in a new concept, at more than twice the annual revenue, and at about 24 times IBM's annual profit, would be an enormous make-or-break gamble.

The reaction from customers was overwhelming. Within the first four weeks, IBM had more than a thousand orders. Within three months IBM had received $1.2 billion in orders. By the end of 1966 the System/360 had generated a billion dollars in pre-tax profits. Within five years over 33,000 units would be sold (compared to a pre-launch total of 20,000 computers of all makes across the US, Japan and Western Europe). System/360 has also left an important legacy, as every subsequent IBM machine can be said to be a descendent of System/360.

Within a short period, System/360 machines were being used by most banks, universities, airlines and government offices. Moreover, five of the machines made NASA's Apollo 11 mission possible, crunching the data relayed by the spacecraft's small onboard computer and displaying it for the support crew in Houston (Cortada, 2019).

Through the 1970s, more than 70 percent of mainframes sold were IBM's. IBM's base of installed computers rose from 11,000 in early 1964 to 35,000 in 1970. IBM itself also grew, more than doubling its workforce from 127,000 employees worldwide in 1962 to 265,000 by the end of 1971. Meanwhile, revenue rose from $2.5 billion in 1962 to $8.3 billion in 1971.

System/360 is associated with facilitating and ushering in the information age. With the benefit of hindsight, the most expensive CPU project in history, which came close to bankrupting the company, had proved to be an enormous business success, which would further ensure an enduring market share in the mainframe computer market. Notwithstanding a significant under-estimation of the cost required to complete the project, and despite consistent efforts from senior management to get the project back on track by repeatedly doubling the size of the project team and virtually destroying the entire initiative, the final product became a success with customers, transforming the entire computer industry and society in the process by enabling many organisa-tions to own and operate their own computers.

Learning the Lessons

Brooks (1995: 30) concludes that the sheer number of minds that need to be coordinated affects the cost of the effort, for a major part of the larger effort *'is in communicating and correcting the ill effects of miscommunication'*. The obvious alternative would therefore be to use as few minds as possible.

> *Indeed, most experience with large programming systems shows that the brute-force approach is slow, inefficient and produces systems that are not conceptually integrated. OS/360, Exec 8, Scope 6600, Multics, TSS, SAGE etc.—the list goes on and on* (Ibid.).

The question is, can a small team still be successful in developing large and significant undertaking?

> *The dilemma is a cruel one. For efficiency and conceptual integrity, one prefers a few good minds doing design and construction. Yet for larger systems one wants to bring considerable manpower to bear, so that the product can make a timely appearance* (p. 31).

Placing conceptual integrity at the core of system design (p. 42) ultimately moves Brooks to declare that the design must proceed from one mind (p. 44) or a small group of agreeing minds (p. 233). Where schedule pressures necessitate involving many hands, he recommends either a division of labour between architecture and implementation or a new way of structuring teams around the key designer. However, in order to ensure conceptual integrity, someone must control the concepts. According to Brooks, *'That is an aristocracy that needs no apology'* (p. 233).

Such a conceptually integrated system is faster to build and to test. Brooks recounts a crucial decision around the writing of external specification for the operating system, where he made the wrong decision about the system (p. 47): The architecture manager had 10 good men and asserted that they could write the specification and do it right, which would take 10 months, three more than the schedule allowed.

The control programme managers had 150 men. He asserted that they could prepare the specifications under the coordination of the architecture team. He contended that they would get it right, do it on schedule, and it would keep his team busy rather than waiting for the architecture team to finish their turn. The architecture manager retorted that if the control team were given the responsibility, the product would *not* be on time, but three months late, and of poorer quality.

Faced with a difficult decision, Brooks decided not to listen to his architecture manager, giving the job to the control team. In the book he admits to being swayed by the allure of having a team of 150 implementers on the case (p. 48). The result . . . was delivered three months late and at a much lower quality. Moreover, he reflects that, *'The lack of conceptual integrity made the system far more costly to build and change, and I would estimate that it added a year to debugging time'* (Ibid.).

Targeted small teams can thus be more effective than large collections of individuals, which need to be coordinated and controlled. Brooks concludes that conceptual integrity does require that a system reflect a single philosophy and that the specification as seen by the user can only flow from one, or very few, minds (p. 49). Indeed, a smaller team results in simplified communication and improved conceptual integrity that can reduce the time needed for implementation (p. 50).

Upon revisiting the work 20 years later, Brooks still emphasises the critical role of the architect this way:

> *'The most important action is the commissioning of some one mind to be the product's architect, who is responsible for the conceptual integrity of all aspects of the product perceivable by the user. The architect forms and owns the public mental model of the product that will be used to explain its use to the user. . . . The architect is also the user's agent, knowledgably representing the user's interest in the inevitable tradeoffs among function, performance, size, cost and schedule. . . . The architect is like the director, and the manager like the producer of a motion picture'.* (p. 256).

The final main point that Brooks reflects on, after 20 years, is to do with creativity and its relationship with control and structure (p. 276). Given his belief that creativity comes from individuals and not from structures and processes, the key question is how to design structure and process so as to enhance, rather than inhibit, creativity and initiative.

Brooks draws on Schumacher (1973), recognising that freedom and enhanced responsibility in smaller units and that individuals can result in happier and more prosperous organisations. Schumacher makes a powerful case for building economies around the specific needs of communities rather than the wishes of large corporations and conglomerates. Brooks maintains that the secret to unlocking improved productivity is through delegated power and the freedom to operate within existing structures (Brooks, 1995: 279).

The key notions of conceptual integrity and creative productivity continue to challenge most constructive endeavours that strive to embrace and balance innovation and creativity with control and structure. Such concerns come to the fore particularly when the contrast between the creativity of the individual, or the small team, contrasts with large or complex organisational undertakings that seem to impose a strong preference for efficiency, structure and control. Attempting to guide and control major undertakings typically dehumanises and deemphasises the role of individuals, resulting in a direct conflict between the overarching need for structure and the human capability for creativity and innovation.

Attempts to balance creativity and control have featured through the history of systems development, project management and organisational behaviour, primarily through a continuing struggle to accommodate talented and creative individuals as part of global initiatives. A fascinating arena that reflects the very same pervading tension can be observed through the emergence, partial disappearance and re-emergence of hackers, the innovative technology-savvy problem solvers able to utilise new approaches and perspectives in delivering creative solutions within the burgeoning software systems domain.

The Emergence of the Hacker: Where Do Hackers Come From?

Hackers are not a new phenomenon. Hackers appear to have always congregated around computer systems and new technologies. In the early days of computers (c. 1950) hackers predominated. Hackers had an in-depth knowledge of programming languages and the hardware on which systems were installed, coupled with a delight in solving problems and overcoming limits. Ince (1988) refers to them as the 'original programming magicians'.

Good hackers were able to use programming 'tricks' in order to reduce memory size, get programmes to run faster, link various devices to computers, bypass faulty or slow functions, create alternative options and subroutines, use fewer punch cards and save precious hours of machine time. Highly skilled individuals could thus practice their craft by attempting to maximise the machine through creative manœuvres (Dalcher, 1999), resulting in elegant solutions that solved problems well, thereby proving that technical problems can have artistic solutions (Erickson, 2008: 2).

The typical approach to programming, known as the 'code and fix' model, used in the early days of computer programming comprised two steps (depicted in Figure 9.1) reflecting the essential elements of the task of creating new software:

- Coding
- Fixing errors in the code

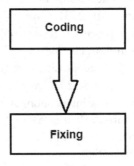

Figure 9.1   The Code and Fix Cycle

The cycle reflects the essence of developing new programmes; software was conceptualised and developed in someone's head, coded and used. The raw code was not structured in any formal way. Hacking was thus a form of art or craft, rather than an engineering discipline. In common with Brooks's notion of conceptual integrity, the initial mental concept for a new programme would be artfully 'sculpted' into a functional programme, much like a sculptor transforming a raw block into a masterpiece.

Over time, frequent corrections would degrade the initial structure and the quality of the programme and make subsequent fixes and corrections far more complex and labour intensive. Without due care, the code-and-fix model could ultimately result in programmes that grow unacceptably large and degrade to a stage where it becomes impossible to continue to use them.

Ultimately, the programmes could become very convoluted. When a hacker left a company, they took with them the contextual knowledge of the programme and the familiarity with the 'magic spells' driving it. As no one else was happy or able to maintain them, many programmes collapsed (see, for example, Macro & Buxton, 1987; Ince, 1988; Glass, 1997).

Over time organisations became more concerned with structure and efficiency. Procedures and approaches have been applied to increase order and add structure and control to the process of development. Indeed, it could be argued that the notion of the waterfall model partly stems from the dissatisfaction with the state of 'the art of programming' (Charette, 1986), the 'hacker running the show' (Booch, 1987; Ince, 1988), and the lack of general control over the programming process (Macro & Buxton, 1987). Structure was thus used to impose order on creative enterprises in an effort to involve larger teams and divide the work according to newly established management approaches emphasising the balanced distribution of man-month effort across wider groups.

The emergence of structured efforts to control programming and the development of concepts such as the waterfall life cycle coincided with the departure of many hackers from their existing organisations. Meanwhile, the widespread adoption of more versatile computing systems, such as System/360, and the subsequent emergence of mini- and microcomputers, enabled hackers to reposition themselves and re-emerge in a wider variety of organisational and institutional settings.

Software houses, established in the fifties and sixties, when manufacturers were developing sophisticated product lines, were working for many of the larger organisations. Software houses were often staffed by outstanding programmers who cut their teeth on some of the early complex systems, before being released by large companies. When large corporations, military and the space agencies needed massive, complex and advanced computer software or encountered problems on their projects, they would hire independent contractors and software houses. The experience these specialists accrued through their earlier projects and the dependence of larger manufacturers on their expertise enabled them to hone their skills and gain market appreciation. Others took advantage of the easily available technology to experiment, develop, grow and position themselves as unquestioned leaders. Indeed, in 1980, when IBM decided to build personal computers, they hired Microsoft to build the operating system, thereby avoiding the need to engage with the development of a significant new operating system.

Many of the old constraints were changing, and the limits of the machine were no longer a key concern. Certainly, by this point experienced hackers in a solid position to compete with the monolithic manufacturers as small start-up companies offered hardware as well as software with amazing capabilities that could reside on the top of a desk. Many hackers were already in business, offering their clients to design complex systems rapidly using innovative machines, code and tools. The result was the encouragement of a new generation of aspiring programmers and hackers able to address a new set of challenges.

Shortages of qualified software professionals, reasonably priced powerful machines, and end-user computing combined to create the 'new age' hacker. New age hackers had a good understanding of the software packages they were using and were capable of utilising the internal features of these packages to produce impressive results. New age hacking was practised by individuals utilising the power on their desk within the confines of their offices, with limited quality assurance support, standards or even professional training. Steven Levy refers to the second generation of hackers, typically involved in the emergence of the PC, in contrast to the hackers of the 1950s and 1960s, which he classifies as first-generation hackers (Levy, 1984; Lin, 2007: 36). Being closer to the problem, the new hackers possessed an intimate knowledge of the problems and the technology, which enabled them to be creative whilst maintaining the principled conceptual integration and developing a wider understanding of the overall architecture required to address the problems.

By 1985, the new generation of hackers, working alone or in small teams, was able to make good use of improved prototyping tools and approaches. Prototyping could utilise newly available higher-order tools and technology to create more suitable computer programmes faster, by way of trial-and-error. Rapid prototyping reduced the cost of producing early programmes through providing the technology for rapid fabrication. The notion of frozen requirements could thus be replaced by communication and ongoing dialogue, while speed of delivery could substitute for the mammoth time spans typical of more traditional approaches involving large teams engaged in more bureaucratic cycles of conceptualisation, development, verification and delivery.

Prototyping is a creative and responsive effort that attempts to address users' needs. Once unleashed, it can prove difficult to control the rate of change, the length of the effort and, indirectly, the cost implications. Many prototyping projects reported problems with controlling the number of iterations or the length of the prototyping/reiteration phase. Costing prototyping projects is therefore done primarily on the basis of timing the length of the prototyping effort or limiting the number of allowed iterations. The pervasive, rational and practical problem of putting a price and a boundary on creativity thus proved to be a major hurdle to utilising a truly creative act.

To address management concerns, more controlled forms of prototyping and coordination were introduced. Approaches like the spiral model, Rapid Application Development (RAD), Scrum, agile development and the Dynamic Systems Development Method (DSDM) place greater emphasis on the management, costing and control of the prototyping or creative effort. The success of prototyping relies on the ability to obtain rapid fabrication of a definitive product. The application of strict management control to the process secures the delivery of rapid functionality according to agreed guidelines. In fact, it represents the imposition of agreed constraints on the creative process. (Interestingly, both the spiral and RAD/DSDM/agile methods respond to the pervasive problems highlighted earlier. The spiral controls the number of iterations through risk management, while RAD/Scrum/agile respond to the length of the effort by imposing the concept of fixed timeboxing.)

Taking Stock: Hackers Gallery

The writing of Brooks conveys a strong admiration for creative programmers and heroic architects and their resulting products. Reflecting back at the end of the anniversary edition, Brooks maintains that the central argument in the book is the critical focus on conceptual integrity and the architect. Brooks maintains that elegant software products are typically designed by a single mind, or at most by a pair of minds (Brooks, 1995: 255), rather than by committee. He contends that the same can be said of well-loved books or musical compositions.

Levy (1984) repositions hackers as the drivers of the computer revolution, profiling the imaginative 'brainiacs' who found clever and unorthodox solutions to computer problems by taking risks, bending the rules and consequently pushing the world in a new direction. Levy traces a daring symbiosis between man and machine, where hackers place the desire to tinker, learn and create technical beauty above all else (p. 39). Levy's sympathetic account traces the hackers from the late 1950s labs to the emergence of desktop machines in the '80s—these would later morph

Table 9.1 Hackers Gallery—A Representative Sample

Name	Association or Key Product)
Bill Gates	Microsoft
John Page	HP
Charles Simoni	Microsoft (MS Word, Excel)
Jonathan Sachs	Lotus 1-2-3
Andy Hertzfeld	Macintosh OS
Wayne Ratliff	dBase III
Peter Roizen	T/Maker
John Warnock	Adobe
Jeff Raskin	Apple Macintosh project
Gary Kildall	CP/M operating system
Bob Frankston	VisiCalc spreadsheet
Dan Bricklin	VisiCalc spreadsheet
Doug Englebart	Computer mouse
Mark Zuckerberg	Facebook
Richard Stallman	Gnu
Linus Torvalds	Linux Kernel
Eric Raymond	Open-Source Initiative

into agile development and are very much alive within the gaming community. Levy also introduces the hacker ethic, which (slightly paraphrased) advocates that (pp. 39–46):

- Access to computers—and any other sources of important information—should be unlimited and total.
- All information should be free.
- Hackers should be judged by their hacking and not by qualifications or position.
- Art and beauty can be created on a computer.
- Computers can change life for the better (and by implication; therefore, hackers play a part in shaping and bringing about that shift).

Hackers have shaped many aspects of life through the development of products and artefacts that have powered further development within wider society. Table 9.1 identifies the names of a number of well-known, self-proclaimed hackers alongside the well-recognised products or companies that they had been associated with. Many of the products have been considered as extremely successful and innovative and have played a part in shaping future generations of products. Intriguingly, the majority have had an active fan club at some point that recognised and appreciated the value and uniqueness of the resulting product.

The inventiveness of the hackers has enabled the wider computer revolution that has transformed society. To put it into perspective, the internet, the personal computer and software such as the Linux operating system and many of the original applications all result from the work of individual hackers tackling a specific challenge, rather than from the concerted and coordinated efforts of governments, or major corporations. Indeed, Castells (2001) frames technology as a fundamental dimension of social change (p. 155). Hackers, it would thus appear, assume agency roles as self-appointed change agents seeking societal or fundamental improvements.

Himanen (2001) portrays hackers as enthusiasts who are energised by truly challenging problems related to programming (p. 4). However, he further maintains that hackers' creations are underlined by the shared hacker values that produced them, promoting passionate and freely rhythmed work, the belief that individuals can create great things by joining forces in imaginative ways, and the need to maintain existing ethical ideals such as privacy and equality, in an increasingly technologised society. Richard Stallman reflects on the values, concerns and work habits of hackers during a conference on the hacker community:

> *What they had in common was mainly love of excellence and programming. They wanted to make their programs that they used be as good as they could. They also wanted to make them do neat things. They wanted to be able to do something in a more exciting way than anyone believed possible and show 'Look how wonderful this is. I bet you didn't believe this could be done* (Stallman, 1985).

Hacking is still alive and well; while the early hackers may have enjoyed the intellectual challenge of overcoming the physical limitations of computer technology and capability, the emerging hacker community appears to still think big and risk failure, whilst continuing to push the computer and what is viewed as possible beyond the current envelope of expectations. Hacking thus appears to revolve around combining an intimate knowledge of the problem to be solved (or the ambition) with knowledge and skill in the tools required to address the problem and the context and environment within which it is to be implemented. The key values, as always, are related to enabling a new capability, achieving a novel and unexpected outcome, outsmarting and extending the technology through unprecedented mastery, and enjoying the process of getting there. Brooks might also add a caveat around the need to maintain conceptual integrity and the ability to delight the client, which chimes with the iconic status of many of the products identified in Table 9.1. The culture, ethics and principles associated with the act of hacking certainly offer an indication of the importance of, and belief in, purpose and the need to focus on the wider perceived value for the user community.

Hacker Communities

Brooks widely acknowledges that, whilst conceptual integrity is essential to delivering significant products, the enormity and complexity of some undertakings requires engaged communities able to work with the architect to deliver useful products. In subsequent talks he alludes to the power of a small sub-community populated with capable and talented programmers to rescue projects that become delayed and threatened. Indeed, working against impossible odds and pushing the boundaries of what can be achieved is a hallmark of the hacker approach. Isaacson (2014) further celebrates the ability of pioneers, hackers and innovators to collaborate and master the art of teamwork, foster new scales and dimensions of innovation and thereby usher in the digital revolution.

Nowadays, hacking is often associated with criminal tendencies (also known as black hat hacking) and security breaches. However, the original spirit of hacking (sometimes referred to as white hat hacking) is a pure form of innovation against all the odds, as technical experts challenge themselves to confront insurmountable problems. A further intriguing concept is the ability of hacking to create communities that are able to share, engage and work collaboratively.

Brooks refers to ancient cathedrals as examples of conceptual integrity, where each generation of architects involved in the ultimate construction is happy to sacrifice some of their own ideas of design so that the whole might be of pure design (1995: 42). In this way, a multigenerational edifice is created that fuses together ideas and thinking into a satisfying whole. It is worth noting that the notion of *cathedral thinking* is increasingly utilised as an intergenerational approach to addressing long-term considerations. Cathedral thinking thus combines a far-reaching vision with a well-thought-out blueprint or integrated conceptual architecture and a shared commitment to responsibility, long-term use, continuous improvement and enduring sustainability.

Raymond (1997) contrasts the cathedral view of development, where between releases or generations, each new element of work is restricted to an elite group, with the Bazaar model. In the Bazaar model, the main work is developed globally over the internet in full view of the public, allowing multiple participants to interact, shape and improve the emerging product. This satisfies Raymond's maxim that *'given enough eyeballs, all bugs are shallow'*. In other words, Raymond maintains that the larger the number of testers and participants, especially through public testing, scrutiny and experimentation, the more rapidly all latent bugs and errors will be uncovered. Therein lies a further potential value that can be derived from the development of communities of capable and interested hackers. However, the assertion that all bugs will be uncovered and more rapidly addressed compared to planned discovery is yet to be rigorously tested and independently verified.

Raymond indirectly advocates for a form of democratisation of creative work. Moreover, the Bazaar approach allows for the mixing of different agendas, styles and approaches, as individuals decide to observe, participate and mingle in different aspects of the work. Rapid and frequent releases allow the content to develop and mature over time, as the wider community gets to engage with it over multiple iterations. The development of Wikipedia by active participants has been described as an exemplar application of the Bazaar model through the engagement of an active community (Poe, 2006). Coleman (2012) refers to the notion of productive freedom as *'the institutions, legal devices and moral codes that hackers have built in order to autonomously improve on their peers' work, refine their technical skills and extend craftlike engineering traditions'* (p. 3). Coleman is particularly impressed with how hackers have managed to build a dense ethical and technical practice that sustains their productive freedom whilst extending and reformulating key liberal ideas such as access, transparency, meritocracy, free speech and equal opportunity. Free and open-source communities—sometimes also known as *hackerspaces* or *makerspaces*—have grown in many parts of software development and therefore carry the potential for speeding up and upscaling innovation (see, for example, von Hippel & von Krogh, 2003; Kostakis et al., 2015; Söderberg & Delfanti, 2015).

It is particularly noteworthy that the example of Wikipedia offers a direct challenge to Brooks' assertion that the addition of person-power can actually delay or complicate the task, as Wikipedia's creation clearly attests to the value of an engaged community who are keen to participate, develop, improve and co-create something better. Indeed, it would appear that adding more human power to some important initiatives can lead to faster, better and richer products. Does this imply that in truly collaborative and voluntary endeavours, adding human power can actually enhance and improve the results? Moreover, does the spirit of true co-creation enable us to overcome the constant struggle between creativity and structure? Does it offer new insights into how to manage or support creative development? And for that matter, given the success of Wikipedia, might the development of the intellectual equivalent of the next System/360 be done on a more public basis and deliver more successful results at a faster pace?

What Are the Wider Implications for Innovation and for Projects?

Having taken a rather wide-sweeping historical perspective of the hacking approach and explored its roots in software development projects, it is time to return the focus to the future of projects. A culture that grew at the margin of the computer industry now seems ready to offer the potential to reposition, recalibrate and realign innovation. As agile thinking, active experimentation ideas and open-source concepts are entering mainstream business, there is an opportunity to utilise some of these new ways of thinking in order to foster better projects, improved outcomes and more satisfied users.

Could the new hacker make a difference in the wider business context? The challenge is to explore the potential and implications of hacking. Our relationship with technology has changed immensely over the past 50 years, as computers have transformed most facets of our society. Digital natives, people brought up during the age of digital technology, are entering the workforce, and the ideas of hacking may simply seem more natural to those who have grown up with computer games, continuous online presence and a wide variety of apps (Prensky, 2001, 2009; Bennett et al., 2008; Palfrey & Gasser, 2011; Albright, 2019). The following section by Tim Rayner is developed from his book *Hacker Culture and the New Rules of Innovation*, published by Routledge, and aims to explore the rich potential of hacking as a timely, creative approach.

Rayner recognises that the organisational landscape has changed. Innovation implies creativity, entrepreneurship, self-organising teams, cheap experimentation and fast learning. It also requires an imaginative new mindset, and Rayner is keen to explore the potential for importing some of the ideas that have transformed our world through new technologies.

Against the backdrop of smart cities, self-driving cars and wearable technologies, this is a good time to reflect on the pace of innovation. How did technology transform our lives so rapidly and so drastically in a span of a mere 50 years? Rayner attributes the fast progress to two main factors: open standards and innovation culture (Rayner, 2018: 2). Sharing and open standards enable entrepreneurs to build on each other's work, to grow innovation combinatorically, to continuously expand, improve and enhance. However, the second factor, the culture of technological innovation, plays a critical role.

It would be simple to focus on the allure of promising technology. However, by resisting the call of the technology sirens to take the easy route, Rayner is therefore able to make a far more important contribution; instead he draws attention to the requisite condition that has enabled the computer industry, and society at large, to benefit from such a tremendous rate of innovation. His focus is on the culture of innovation, the way people share, coordinate, work and collaborate to produce innovation.

In many ways Rayner's perspective provides a much-needed refresh and update to the view of a large firm engaged in a major innovation project that is imposed on the workforce. Here instead we have a democratised approach to the co-creation and co-development by consensus of cutting-edge innovation that is not limited by pre-ordained ambition or by accidental constraints. By looking at hacking as the vehicle for improvement and development, Rayner is able to offer a significant alternative to conventional technological innovation models.

Whilst the factor that appears to make the difference is hacking, it is hacking-in-the-large, in a wider social setting, rather than the initial hacking by very capable individuals, that comes to the fore. The power of hacking seems to be multiplied when it is used to engage and connect complete communities, enabling people to stand on the shoulders of others, and thereby continually grow, stretch and expand what is possible and attainable. In a true community spirit, where there is interest and commitment, hacking can act as a powerful multiplier that enables entrepreneurship to flourish. The *hacker culture* that Rayner talks about seems to be particularly important in establishing the dynamics needed to engage the multiplier and benefit from a more involved and passionate form of social and communal problem solving.

Cultures that are shaped by hierarchy, tradition, obedience, egos, targets and KPIs will continue to struggle to deliver in an increasingly dynamic and evolving marketplace. Start-ups have a lot to offer and a great potential to benefit from such fresh thinking: Start-ups that embrace the technological revolution have been able to transform their offerings by taking a customer-centric approach and engaging with their emerging markets. Rayner is therefore documenting a new stage in the development of hacker culture as a wider and more encompassing precondition for achievement of a hitherto unexpected and unimaginable new level of innovation.

Rayner's re-focus is on the all-important social space. The hacker entrepreneurs are far better connected and therefore more powerful than their poor cousins, the technical magicians, from 50 years ago. Leaders interested in successful transformation in the digital age would do well to begin by looking at the principles identified by Rayner in the context of starting to embed innovation within more agile and flexible organisations with better designed innovation space. The principles he sets forth are essential for setting the scene required for introducing and embedding meaningful innovation.

Is Hacking Ready to Take the Next Big Step?

Hacking thrives in the undefined and often overlooked interface between small and big, between creativity and structure, often empowering individuals to attempt the impossible against bureaucratic and overwhelming structures, monolithic machines and inflexible systems. As hacking becomes more apt as a strategy adopted by start-ups and innovators who have graduated from grappling computers to tackling more pervasive and wicked challenges, hacking offers the potential to solve significant problems in new entrepreneurial ways.

Hackers, it seems, are ready to tackle bigger and bolder challenges. Evan Burfield (2018: 2–6) identifies five important trends in an increasingly regulatory era:

1. Tech start-ups are diversifying beyond Silicon Valley, both in terms of geography and strengths, and therefore offer the potential to expand and encroach into new ecosystems.
2. They are increasingly trying to solve more pervasive problems, as entrepreneurs engage with transforming meaningful 'real-world' sectors such as health, education, transportation, energy and food, and in the process altering both business and society (Case, 2017).
3. There is a backlash against big tech, such as Facebook® (now Meta˚), Amazon®, Google® or Apple®, and an increasing concern with privacy, security and democracy.
4. Start-ups are solving urgent problems that would previously have been left to governments or nonprofits.
5. New technologies ranging from robots to artificial intelligence, and from cryptocurrencies to synthetic biology, offer the potential for technology-driven innovation to solve previously intractable challenges.

The clash between creative start-ups—which can see potential for the hacking needed to marshal new technologies and opportunities, and governments, which previously controlled this space but are increasingly tempted by the power of new technology to embrace game-changing impacts—introduces the potential for a new form of regulatory hacking. Rather than breaking the law, regulatory hacking is concerned with *finding a much more nuanced and strategic approach to navigating complex markets*', which Burfield (2018: p. 7) views as the stretching and bending of red tape to make room for (much-needed) progress.

> *Regulatory hacking is the application of hacker culture to complex markets that are deeply intertwined with government because they meaningfully impact the public interest. Regulatory hacking—when done thoughtfully and with the right motivations—is **hacking in the public interest*** (Ibid.: 8).

Successful hackers experiment, challenge and test the boundaries and capabilities of systems to arrive at elegant new solutions. Burfield views regulatory hacking as the natural application and extension of hacking ideas in the public interest so that it becomes a continuous process infused by experimentation, rather than a predefined gameplan that requires implementing (p. 28).

Indeed, hacking and entrepreneurship appear to be able to forge a synergistic alliance. Jensen and Klein (2010: 21) make a case for embracing hacking as an amazing innovation engine. They contend that the motivation to hack falls within three categories: curiosity, imagination and drive, which makes hacking so powerful (p. 18). In a similar vein, Butler observes that entrepreneurs aren't always more creative than general managers; however, they enjoy pushing the boundaries and thrive under conditions of uncertainty:

> *In reality, what sets entrepreneurial individuals apart is something both broader and deeper than what is typically evoked in the word 'creativity'. It is the ability to thrive in uncertainty . . . A critical aspect to this dimension is openness to new experiences. In my research I've found that it is the single trait and most distinguishes leaders who are entrepreneurial from their more conventional peers* (Butler, 2017: 86).

Butler defines *openness to new experiences* as having a restless need to explore and learn (Ibid.). It requires a willingness to proceed in uncertain, untried and unpredictable environments, as

---

˚ Meta trademark status uncertain as of this writing.

well as a heightened state of motivation at the edge of the unknown and untried. Individuals who score high in this dimension therefore view the unknown as a source of excitement rather than the underpinning factor for anxiety. Many entrepreneurs assume that things can be done better and are happy to experiment and explore that vision, leading serial entrepreneur Richard Branson to summarise his essential take on entrepreneurship as the need to listen, learn and lead (Branson, 2014). His most recent biography features his never-ending quest to push boundaries, break rules and seek new frontiers through an insatiable urge to learn and a willingness to embrace an extended learning journey (Branson, 2017). Crucially, the learning comes from continuous engagement through an ongoing attempt to improve, make sense and accomplish something useful, meaningful and significant.

Experimentation, trial-and-error and constant readjustment are part of the standard repertoire of successful hackers and effective entrepreneurs. As we move to the realm of more social and strategically positioned hacking, perhaps the next iteration of the hacker gallery (represented in Table 9.1 on page 223) would feature specific communities and wider sections of society, as organisational and global leaders become more comfortable with their role in facilitating large-scale social experiments and transformations in the public interest.

It would be interesting to see how larger systems developed through hacking solutions would evolve over time. At the very least, it gives us another experiment and another approach to test as we continually seek to improve, progress and grow. Furthermore, it enriches the conversations and provides much-needed inspiration and the beginning of an important new dialogue in this arena. The tension between creativity and structure through various management regimes has shaped development and progress over generations.

Ultimately, the thinking put forward by Rayner offers the potential to reignite innovation, create a connected social focus within the enterprise, and prepare the ground for delivering a new form of entrepreneurial management—a much-needed strategic capability in uncertain and unpredictable times.

References

Albright, J. M. (2019). *Left to Their Own Devices: How Digital Natives Are Reshaping the American Dream*. New York, NY: Prometheus Books.

Ascher, W. (1993). The ambiguous nature of forecasts in project evaluation: Diagnosing the over-optimism of rate-of-return analysis. *International Journal of Forecasting, 9*(1), 109–115.

Bennett, S., Maton, K., and Kervin, L. (2008). The 'digital natives' debate: A critical review of the evidence. *British Journal of Educational Technology, 39*(5), 775–786.

Booch, G. (1987). *Software Engineering with Ada*. San Diego, CA: Benjamin-Cummings Publishing Co.

Branson, R. (2014). *The Virgin Way: How to Listen, Learn, Laugh and Lead*. London, UK: Random House.

Branson, R. (2017). *Finding My Virginity: The New Autobiography*. London, UK: Penguin Random House.

Brooks, F. P., Jr. (1975). *The Mythical Man-Month: Essays on Software Engineering*. Reading, MA: Addison-Wesley.

Brooks, F. P., Jr.. (1995). *The Mythical Man-Month: Essays on Software Engineering*. (Anniv. Ed.). Reading, MA: Addison-Wesley.

Burfield, E. (2018). *Regulatory Hacking: A Playbook for Start-Ups*. New York, NY: Portfolio Penguin.

Butler, T. (2017). Hiring an entrepreneurial leader: What to look for. *Harvard Business Review, 95*(2) 85–93.

Case, S. (2017). *The Third Wave: An Entrepreneur's Vision of the Future*. New York, NY: Simon & Schuster.

Castells, M. (2001). Epilogue. In: P. Himanen (Ed.). *The Hacker Ethic and the Spirit of the Information Age*, 155–178. London, UK: Secker & Warburg.

Charette, R. N. (1986). *Software Engineering Environments: Concepts and Technology*. New York, NY: McGraw-Hill.

Coleman, E. G. (2012). *Coding Freedom: The Ethics and Aesthetics of Hacking*. Princeton, NJ: Princeton University Press.

Cortada, J. W. (2019). *IBM: The Rise and Fall and Reinvention of a Global Icon*. Cambridge, MA: MIT Press.

Dalcher, D. (1999). Simplicity and power: When more means less. *IEEE Computer, 32*(5), 117.

Dalcher, D. (2013). Project economics: Wishful thinking, conspiracy of optimism or a self-fulfilling prophecy? *PM World Journal, 2*(12), 1–4.

Erickson, J. (2008). *Hacking: The Art of Exploitation*. San Francisco, CA: No Starch Press.

Fishman, K. D. (1981). *The Computer Establishment*. New York, NY: McGraw-Hill.

Flyvbjerg, B. (2008). Curbing optimism bias and strategic misrepresentation in planning: Reference class forecasting in practice. *European Planning Studies, 16*(1), 3–21.

Flyvbjerg, B. (2009). Optimism and misrepresentation in early project development. In: T. Williams, K. Samset, and K. Sunnevåg (Eds.). *Making Essential Choices with Scant Information: Front-End Decision Making in Major Projects*, 147–168. London, UK: Palgrave Macmillan.

Glass, R. L. (1997). *In the Beginning: Recollections of Software Pioneers*. Los Alamitos, CA: IEEE Computer Society Press.

Himanen, P. (2001). *The Hacker Ethic and the Spirit of the Information Age*. London, UK: Secker & Warburg.

von Hippel, E., and von Krogh, G. (2003). Open source software and the 'private-collective' innovation model: Issues for organization science. *Organization Science, 14*(2), 209–223.

Ince, D. (1988). *Software Development: Fashioning the Baroque*. Oxford, UK: Oxford University Press.

Isaacs, W. (1999) *Dialogue and the Art of Thinking Together*. New York, NY: Currency Doubleday.

Isaacson, W. (2014). *The Innovators: How a Group of Inventors, Hackers, Geniuses and Geeks Created the Digital Revolution*. London, UK: Simon & Schuster.

Jensen, B., and Klein, J. (2010). *Hacking Work: Breaking Stupid Rules for Smart Results*. London, UK: Penguin UK.

Jordan, T., and Taylor, P. (1998). A sociology of hackers. *The Sociological Review, 46*(4), 757–780.

Kostakis, V., Niaros, V., and Giotitsas, C. (2015). Production and governance in hackerspaces: A manifestation of commons-based peer production in the physical realm? *International Journal of Cultural Studies, 18*(5), 555–573.

Levy, S. (1984). *Hackers: Heroes of the Computer Revolution*. New York, NY: Bantam Doubleday.

Lin, Y. W. (2007). Hacker culture and the FLOSS innovation. In: *Handbook of Research on Open Source Software: Technological, Economic, and Social Perspectives*, 34–46. Hershey, PA: IGI Global.

Love, P. E., Edwards, D. J., and Irani, Z. (2011). Moving beyond optimism bias and strategic misrepresentation: An explanation for social infrastructure project cost overruns. *IEEE Transactions on Engineering Management, 59*(4), 560–571.

Macro, A., and Buxton, J. N. (1987). *The Craft of Software Engineering.* Wokingham, UK: Addison-Wesley.

Palfrey, J. G., and Gasser, U. (2011). *Born Digital: Understanding the First Generation of Digital Natives.* New York, NY: Basic Books.

Poe, M. (2006). The hive—Can thousands of Wikipedians be wrong? How an attempt to build an online encyclopedia touched off history's biggest experiment in collaborative knowledge. *Atlantic Monthly, 298*(2), 86.

Prensky, M. (2001). Digital natives, digital immigrants, Part 1. *On the Horizon, 9*(5), 1–6.

Prensky, M. (2009). H. sapiens digital: From digital immigrants and digital natives to digital wisdom. *Innovate: Journal of Online Education, 5*(3), 1–9.

Raymond, E. S. (1997). *The Cathedral and the Bazaar.* Sebastopol, CA: O'Reilly Media.

Rayner, T. (2018). *Hacker Culture and the New Rules of Innovation.* Abingdon, UK: Routledge.

Schumacher, E. F. (1973). *Small Is Beautiful: A Study of Economics as if People Mattered.* New York, NY: Random House.

Sharot, T., Riccardi, A. M., Raio, C. M., and Phelps, E. A. (2007). Neural mechanisms mediating optimism bias. *Nature, 450*(7166), 102.

Sharot, T., Korn, C. W., and Dolan, R. J. (2011). How unrealistic optimism is maintained in the face of reality. *Nature Neuroscience, 14*(11), 1475.

Sharot, T., et al. (2012). How dopamine enhances an optimism bias in humans. *Current Biology, 22*(16), 1477–1481.

Söderberg, J., and Delfanti, A. (2015). Hacking hacked! The life cycles of digital innovation. *Science, Technology, & Human Values, 40*(5), 793–798.

Sparkes, M. (2016, April 7). IBM's $5bn gamble: Revolutionary computer turns 50. *Telegraph.* Accessed 23 June, 2019, at: https://www.telegraph.co.uk/technology/news/10719418/IBMs-5bn-gamble-revolutionary-computer-turns-50.html

SPREAD Task Group (1961). *Final Report of SPREAD Task Group* (28 December). (Reprinted in *IEEE Annals of the History of Computing,* Vol. 5, 1983, 6–26.)

Stallman, R. (1985). Interview. *Hackers—Wizards of the Electronic Age.* Documentary, KQED.

Wise, T. A. (1966). IBM's $5,000,000,000 Gamble. *Fortune Magazine,* 118–119.

How to Herd Cats: The Art of the Hacker Paradigm Leadership

Tim Rayner

Abstract: This section defines six core elements of hacker paradigm leadership—a style of leadership required in agile, lean, and collaborative design environments. Hacker paradigm leaders start with human connection, creating a foundation of trust and ownership in teams. They give people a sense of purpose. They cultivate a tribal mindset, focused on shared potential and rewards. They challenge teams to identify unverified assumptions and resolve unknowns through experiments. They spur teams to create value for customers and to work collaboratively to sustain a generative space where life is good and great things get done.

Hackers have a bad reputation. Thanks to the high-profile Distributed Denial of Service (DDoS) attacks of hacktivist groups like Anonymous, political hacks such as attempts to interfere with voter registration databases in the 2016 US election, and criminal hacks like the Sony cyber attack of 2014, in which hackers stole over 100 terabytes of data and planted malware to erase content from the company's servers, many people have a dim view of hacking. Hacking is seen as a subversive, immoral activity. Films like *Hackers* (1995) and the HBO series *Mr. Robot* portray hackers as lonely outsiders who fight governments and corporations. When hackers appear in the media, the article is typically headed with a shot of a shadowy figure hunched over a keyboard, looking like the Grim Reaper in a hoodie.

While the media's depiction of hackers is not factually incorrect, it is a partial and misleading view, focused exclusively on 'black hat hackers', or file breakers. Steven Levy's seminal book, *Hackers: Heroes of the Computer Revolution* (1984/2010), offers a different perspective on hacking that is vital for understanding the broader impact and influence of hacking today. Levy's account focuses on the True Hackers, a tradition that started at Massachusetts University of Technology (MIT) in the 1960s, where a ragtag band of young electronics engineers volunteered their passion, knowledge, and coding skills to write software for the first generation of user-programmable computers. These hackers created a culture of open, collaborative, exploratory coding (Levy, 2010). In subsequent decades, this tradition fueled the rise of personal computing (and Apple computers), inspired the free and open-source software (FOSS) movement, and contributed massively to the culture and technical infrastructure of the internet. It continues to shape the world of technology today.

In the wake of the dot.com crash of 2001–2002, a new generation of tech entrepreneurs emerged inspired by the practices and principles of hacking. Entrepreneurs like Facebook's CEO Mark Zuckerberg and Twitter's Jack Dorsey cut their teeth on open-source hacking. The success of their companies helped drive a new wave of interest in fast, cheap, exploratory approaches to product design and small business development. This interest subsequently cohered around three methods: agile development, lean start-up and design thinking. These methods, used today by developers, entrepreneurs, and designers internationally, are deeply indebted to the positive tradition of hacking that started at MIT (Rayner, 2018).

Today, hacking is a ubiquitous approach to innovation, a way of solving problems through collaborative, iterated sprints. It is not just for programmers. Anyone can be a hacker, assuming an experimental mindset and a willingness to get hands on, build and learn.

Hacker Paradigm Leadership

Project managers should attend to these developments. They imply new challenges and vast new opportunities. They require a new kind of leader and a new style of leadership.

We see this new style of leadership in the start-up sector. The kind of leadership required to get an early-stage start-up off the ground is radically different to that required to run an established business. As entrepreneur and author Steven Blank argues, a start-up is not a small version of an established business. It is a different entity—an idea in search of a workable business model, requiring a different set of strategies, mindsets and practices to get up and running. In an early-stage start-up, the ultimate shape and nature of the enterprise is fundamentally unknown. It must be discovered before it can be developed. This is the advantage of hacking, which is essentially a method for treating the unknown, teasing out new paths and possibilities through lightweight experiments.

Hackers' creative response to the unknown explains why the hacker way has proved so successful in new business and product development environments, especially in contexts where time is short, customer preferences are uncertain, and there are many complexities to be resolved. Methods like agile development, lean start-up and design thinking cut through complexity by empowering small teams to rapidly ideate, prototype and test ideas, exploring possibilities rather than leaping forth to execute on a plan.

The style of leadership required to enable these kinds of teams is light touch, inspirational, customer-focused and geared towards experimentation. Hacker paradigm leaders *make space* for innovation, in the sense of empowering teams to autonomously hack their way to success. Instead of stipulating what needs to be done by when, these leaders champion an ambitious vision and invite people to participate to figure out how to deliver on it. They cultivate a tribal mindset, coaching teams to believe in their potential, so that people contribute for intrinsic rewards like autonomy, mastery and purpose, not just a paycheck.

If you want troops, act like a general. If you want to make space for innovation and inspire self-motivated individuals to collaborate on solutions, you need a different style of leadership and a different set of people management skills. The best hacker paradigm leaders are transformational leaders (Bass, 1999). These leaders inspire and motivate teams by championing a vision that people *want* to make their own. There are few things more important for a team than a leader who can inspire people to rise to great heights, without trying to control them. This encourages team members to take risks and embrace uncertainty, trusting in their leader's support and the camaraderie of the team.

This section defines six core elements of hacker paradigm leadership—a style of leadership required for success in agile development, lean start-up, and collaborative design contexts. These six elements build on one another to form a coherent leadership system. Hacker paradigm

Hacker paradigm leaders:

1. Trust in people
2. Lead with purpose
3. Cultivate a tribal mindset
4. Are 'Chief Experimenters'
5. Create user value
6. Makes pace for innovation

leaders start with human connection, creating a foundation of trust and ownership. They give people a sense of purpose. They cultivate a tribal mindset, focused on shared potential and rewards. They challenge teams to identify unverified assumptions and resolve unknowns through experiments. They spur teams to create value for customers and to work together to sustain a generative space where life is good and great things get done.

Hacker paradigm leaders do more than just steer people into work. They create meaningful work and the opportunity for meaningful lives.

Trust in People

Learning to trust in a team and communicating this trust to every member of the team is a prerequisite for creating a safe environment in which people feel comfortable taking risks, running experiments and exploring new terrain. Accordingly, the best hacker paradigm leaders automatically defer to trusting in people's capacity and potential. They trust in people's inventiveness and resourcefulness, their capacity to deliver under pressure, and their ability to put their heads together and create. Based on this trust, they set their people free, empowering them to try things out, make mistakes and learn from them.

This level of trust can terrify leaders who are used to being in control of things. Certain of these leaders have reason to feel nervous. Leaders can put their reputations, and even livelihoods, on the line when investing trust in teams. If the team fails, it is the leader who takes the hit. Yet, carrying risk is the only way that leaders can demonstrate to their team how much they trust them, believing in them and the project. Hacker paradigm leaders carry risk so that their teams feel trusted and supported to take risks of their own. They inspire people to believe in themselves by standing tall for the team, defending it against the intrusion of outside forces and championing its capacities and mission.

Smart leaders don't gamble on just any team. Good business involves minimising risk, and so does hacker paradigm leadership. Smart leaders take calculated risks on teams and projects they truly believe in. They invest in projects in an entrepreneurial way, carrying risk strategically so that trustworthy teams can cut loose and innovate for mutual reward.

Teams are only as strong as the people who contribute to them. To create a trustworthy team, leaders need to recruit a set of trustworthy people. Leaders also need to ensure that these people can work as a team. The fact of working together does not make a group of people a team. Unless these people can communicate and collaborate effectively, they are unworthy of the title 'team' and unworthy of the leader's trust in them to perform as such.

The upshot is that there are two entities hacker paradigm leaders must learn to trust: individuals and teams. Since teams are only as strong as the people who contribute to them, it makes sense that we start by reflecting on trustworthy individuals.

Trusting People

Recruiting is critically important in the start-up industry. Start-up founders need to find people they can genuinely believe in, and so they typically put applicants through a rigorous recruiting process. In addition to looking for evidence that the applicants can perform the tasks required of them, founders look for a T-shaped skill set and cultural fit.

T-shaped people have core expertise in a certain area (for example, UX design, software development, marketing and so on), as well as a broad range of additional skills, talents and interests. This mix of core and ancillary skills makes T-shaped people ideally suited for working in cross-functional team environments. These people can head up key aspects of projects by leading with their core expertise, playing to their strengths in design, programming, strategy or whatever their skills may be. Because they have a broader range of skills and talents to draw on, they can also slot in with and contribute to other parts of the project, standing in for other team members and tackling various tasks as they arise.

Cultural fit implies both an intuitive understanding of hacker culture and the desire to apply it. Hacker paradigm leaders look for people who are passionate about collaboration, who enjoy getting hands-on with problems and figuring things out, and who aren't afraid to work in environments of high stress and uncertainty. They seek out candidates who see challenges as opportunities to learn, and who want to contribute to changing the world.

When a start-up founder finds an applicant with both a T-shaped skill set and a hacker sensibility, they know they have someone they can believe in and potentially trust. The decisive factor is whether the applicant is prepared to step up and unleash their abilities, investing themselves conceptually, emotionally and behaviourally in the work of the team.

The best way to test an applicant's commitment to the job is to give them the opportunity to demonstrate it in practice. New recruits to start-ups are often invited to spend a day or two working with the team, to see how they fit. Rather than give them a specific task to perform, leaders should introduce them to the team and leave it up to them to figure out how they can contribute to the work in progress. This quickly establishes whether the applicant has what it takes to work in a self-organising hacker environment.

Trusting Teams

Hacker paradigm leaders also look for potential in teams. This shared potential is underwritten by the trustworthiness of the individual team members. Team potential is defined by the chemistry amongst team members, together with their ability to communicate and combine their powers. Until the leader can trust in a team's potential, he will remain ambivalent about the team's capacity for success, which invariably impacts on team members' confidence and the performance of the team as a whole.

Hacker paradigm leaders are always on the lookout for teams with extraordinary potential. These teams comprise people with unique qualities, who also possess critical interpersonal abilities, such as an enhanced ability to communicate and exchange ideas, to build, test and learn at speed, to manage time in a productive way, and to support one another and invest emotional energy in the work, feeding the spirit and vitality of the team.

When leaders identify these qualities in a team, they can feel confident they have a team they can trust. Leaders should not be shy to express this trust. Here are some characteristic statements leaders use to express their trust in teams:

'You people are great!'

'I see amazing potential on this team'.

'I'm convinced we can do incredible things together'.

'You are always teaching me things. I love learning from you'.

Lead with Purpose

The greatest hacker teams through history have been driven by a sense of purpose. The MIT hackers didn't stay up late at night playing around with computers just because they were curious about the machines. A powerful sense of purpose drove them. They believed that computers could, and one day would, change the world. Their goal was to make it happen.

Thanks to their sense of purpose, the MIT hackers were unstoppable. Few people outside their circle were aware they existed, but the hackers knew they were creating value nonetheless. Their sense of purpose gave meaning to their work. It transformed them from a rag-tag collective into a learning organisation and tribe.

Purpose is a buzzword in business today. Behind the hype, it reflects a major transition in the nature of work, as teamwork and innovation become central features of organisational productivity. Aaron Hurst, author of *The Purpose Economy* (2014), argues that running a business today without an emphasis on purpose 'is like running an organisation in the early 1990s and failing to implement technology.' Like enterprise software, purpose brings teams together, creating efficiencies and maximising engagement and commitment. Purpose catalyses magic by inspiring people to believe in their work and to give it everything they've got.

Simon Sinek was one of the first people to see the new paradigm emerging. In *Start with Why* (2009), Sinek explains how great leaders use purpose to inspire their followers to action. For great companies, purpose is more than just sexy marketing and sales patter. It is an answer to the question: 'Why are we doing this?' This answer changes everything. Sinek cites Apple as an example of a company that is guided by purpose. Apple, Sinek points out, isn't just in the business of selling computers, phones, watches and services. Apple is selling a mindset and a way of life. Apple sells an echo of the hacker ethos that animated the company in its formative years, when it was a start-up launched by a hacker and a college dropout who dreamed of changing the world by giving everyone a computer.

Steve Jobs crystallised this ethos in Apple's famous 'Think Different' campaign. '*Here's to the crazy ones*', the campaign ran. '*They push the human race forward. . . . Because the people who are crazy enough to think they can change the world, are the ones who do*'.

Apple's sense of purpose is essentially Jobs's sense of purpose, infused in the company. Inspiring and enabling people to 'think different' has become key to Apple's brand. This answer to the question 'why?' has accelerated Apple's success over the years. In Apple's early days, it inspired hacker teams to work around the clock and endure Jobs's volatile temperament to get the job done. Apple's sense of purpose continues to inform design decisions on every product it releases and every marketing decision it makes.

Drop into an Apple Store, and you can feel this sense of purpose at work. Apple Store employees are clearly proud of the job they are doing and thrilled to be associated with the brand. They engage you directly, listen to your problem, solve it, take your payment and send you on your way in a matter of minutes. Microsoft has tried to replicate the model in its stores, but there is a reverence among Apple employees that is hard to replicate. This is because Apple offers its employees a clear sense of purpose. As Apple Store employees see it, in serving customers, they are contributing to changing the world.

Early-stage start-up founders need to lead with purpose. Consider the work that is involved in getting an early-stage start-up off the ground. At first, the work is fun, as ideas get thrown around and everyone figures out what to do. But once the work gets underway, things get hectic, and it takes a lot of energy to maintain momentum.

People are working long hours on the project. Employees sweat through endless cycles of hacking and customer development. The pressure and anxiety ratchet up as the company scales. Budgets are tight, and there is never enough cash. Sometimes people don't get paid. No one sees a share of equity if the company fails. Employees need a good reason to continue giving their best under these conditions, day after day. When they ask the founder: 'Why am I doing this?', there better be a good answer, or the company will lose employees.

Leading with purpose requires that leaders genuinely engage with people and connect with them on an emotional level. It requires that leaders speak to people's intrinsic passions, celebrate their potential and cultivate their desire to make a difference. Most importantly, it requires that leaders articulate why the work is important and shouldn't be treated lightly. When employees ask: *'Why am I doing this?'* the right answer is: *'Because it matters'*.

Here are the mission statements of five of the most valuable tech companies in the world. All of them offer an answer to the question: *'Why?'*

- Google: To organise the world's information and make it accessible to everyone
- Facebook: To enable the world to connect and share
- Airbnb®: To create great travel experiences defined by authenticity and connection
- Uber®: To provide safe and reliable transpiration, everywhere to everyone
- Tesla®: To accelerate the transition to a global clean-energy regime

Cultivate a Tribal Mindset

A third component of hacker paradigm leadership concerns how leaders catalyse the collective energies of their teams. Purpose works as a broad motivational tool, but something more specific is required to cultivate top performance in teams. We touched on this earlier when we considered how a leader should speak to a team to express trust in its potential. Trusting a team involves believing in team members' collective potential for greatness. When a team believes it can do amazing things, people commit beyond the call of duty. They work hard, help each other out and move mountains to achieve their goals.

Some people feel uncomfortable with the word 'greatness'. Applied to individuals, the term sounds egoistic. But there is nothing egoistic about a team aspiring to greatness. This is something that the best sports teams do all the time. On great teams, team members bury their egos and focus on the shared prize. They work together to achieve something great that none of them could achieve alone, and they share the kudos equally across the team.

Every talented team is capable of greatness. The art of hacker leadership hinges on seeing the potential for greatness in a team, affirming it and teaching the team members to affirm it themselves. Leaders need to coach individuals to appreciate what they're capable of achieving in concert with others and to see their potential for greatness. They need to help the team as a whole to understand what it can achieve by working as a unit and to inspire team members to commit to realising this potential in practice.

In their book *Tribal Leadership* (2008), Dave Logan, John King and Halee Fischer-Wright offer a set of coaching techniques for leaders who want to build high-performing teams inspired by a sense of greatness. Their approach hinges on creating a shared mindset in teams, such that team members appreciate their collective potential. By coaching teams to appreciate their collective potential, tribal leaders instil a collaborative mindset in teams. Teams affirm collaboration as an intrinsically valuable feature of work—one that enables the whole team to enjoy an extraordinary sense of empowerment and achievement.

Tribal leadership requires leaders to diagnose and change the cultural status quo in their organisations. Logan, King and Fischer-Wright distinguish five levels of organisational culture, each with its characteristic vocabulary and mindset:

Stage 1 cultures are pathological. People with Stage 1 mindsets believe that life sucks—end of story. The authors claim that Stage 1 mindsets are mostly found in criminal subcultures. They calculate that *about 2% of American professionals operate [at the Stage 1 level]*. They wryly suggest that these are the *people who come to work with shotguns* (Logan et al., 2008: 18).

The Stage 2 mindset is more widespread, accounting for about 25 percent of workplace cultures. People at a Stage 2 level have the mindset that 'my life sucks', while conceding that others have it better. Stage 2 agents tend to be depressive, resigned and hostile to management. The authors observe that in Stage 2 cultures *[t]here is little to no innovation and almost no sense of urgency* (p. 19).

Most coaching strategies focus on hauling people up to the Stage 3 level. Stage 3 cultures are intrinsically individualistic and highly competitive. People in these cultures behave like lone wolves, each convinced that he or she is the only capable person in the company. The governing language and mindset of Stage 3 is: 'I'm great (and you're not)'. The authors estimate that around 50 percent of companies operate at this level.

Stage 4 cultures can also be highly competitive. But at the Stage 4 level, competition is played out in the struggle between teams, not individuals. The governing language and mindset of a Stage 4 level is: 'We're great (and they're not)', where 'they' is the opposing team. Precisely who a Stage 4 team selects as their 'they' is important. The authors reflect: *The bigger the foe, the more powerful the tribe* (p. 23). Stage 4 teams reflect the extraordinary cultures that hacker paradigm leaders should try to create. Within each team, individuals compete in a virtuous manner, trying to outperform one another to advance the tribe. Every individual works to empower the team, seeking to unleash the team's potential. Leaders rarely need to crack the whip on Stage 4 teams. They often feel like they're being 'pulled by the group' as it seeks to achieve its goals (p. 23).

Stage 4 teams are the springboard to the highest and most fulfilling form of workplace culture, the Stage 5 form. Stage 5 level cultures emerge when a Stage 4 team chases a world-changing vision and a noble cause, like curing cancer or developing the next generation of renewable energy technologies and finds itself on the winning side of history.

At Stage 5 level, teams have a sense that 'life's great'. This sensibility is borne out in their language and relationships with one another. Stage 5 level teams are not interested in competing with one another or competing with other teams, companies or organisations. They are too busy making history. Rather than compete, Stage 5 teams would rather look for opportunities to collaborate with other teams working in the same direction. At the Stage 5 level, competitors become 'frenemies', collaborating for mutual benefit and the opportunity to learn from one another (Gupta et al., 2013).

Stage 5 culture is hard to maintain. Logan, King and Fisher-Write claim that, typically, a Stage 4 team spikes to Stage 5 at the height of its achievements, then *recedes to Stage 4 to regroup* before making a fresh attempt (Logan et al., 2008: 25). Under the steady hand of a tribal leader, however, it is possible to sustain a team at Stage 4 level, taking tilts at Stage 5. The authors suggest that the team that built the Apple Macintosh sustained a Stage 5 culture throughout its life (p. 25). The purpose-driven hacker-generation companies listed at the end of the previous section are all Stage 4 organisations and launching pads for Stage 5 team experiences.

Logan, King and Fischer-Wright's focus in *Tribal Leadership* is on how to transform organisations from Stage 3 to Stages 4 and 5. Leading with purpose is a prerequisite for levelling up. Higher-level cultures are powered by a sense that the tribe is doing something extraordinary together. Greatness is not a confidence trick. Companies and individuals need to aspire to great things, otherwise the language of greatness rings hollow.

Purpose alone is rarely enough to shift a team of people out of a Stage 3 mindset. In a lone-wolf culture, no one wants to let their guard down for fear of being savaged by the pack. To get a team out of a Stage 3 rut, leaders must do two things: First, they must coach lone wolves to see the limits of a Stage 3 mindset by reflecting on what they could achieve by working collaboratively with others. Second, they should create the conditions for a Stage 4 epiphany by challenging lone wolves to form empowering workplace triads.

- The first strategy involves teaching people that no matter how great they are independently, there are many things they will never be able to achieve alone. Logan, King and Fischer-Wright recommend that leaders encourage lone wolves to work on projects that require collaboration as a condition of success. This teaches people to see the limited nature of lone-wolf mindsets. Meanwhile, leaders should offer these individuals Stage 4 mentorship, coaching them to see that real power comes from relationships and networks, not from personal expertise.
- The second strategy involves teaching lone wolves to build and lead collaborative cultures. Lone wolves tend to form dyadic relationships with other Stage 3 operators, shutting themselves off from others. To get the wolves mingling with friendlier animals, leaders should encourage them to proactively create triadic relationships in the workplace, introducing co-workers to talented third parties they would benefit from knowing.

    By pushing lone wolves to broker profitable encounters between two or more parties, tribal leaders teach wolves to see themselves as bonding elements in a team, as opposed to isolated nodes. It is important that lone wolves reflect on how good it feels to create a 'we' environment. Finding themselves in a great team of their own making, they embrace a Stage 4 mindset as a matter of pride. As the people they have brought together express their gratitude, it creates a sense of friendship and mutuality that helps concretise and maintain a Stage 4 perspective.

Be a 'Chief Experimenter'

In December 2009, Dean McEvoy was at the Pollenizer Christmas party in Sydney, Australia. Pollenizer, a start-up incubator, was a growing force in Sydney's start-up scene, and the party was packed with hustlers, hackers and hipsters, soaking up the energy of the night.

McEvoy's start-up, Booking Angel, was part of the Pollenizer stable. As of December, McEvoy had been working on Booking Angel for about five years. While he maintained a brave face at the party, McEvoy was worried that the business was failing to grow.

Recently, McEvoy had been nosing around for new opportunities. Earlier that year, a Silicon Valley investor had introduced him to Groupon, a Chicago group buying site that had recently pivoted its model and was growing fast. McEvoy was impressed with the group buying concept. He could see that it resulted in an exciting user experience that kept customers coming back.

Booking Angel's pay-per-booking model lacked this spark. McEvoy was wondering what an Australian Groupon might look like and how it might work.

Pollenizer co-founder and CEO, Phil Morle, was also at the party. After a couple of drinks, McEvoy mustered up courage and pitched Morle on his idea for a group buying site. McEvoy knew Pollenizer had a couple of developers kicking around over the summer without much to do. Why not set them on the job, he suggested, and see what they could create?

Morle was intrigued. He liked the idea, but he wanted to test it. Morle said, *'Let's do this lean. We don't want to waste time and money. Let's find out if the model works'.*

McEvoy and Morle sprang into action. Between Christmas and New Year, they mapped out the dimensions of their business concept, making educated guesses about who their customer was, the value the business created for the customer, how the sales and marketing channels worked and where the money would come from. They knew that possibly some of these assumptions were false. They also knew that some of them had to be true for the business model to work. They focused on identifying their *riskiest* assumptions—the assumptions that needed to be right for the business to succeed. These were the assumptions they needed to test.

Working with a developer, McEvoy and Morle built a series of prototypes that would enable them to test these assumptions. Tapping into Pollenizer's networks, they began running experiments with potential customers to see if the group buying concept had traction. For one experiment, they hosted a private party and invited guests to use their prototype to 'group buy' drinks. It was a simple face-to-face experiment. McEvoy and Morle figured that if the group-buying concept worked, it should work for people standing together in a room. The participants loved the experiment. Their contributions helped the team learn more about user behaviour and perfect their prototype design.

McEvoy and Morle continued testing their ideas in online and offline environments. They ran tests with a range of products from pizzas to fashion footwear. They ran A/B tests to isolate and measure the impact of their design ideas. They set up 'Wizard of Oz' environments in which customers would interact with a web interface, with human beings manually performing the back-end processes. The whole time, they sought to validate or disprove key aspects of their business model. Those assumptions they successfully validated they baked into the model. Those that they disproved were dumped or reworked.

By the end of January, McEvoy, Morle and their new business partner, Justus Hammer, had a business model they felt confident about, with hard data to dispel any doubts. Through many iterations, their start-up had evolved into a 'deal of the day' site that gave customers the opportunity to scoop deals on the most exciting things happening in their city. They called the start-up 'Spreets'—a mashup of 'spree' (as in 'shopping spree') and 'treats'.

Spreets went live on February 4, 2010 (which happened to be McEvoy's birthday). The site processed $4,000 worth of sales in the first 24 hours. The team immediately knew they were onto something. They buckled in, hit overdrive and clung on for the ride.

Spreets grew rapidly through the following months. The founders went looking for venture capital investment as memberships soared and traffic went through the roof. By June, Spreets was opening internationally in one new city a week. By September, it was bringing in $1 million dollars a week. By December 2010, Spreets had 500,000 members and had processed 270,000 voucher sales. The team could barely keep up with the pace of growth.

Then, in January 2011, the gods of start-up entrepreneurship reached down and anointed the team. Yahoo!7 made an offer to buy Spreets for $40 million Australian dollars. This is what the start-up game is all about. McEvoy, Morle and Hammer scarcely hesitated. They accepted Yahoo!7's offer, sold the company and became wealthy entrepreneurs as a result.

The story of Spreets is the start-up entrepreneur's dream. A small team of disruptors design a novel business that launches fast and scales faster, and which is snapped up by a corporate buyer for a multimillion-dollar sum. Most large companies spend as much time planning new ventures as it took Spreets to scale and exit. Morle told me, *'Spreets got [Pollenizer] a lot of attention from corporates, because they said, "Wait—that took you 11 months to go from an idea to $40 million? We're still thinking about things in that time"'*.

It is hard for a corporation to innovate at this speed. Hard—but not impossible. The key to enabling any organisation to innovate like a start-up is to build a culture of experiments. To achieve this, the organisation needs Chief Experimenters, who lead by the power of example. This is how McEvoy, Morle and Hammer got Spreets off the ground. The founders led with experimental method, questioning the tenets of their venture and testing every assumption. A lean feedback cycle doesn't run itself—it requires the will and determination of a hacker paradigm leader to initiate the cycle, help teams identify assumptions that need to be tested and keep the learnings coming fast.

Nathan Furr and Jeff Dyer (2014: 49–51) coined the idea of a Chief Experimenter to counter the command-and-control mentality of traditionally minded business executives. Most executives see themselves as 'Chief Decision Makers'. In their view, their job is to anticipate the future, decide on a direction and set their company on a course to success. This attitude is reasonable enough in well-defined environments with clear challenges, opportunities and risks. It is foolishness or lunacy in uncertain and unstable environments in which no one understands the opportunities and risks, or even what success looks like.

The challenge of leading innovation projects calls for a different kind of leadership. Leaders must think and act like hackers, teaching teams to acknowledge their assumptions and to run experiments to test them. Instead of making decisions on behalf of teams, Chief Experimenters *'[let] decisions move downwards in the hierarchy'*, letting data reveal *'what the next experiment should be'* (Ibid.: 50). They work with teams to identify 'leap-of-faith' assumptions that need to be tested and support them as they validate these assumptions through customer experiments.

Insisting on experiments can be a thankless task. When a team has struck on a great idea, people like to think they are on the road to success. Enthusiasm levels run sky high. Egos bloat out of proportion. No one wants to hear it when someone says: 'Hold on. We have no idea if this will work. Let's run some experiments to figure it out'. This pops everyone's bubble. But this is precisely what the Chief Experimenter must do.

The most important thing a Chief Experimenter must do is set an example by running experiments every day. Running experiments doesn't always involve building prototypes and minimum viable products (MVPs). Hacker paradigm leaders run regular workplace experiments to streamline processes and improve team performance. They start with a problem and take the measure of the situation, trying to figure out what is going wrong. They make a guess about how to fix things and formulate a practical hypothesis, along the lines of: 'If I try X, I'll get Y'. They run an experiment, intervening in the situation in a constructive way, and monitor the results. If their hypothesis plays out, the leader may institute a new rule or process. If the hypothesis doesn't stand up to testing, the leader tries something different.

This is how Chief Experimenters hack the workplace every day. They lead with experiments and encourage their teams to do the same.

Create User Value

When Brian Chesky and Joe Gebbia decided to rent out their loft apartment in 2007, they weren't thinking of launching a billion-dollar business. It was a way to cover the rent while they hatched their big idea. Chesky and Gebbia figured they could earn some money and perhaps make some friends in the process. They were proud of their apartment, and they looked forward to showing it off to guests.

Chesky and Gebbia called their venture AirBed and Breakfast.com. They built a website and put out a call: three airbeds for rent, with a homecooked breakfast thrown in. Three guests booked, followed by a flurry of emails from all over the world asking if Airbed and Breakfast's services were available in other cities. Inspired by this response, Chesky and Gebbia wondered if there might be a business model in the idea. They started brainstorming plans for a start-up, one that would enable people to rent out their homes to strangers.

Nathan Blecharczyk, a former roommate, was impressed with Chesky and Gebbia's idea, but he thought their website sucked. Blecharczyk came on board and helped the team build a more sophisticated site. The three founders ran a second experiment to test the AirBed and Breakfast.com idea, offering the service during the 2008 Democratic National Convention in San Francisco. Once again, the experiment was a success. But when the convention finished, traffic on the site slowed to a crawl. Clearly, world domination was a long way off.

Uncertain of how to proceed, Chesky, Gebbia and Blecharczyk enrolled in Y Combinator, a Silicon Valley start-up incubator. Paul Graham, CEO of Y Combinator, was sceptical that anyone would want to rent rooms in other people's homes, but he liked the chutzpah of the founding team and thought their idea was worth testing. Y Combinator was a fresh start for the team. They shortened their name to Airbnb and dedicated themselves to making the company a success.

Graham gave the Airbnb team permission to think small. To this point, the team had focused on building a robust back-end system ready to scale. Inspired by the Silicon Valley mantra of scaling and growth, they'd obsessed over how their site would handle one million or more users a day. Graham proposed a counterintuitive experiment. Instead of making something for millions of people, what if you were creating a special experience for one hundred people. It is better to create something awesome for a core group of customers than something mediocre that is targeted at everyone. If you can create real value for these customers, they will market the product for you. Scaling comes later in the sequence. First, define an offering that changes people's lives.

Thinking small forced the Airbnb team to acknowledge that they didn't really know who their customer was. To find out, they needed to get out of the building. New Yorkers were using Airbnb, so the founders travelled to New York and started renting rooms on the site and interviewing the hosts. What did they love about Airbnb? What did they think could be improved? Meanwhile, the founders were drilling down into the deeper question: 'Who are you, anyway?'

The founders were encouraged to learn that many of the hosts using Airbnb were doing it for the same reasons as Chesky and Gebbia had initially rented out their own apartment. They wanted to make some extra money, but they were also keen to show off their spaces to guests. The problem was, the photos they were uploading to Airbnb failed to achieve this. They were poor-quality photos that didn't reflect the charm of the spaces themselves.

Intrigued by this disjunction, the team decided to try another experiment. They went about New York taking glossy colour photographs of select lodgings that captured their spaces in their full glory. When these photos were posted on the Airbnb site, the lodgings secured two to three times the number of rentals of other spaces in the city.

This was an 'aha' moment for the Airbnb team. It turned out to be the cornerstone of a remarkable insight. After several experiments of this nature, Chesky, Gebbia and Blecharczyk realised that Airbnb's guests weren't just looking to find cheap accommodation—they wanted to have unique travel experiences. They specifically wanted a personalised experience—something friendly, authentic and human—the kind of experience they'd rarely enjoy when booking a room at a standard hotel.

Reversing this insight, Chesky, Gebbia and Blecharczyk reflected on what the best Airbnb hosts offered their guests. The highest-rating hosts in New York were passionate about providing guests with unique experiences. They loved their homes and neighbourhoods and they wanted guests to enjoy them too. Chesky and Gebbia had wanted much the same thing when they started their venture. When they'd rented out their loft apartment, they'd sought the simple pleasure of showing off their space, in addition to earning extra cash. Since then, they'd lost focus on the values that first inspired them. Caught up in the challenge of creating a scalable platform, they had forgotten why it was that Airbnb had seemed like such a great idea from the start.

Airbnb's mission from this point was clear. Airbnb would bring together people who wanted to create and enjoy unique travel experiences. Inspired by this insight, Chesky, Gebbia and Blecharczyk leapt into a wholesale redesign of the Airbnb website, enabling hosts to post large, colour pictures of their spaces, thereby selling them on character as much as price. They enabled hosts and guests to profile themselves in detail, so that individuals felt like they were connecting with real human beings, not just parties to a commercial transaction.

The strategy worked. By the end of 2010, Airbnb was scaling fast. Through 2011, the start-up grew from two million, to four million, to 10 million users by mid-2012. With investment capital flooding in, the founders shifted gear, from being struggling entrepreneurs to leaders of a ground-breaking company, the poster child of the so-called 'sharing economy'.

The story of Airbnb reflects an important lesson for hacker leaders and their teams. A hacker team's foremost concern should be to create value for customers or users, whether this is by simplifying or enhancing their lives or enabling them to achieve something they would struggle to achieve independently. The leader's role is to challenge and assist the team in zeroing in on *how* they are creating value, and to ensure that they maintain this focus through the design, development and delivery of work. Ideally, the value the team seeks to create will be an extension of their own values. This ensures that a clear and consistent set of values runs through the project and, in the case of a company, the brand.

Great companies are defined not just by the value they create in the world, but by the way they embody their mission in the core values their employees live out every day. Airbnb is a fine example. Thanks to its founders' insight into their core values and motivations, Airbnb is staffed by people who are genuinely passionate about creating unique travel experiences. This creates an emotional connection between the company and its customers, reflected at every point of the customer journey, from the first visit to the final review.

Great companies and teams are defined by people who pull together because they passionately believe in what they're doing and the value they are creating for customers. Value, in this case, is more than just a set of abstract nouns (such as 'honesty' and 'integrity') on the company's value statement. To build a great company, leaders must identify the core values that *really* drive them and build these values into the DNA of the culture and brand. This enables employees to say, 'Life's great', and believe it, because they know they are living by their values and making the world a better place.

Make Space for Innovation

In August 1983, the Apple Macintosh team moved into the Bandley 3 building, across the street from their previous digs in Texaco Towers. A few days before the shift, Steve Capps, an engineer on the team, had a flash of inspiration. Capps was thinking about Steve Jobs's speech at the Carmel retreat earlier that year. Something Jobs said at the retreat had stuck in Capps's mind: *'It's better to be a pirate than join the navy'*. This was one of Jobs's pet maxims. The Macintosh team had recently celebrated Jobs's birthday by paying for a billboard that read: *'Happy 28th Steve. The Journey is the Reward. The Pirates'*.

Capps had a blazing insight. If the Macintosh team were pirates, then Bandley 3 should fly a Jolly Roger! It was the perfect prank. Capps shared the idea with Andy Hertzfeld, lead developer on the team, who declared he was on board. The night before the team took occupancy of Bandley 3, Capps, Hertzfeld and a band of miscreants crept out and hung a handcrafted, black and white, skull and crossbones flag from the roof of the building, with a rainbow Apple decal in place of an eyepatch (Hertzfeld, 2013).

The Bandley 3 pirates weren't sure how their prank would be received. They were thrilled to discover, the following morning, that Jobs and other senior people at Apple loved the flag. The pirate flag became a permanent fixture on the roof of Bandley 3 during the Macintosh team's tenure at the building. Jobs defended the flag right up to the launch of the Macintosh in 1984. He loved the pirate metaphor. *'We were the renegades, and we wanted people to know it'*, Jobs recalled (Isaacson, 2015: 133).

Bandley 3 was nothing special. But the pirate flag transformed the building into a home base and play space for hackers. In their time at Bandley 3, the Macintosh team took high performance hacking to a new level. They built on the work of the Bandley pirates to create a generative environment within the space, an environment defined by energy and limitless possibility, in which the future was open and life was great.

Given Jobs's familiarity with hacker culture, it is no surprise that he affirmed the pirate flag prank. When team members establish cultural norms in this way, the leaders' work is done. Leadership on hacker teams should ultimately come from team members themselves, as they model the attitudes and behaviours of the Chief Experimenter. A good leader trusts the team to culture hack their environment to define a space that's right for them.

Making space for innovation is the ultimate task of hacker paradigm leadership. It starts with establishing a physical space for work, but it doesn't end there. It fundamentally concerns the mindsets and values the leader brings to the space and the behaviours through which the leader expresses and consolidates these mindsets and values in teams. The other five elements of hacker paradigm leadership feed into this activity. Hacker paradigm leaders create an opportunity space for hacking, which they work to sustain with their teams.

Making space for innovation involves a variety of actions and initiatives. Leaders must establish a physical environment suitable for hacking. They must work to cultivate a social space within the environment, so that people take ownership of the space and contribute to it. Crucially, leaders must seed appropriate cultural mindsets and values within the space. This

> **Innovation space has three dimensions:**
>
> 1. Physical space
>   - Space design
>   - Messaging
>   - Props
> 2. Social space
>   - Trust
>   - Authenticity
>   - Ownership
> 3. Cultural space
>   - Values
>   - Mindsets
>   - Practices

work of cultural engineering draws on all the elements of hacker paradigm leadership. It involves establishing trust, purpose, a collaborative sensibility, an experimental mindset and a customer orientation. It involves creating a shared understanding of 'how we get things done around here', which is ultimately the most important hack of all.

To complete our inquiry into hacker paradigm leadership, we will consider these elements in brief.

- **Create a physical space.** This might involve requisitioning office space or designing a bespoke workshop for team activities. A raw, unfurnished warehouse space typically sets the right tone, conjuring up notions of tinkering and experimentation and reminding people of the long history of start-ups that have launched from garages.

  Hacker generation companies tend to emphasise the cultural dimensions of innovation space and consequently fill their physical environments with messaging and props reflecting a playful, anarchic culture. Facebook, for example, covers its walls with motivational posters that encourage its employees to 'Keep on shipping' and 'Move fast and break things'. Google fills its spaces with toys, exercise balls, Ping-Pong tables and more.

  Messaging and props can be valuable cultural signifiers. But it is easy to overdo a playroom atmosphere. Every company is different, and an innovation space should be customised to suit a company's unique culture and its situation. The important thing is that team members feel they belong in the environment. People should feel comfortable, relaxed and at home.

- **Cultivate a social space.** An innovation space should be a fun and relaxed environment. People should feel free to hang out and socialise between bouts of work. Videos of Jobs working with the Macintosh team indicate the kind of social atmosphere that leaders should try to create. The mood is cheerful and relaxed. Team members talk to one another as equals. In team meetings, Jobs sits on the floor in lotus position. The laid-back vibe of the counterculture is in full effect.

  The contents and layout of an innovation space can contribute to a social atmosphere. Jobs installed video games in the foyer of Bandley 3 to underscore that hacking and play are of a piece. When people felt blocked or frustrated, they could loosen up by playing Defender or Joust and return to work when they were ready. Hacker leaders should enable people, as much as reasonably possible, to determine the pace of work. This is all a matter of trusting teams to deliver, letting their sense of purpose be their guide.

  The ideal social environment makes people feel comfortable being authentic with one another and to contribute to work as they see fit. The payoff for hacker teams is to enable T-shaped people to unleash their full range of talents and skills. When people feel threatened by authority and under pressure to perform, they tend to play to their professional roles, trying to meet their manager's expectations. This stifles creative self-expression and limits the range of contributions that people offer their teams. In a safe environment, where diversity is affirmed and eccentric behaviour is tolerated or even encouraged, people can freely share ideas without worrying about being shot down by others. This unleashes the creativity in T-shaped people and boosts the realm of resources that teams can apply to work.

  Creating space for trust, authenticity and personal expression inspires people to take ownership of their work. With ownership comes engagement and a sense of commitment. People give more to the work and to the innovation space itself. Teams will *do amazing things—even and particularly in the face of rapid change and uncertainty*' (Pixton et al.,

2014: 3). Teams work at holding space because they identify with the work on a personal level and believe in the people they work with. United in a shared sense of purpose, they become a Stage 4 tribe, aspiring to greatness.

- **Seed cultural mindsets and values in the space.** Culture catalyses the psycho-social dimensions of an innovation space. It is the 'operating system' that guides team activities and determines what is possible in the space. If the culture is vague and inconsistent, nothing works. With a clear set of cultural values in place, work happens fast and organically, and management can be pared back to a minimum.

  Culture is mindset. This makes it difficult to perceive. When you walk into an innovation space, you can see that work is taking place and perhaps see that people are enjoying doing it too. But, unless you observe people's practices over time, it is impossible to tell *how* the work is being done (beyond making basic observations, such as, 'They are using computers'). The 'how' is invisible, embedded in people's hearts and minds. It is manifested when team members engage in collaborative activities and engage in discussion to figure out how to tackle problems. But it happens behind the scenes. Like the operating system of a computer, culture determines everything that happens, but is fundamentally hidden from view.

  A good way to think about culture is to see it as the collective imagination of a team. Culture is the way that a team imagines what it can do and achieve together. It is how the team imagines 'how we get things done around here'. On this count, the fundamental task of the hacker paradigm leader is to inspire teams to imagine themselves into being. Teams that are incapable of imagining what they could do and achieve together are really just groups of individuals. It takes a transformational leader to convince people to see life through the lens of their collective potential and to dream a common dream.

  Capturing a team's imagination in this way requires leaders to do several things at once: Leaders must establish that they trust their team, so that the team trusts them. They must lead with purpose, focus people on their potential for greatness, offer them a roadmap to running experiments, and excite them about the idea of creating customer value. They must provide the team with a physical environment for completing work and ensure this space has a social vibe, so that work and play are of a piece.

Only once these pieces are in place can the hacker paradigm leader ignite a shared cultural mindset. Once these pieces are in place, a simple suggestion can set a team on fire. The leader says: *'People! Let's imagine we can change the world'.* The team understands precisely how to set to work. They start brainstorming possibilities and begin to hack.

References

Bass, B. M. (1999). Two decades of research and development in transformational leadership. *European Journal of Work and Organizational Psychology* 8(1): 9–32.

Furr, N., and Dyer, J. (2014). *The Innovator's Method: Bringing the Lean Start-up into Your Organization.* Boston, MA: Harvard Business Review Press.

Gupta, P., Kim, M, and Levine, D. (2013). Insight: Apple and Samsung, frenemies for life. *Reuters.* Accessed 03/06/17 at: http://www.reuters.com/article/net-us-apple-samsung-idUSBRE 91901Q20130210

Hertzfeld, A. (2013). Pirate flag. *Folklore.* http://www.folklore.org/StoryView.py?story=Pirate _Flag.txt. Accessed: 04/06/17.

Hurst, A. (2014). Welcome to the purpose economy. *Fast Company.* Accessed 02/06/17 at: https://www.fastcompany.com/3028410/welcome-to-the-purpose-economy

Isaacson, W. (2015). *Steve Jobs.* London, UK: Abacus.

Levy, S. (2010). *Hackers: Heroes of the Computer Revolution.* Sebastopol, CA: O'Reilly Media.

Logan, D., King, J., and Fischer-Wright, H. (2008). *Tribal Leadership: Leveraging Natural Groups to Build a Thriving Organization.* New York, NY: Harper Business Press.

Pixton, P., Gibson, P., and Nicolaisen, N. (2014). *The Agile Culture: Leading Through Trust and Ownership.* Upper Saddle River, NJ: Addison-Wesley.

Rayner, T. (2018). *Hacker Culture and the New Rules of Innovation.* London/New York: Routledge.

Sinek, S. (2009). *Start with Why: How Great Leaders Inspire Everyone to Take Action.* New York, NY: Penguin Random House.

Chapter 10

Stewardship

Taking Responsibility for Our Actions: Why It Is Time to Think About Stewardship

Darren Dalcher

Do our actions matter? Can we, or the actions that we take, make a difference beyond our own sphere and influence? Should we therefore consider the global impact of our intentions?

We are often far too occupied with our own interests, preferences, priorities, issues, concerns and tribulations to observe the wider implications and impacts beyond our immediate context. Yet, it increasingly appears that our private little arrangements and engagements can still make a difference to the wider world beyond our immediate and obvious concerns. This chapter aims to encourage a more responsible and considerate mindset and revisit the critical role of stewardship in a constrained resource world.

Love Unchained

Love padlocks, or lovelocks, are padlocks attached to a bridge, fence, gate, post or monument by couples to symbolise and attest to their everlasting love. Couples typically inscribe their names or initials onto the lock before affixing it to a public monument or gateway and throwing the key into a river or waterway to symbolise the unbreakable bond that has been sealed through such action.

For the individuals involved, lovelocks are a harmless phenomenon demonstrating an aspiration for a life-long, unbreakable commitment to their partnership. Indeed, one could argue that lovelocks are significantly less obtrusive than carving, daubing or plastering the names onto a bridge, monument, ancient wall, prehistoric ruin, subterranean cave or natural beauty spot.

Lovelocks appear to have proliferated in many countries and regions since the early 2000s, particularly adorning bridges in the centre of main cities. In Rome, the attaching of lovelocks to the Ponte Milvio bridge was documented in a popular book, *I Want You (Ho voglia di te)*, by Federico Moccia (2007), which was further immortalised when it was adapted into a film.

Nonetheless, many people associate lovelocks with the Pont des Arts bridge in the centre of Paris. Pont des Arts, also known as Passerelle des Arts, is an extremely popular pedestrian bridge which crosses the River Seine, connecting the Institut de France to the central square of the Palais Du Louvre. It was the first iron bridge built in France, opening in 1804 as a toll footbridge. In 1991, UNESCO listed the entire Parisian riverfront between the Eiffel Tower and the Ile Saint Louis, including the Pont des Arts, as a World Heritage Site. Since 2008 lovelocks have been appearing on the Pont des Arts bridge. By 2012, the number of locks covering the bridge had become overwhelming, with locks being placed upon other locks. In February 2014, Le Monde estimated that there were over 700,000 locks on the bridge. With little free space remaining on the bridge, lovelocks have since spread to at least 11 other Seine bridges, the footbridges on the Canal St. Martin, and, more recently, to fences and posts in parks and to public monuments all over the city, including the site of the Eiffel Tower.

So, does a personal gesture and intimate bond sealed between two lovers by affixing a lovelock to the side of a bridge impact others?

Well, so it would appear, as many little gestures can add up to significant unintended consequences. As a result of the continuous addition of individual locks, the historic bridge at Pont des Arts historic started experiencing new problems. The city of Paris would later remove one million locks attached to the Pont des Arts, with a total weight in excess of 45 tonnes. In May 2014 the Paris Mayoress, Anne Hidalgo, concerned about the safety of the historic bridge and the wider impact on the city, had tasked her First Deputy Mayor with finding alternatives to lovelocks in Paris. A month later, in June 2014, the parapet on the bridge collapsed under the combined weight of the lovelocks (BBC, 2014). Under the added weight, one side of the railing simply crumpled into the water. The railing was replaced, and notices were left requesting that people stop the lovelock habit. Still, the love tokens started reappearing, ultimately forcing the city to replace the railings with protective glass panels in search of an alternative material to which lovelocks could not be attached.

The original bridge had featured in many films and TV shows and had been enjoyed by millions of tourists and locals over the years. It had survived aerial bombardments during the First and Second World Wars, as well as multiple collisions with boats (although it had been replaced after a barge crashed into it in 1977); however, over one million individual acts of demonstrative love overwhelmed the structure and its built-in safety margins and tolerances, causing the side to collapse.

The Paris City Council reports two main concerns for the city resulting from the trend of leaving lovelocks on bridges: degradation of property heritage and a risk to the safety of visitors and locals. Locals also complain about the resulting graffiti, pickpockets and vendors selling cheap padlocks, turning former heritage areas into unpleasant no-go zones. Some would even argue that the entire UNESCO World Heritage designation was endangered by the lovelock phenomena. Furthermore, the rust from the locks (and the rust and pollution caused by keys discarded into river beds) has also been cited as problematic.

Throughout Paris, workers have been regularly removing lovelocks from bridges. Chicago has been removing lovelocks from the city's moveable bridges, which are raised for boat traffic, out of fear of damaging boats and hurting people on them. Paris and other cities have been experimenting with legislation to ban the practice. In Berlin affixing a lovelock to a bridge is a misdemeanour and can generate fines of €35. The city of Venice has introduced a €3,000 fine for the same offence. Moscow offers a different and more creative approach by installing metal trees for lovers to hang their locks from, whilst creating a dynamic new form of street art. Meanwhile, while it is now possible to pre-order and customise engraved physical love padlocks online, entrepreneurs offer lasting virtual lovelock-free alternatives to replace the physical artefacts.

Extending Our Scope of Interest

Individuals appear to be focused on their own actions, needs and motivations, often ignoring the wider consequences, which are not framed within their direct and immediate context. This shift enables consequences of actions that may impact others to escape closer scrutiny, as they reside in a different time frame that persists beyond the action space and therefore defies attention and consideration. A noteworthy warning to consider wider impacts is encapsulated through the ancient proverb *'For Want of a Nail'*[*]:

For Want of a Nail

For want of a nail the shoe was lost.
For want of a shoe the horse was lost.
For want of a horse the rider was lost.
For want of a rider the message was lost.
For want of a message the battle was lost.
For want of a battle the kingdom was lost.
And all for the want of a horseshoe nail.

The proverb has been expressed in different forms, through many variations and multiple languages, over hundreds of years, dating back to the beginning of the 13th century. It serves notice that seemingly unimportant actions, small dysfunctions or omissions can become amplified and have grave and unforeseen consequences. Actions can thus initiate chains of causality or wide impacts over different levels and systems.

Perhaps a key lesson is that we need to become more mindful of our actions and their impacts, however well-intentioned. If a relatively inconsequential padlock can multiply and lead to collapsing bridges, boat accidents, the deterioration of neighbourhoods and the destruction of recognised international monuments, perhaps it is also time to consider the longer-term implications of more significant and pre-planned undertakings, such as projects, programmes and change initiatives.

As individuals become more obsessed with their own personality, image, appearance and actions, online and more generally, and as social tools perpetuate and encourage positioning ourselves at the centre of things, both the rhyme and the lovelocks on the bridge can encourage a readjustment—a repositioning of our self-interest in a wider, richer and more responsible context. Santos et al. (2017) report the results of their extensive study indicating that there is a tremendous shift towards individualism and self-centrism across the globe, translating into a move away from collectivism and towards individualistic practices and values.

Indeed, if only one individual were to deposit a padlock on a single bridge, the overall impact of a relatively harmless action would be negligible. However, if everyone starts to behave in that same manner, impacting overall resources or common assets, it is no longer harmless. Ecologists, economists and social scientists refer to this effect as the *Tragedy of the Commons* (Hardin, 1968), as a shared resource is destroyed as a result of mass action and exploitation by many individuals all acting independently according to their self-interest. The combined effect of many such collective actions is to erode, deplete, spoil and destroy the common resource. In this context, 'the commons' is taken to mean any shared and unregulated resource, ranging

---

[*] https://www.goodreads.com/quotes/626466-for-the-want-of-a-nail-the-shoe-was-lost

from the natural atmosphere, beauty spots, open space, rivers, oceans, lakes, energy, trees, oil, coal and animals, bird and fish stock, to the artificial, man-made artefacts including roads, highways, bridges, parks and monuments.

Common resource systems can collapse due to overuse by the wider community unless an effort is made to regulate or govern such use (Ostrom, 1990; Ostrom et al., 2002). Such regulation could be done by the wider community or group or emerge from the responsible actions of cognisant individuals.

> *Individualism is cherished because it produces freedom, but the gift is conditional: The more the population exceeds the carrying capacity of the environment, the more freedoms must be given up* (Hardin, 1998: 683).

The Case for Stewardship

An alternative to imposed governance and top-down regulation can come from informed stewardship, whereby interested and engaged local members cooperate and coordinate their actions in order to avoid the collapse of common resources. The notion of stewardship embodies responsibility, added consideration and a focus on sustaining the common interest.

The *Oxford English Dictionary* describes stewardship as *'the act of taking care of or managing something, for example property, an organization, money or valuable objects'*.

Merriam-Webster defines stewardship as *'the conducting, supervising or managing of something, especially the careful and responsible management of something entrusted to one's care'*, offering the specific example of stewardship of natural resources. Stewardship thus seems to refer to the way we protect, utilise, share and manage special resources or a specific capability or value. In theological discourse, across multiple religions, including the Judeo-Christian tradition, it is often referred to as the theological belief that humans are responsible for the world, or the universe, and should therefore cherish and take care of it.

The term was popularised by Peter Block's book *Stewardship: Choosing Service over Self-Interest*, published in 1993 to great acclaim. The book became a best seller, selling over 200,000 copies before being reissued in a revised anniversary edition in 2013. Block (2013: *xxiv*), defines stewardship as *'the choice to preside over the orderly distribution of power'*. This entails giving people at the bottom and the boundaries of the organisation choice over how to serve a customer, a citizen, a community, whilst recognising that they are operating in service rather than in control. In a nutshell, stewardship is accountability without control or compliance (Ibid.). This is done through deepening the commitment to service and to supporting the wider community. In analysing developments over the 20 years between the two editions, Block repositions stewardship as *'a choice to (1) act in service of the long run, and (2) act in service to those with little power'* (Ibid.: 1).

Block views stewardship as an intention to distribute power more widely across the organisation, especially to the lowest levels of the organisation, emphasising the common good for the communities. The starting point is the willingness to be accountable for some larger body than ourselves—a team, an organisation or a community—through the notions of service and commitment.

> *Stewardship is the set of principles and practices that have the potential to make dramatic changes in the governance of our institutions. It is concerned with creating a way of governing*

ourselves that creates a strong sense of ownership and responsibility for outcomes at every level of the organization. It is a buck that stops everywhere. It means having more of a partnership with customers and creating self-reliance on the part of all who are touched by the institution. It says that the answer to economic problems is not reduced costs or better funding; it is to focus on relationships, reciprocity, and participation first. These are the elements that produce the service we seek. This is what will put us closer to our employees and our marketplace. Stewardship is creating a sustainable connection with the people in our playing field that is the answer to our concerns about economics (Ibid.: 15).

Block argues compellingly for a move away from typical patriarchy and hierarchy as the core forms of governance. The purpose of the shift is to liberate initiative and spirit within organisations and their employees by fostering empowerment, ownership and responsibility.

The position distinguishes the capacity to decide and the responsibility for our thoughts and actions. The change in attitude and approach requires a number of fundamental adjustments and intentional choices, which Block poses as:

- Replacing leadership with stewardship
- Choosing partnership over patriarchy
- Choosing adventure over safety
- Choosing service over self-interest

Block's emphasis on ownership and responsibility is essential to securing the success of organisations and must be implemented at every level of the organisation. The reform is particularly important to enable management and stewardship systems to deal with the following organisational challenges (pp. 28–30):

1. **Doing more with less.** There is a need to own accountability and responsibility for product, service and the customer, especially with fewer people and growing demands.
2. **Learning to adapt to customers and the marketplace.** As customers become more important, there is a need to enable and empower those at the front line who deal with customers to respond and address customer needs without resorting to authority.
3. **Creating passion and commitment in employees.** Creating commitment relies on developing a sense of ownership and responsibility, especially when job security is no longer guaranteed.

Davis et al. (1997) position stewardship as an alternative to agency theory, thereby eschewing an economic basis for governance considerations, focusing instead on sociological and psychological approaches and considerations. Individuals can thus be viewed as collectivists, pro-organisational and trustworthy (p. 20). Hernandez (2012: 174) defines stewardship as, *'the extent to which an individual willingly subjugates his or her personal interests to act in protection of others' long-term welfare'.*

Stewardship does not require a formal position, power or authority; stewardship behaviours can be enacted across all levels of an organisation. The underlying assumption is that managers and workers will act as responsible stewards of assets and resources at their disposal, preferring pro-organisational behaviour to self-serving individualism. Stewards typically pursue a more responsible, long-term and trustworthy agenda. The concept of stewardship has been applied to many different aspects, including nature, the environment, resources, economics, health and data.

Product Stewardship

Moving from self-interest towards service, as advocated by Block, is a revolutionary idea which overcomes the artificial separation between doing and managing, as conceived and encouraged through the lens and practice of scientific management (Dalcher, 2017). Stewardship encourages individuals to operate beyond their self-interest. It restores power to frontline workers, enables the creation of positive organisations and builds on their power to change and transform (see Chapter 8). Moreover, it places a greater emphasis on the extended products, outputs and outcomes of change initiatives and on the longer-term considerations regarding intervention and lasting improvement for the concerned community.

Until recently this area has escaped significant consideration within project work; however, the 7th edition of the *APM Body of Knowledge* points out that many projects need to include consideration of the management of change and the realisation of benefits, thereby requiring the use of extended life cycles (Murray-Webster & Dalcher, 2019: 24). The consideration of benefits extends beyond the handover of defined project outputs, encompassing additional adoption and realisation activities and considerable subsequent contact with change subjects. More crucially, however, there is a need to account for the full product life span from initial idea, through development, evolution and upgrades, to removal from service and ultimate dismantling (Ibid.: 26). Whilst such considerations extend beyond the traditional project boundaries, issues regarding operation, upgrade, decommissioning and disposal can be supported through the application of a stewardship stance to the wider project context.

> *The product life cycle helps in making sustainable choices and embraces the principles of product stewardship, advocating that everyone who benefits commercially from a product has a shared responsibility to minimise its environmental impacts. Adopting a whole life cycle or a full product life cycle perspective enables executives and managers to responsibly engage with the long-term future implications of their project-related actions, and discharge their increasingly emerging responsibility for proper end of life disposal of systems and assets in a responsible, affordable and effective manner* (Ibid.).

Nonetheless, very little has been written about the application of the product life cycle and the underpinning need for stewardship in the context of project work. New thinking on environmental impacts of products and projects is essential to developing enhanced understanding of pragmatic practice in this area. Moreover, as product stewardship has become more mainstream, there is a fundamental need to access this content and make it available to the project community. The following section by Dr. Helen Lewis addresses this important gap by offering much-needed thought leadership and practical guidance. The contribution is derived from her book *Product Stewardship in Action: The Business Case for Life-Cycle Thinking*, published by Greenleaf Publishing/Routledge (Lewis, 2017).

Dr. Lewis's work offers an important introduction to product stewardship and describes how and why leading companies are taking responsibility for the environmental impact of their products and packaging. The work draws on the knowledge and experience of industry practitioners and other experts to provide a structured approach to product responsibility within organisations.

Lewis views stewardship as an amalgamation of voluntary action by organisations with regulated schemes which encompass social and environmental impacts. In doing so, she extends product stewardship beyond the realm of regulated schemes and compliance to include ethical and social responsibility for actions. Product stewardship is therefore duly defined as the *'principle that everyone involved in the manufacture, distribution or consumption of a product shares responsibility for the environmental and social impacts of that product over its life cycle'* (Ibid.: 5).

Lewis's definition is significant, as it extends beyond the manufacturing (or project delivery or deployment team) to include various agencies such as distributors, suppliers, retailers and brand owners. Most notably, it also encompasses the consumption side of products, drawing consumers and users into the pool of responsible stewards. Project teams may form an inevitable part of the manufacturing concerns, but they must also be aware that the responsibility extends throughout the fully extended life cycle. The inclusion of distributors and consumers could thus place an additional responsibility on the production and project teams to consider the ensuing interaction and impacts and to design products and projects with such considerations in mind. A further implication is that product responsibility clearly extends beyond the formal handover and commissioning. Indeed, nor is it limited to decommissioning and disposal, but to the full range of potential actions during use and utilisation.

Lewis introduces an extremely useful framework for considering the scope of product stewardship across four key areas of activity (pp. 10–11):

- Policies that establish goals and targets for product sustainability
- Design processes that consider sustainability impacts across whole life cycles
- Procurement policies and guidelines
- Recovery of products at end of life, fully or partially funded by producers

Product stewardship can be contrasted with extended producer responsibility (EPR). EPR places the responsibility for the product throughout its entire life cycle with the manufacturer, especially in terms of recycling and disposal. EPR can therefore be viewed as a strategy to add all of the environmental costs associated with the product throughout its life cycle to the market price for the product (OECD, 2001). Lewis points out that EPR is widely accepted as the basis for product-related environmental policies, particularly in the European Union, Japan, South Korea, Taiwan and many Canadian provinces (Lewis, 2017: 9). Although EPR and product stewardship overlap to some extent, Lewis concludes that EPR focuses on mandatory aspects, whilst product stewardship also encompasses the voluntary aspects (p. 5); it thus comes closer to Block's take on stewardship (1993, 2013). If EPR forms the basis for establishing product responsibility, the framework introduced by Lewis provides a sound basis for establishing product stewardship as a responsible extension beyond compliance and regulation.

Lewis's work makes a powerful case for product stewardship as a business strategy rather than a philanthropic exercise. It highlights the benefit from achieving public and commercial shared value by responding effectively to stakeholder concerns regarding the environment. Lewis positions stewardship as an ethical and social obligation, yet one that can also be viewed as a source of competitive advantage for the business. Ultimately it is an imperative if we want to guarantee a sustainable future for our community and its cherished resources.

Stewardship Reprised

Product stewardship places the spotlight on the product and its overall impact. Its value is in getting manufacturers and managers to rethink and reconsider its wider impacts—and possibly redesign or reposition the resulting product accordingly. Rosselot and Allen (2001) note that engineers and managers must address changing needs and consider how their products will be recycled, how their customers will use their products and what environmental hazards might arise. *'Simply stated, engineers must become stewards for their products and processes throughout their life cycles'* (Ibid.).

Making use of the whole life cycle encourages a process perspective encompassing the full production–utilisation–disposal chain, thereby leading to better informed and more responsible decision-making regarding the product and its intended use. A life cycle approach therefore enables the impacts of all life cycle phases to be considered comprehensively by all participants and inform choices for the longer term.

Product stewardship extends the responsibility to everyone involved in the product chain through the extended life cycle of the product: Whoever designs, produces, sells or uses a product is called to take responsibility for minimising the product's impacts throughout all stages of its life cycle. Ultimately, managing a product through an extended life cycle decreases environmental impacts, allows consideration of the long-term implications and shares the burden and ownership of responsibility with all actors and participants.

Product stewardships also relates to the increasingly popular notion of the impact economy, which extends beyond consideration of financial returns to encompass the effects of action, or in some cases investments, on society at large and on the global environment. This enables companies to consider both profit and overarching purpose. The impact economy recognises that companies cannot divorce themselves from the impact that they, and their actions, make on the global world. The implication is that responsible companies may need to pay more so that all the people down the value chain will benefit, or avoid harm, implying an assumed stewardship related to products and their use.

Lane and Watson maintain that product stewardship has radical potential as a means to promote significant change in the relationship between society and the material world (2012; p. 1254). The Product Stewardship Society frames product stewardship as an emerging and evolving profession. Product stewardship is defined as *'responsibly managing the health, safety, and environmental aspects of raw materials, intermediate, and consumer products throughout their life cycle and across the value chain in order to prevent or minimize negative impacts and maximize value'* (PSS, 2014: 4). Whilst different industries and sectors may have divergent definitions and approaches, Lewis's work provides an important and timely guide to the application of product stewardship in practice.

The notion of stewardship is an important addition to the discourse around responsibility, particularly in terms of the commitment to future generations. While producer responsibility accounts for some of the impacts, shared responsibilities, in the form of stewardship, extend to include all other users and participants, developing a wider set of accountable and responsible actors. Adopting the lens of stewardship enables, facilitates and encourages important development in considering the wider implications of actions that extend beyond self-interest, short-term concerns and selfish acts by individuals.

Stewardship begins with recognition of the value of a precious resource or prized commodity that requires conserving. Stewardship is then tasked with protecting and cherishing the public interest. This can be done by adopting the commons imperative and considering the greater good, which adds a social dimension to the environmental considerations. Stewardship extends beyond prohibition and regulation to develop a more systemic and comprehensive mindset that allows ownership and empowerment of all participants. Stewardship is thus entrusted to individuals, who are in a position to consider the wider implications of their actions and safeguard common global resources.

Developing through stewardship requires new ways of building organisations, making decisions, prioritising and managing. By encouraging individuals to consider the implications of potential actions, the collective can become more responsible and more accountable for shared resources ranging from bridges and beauty spots to water, livestock and the environment. It can also offer social and societal empowerment which is needed to underpin wider considerations. Collaborating for the greater good is essential if we want to protect our entrusted commons. If we accept the essence of stewardship as a concern with leaving the world a better place than when we found it and ensuring that our systems, structures, actions and undertakings subscribe to that view, we will find that we are embracing the calling of stewardship to serve others. The key to the prosperity of future communities may well be in fostering stewardship skills and capabilities in all aspiring members as we begin to collaborate towards creating, facilitating and securing a better common future.

References

BBC (2014). 'Lovelocks' collapse Paris bridge rail. Accessed July 2019 at: https://www.bbc.co.uk/news/av/world-europe-27758940/lovelocks-collapse-paris-bridge-rail

Block, P. (1993, 2013). *Stewardship: Choosing Service over Self-Interest*. San Francisco, CA: Berrett-Koehler Publishers.

Dalcher, D. (2017). What has Taylor ever done for us? *PM World Journal, 6*(4).

Davis, J. H., Schoorman, F. D., and Donaldson, L. (1997). Toward a stewardship theory of management. *Academy of Management Review, 22*(1), 20–47.

Hardin, G. (1968). The tragedy of the commons. *Science, 162*(3859), 1243–1248.

Hardin, G. (1998). Extensions of 'the tragedy of the commons'. *Science, 280*(5364), 682–683.

Hernandez, M. (2012). Toward an understanding of the psychology of stewardship. *Academy of Management Review, 37*(2), 172–193.

Lane, R., and Watson, M. (2012). Stewardship of things: The radical potential of product stewardship for re-framing responsibilities and relationships to products and materials. *Geoforum, 43*(6), 1254–1265.

Lewis, H. (2017). *Product Stewardship in Action: The Business Case for Life-Cycle Thinking*. Austin, TX: Greenleaf Publishing/Routledge.

Moccia, F. (2007). *Ho voglia di te (I Want You)*. Nord. ISBN: 8842930229.

Murray-Webster, R., and Dalcher, D. (Eds.) (2019). *APM Body of Knowledge* (7th Ed.). Princes Risborough, UK: Association for Project Management.

OECD. (2001). *Extended Producer Responsibility: A Guidance Manual for Governments*. Paris, FR: Organisation for Economic Co-operation and Development, OECD Publishing.

Ostrom, E. (1990). *Governing the Commons: The Evolution of Institutions for Collective Action*. Cambridge, UK: Cambridge University Press.

Ostrom, E. E., Dietz, T. E., Dolšak, N. E., Stern, P. C., Stonich, S. E., and Weber, E. U. (2002). *The Drama of the Commons*. Washington DC: National Academy Press.

PSS (2014). *Core Competencies for the Product Stewardship Professional*. Falls Church, VA: Product Stewardship Society.

Rosselot, K., and Allen, D. T. (2001). Life cycle concepts, product stewardship and green engineering. In: D. T. Allen and D. R. Shonnard (Eds.). *Green Engineering: Environmentally Conscious Design of Chemical Processes*. Upper Saddle River, NJ: Prentice Hall.

Santos, H. C., Varnum, M. E., and Grossmann, I. (2017). Global increases in individualism. *Psychological Science, 28*(9), 1228–1239.

A Strategic Approach to Product Stewardship

Helen Lewis

Introduction

Product stewardship is no longer a discretionary activity confined to businesses that want to 'do the right thing'. There is growing government and consumer interest in the social and environmental impacts of products, from their supply chain through to end of life. This represents both a risk and an opportunity for businesses that make, sell or recover products.

Most product stewardship programmes are a reaction to regulations or pressure from external groups. Responsiveness to stakeholder expectations on issues such as worker safety, hazardous substances and recycling can be beneficial—for example, by improving a company's reputation. A more proactive and strategic approach is to look for opportunities that create 'shared value'—that simultaneously achieve social and environmental objectives while building long-term competitiveness (Porter & Kramer, 2011).

This section presents a strategic, shared value approach to product stewardship. It can be used by companies to reduce the life cycle impacts of their products while building business value—for example, by reducing costs, improving access to raw materials or building customer loyalty.

Drivers for Product Stewardship

While product stewardship is often driven by stakeholder perceptions or expectations about a specific issue in the product life cycle, a more strategic approach also considers the available scientific evidence and how stakeholder concerns interact with business priorities. As Porter and Kramer argue, stakeholder views are important, but:

> . . .these groups can never understand a corporation's capabilities, competitive positioning, or the trade-offs it must make. Nor does the vehemence of a stakeholder group necessarily signify the importance of an issue—either to the company or to the world (2006: 8).

In practice most companies are driven to act by a combination of factors, including stakeholder expectations, evidence of product impacts and business goals and priorities. A systematic approach to product stewardship involves careful evaluation of all three drivers to guide decision-making within firms (Figure 10.1).

The following section considers each one of the three drivers for product stewardship individually: stakeholders, product research and business priorities.

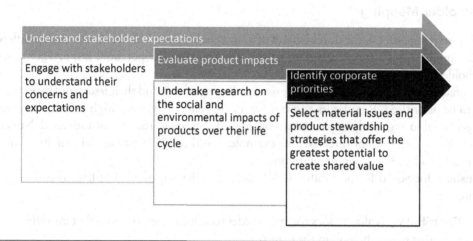

Figure 10.1 Three Steps Towards a Product Stewardship Strategy

Stakeholder Engagement

Ongoing stakeholder engagement through surveys, workshops or informal dialogue is essential to the success of product stewardship initiatives. Many existing schemes were developed in response to pressure from environmental groups or regulators. In the 1990s Greenpeace International campaigned to stop companies using chlorine-containing products, including PVC plastic. In Australia, following similar developments in Europe, resin suppliers and converters responded by developing a comprehensive environmental programme in consultation with stakeholders. This included a voluntary phase-out of heavy metal additives and support for collection and recycling of PVC products.

In contrast, the Call2Recycle battery recycling programme was set up by battery manufacturers in the US to avoid product bans and mandatory recycling mandates. In 1991 the Environmental Protection Agency announced that rechargeable nickel cadmium batteries would be classified as a hazardous waste and delegated responsibility to the states for regulation. After a number of states introduced laws mandating producer responsibility for recycling, and others threatened to ban the sale of mercury- and cadmium-containing products, including rechargeable batteries, the industry established a voluntary national recycling scheme to avoid any further regulation.

Over time these organisations, and many others like them, have shifted from a reactive and defensive approach to a more proactive engagement strategy. The Vinyl Council of Australia, for example, seeks input to its programme through an external Technical Steering Group that meets quarterly, and a larger stakeholder round table every two to three years. Some of the significant changes that have been made in response to stakeholder feedback include a commitment to open disclosure of material components and actions to address climate change.

Companies can minimise the risks associated with negative stakeholder perceptions and influence by taking steps to engage with groups that are important to their business. The most appropriate engagement tools will vary depending on the purpose—for example, whether stakeholders are being approached to help identify corporate social responsibility priorities to guide product development and marketing strategies or to inform product take-back programmes.

Stakeholder Mapping

A useful starting point is the development of a 'stakeholder map'. This can take many different forms, ranging from a simple diagram to a matrix showing the potential importance of each stakeholder to the business.

In practice a firm's stakeholders are never equally important, and their issues and expectations need to be prioritised. Regulators and customers are generally given a high priority because of their potential to negatively impact on the business if their concerns are not addressed. Noncompliance with a government directive, for example, could result in a financial penalty or (more importantly) a loss of corporate reputation.

Business for Social Responsibility (BSR, 2011) has developed a list of five criteria to guide this process :

- **Contribution (value).** Does the stakeholder have information, counsel or expertise on the issue that can be helpful to the company?
- **Legitimacy.** How legitimate is the stakeholder's claim to engagement?
- **Willingness.** How willing is the stakeholder to engage?
- **Influence.** How much influence does the stakeholder have, and on whom?
- **Necessity of involvement.** Is this someone who could derail or delegitimise the process if they are not included?

Engaging with Consumers

A successful product stewardship strategy requires a good understanding of consumer attitudes and behaviour. Consumers can influence the environmental impact of products in several ways:

- **Through their purchasing decisions.** For example, whether to buy a 'green' or environmentally improved product.
- **Through the way they use products.** For example, whether they choose to wash clothes with hot or cold water.
- **Through their disposal decisions.** For example, whether to give something away when they no longer want it, recycle it, or put it in a rubbish bin.

For these reasons, individual companies, stewardship organisations and government environment agencies often undertake market research to inform their environmental programmes.

Numerous surveys have been undertaken on consumer attitudes to the environment, their purchasing preferences and their willingness to buy more sustainable products. These often identify a gap between consumers' expressed concerns about social and environmental issues and their willingness to reflect these concerns in their purchasing behaviour (Belz & Peattie, 2009).

BBMG, GlobeScan and SustainAbility surveyed over 6,000 consumers in six international markets (Brazil, China, Germany, India, United Kingdom and United States) and identified strong demand for more sustainable products (BBMG, 2012). Almost two-thirds of respondents (65%) said that they '*feel a sense of responsibility to purchase products that are good for the environment and for society*' (p. 7). When asked about which social and environmental issues were most important for companies to address as part of their products, services or operations, there was universal agreement in all markets that 'safe drinking water' was the most important issue overall, followed by several other social issues such as healthcare and jobs. Waste reduction was supported by 85 percent of respondents, which made it the highest-ranking environmental issue on the list (p. 15).

In the same survey, most consumers (75%) agreed that they would 'purchase more products that are environmentally and socially responsible' if they 'performed as well as, or better than, products they usually buy'. This clearly presents a marketing opportunity for companies with the ability to change their product mix or redesign products to reduce their environmental or social impacts.

Understanding Product Impacts

Additional research is often required to test stakeholder perceptions or to gather further information on product impacts. The PVC industry in Australia, for example, commissioned a literature review from Australia's preeminent scientific organisation, the Commonwealth Scientific and Industrial Research Organisation (CSIRO), to investigate stakeholder claims that PVC was more hazardous than other building materials and should be avoided in construction of infrastructure for the 2000 Olympic Games in Sydney.

CSIRO's report concluded that PVC building products were generally sound from an environmental perspective, but there were issues that could be addressed to improve their performance (Smith, 1998). The findings of this study and a later update have helped to shape the industry's product stewardship programme (Coghlan, 2001).

Life-Cycle Mapping

A literature review is useful to investigate specific issues raised by stakeholders. A visual 'life-cycle mapping' exercise can also provide insights into the product life cycle and some of the sustainability benefits and impacts associated with each stage. This can be as simple as a hand-drawn flow chart, compiled by a cross-functional and knowledgeable group of people within the company, showing the different stages in the product life cycle and some of the inputs and outputs at each stage. An exercise like this has some advantages compared to a literature review:

- It is specific to a particular company, product and supply chain.
- A visual map, particularly when undertaken as a group exercise, can identify materials, components or activities that may have been overlooked.

A more detailed explanation and step-by-step guide to developing a life-cycle map is found in Verghese and Lockrey (2012).

Life Cycle Assessment

Life cycle assessment (LCA) is an internationally recognised method for evaluating the environmental impacts of a product over its total life cycle. LCA is useful when an organisation needs to evaluate the environmental impacts of a product or system with a high degree of accuracy—for example, to support product claims (Verghese & Carre, 2012). Nestlé, for example, commissioned an LCA to calculate the environmental benefits of a new laminated pouch for coffee, and the results were promoted on the label. The LCA found that the pouch used 73 percent less non-renewable energy, 66 percent less water and emitted 75 percent fewer greenhouse gas emissions over its entire life cycle than a glass jar, challenging a common perception that glass is superior to plastics from an environmental perspective (RMIT, 2015).

An LCA can also make an important contribution to understanding and managing environmental problems—for example, by revealing 'blind spots' in the knowledge base (Grant &

MacDonald, 2009). While batteries are often perceived as a hazardous waste issue, for example, there are also significant issues in raw materials extraction and processing (Olivetti et al., 2011). One of the benefits of an LCA is that it generally highlights a range of different impacts that may require trade-offs in the selection of appropriate strategies.

The cost of an LCA can be a valuable and worthwhile investment if it helps to generate new business opportunities. Interface Carpets, for example, used an LCA to identify and promote design improvements, such as the use of lower yarn weights, which gave the company a competitive advantage (Hensler, 2014).

There are a number of LCA software tools which are available to assist practitioners (Verghese & Lockrey, 2012). These include publicly available inventory data and also allow the user to add their own product-specific data to improve its accuracy and therefore value.

Identifying Priority Issues and Strategies

Stakeholder engagement and product research can both help to identify social issues that could be considered 'material' to a business. These have been defined as issues that:

- Reflect the organisation's significant economic, environmental and social impacts.
- Substantially influence the assessments and decisions of stakeholders (GRI, 2016: 11).

Businesses are not responsible for all of society's problems, nor are they always in the best position to address them (many issues are better addressed by governments or civil society actors). Porter and Kramer (2011) advise companies to select social issues that intersect with their particular business interests:

> The essential test that should guide CSR is not whether a cause is worthy but whether it presents an opportunity to create shared value—that is, a meaningful benefit for society that is also valuable to the business (p. 10).

Porter and Kramer distinguish between three types of issues: generic social issues, those directly related to a company's value chain, and social issues in the external environment that affect competitiveness (Table 10.1). To maximise the overall benefits of a corporate social responsibility (CSR) programme, the authors recommend that companies choose CSR strategies that either transform their value-chain activities to benefit society and improve competitiveness at the same time or change aspects of the external environment to improve the 'competitive context' in which they operate. External issues that affect productivity include the availability of raw materials and labour, the nature of regulations and standards, demand from local consumers or access to firms in related fields (Porter & Kramer, 2006).

This framework for strategic CSR can also be used to identify material issues and priorities for product stewardship. Changes to products or packaging to reduce material consumption, eliminate toxic components or improve recovery can transform a company's value chain in ways that achieve both societal and business benefits.

Product Stewardship Policy and Strategies

To be effective, product stewardship needs to be considered in every aspect of a business, from corporate policy and targets through to the product portfolio, design, procurement and distribution. It has implications for every function within the business.

Table 10.1 Prioritising Social Issues

Generic Social Issue	Value Chain Social Impacts	Social Dimensions of Competitive Context
Social issues that are not significantly affected by a company's operations nor materially affect its long-term competitiveness	Social issues that are significantly affected by a company's activities in the ordinary course of business	Social issues in the external environment that significantly affect the underlying drivers of a company's competitiveness in the locations where it operates

After: Porter, M., and Kramer, M.(2006, December). Strategy and society: The link between competitive advantage and corporate social res ponsibility. *Harvard Business Review,* 9.

This section outlines some of the strategies that companies are commonly using to manage the environmental and social aspects of their products. It focuses on four key areas of activity: corporate policy (leadership), design, procurement and product recovery (Figure 10.2).

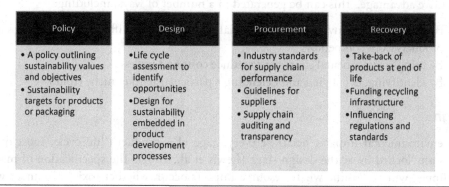

Figure 10.2 Examples of Product Stewardship Strategies

Policy

Many businesses have a CSR or sustainability policy that outlines their corporate values and objectives. These should reflect the knowledge and insights gained through stakeholder engagement and product research. To be effective, a sustainability policy must be relevant and meaningful to employees and customers.

Product Goals and Targets

Sustainability or CSR policies provide a broad framework for action, but more specific product goals and targets are needed to guide product stewardship strategies in design, procurement and recovery. Foodstuffs New Zealand, for example, has a goal to ensure that all of its own-brand packaging is recyclable. This has helped to guide the development of environmentally improved packaging, including the launch of a new recyclable plastic meat tray in 2015. Foodstuffs uses around 100 million meat trays a year, and previously these were all manufactured from non-recyclable foamed polystyrene. The new tray is made from recyclable polyethylene terephthalate (PET), which can be collected through municipal recycling programmes.

The achievement of product-related policies, goals and targets must be supported by procedures to ensure that these are implemented in everyday practices, including design and procurement (explored further below).

Within the marketing function, a strategic approach to product stewardship integrates sustainability objectives in the product portfolio, the product development process and the marketing mix. In their book *Sustainability Marketing*, Belz and Peattie (2009) suggest two important questions that need to be answered:

- Which markets should we compete in?
- Within each of our markets, how shall we compete?

They argue that the choice of products will depend on a range of factors, including the perceived attractiveness of the market and the potential strength of the company's competitive position within it. The process of strategic portfolio planning involves decisions about which products the company should withdraw from as well as those it will invest in, and sustainability considerations may influence these decisions (p. 10).

Marketing practitioners need to consider when and how sustainability can be a source of competitive advantage. This can be generated in a number of ways, including:

- By using superior environmental or social performance to differentiate a business and its products from competitors
- By using environmental strategies to reduce costs and prices
- By identifying, occupying and defending a particular market niche (Ibid.)

Design

While environmental impacts occur at every stage of a product's life cycle, most of these impacts are 'locked-in' at the design stage (Lewis et al., 2001). The specification of materials, for example, will determine where resource impacts occur, whether toxic substances will be released during manufacture, and whether or not the product is recyclable. Impacts such as energy and water consumption during use, or recycling rates at end of life, are also influenced by consumer behaviour and may require alternative strategies (Figure 10.3).

'Design for sustainability' means thinking about the environmental and social impacts of a product during the design process. Implementing design for sustainability requires new skills and capabilities, including life-cycle thinking. A simple life-cycle mapping exercise, common sense and a good understanding of the supply chain will almost always identify opportunities for improvement. Many larger companies also use LCA to inform product development.

A commitment to product stewardship in the design process can generate a range of business benefits. Resene (New Zealand) reformulated its products to meet the 'Environmental Choice' ecolabeling standard for decorative paints, which restricts the use of pigments, solvents, additives and volatile organic compounds that are environmentally damaging or hazardous to human health (The New Zealand Ecolabelling Trust, 2015). Initiatives such as this have helped to build a positive reputation for the company with commercial markets and specifiers.

Procurement

Companies are increasingly being held accountable for the social and environmental impacts of products and materials in their supply chain. Many of these impacts are outside the direct

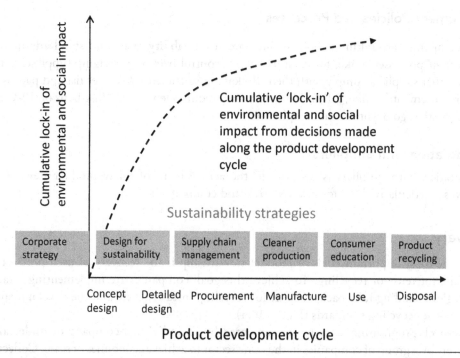

Figure 10.3 Environmental 'Lock-In' over a Product's Development Cycle. (*Source:* Adapted from Lewis, H., et al. [2001]. *Design + Environment: A Global Guide to Designing Greener Goods.* Sheffield, UK: Greenleaf Publishing.)

control of a product manufacturer or brand owner, but there are a number of ways that companies can influence or control the actions of suppliers. These include:

- The development of voluntary or mandatory industry standards in collaboration with industry peers
- Specifying minimum standards in procurement guidelines and contracts
- Collaborating with suppliers to develop more sustainable materials or products.

Industry-Wide Guidelines and Standards

Media coverage of a factory fire in Bangladesh in 2013 revealed that many well-known clothing brands were being manufactured in unsafe conditions. As a direct result of the fire, Walt Disney Company announced that it would no longer allow the manufacture of its branded merchandise in Bangladesh (Greenhouse, 2013). However, labour groups suggested that Western companies should 'stay and fix the problem' rather than leave. The outcome was the development of the legally enforceable 'Accord on Fire and Building Safety in Bangladesh', which has been signed by over 100 international brands and retailers, local and global labour unions and non-government organisations (Clean Clothes Campaign).

Other sustainability issues are being addressed in response to actions by government. The Conflict-Free Sourcing Initiative (2013) was developed by consumer electronics manufacturers after President Obama signed the Dodd-Frank Consumer Act into law. The resources available through the initiative help companies to comply with a requirement to verify and report on their use of 'conflict minerals' that may be contributing to conflict or human rights abuses.

Procurement Policies and Processes

Many companies are taking action to integrate sustainability goals and standards in their procurement processes. Nike, for example, exerts control over its packaging supply chain by requiring that suppliers comply with their 'Packaging restricted substances list and packaging design requirements' (Nike, 2015). Many of Nike's requirements, including bans on PVC and foamed plastics, go beyond legal compliance.

Collaboration with Suppliers

Collaboration with suppliers is essential to the achievement of many product stewardship objectives, particularly those for raw materials and components.

Recovery

One of the most important goals of product stewardship is the recovery of used products at end of life for reuse or recycling. To achieve this goal, companies are implementing a range of strategies including take-back, support for recycling infrastructure and the development of industry-wide recycling standards (Figure 10.4).

Take-back programmes may be implemented by an individual company or undertaken collectively by a group of companies in the same sector to achieve economies of scale. Collective industry programmes can be further categorised as either industry-led, as is the case for most producer responsibility organisations (PROs); provided by a more conventional waste management service provider on behalf of an industry sector; or entrepreneur-led, where a company develops a programme and then works with industry stewards to implement it.

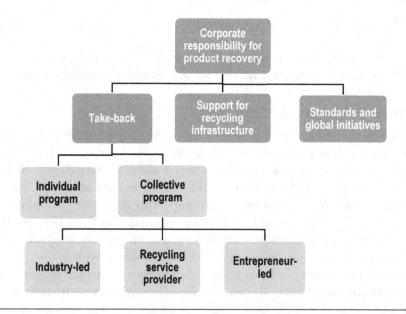

Figure 10.4   Producer Responsibility Strategies for Product Recovery

Take-back

Extended producer responsibility laws shift financial and/or physical responsibility for recycling from local government to producers. Most regulations give producers a choice of complying individually or collectively, which means they can either implement their own take-back and recycling programme or join a collective PRO.

In certain circumstances a company might choose to implement their own individual programme—for example, if they have an efficient reverse logistics system, if they think they could do it more cost effectively than an established PRO, or if they want more control. There are indications that some companies are reviewing whether their objectives could be better serviced by fulfilling their EPR obligations individually and not as part of a collective scheme (Bury, 2010).

There are three common models for take-back. The first and most common is the industry-led and industry managed model, which usually involves a not-for-profit PRO developed by a group of companies with the purpose of meeting compliance obligations.

The second collective model involves a waste management or logistics company providing a compliance service to producers, with the total cost shared between a number of different companies.

The third option for a collective programme is one initiated by an entrepreneurial organisation in response to a perceived need rather than a compliance obligation. RED Group, for example, developed a national retail recycling initiative for 'soft plastics' (bags and film) in Australia with the support of food and consumer product manufacturers. This was driven by its founder, Liz Kasell, who had become concerned about the amount of soft plastic packaging going to land-fills. She convinced retailers and manufacturers to support her vision for an industry-funded recycling programme called REDcycle.

Other Options to Support Product Recovery

Where product take-back is not regulated, some companies have chosen to support recycling of their products in other ways—for example, by providing financial support for collection or recycling infrastructure. The Closed Loop Fund (2019) in the US, which is supported by consumer goods manufacturers, provides financial support for packaging collection, sorting, reprocessing and manufacture into new products.

Another way that companies support recovery of their products is through global initiatives. Dell, for example, is working with the United Nations Industrial Development Organization (UNIDO) to facilitate the development of appropriate e-waste regulations in developing countries.

Conclusions

Product stewardship is being implemented by organisations and regulators in response to increasing community concern about the environmental impact of everyday products. Companies that take a strategic and knowledge-based approach to product stewardship understand the perceptions and expectations of their stakeholders, investigate sustainability issues over the total life cycle of their products, and use this knowledge to identify material issues and priorities for their business (Lewis, 2017). This approach helps to ensure financial sustainability within an environment that places more emphasis on corporate responsibility and shared value for business, employees and the community.

References

BBMG, GlobeScan, and SustainAbility (2012). Re:Thinking consumption: Consumers and the future of sustainability. http://www.globescan.com/component/edocman/?view=document &id=46&Itemid=591

Belz, F. M., and Peattie, K. (2009). *Sustainability Marketing: A Global Perspective*. Chichester, UK: John Wiley & Sons.

BSR (2011). *Stakeholder Mapping*, 2. http://gsvc.org/wp-content/uploads/2014/11/Stakeholders -Identification-and-Mapping.pdf

Bury, D. (2010). Policy forum: Should extended producer responsibility programs use eco-fee-included pricing? *Canadian Tax Journal, 58*(4), 927–950.

Clean Clothes Campaign (n.d.). *Frequently Asked Questions (FAQs) about the Bangladesh Safety Accord*. Retrieved from http://www.cleanclothes.org/issues/faq-safety-accord/#1---what -is-the-accord-on-fire-and-building-safety-in-bangladesh

Closed Loop Fund (n.d.). *About the Closed Loop Fund*. Accessed 2019 at: http://www.closedloopfund .com/page/about

Coghlan, P. (2001). A discussion of some of the scientific issues concerning the use of PVC. *Report by CSIRO Molecular Science and Australian National University*. Canberra, AU: Vinyl Council of Australia.

Conflict Free Sourcing Initiative (2013). *Reasonable Practices to Identify Sources of Conflict Minerals: Practical Guidance for Downstream Companies*. Electronic Industry Citizenship Coalition and the Global e-Sustainability Initiative. http://www.conflictfreesourcing.org/media/docs /news/CFSI_DD_ReasonablePracticesforDownstreamCompanies_Aug2013.pdf

Grant, T., and MacDonald, F. (2009). Life cycle assessment as decision support: A systemic critique. In: R. Horne, T. Grant, and K. Verghese (Eds.). *Life Cycle Assessment: Principles, Practice and Prospects,* 33–41. Melbourne, AU: CSIRO Publishing.

Greenhouse, S. (2013). Some retailers rethink role in Bangladesh. *New York Times*. http://www .nytimes.com/2013/05/02/business/some-retailers-rethink-their-role-in-bangladesh.html

GRI (2016). *GRI 101: Foundation*. Amsterdam, NL: Global Sustainability Standards Board.

Hensler, C. D. (2014). Shrinking footprint: A result of design influenced by life cycle assessment. *Journal of Industrial Ecology, 18*(5), 663–669.

Lewis, H., et al. (2001). *Design + Environment: A Global Guide to Designing Greener Goods*. Sheffield, UK: Greenleaf Publishing/Routledge.

Lewis, H. (2017). *Product Stewardship in Action: The Business Case for Life-Cycle Thinking*. Austin, TX: Greenleaf Publishing/Routledge.

Nike Inc. (2015). Restricted Substance List and Design Requirements: Update Log. www.nikeinc chemistry.com/restricted-substance-list/prsl-pdr-3.0-feb-2015.pdf

Olivetti, E., Gregory, J., and Kirchain, R. (2011). Life cycle impacts of alkaline batteries with a focus on end-of-life. *Report by Massachusetts Institute of Technology for the National Electrical Manufacturers Association*. http://www.epbaeurope.net/documents/NEMA_alka linelca2011.pdf

Porter, M., and Kramer, M. (2006, December). Strategy and society: The link between competitive advantage and corporate social responsibility. *Harvard Business Review*, 1–16.

Porter, M., and Kramer, M. (2011). The big idea: Creating shared value. *Harvard Business Review*. https://hbr.org/2011/01/the-big-idea-creating-shared-value

RMIT (2015). *Life Cycle Assessment of Nestle NESCAFE Gold Packaging.* https://www.rmit
    .edu.au/research/research-institutes-centres-and-groups/research-centres/centre-for-design
    -and-society/research-areas/sustainable-prodcts-and-packaging/projects/life-cycle-assessment
    -of-nestle-nescafe-gold-coffe/

Smith, R. (1998). The environmental aspects of the use of PVC in building products. *Report by
    CSIRO Molecular Science for the Plastics and Chemicals Industries Association.* Clayton, AU.

The New Zealand Ecolabelling Trust (2015). *Licence Criteria for Paints EC-07-13.* Auckland, NZ.
    http://www.environmentalchoice.org.nz/docs/publishedspecifications/ec0715_paints.pdf

Verghese, K., and Carre, A. (2012). Applying life cycle assessment. In: K. Verghese, H. Lewis, and
    L. Fitzpatrick (Eds.). *Packaging for Sustainability.* London, UK: Springer.

Verghese, K., and Lockrey, S. (2012). Selecting and applying tools. In: K. Verghese, H. Lewis,
    and L. Fitzpatrick (Eds.). *Packaging for Sustainability,* pp. 251–283. London, UK: Springer.

Chapter 11

Knowledge

The Mind of the Maker: Making Sense of Knowledge

Darren Dalcher

Knowledge management is a relatively new addition to the project management bodies of knowledge but nonetheless is increasingly recognised as an area that is crucial for the success of projects, programmes and portfolios. The big challenge for many project managers is to figure out what knowledge management is, what it entails and what it can do for you.

Peter Drucker famously proclaimed that a manager is responsible for the application and performance of knowledge.* However, in practice, knowledge is highly contextual and innately dynamic. Knowledge is deeply entwined with meaning, understanding and interpretation, making it difficult to grasp, let alone manage. As a result, some scholars even suggest that there is a fundamental incongruity and mismatch between the concepts of knowledge and management.

For one thing, knowledge is not manageable in the same way as a tangible resource. The intellectual capital of an organisation resides in the individuals and the communities that make up the different facets of the organisation. Management of the knowledge embedded within people requires engagement, understanding and skills related to the management of and interaction with people and their perceptions. It also necessitates intimate and ongoing engagement with the individuals and their communities in order to share, shape and co-develop the knowledge.

So, Why Manage Knowledge?

Knowledge is essential to making informed decisions. Moreover, innovation and increased productivity both arise through the creation and application of knowledge-based assets.

Yet, Alvesson and Kärreman (2001: 995) assert that *'knowledge is an ambiguous, unspecific and dynamic phenomenon, intrinsically related to meaning, understanding and process, and therefore difficult to manage. There is thus a contradiction between knowledge and management'*.

Hislop (2009: 59) positions knowledge management as a deliberate effort to manage the knowledge of an organisation's workforce. In a more recent update, Hislop and colleagues (2018) further encourage a practice-based perspective, which views knowledge as a process:

> *The practice-based perspective considers knowledge as embodied in human beings and therefore focuses on facilitating interpersonal knowledge-sharing and processes. This requires an organizational*

---

* https://quotepark.com/quotes/1217999-peter-f-drucker-a-manager-is-responsible-for-the-application-and-p/

approach and involves establishing a culture in which knowledge is shared and where managers evaluate their employees on their contribution to knowledge management (Hislop et al., 2018: 51).

Knowledge can be embedded in tangible assets such as finished goods, completed project outputs and results, machinery and manuals. However, Hislop calls attention to the need to engage with knowledge embedded within the people that make up the organisation, thereby presenting an enormous challenge for traditionally structured organisations.

Managing knowledge, or intellectual capital, that resides in the individual employees poses significant challenges to managers—not least, the problem of asymmetric information, where managers have significantly less knowledge than the experts or highly skilled knowledge workers that they oversee (Roberts, 2015: 51–52). Adler's solution is to advocate community forms of organisation as an alternative to knowledge-based organisations (Adler, 2001).

Defillippi et al. (2009) note that knowledge work is neither created nor used in a social vacuum. Participants in knowledge work deal with a complex web of relationships among people and activities. Typically, there is a tendency to focus on a single type of participant and their interactions and processes. However, Defillippi et al. contend that there is a need to explain how each of the participants in knowledge work influences and is in turn influenced by the other participants. To gain a fuller picture of the different types of knowledge participants and their interactions, they construct the knowledge diamond (p. 19), with four focal groups of participants (summarised and paraphrased below, after pp. 17–18):

- **The individual.** Single actors who bring knowledge to and have the opportunity to take knowledge from an activity or a project.
- **The community.** Occupational communities that join together in completing tasks and activities; includes different specialisms that come together on a project.
- **The organisation.** One or more organisations that provide the infrastructure through which the work gets done.
- **The industry.** The wider industry can be seen as a participant in and a contributor to the knowledge economy; will ultimately absorb the knowledge workers that participate in current projects, and any new learning that has been gained.

The model draws attention to the wider knowledge context and identifies different groupings of participants and their interconnected impacts. Focusing on a single entity in isolation is limiting, as interactions and influences are created between the different participating groupings. The knowledge diamond proposed by Defillippi et al. indicates that each individual participant may also interact with the community, organisation and industry, implying that in every project or undertaking, all four types of knowledge work are likely to be involved (p. 20).

Engaging with the Mind of the Maker

The starting point for a lot of project work is around understanding the original intention. The 7th edition of the *APM Body of Knowledge* (2019: 6) starts with the notion of strategic intent as a way of capturing the direction of travel for a new undertaking. A key challenge is to develop an emerging knowledge and understanding of the intention and main purpose of proposed initiatives.

Organisational activities are increasingly analysed in terms of value capture and value creation. Value creation chains encompass multiple activities ranging from planning (value proposition), to creation and delivery, and ultimately to value capture and communication. The implication is that a concept undergoes an extended journey between the initial idea generation and the ultimate realisation of business value.

The knowledge interaction related to the development of a project, endeavour or initiative starts with the maker, visionary or thinker who has come up with a new concept, need or another enticing proposition for the future. Fred Brooks, the manager entrusted by IBM with what is possibly the largest software development project ever undertaken (see Chapter 9), reflects on the nature of the creative process:

> Dorothy Sayers, in her excellent book The Mind of the Maker *(1941), divides creative activity into three stages: the idea, the implementation, and the interaction. A book, then, or a computer, or a program comes into existence first as an ideal construct, built outside time and space, but complete in the mind of the author. It is realized in time and space, by pen, ink, and paper, or by wire, silicon, and ferrite. The creation is complete when someone reads the book, uses the computer, or runs the program, thereby interacting with the mind of the maker* (Brooks, 1995: 15).

There are numerous implications resulting from the value chain highlighted by Brooks and Sayers. The cycle comprising the three major phases of idea, implementation, interaction is quite appealing. While it recognises the role of implementation as a core activity, it also positions the initial front-end concerned with conceptualising and formulating the idea firmly within the wider scope of conversation. Moreover, the subsequent emphasis on use, or interaction, extends the cycle into the realm of intended and actual use. Projects are carried out for a purpose, and recognising that the creation cycle is complete when the user is able to utilise the artefacts that emerge from the creative process implies an understanding of the intended outcome and expected impacts (as highlighted in Chapter 5). This shift of emphasis indicates that both initiation and implementation should be concerned with interaction and use and aim to ensure that the concepts being developed make a beneficial difference to the intended user.

Engaging with the mind of the maker requires an understanding of the intention embedded and implied in every change and innovation. Crucially, it also implies that the planner grasps the intended use and outcomes that transpire from new initiatives, and that all that follow downstream in the subsequent process can engage with the planner/maker's intention and understanding. Extending the scope of conversation to include the interaction means that knowledge of the intended use (and expected benefits) is crucial to the design effort, so that intention ultimately encompasses the spheres of idea, implementation and interaction. Successful delivery would therefore encompass sustainable engagement with idea, implementation and interaction.

Reflecting on his management experiences during the development of a complex operating system programme for IBM (as highlighted in Chapter 9), Brooks yearns for the conceptual integrity that comes from only engaging with one mind or a very small team of decision makers:

> The dilemma is a cruel one. For efficiency and conceptual integrity, one prefers a few good minds doing design and construction. Yet for larger systems one wants to bring considerable manpower to bear, so that the product can make a timely appearance (Brooks, 1995: 31).

Engaging fully with the mind of a single maker is difficult enough, embracing the thoughts ideas and knowledge of a wider grouping would require better organised methods for engaging with communities and ecologies of doers, makers and creators. Indeed, as more individuals seek to adopt a new role as craftsman (Sennett, 2008; Korn, 2015) or maker (Dougherty, 2012; Hatch, 2013, 2017), and as technology enables many more to assume such roles (Anderson, 2012; Browder, 2017; Davies, 2017), we must find new ways of engaging with the minds of diverse communities and constellations of makers and embrace new forms of more meaningful and fruitful co-creation.

Managing Knowledge in Project Environments

Knowledge can offer a source of competitive advantage, and the purpose of projects and programmes is to enable beneficial change in behaviour and create new capabilities utilising new and existing knowledge. The establishment of the temporary organisations required for project work further defies traditional and functional organisational structures and settings. If project teams only exist for a short and limited period, it becomes more important to engage with them in order to share meaning and understanding and thus enable work to progress. Moreover, given the personal nature of knowledge within different communities and stakeholder groups, managing knowledge becomes deeply concerned with opening up boundaries, enabling communication, and facilitating meaningful exchanges.

Defillippi et al. maintain that *'projects are interconnected to each other in an evolutionary sequence involving the successive exploitation of existing knowledge and exploration of new knowledge, thereby contributing to an organization's long-term position in the market-place for goods and services'* (2009: 130).

Projects can thus be viewed as episodes in knowledge work. A key challenge is to develop knowledge management capability to support effective project work.

Turning to guidance related to the application of knowledge management practice within projects and programmes is limited by the lack of adequate resources that enable managers and leaders to make sense of their landscape. The following section by Judy Payne, Eileen Roden and Steve Simister draws on their book *Managing Knowledge in Project Environments*, published by Routledge, which endeavours to provide such a resource (Payne, Roden & Simister, 2019).

The authors recognise the confusion within the project context. They acknowledge that while projects empower change and improvement, no individual or repository 'owns' all the knowledge required to bring about effective change. Their work offers a new way of making sense of project work through knowledge and its management. Projects create, explore and exploit knowledge. This implies different needs and processes that can be viewed through a knowledge lens.

Crucially, the authors avoid the all-too-familiar temptation to provide recipes and prescriptions in the form of templates, tools and registers that can be copied or replicated. In recognition of the contextual and situated nature of knowledge and the need to make informed decisions, their approach emphasises the development of a set of underlying principles that can be applied to knowledge work. The principles combine with management choices and contextual factors to develop a detailed framework for making sense of knowledge in projects.

Their framework also helps to make sense of the choice of development approaches and life cycles used in project work. It takes into account what is known and recognises the uncertain and ambiguous dimensions, enabling managers to respond to their context. Payne, Roden and Simister (2019) make an important distinction between creating new knowledge and exploiting existing knowledge. Both are important; however, they require fundamentally different approaches and will be applied at different times. Recognising the distinctions and working through the set of principles can make a big difference to devising effective knowledge management in projects and programmes.

The perspective adopted by Payne, Roden and Simister offers many new insights into the practice of knowledge management. It innovates and encourages new approaches and a fresh viewpoint. The resulting guidance is aimed at practitioners who are looking to transform their individual practice and create more effective and efficient projects. The framework and principles provide an important starting point for managing knowledge in projects. In this way, the authors make an important and much needed contribution to project management literature and advance the discussion related to the management of knowledge in social and temporary settings.

Learning to Work with Knowledge

The case for better and more nuanced management of knowledge is overwhelming. Knowledge is central to decision making, progress making and ultimately to long-term survival (Dalcher, 2014).

However, knowledge is not simply an asset that can be captured. Nagel points out that knowledge always belongs to someone, be it an individual or a group (2014: 3). It is therefore always highly contextualised, personalised and subjective. Consequently, the act of knowing is an ongoing social phenomena. However, it not always what we know that makes a difference.

O'Dell et al. (1998) assert that *'what you don't know will cost you—or even ruin you'.* They recall a poignant observation by Arthur C. Clarke that cave dwellers froze to death on beds of coal (p. *ix*). Sadly, while the coal was immediately underneath them, they couldn't see it, mine it or use it. This supports the notion that sometimes we simply don't know what we don't know. This chimes with Confucius' notion that *'Real knowledge is to know the extent of one's ignorance'.*[*]

Sometimes, we simply don't know what we know. Lew Platt, former CEO of Hewlett Packard, was keen to point out that *'If HP knew what HP knows, we would be three times more profitable'.*[†]

The key then is having the ability to organise knowledge in a useful form for a given situation and to understand what it entails. In those terms, Immanuel Kant's perspective that *'Science is organised knowledge; and wisdom is organised life'*[‡] provides the idealised model to aim for.

However, Nicolaus Copernicus was perhaps better able to identify the connection between the ideas of knowing and knowledge: *'To know that we know what we know, and to know that we do not know what we do not know, that is true knowledge'.*[§] The meta-knowledge perspective, or the ability to step back and see patterns, connections and links, is often more important than the minutia of detail. In Benjamin Franklin's words, *'The doorstep to the temple of wisdom is a knowledge of our own ignorance'.*[¶]

---

[*]　https://www.brainyquote.com/quotes/confucius_101037

[†]　https://weirdblog.wordpress.com/2007/10/24/quotable-quote-lew-platt/

[‡]　https://quoteinvestigator.com/2015/05/19/wisdom/#:~:text=%E2%80%94Immanuel%20Kant.

[§]　https://www.brainyquote.com/quotes/nicolaus_copernicus_127510

[¶]　https://www.brainyquote.com/search_results?x=0&y=0&q=The+doorstep+to+the+temple+of+wisdom+is+a+knowledge+of+our+own+ignorance

Perhaps it is also time to start taking stock of our own ignorance and allow what we know and need to shape the approaches that we adopt for experimenting, exploring and exploiting knowledge opportunities. Payne, Roden and Simister do a good job reminding us that knowledge is situated and context is key; therefore, we need to strategically tailor interventions to match our ambitions and intentions, the organisational appetite for risk and change, and the penchant for learning. But the final word goes to Anton Chekov for observing that *'knowledge is of no value unless you put it into practice'.* That gives us a basis for developing knowledge for, in and of practice so that it can improve our interactions and condition over time as we continue to experiment, grow and develop the capability to leverage our intellectual capital for the greater good of our joint endeavours.

References

Adler, P. S. (2001). Market, hierarchy, and trust: The knowledge economy and the future of capitalism. *Organization Science, 12*(2), 215–234.

Alvesson, M., and Kärreman, D. (2001). Odd couple: Making sense of the curious concept of knowledge management. *Journal of Management Studies, 38*(7), 995–1018.

Anderson, C. (2012). *Makers: The New Industrial Revolution*. London, UK: Random House.

APM (2019). *APM Body of Knowledge* (7th Ed.). R. Murray-Webster and D. Dalcher (Eds.). Princes Risborough, UK: Association for Project Management.

Brooks, F. P., Jr. (1995). *The Mythical Man-Month: Essays on Software Engineering* (Anniv. Ed. 2/E). Reading, MA: Addison-Wesley.

Browder, R. E., Aldrich, H. E., and Bradley, S. W. (2017, January). Entrepreneurship research, makers, and the maker movement. In: *Academy of Management Proceedings, 2017*(1), 14361. Briarcliff Manor, NY: Academy of Management.

Dalcher, D. (2014). Beyond knowledge: Growing capability for an uncertain future. *Cutter IT Journal, 27*(3), 6–11.

Davies, S. R. (2017). *Hackerspaces: Making the Maker Movement*. New York, NY: John Wiley & Sons.

Defillippi, R., Arthur, M., and Lindsay, V. (2009). *Knowledge at Work: Creative Collaboration in the Global Economy*. New York, NY: John Wiley & Sons.

Dougherty, D. (2012). The maker movement. *Innovations: Technology, Governance, Globalization, 7*(3), 11–14.

Hatch, M. (2013). *The Maker Movement Manifesto: Rules for Innovation in the New World of Crafters, Hackers, and Tinkerers*. New York, NY: McGraw-Hill Professional.

Hatch, M. R. (2017). *The Maker Revolution: Building a Future on Creativity and Innovation in an Exponential World*. New York, NY: John Wiley & Sons.

Hislop, D., (2009). *Knowledge Management in Organizations: A Critical Introduction* (3rd Ed.). Oxford, UK: Oxford University Press.

Hislop, D., Bosua, R., and Helms, R. (2018). *Knowledge Management in Organizations: A Critical Introduction* (4th Ed.). Oxford, UK: Oxford University Press.

Korn, P. (2015). *Why We Make Things and Why It Matters: The Education of a Craftsman*. New York, NY: Random House.

---

* https://www.brainyquote.com/quotes/anton_chekhov_119058

Nagel, J. (2014). *Knowledge: A Very Short Introduction (Very Short Introductions)*. Oxford, UK: Oxford University Press.

O'Dell, C. S., Grayson, C. J., and Essaides, N. (1998). *If Only We Knew What We Know: The Transfer of Internal Knowledge and Best Practice*. New York, NY: Free Press.

Payne, J., Roden, E., and Simister, S. (2019). *Managing Knowledge in Project Environments*. Abingdon, UK: Routledge.

Roberts, J. (2015). *A Very Short, Fairly Interesting and Reasonably Cheap Book About Knowledge Management*. London, UK: SAGE Publications.

Sayers, D. L. (1941). *The Mind of the Maker*. London, UK: Methuen.

Sennett, R. (2008). *The Craftsman*. New Haven, CT: Yale University Press.

Through the Knowledge Lens: KM Adventures in Project-Land

Judy Payne, Eileen J. Roden and Steve Simister

Knowledge management (KM) is a holistic, cross-functional approach focussed on ways organisations create and use knowledge to improve outcomes (Association for Project Management, 2019; BSI, 2018). KM has been around as a discipline and organisational practice since the early 1990s, but it is still a relatively new concept in project environments. Although KM is widely practised in project work, managers don't always recognise the knowledge aspects of their work and tend to treat KM as a series of discrete activities rather than as a way of making project work produce better outcomes in different contexts. What is labelled 'KM' is often not KM at all—and the real KM is hidden.

Does this matter? We think it does. KM adds value and can contribute significantly to project, programme and portfolio success—and project management is missing out on it. KM experience and thinking from beyond the project management world can change this, but only if managers recognise the knowledge and KM aspects of their work.

The ideas in this section are based on the book *Managing Knowledge in Project Environments* (Payne, Roden & Simister, 2019), which looks at project work through a knowledge lens and explores how knowledge contributes to success. The book argues that actively considering and managing the knowledge aspects of project work leads to better organisational outcomes—and provides a framework for understanding and improving KM in different organisational contexts. The section briefly introduces the framework of KM principles, KM context and KM scope, then applies the knowledge lens to take a deeper look at the interplay between three of the context factors: strategic KM purpose, project delivery method and project type.

KM Principles, the KM Context and KM Scope

KM Principles

Seven KM principles capture the *why* of managing knowledge: the fundamentals of KM that apply to KM the world over—not just to KM in project environments. The principles and underlying fundamentals are summarised in Table 11.1 and covered in more detail in *Managing Knowledge in Project Environments* (Payne, Roden & Simister, 2019).

The KM Context

Different kinds of knowledge (and therefore project) work require different working environments and different KM activities (Principle #4). The working environment is heavily influenced by the

Table 11.1 KM Principles and Underlying KM Fundamentals

KM Principle	Underlying KM Fundamentals
Principle #1 Be clear about what you want to achieve with KM.	Knowledge is intangible and has no inherent value. KM adds value by making sure knowledge contributes to what matters to organisations and projects. Two strategic KM purposes reflect the way knowledge adds value: the use of existing knowledge and the creation of new knowledge.
Principle #2 Develop working definitions of knowledge and KM.	There are no universally accepted definitions of knowledge or KM. Three perspectives on knowledge: 'thing', 'knowing' and 'doing' thinking lead to different KM approaches and practices. Knowledge can be explicit or tacit and individual or collective. 'Thing' thinking is essentially information management (IM).
Principle #3 Be clear about the difference between KM and IM.	KM is more than IM. Knowledge can't be shared simply by transmitting it. Shared understanding is reached through interaction between people. IM is used in KM but it isn't the same thing. Knowledge should flow, not be collected as stocks of information.
Principle #4 Create different working environments for different kinds of knowledge work.	Knowledge can't be managed directly, and people can't be forced to do KM, so KM in practice focusses on creating working environments that motivate people to engage in KM. KM tools and techniques won't work unless people are motivated to engage in KM. The ideal environments for using existing knowledge and creating new knowledge are different. All organisations and projects need to use existing knowledge and create new knowledge. The two kinds of knowledge work and their supporting environments are often separated to avoid sending mixed messages to workers.
Principle #5 Focus on the big KM picture rather than the detailed KM tools and techniques.	KM is everyone's responsibility, but requires leadership. Some knowledge needs to be shared, some needs to be protected. Knowledge is both sticky and leaky. KM can be formal or informal. In-the-flow KM is better than above-the-flow KM. Demand-driven KM is more effective than supply-driven KM but less efficient in the short term. Technology is more than an enabler of KM—it enhances KM. Rich, face-to-face communication is not always the best.
Principle #6 Experiment, use feedback and adapt.	KM is complex. Managing knowledge is iterative, evolutionary and adaptive. Different levels of learning support KM in different situations.
Principle #7 Beware of elephant traps.	Common KM pitfalls are related to Principles #1 to #6. Disciplines related to KM and alternative names for KM can cause confusion.

way projects are managed, the way knowledge is managed, and, to some extent, by the KM activities themselves. We call these overlapping influences the *KM context* (see Figure 11.1) and further define it using clusters of context factors: things that make a difference to the success of KM.

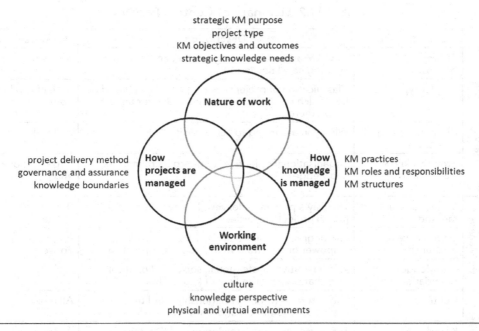

Figure 11.1   The KM Context: Clusters and Factors

The context factors and clusters are the *how* of managing knowledge in project environments: the basis of a KM strategy for project work. The 'how' focuses on project management decisions about the nature of the work and the supporting environment (Principle #4) and KM decisions such as the characteristics of KM practices (Principle #5).

The common thread running between the clusters is people. Decisions made in all four clusters affect the motivation and ability of people to work effectively. The success of KM in project environments depends on alignment among the four clusters. The individual context factors are the levers a KM actor can pull to create or improve alignment and increase the chances of KM contributing to project success. The individual context factors are summarised in Table 11.2 (on next page).

The factors, clusters and the way they work together can be used to understand an existing situation; to improve KM in existing projects and programmes, as an input to planning new projects and programmes; and to manage knowledge across a whole portfolio.

Ignoring KM for a moment, *how projects are managed* and the *working environment* should match the *nature of the work* being carried out.

This principle is already built into project management practices and is common sense to project managers. You wouldn't choose an iterative, emergent delivery method for a project to build six identical houses to a standard design—this would be poor alignment between the way projects are managed and the nature of work. In a session to brainstorm options for a project, you wouldn't lock stakeholders in a dark basement and stand over them with a whip—this would be poor alignment between the nature of work and the working environment.

Including *how knowledge is managed* is an extension of this thinking that focuses attention on the knowledge dimension of project management. Considering how knowledge is managed is a way of making better project management decisions, not an additional task that makes project management decisions more difficult.

Table 11.2 Summary of Context Factors

	Context Factor	Description	Most Useful At
Nature of Work	Strategic KM purpose	How KM adds value: using existing knowledge or creating new knowledge	All levels
	Project type	Classification of projects or project stages based on how much is known about what to aim for and how to get there	Project level and above
	KM objectives and outcomes	What you are trying to achieve with KM	All levels
	Strategic knowledge needs	Organisational objectives and targets related to knowledge	Organisational and portfolio levels
How Projects Are Managed	Project delivery method	The way a project is delivered: linear, iterative or hybrid project life cycles	Project level and above
	Governance and assurance	The degree to which standard ways of working empower or constrain what happens in practice	Project level and above
	Knowledge boundaries	Administrative, professional, social and political barriers that prevent the flow of knowledge	All levels
Working Environment	Culture	The nature of working relationships and the value placed on knowledge and learning	All levels
	Knowledge perspective	The perspective on knowledge and KM: thing, knowing or doing thinking	All levels
	Physical and virtual environments	The physical and virtual working environments and how they are used	All levels
How Knowledge Is Managed	KM practices	The high-level characteristics of the way people create, share and use knowledge	All levels
	KM roles and responsibilities	Leadership, consultants and PMOS	Project level and above
	KM structures	Tangible elements of KM: definitions, standard terminology, policies, accreditation against standards	Organisational and portfolio levels

KM Scope

KM can be applied at any level in a project environment: to an activity within a project, to a project stage or programme phase, to a whole project or programme, a portfolio, a whole organisation, or between two or more organisations.

The KM actor needs to define the KM scope. Although KM scope describes the level at which KM is applied, it is not always the level at which the KM actor is working. What is included in the KM scope is a judgement based on the KM actor's project management role, sphere of interest and sphere of influence. The three do not necessarily coincide.

The KM scope should be within the sphere of influence of the KM actor. If the KM actor's sphere of interest is wider than the actor's sphere of influence, there might be opportunities to widen the sphere of influence through relationships with influential stakeholders. Sometimes there will be little choice: a project team member might have to take activity-level KM opportunities when they arise; a projects director might have already identified the need to introduce KM across a whole portfolio.

Note that KM scope is different from the starting point for KM. Introduction of portfolio-wide KM can start with a single project or programme but will be approached from a wider perspective than KM in a single project or programme.

The KM principles apply whether you are working on KM in a single project or across multiple organisations, but the way the principles are applied and the way the context factors are used changes as the scope becomes more strategic.

Different context factors and clusters are useful at different levels. At the activity level in an existing project, it is enough to identify the desired KM outcome, choose a KM activity that will lead to the desired outcome, and create a local working environment that supports the activity. Some iteration will be needed between these three elements. It is not necessary to create KM roles and responsibilities or KM structures such as definitions of knowledge and KM—but the KM actor does need an understanding of the perspective on knowledge that will lead to the desired outcome. At the portfolio level, the KM actor needs to consider KM roles and responsibilities and KM structures and will be more concerned with providing guidance on how to identify activity-level KM outcomes than with doing it themselves.

Context Factor: Strategic KM Purpose

Strategic KM purpose describes how KM adds value by influencing the way existing knowledge is used and the way new knowledge is created. Strategic KM purpose matters because it defines the nature of the work that the rest of the KM context (how projects are managed, how knowledge is managed and the working environment) has to support.

The strategic KM purpose of a single activity within a project is usually obvious. An activity to generate options for a project is creating new knowledge; an activity to build a pre-fabricated structure is using existing knowledge. Sometimes there is a choice: the layout of furniture and equipment in an office can be produced by starting from scratch or by copying the layout from another floor.

At the project level, things become more complicated. Almost all projects create new knowledge *and* use existing knowledge. New knowledge is usually needed to understand what the project is going to achieve and how it will be managed. When the project outputs are delivered, a different kind of knowledge ('doing' knowledge) has to be created by users of the outputs so that they understand how to use them.

In a single project, KM actors therefore need to decide how to create supporting contexts for both kinds of knowledge work. One way of doing this is to adopt a separation strategy (Principle #4) in which the creation of new knowledge is separated from the use of existing knowledge through structure or through time. Dividing the project into stages in a linear, sequential life cycle (often referred to as a waterfall approach) is a separation strategy. The knowledge about what the project is going to achieve and how it is to be managed is created through development of the business case and project management plan, and the execution stage involves using this knowledge by following the plan. When the outputs are delivered, change managers and users create knowledge of how to use them in a benefits realisation stage.

If the knowledge about what the project is going to achieve cannot be worked through at the start of a project—for example, because the organisation's external environment is changing rapidly—an alternative is to allow the missing knowledge to emerge during the project. This might lead to an iterative approach (often referred to as agile) which cycles rapidly between creating new knowledge about requirements and using this knowledge to deliver outputs. Users and other stakeholders are typically much more involved throughout iterative projects, so are able to create the knowledge needed to use the outputs as they emerge. An iterative, emergent approach is the alternative to a separation strategy: knowledge is created and used almost simultaneously all through the project.

Project Work as a Separation Strategy

Project working is itself a way of separating activities through structure. An organisation's portfolio is separate from business as usual, and projects and programmes are separate from each other.

The existence of projects and programmes is an opportunity to create working environments that are different from business as usual—an opportunity to apply a different set of rules and develop different behavioural norms. Unfortunately, this doesn't always happen. A business-as-usual culture that works for using existing knowledge might spill over into innovation projects and programmes, and policies designed for efficiency might be applied to creative projects.

Projects, programmes and business as usual should have different working environments *by design*. This is an important KM consideration for KM actors, such as PMO members working at the portfolio level.

Context Factor: Project Delivery Method

Linear and iterative approaches are often considered as two distinct project delivery methods. If we unpick the built-in assumptions about knowledge and KM associated with each, it becomes clear that this is not the case: almost all projects need elements of both.

Linear and Iterative Life Cycles as Two Extremes

The assumptions about knowledge and KM in linear and iterative project life cycles are summarised in Table 11.3. We have used extremes to highlight the differences in the assumptions.

It is clear from Table 11.3. that neither extreme works. In knowledge terms, many of the assumptions and practices associated with linear life cycles practices are questionable:

- The knowledge needed to complete the project doesn't always exist at the start.
- Knowledge is not static: changes in the organisation's environment lead to changes in requirements.
- Knowledge cannot be captured completely in documents.
- If knowledge of how to use outputs isn't created until a project is complete, it is too late (or too expensive) to modify the outputs.

These criticisms of linear project life cycles are used to argue in favour of iterative life cycles, but some of the iterative life-cycle assumptions and practices are questionable too:

- Some of the knowledge needed to complete the project usually does exist at the start.
- Knowledge created during the project doesn't necessarily need to be developed from start to finish.

Table 11.3 Knowledge and KM in Extreme Linear and Iterative Project Life Cycles

	Extreme Linear Life Cycles	Extreme Iterative Life Cycles
Description	Linear, sequential approach in which projects move through initiation, planning, execution and closure. Each stage is completed before the next can begin.	Iterative, emergent and adaptive approach in which work is progressed through a series of sprints. Requirements emerge and evolve throughout the project, while subsets of requirements are taken through design and delivery.
Knowledge perspective and assumptions	'Thing' thinking. Knowledge isn't so much created as found in the heads of project managers and stakeholders. Knowledge is static. At the start of each stage, the knowledge needed to complete it already exists. Knowledge doesn't change during the project.	'Knowing' and 'doing' thinking. Knowledge is created through social interactions ('knowing') and through practical experience ('doing'). Knowledge is dynamic. None of the knowledge needed to complete the project exists at the start. Knowledge should be allowed to develop throughout the project.
Strategy for knowledge creation and use	Separate the work into stages. Knowledge of what the project is going to achieve and how the outputs will be delivered is gathered up front, then used in the execution stage.	Integrate knowledge creation and use. New knowledge is created and used in each sprint.
How knowledge of using project outputs is created	Change management for benefits realisation after the outputs are delivered.	Hands-on user experience of outputs as they are delivered.
Typical approach to KM	Codification of knowledge into documents.	Frequent face-to-face interaction between project team and stakeholders.
Stakeholder involvement	Highest in the early stages. Stakeholders contribute knowledge as part of requirements gathering.	High throughout. Stakeholders provide feedback on outputs as they emerge.
Knowledge boundaries	Boundaries to knowledge flow exist between stages.	Boundaries to knowledge flow often exist between the project and management.

- Simultaneously creating new knowledge and using existing knowledge requires flexible, committed people and skilled leadership.
- Many organisations lack the capability to cope with iterative life cycles.

The Best of Both Worlds

Many organisations are far more comfortable and capable of delivering projects with linear life cycles. Modifications to linear life cycles are already widely used to overcome the questionable knowledge assumptions and practices: the project life cycle is extended to include benefits realisation, users are involved early in projects, and mechanisms exist for changing project scope.

Delivering projects in stages provides the opportunity to separate the creation of new knowledge from the use of existing knowledge: each stage can focus on one or the other. Different working environments can be designed to support the knowledge work in different stages. Separation through time is built in and can be emphasised through structure. In project stages where knowledge needs to be created, iteration can be injected through KM practices. Iteration is good for creating new knowledge because of the environment associated with iterative projects: self-managed teams, relative autonomy and frequent face-to-face contact.

The downside of delivering projects in stages is that it creates knowledge boundaries—barriers to the flow of knowledge between stages. These need to be overcome through KM.

None of this is an argument against adopting an iterative life cycle for entire projects. Organisations that have the capabilities to manage iterative life cycles should use them when they support the nature of the project. Organisations that work in fast-changing environments might benefit from developing such capabilities. Iterative life cycles should be used for the right reasons, though—not just because the developers prefer the relative freedom of allowing knowledge to emerge throughout the project, not because of pressure to 'start the project' and definitely not as an easy option when the knowledge required for a project isn't obvious. Some of these ideas are explored further in the next context factor: project type.

Project Type

Project type is a classification that can provide insights into the strategic KM purposes of different projects. It can be used to decide when, over the life cycle of a project, new knowledge needs to be created and existing knowledge used. It can be used to decide on a linear or iterative project delivery method—or, more helpfully in many cases, a combination of the two.

Projects can be classified into four types based on a combination of how much stakeholders know about what the project is aiming for (the 'what') and how much they know about how to get there (the 'how'). Several versions of this classification exist. Figure 11.2 is based on Eddie Obeng's (2002) classification. The 'known' and 'unknown' labels make it clear that project

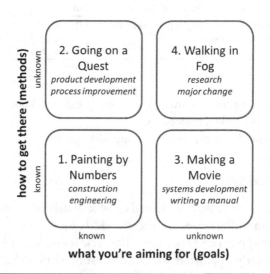

Figure 11.2   Project Types. (*Source:* Adapted from Obeng, E. [2002]. *Perfect Projects.* Beaconsfield, UK: Pentacle Works: The Virtual Media Company.)

management thinkers have for many years recognised the importance of knowledge in making decisions about how to manage projects.

Projects typically move through more than one type during their life cycle. Only projects that start out in the painting-by-numbers quadrant can be completed using existing knowledge. Any project with an 'unknown' element requires some knowledge creation before the project can be completed. Effective KM can propel projects from walking in fog to going on a quest or a making a movie, or from a quest or movie to painting by numbers. All projects need to get to the painting-by-numbers quadrant eventually—even if it is just for a few days.

Walking in Fog

Projects that start with the team walking in fog are those where you know something needs to change, but no one is sure exactly what it is or how they are going to get there. Foggy projects are usually things the organisation hasn't done before and are typically initiated because of a change in the organisation's environment, such the 2016 referendum in which the UK voted to leave the European Union.

Walking-in-fog projects have to create the missing knowledge about what it is that needs to change *and* about how the team is going to get there. The temptation is to jump straight into an iterative life cycle because there are so many unknowns, but this isn't necessarily the best strategy. The hard work of creating the missing knowledge needs to be done at some point, and an iterative approach is no excuse for avoiding it. If the missing knowledge can be created up front, the project will be more effective and more efficient.

An alternative strategy is to focus initially on clarifying the 'what' so the project turns into a quest. The transition from walking in fog to a quest project is typically managed in small, iterative steps to edge towards clarity in the initiation stage of the project. This requires the commitment of stakeholders and KM processes that enable them to explore potentially conflicting requirements and perspectives to generate multiple options, then reach agreement. The initiation stage is likely to be intense and might be long. The KM actor needs to create a working environment of trust, flexibility and autonomy so that the stakeholders can create a shared vision they can all sign up to. Practices and controls designed for projects that use existing knowledge will not work here!

This strategy works only if the requirements can be clarified in time to work out the 'how' and deliver the benefits when they are needed. If the 'what' is likely to change (as in a project to prepare an organisation for the UK leaving the European Union), following this strategy will turn the initiation stage into a tail-chasing exercise and nothing will change. An iterative approach for the whole project is a possible solution in this scenario. An alternative is to proceed with several options simultaneously so that stakeholders gain practical experience ('doing' knowledge) of them—and then decide on which option(s) to take forward.

Making a Movie

Movie projects are those where you know the methods to apply but don't know exactly what you are going to end up with. The movie analogy is perfect: there are well-known processes, but the end product emerges with time, and its success can't be judged until the movie reaches the box office.

Because movie project teams are experienced in following a method (using existing knowledge), the temptation is to focus immediately on activity scheduling. What is actually needed is time in the initiation stage to create some of the missing knowledge about the outputs. This is an iterative process in which the project team generates ideas and seeks feedback from users and other stakeholders. Iteration is needed in the initiation stage, not for the whole project.

The initial focus could be on developing one or more pilot or prototype outputs with limited functionality so that users can try them out. Once the user requirements are fully understood, the work can proceed as a painting-by-numbers project.

At HR Wallingford in the late 1980s, a multidisciplinary project produced the first ever simulation model of an urban drainage system. The team had to design a user interface, and knew exactly how to go about creating it, but couldn't ask users what it should be like because the users had no idea what it could be like. The team imagined what the user interface could be like and produced a user manual before any coding took place. Users' feedback on the manual was then used to plan the detailed activities to complete the project.

The KM actor needs to give the team freedom to generate ideas and prototypes, support the team in understanding and incorporating feedback, then switch to painting-by-numbers mode.

Going on a Quest

Quest projects are those in which the aim is clear from the start, but it isn't clear how the project is going to get there. Process improvement and new product development projects typically start as quests. Foggy projects can turn into quests when they clarify what it is they are trying to do.

The project can't simply be planned, because the knowledge of how to deliver it doesn't exist. The missing knowledge needs to be created through an iterative process of generating and evaluating options—as for a movie project, but focusing on the 'how' rather than the 'what'. If this can be done in the initiation stage, the project turns into a painting-by-numbers one. If it can't be done, the project can proceed in phases where the team works out how to deliver components of the product or process. This can lead to adoption of an iterative life cycle for most of the project, or to a programme in which some components are delivered in parallel.

To clarify the 'how', the KM actor needs to create an environment that supports knowledge creation and support the team through KM processes such as brainstorming to generate options, and workshops to evaluate them.

Painting by Numbers

Painting-by-numbers projects are those where you are sure about what you're aiming for and know how to get there—either from the start or because a quest, movie or walking-in-fog project has clarified unknowns.

Projects that start and end in the painting-by-numbers quadrant are those where the project team or organisation is repeating something that has been done before, such as building a new housing development with standard house types.

Wherever the project started, once it is in the painting-by-numbers quadrant, it focuses on using existing knowledge. The project can be delivered using a linear life cycle with detailed activity scheduling.

The KM actor has to create an environment that supports the use of existing knowledge: control, order and standard processes. Information management is used to support knowledge management, typically through supply-driven KM processes based on codified knowledge. Informal and demand-driven KM processes are needed to supplement this approach and ensure shared understanding of the project.

Separate or Integrate?

Any project that starts with an unknown has to create the missing knowledge before it can be completed. This takes time, commitment of the team and stakeholders, a supporting environment and appropriate KM processes and activities—wherever it happens. Once the missing knowledge has been created, it needs to be used to complete the project. This requires a different supporting environment and different KM processes and activities.

In project environments where people are used to linear life cycles designed for painting-by-numbers projects that succeed by using existing knowledge, creating knowledge is hard work. It is necessary to create a working environment that people will initially find unusual and uncomfortable. You can't avoid the hard work, but you can make it easier to manage by placing knowledge creation in a single project stage. This is separating knowledge creation from the use of existing knowledge through time.

The different environments for the two kinds of knowledge work can also be separated through structure—in two ways. The first is a change in leadership, by having one manager for the creative, early stages of projects and a second manager for the execution stage that focuses on using existing knowledge. The two leaders can adopt different styles, and the change of leader is a signal to team members that something has changed. Ideally, the project should include a long handover period where both managers are involved: to provide continuity and avoid loss of knowledge between stages. The second is to separate the early stages of projects from execution completely, by making one team responsible for business case and project plan development and another for execution. Although this makes it easier to create different working environments with different people, it can create knowledge boundaries between the two groups and leave the team responsible for execution without the in-depth knowledge they need.

The alternative to separation is to integrate the two kinds of knowledge work by adopting an iterative life cycle for all or most of the project. This is best suited to situations where the 'what' of a project is likely to change because of a volatile external environment, not because stakeholders might change their minds. Unless your organisation has mastered the art of jumping between the two different kinds of knowledge work on a daily basis, separation is easier. If you want to develop the flexible capabilities needed for iterative working, introducing some iteration in the initiation stage is a good place to start.

Pressure to 'Start' the Project

Project managers are often under pressure to 'start' the project, in other words get to the execution stage. We can't emphasise enough that the pre-execution stages are *part of the project*. Creating missing knowledge up front takes time, but if it can be done, it should be—even if it makes the initiation stage longer than the execution stage.

At the programme and portfolio levels, decisions about how to create new knowledge and use existing knowledge can be standardised to some extent so that projects are easier to plan and support—and so that everyone knows what to expect.

> Supermarket X classifies projects as routine or innovation projects. Routine projects are those where they are confident they can create the necessary knowledge quickly at the start. Innovation projects are those where they realise a lot of knowledge needs to be created and it will take longer. Both are delivered with a linear life cycle. In routine projects, the initiation stage is typically short and the execution stage is longer. In innovation projects, the initiation stage is longer to allow time for knowledge creation before the shorter execution stage. For each class of project, everyone knows what to expect, which makes it easier for everyone involved to plan and support the work.

Sometimes it is tempting to jump to execution before the missing knowledge has been created or to adopt an iterative life cycle because that will fill all the knowledge gaps and you can say you have started the project. The missing knowledge still has to be created, and it is still going to take time, commitment and a supporting environment.

Is That All There Is to KM?

No, there's a lot more. Our exploration has focused on using the knowledge lens and three of the context factors to understand and make decisions in the early stages of projects. KM doesn't end there—it should be planned and applied throughout project and programme life cycles and used to overcome the difficult knowledge boundary between project closure and benefits realisation.

We refer you to *Managing Knowledge in Project Environments* for further explanation of KM principles, the KM context, how to identify hidden KM throughout the project life cycle, how to build KM into a single project and portfolio-wide KM.

For a high-level explanation of the KM must-haves in any organisational context, see the first ever international standard on KM: *BS ISO 30401 Knowledge management systems: requirements* (BSI, 2018). For a summary of KM in project work, see the 7th edition of the *APM Body of Knowledge* (2019).

Finally, don't believe everything you read about KM. KM thinking and practice has changed significantly over the last 30 years, and much of the available information is out of date. Even recently published material is sometimes rooted in out of date thinking. Project management is at last catching up with current KM thinking. Don't get left behind!

References

Association for Project Management (2019). *APM Body of Knowledge* (7th Ed.). Princes Risborough, UK: Association for Project Management.

BSI (2018). *BS ISO 30401: Knowledge Management Systems: Requirements*. London, UK: BSI.

Obeng, E. (2002). *Perfect Projects*. Beaconsfield, UK: Pentacle—The Virtual Media Company.

Payne, J., Roden, E. J., and Simister, S. (2019). *Managing Knowledge in Project Environments*. Abingdon, UK: Routledge.

Conclusion

Rebooting Project Management for a Brighter Future

Darren Dalcher

Project managers have an amazing job—they get to turn vague ideas, half-formed dreams and fanciful, wishful ambition into reality. In the process, they engage with stakeholders, users, team members, sponsors, project boards, clients, other experts, managers, suppliers and analysts. In order to translate their ambition into action, they influence, partner, cajole, encourage, support, motivate, coach, mentor, involve, inform, sell and engage; meanwhile on the technical side, their teams also plan, scope, schedule, chart, estimate, budget, assess, analyse, allocate, establish, set up, mitigate, prototype, execute, monitor, assure, coordinate, document, check, confirm, report, inform, approve and deploy. This requires a rather diverse set of skills and capabilities. When all is finally achieved, they are ready to move on to embrace the challenge of realising the next ambition.

Project work appears to be thriving across most sectors and domains; however, the set of skills required to deploy projects and secure enduring, sustainable results for users is expanding rapidly, especially when dealing with uncertain, ambiguous and turbulent environments. As can be seen throughout this volume, successful projects rely upon intense engagement with people, teams, communities, neighbourhoods and society at large, and often require concerted deliberation about long-term implications and impacts on the people, planet and purpose, as well as profits.

Project management is not simply a suite of tools and techniques. Projects entail complex and uncertain dynamics operating across constellations of temporary and established organisations. They require a deeper and more nuanced understanding of contexts and culture. The new edition of the *APM Body of Knowledge* (2019) also refers to beneficial change, innovation and strategic intent, as well as alignment and appetite. The key implication is that projects desperately need to extend beyond the limiting constraints of instrumental rationality. Seeing the world through projects as depicted by the authors in this volume requires a significantly updated and refined mindframe regarding the role and potential of projects. Yet, it also enables organisations and nations to deliver against their ambition and to progress towards enduring success in project practice.

The UK's Rethinking Project Management network (explored in Chapter 5) brought together senior practitioners and leading researchers for a series of workshops over a two-year period, in order to develop a research agenda aimed at extending and enriching project management ideas in relation to developing practice (Winter & Smith, 2006). A key finding was the need to shift the dialogue from a singular focus around product creation, emphasising the staged delivery of an asset, towards a wider focus on stakeholders, value, benefits and complexity as befitting twenty-first century project management (Dalcher, 2016). The implication is that the development of practitioner capabilities that address the challenges of a growing and developing profession in a modern society must now take centre stage and replace a fixation with the prevailing instrumental rationality that presumes a linear interpretation of how projects ought to be performed under well-understood and stable conditions. The authors in this volume emphasise and celebrate the role of human contribution to the project setting, indicating a similar shift emanating from a multitude of domains and contexts.

The Rethinking Project Management network was thus able to call for a strategic departure from a position that emphasised the following (adapted from Dalcher, 2016: 800):

- Simplistic life cycle–based models of projects
- The assumption that the life cycle is the terrain
- Instrumental processes accentuating projects as temporary apolitical production processes
- A presumed focus on product and artefact creation
- Narrow conceptualisation of projects that implies a well-defined underpinning objective at the start
- Framing around a singular discipline
- Practitioners as trained technicians, able to follow procedures and techniques

The reality of project work coupled with the escalating ambitions of society require a richer interpretation of projects and their role in enabling change and delivering value and benefit to organisations. The authors featured in this volume have been able to demonstrate a richer and more diverse use of projects embedded within a societal and communal perspective that fosters a deeper integration with users, purpose and context. The contributions and main topics of novelty and innovation presented by the authors are highlighted in Table 2 (against a list of revised focal areas and needs identified by the Rethinking Project Management network, summarised in Winter et al., 2006, revisited in Dalcher, 2016 and contextualised in Chapter 5).

Many of the concepts and models explored by the authors address more than one area and could be legitimately positioned in multiple, or alternative, boxes. Indeed, a feature of a significant portion of the work presented in this volume is that it makes important connections and links across different areas, reflecting a broadening understanding of the role and wider impacts of projects in organisational settings. Such rich positioning reflects an ability to draw on other areas that and strengthen the discourse related to projects and project management. It also shows that project management is maturing beyond the singularity of approach and overly simplistic instrumental rationality that have long been advocated in some quarters.

The principles highlighted in the introductory chapter resonate throughout the contributions, and this seems to be a good juncture to revisit the main ideas and reinforce a mini manifesto based on the notions explored throughout the work. The labels are slightly reworked to reflect the journey and the fresh insights, as follows:

People first. Human orientation is essential for success in project work. Projects hinge on people and relationships, rather than on methods and tools. Success is determined by use and therefore implies getting both employees and users on board before we can deliver the benefits that organisations and society depend upon. This implies recognising the primacy of people in projects, organisations and society and developing their needs.

Purpose means value. Successful projects are guided by a deep, defining sense of purpose that enables individuals and organisations to find a meaning, make sense of events and

Table C.1 Mapping of New Focal Areas— Central to Future Project Management Thinking

Key Concerns and Needs	Exemplar Areas and Approaches Covered Within This Volume
New models and theories recognising complexity in projects and project management	• Human-centred management • Rethinking project management • Entrepreneurship modes in project work • Social process for project leaders • Conceptual integrity • Using the knowledge lens
New models and theories which are presented as only partial theories of a complex terrain	• Teaming for project success • Turn the ship around • Action in societal relationships • The project framework • Rethinking progress in projects • Managing knowledge in project environments
Concepts and images focusing on social interaction amongst people, illuminating flux of events and human action	• Communicating leadership in projects • Trust and psychological safety in teams • Strategic goal alignment • Empowering followers • Putting your people first • The power of social organisation • Leading with purpose
Framing of projects within an array of social agenda, practices, stakeholder relations, politics and power	• The power and peril of hidden assumptions • Leading brainy teams • The role of strategic initiatives • Portfolio stakeholders • Strategic stakeholder alignment • Hacker paradigm leadership • Strategic approach to product stewardship • Strategic knowledge management
Concepts and frameworks which focus on value creation as the prime focus of projects	• Lean quality for improved outcomes • Progressing from a culture of delivery to an ethos of value • Project portfolios to enhance innovation • Strategic goal alignment • Effectuation • The role of experimentation
Broader conceptualisation of projects, including multi-disciplinary, multi-purpose, not predefined, permeable, contestable and negotiable	• Multi-stakeholder dialogues • Organising for project work • Creating positive organisations • Hacker communities • Creative hacking • The case for stewardship
Development of reflective practitioners who can learn, operate and adapt in complex settings, through experience, intuition and pragmatic application	• Benchmarking across sectors as a tool for creative innovation • The role of reflection in practice • Understanding product impacts • Engaging with the mind of the maker

Source: Adapted from Dalcher, D. (2016). Rethinking project practice: Emerging insights from a series of books for practitioners. *International Journal of Managing Projects in Business*, 9(4), 798–821.

decisions and subscribe and buy into a shared and well-communicated purpose. Purpose can drive an entrepreneurial search for maximising opportunities and delivering value and enable the development of portfolios that balance and take account of the organisational appetite for innovation and risk. Further downstream, users are able engage with newly deployed artefacts and capabilities, enabling organisations and society to derive the benefits from intended and well-managed change efforts.

Continuous innovation. Experimentation and entrepreneurship drive the quest for improvement, enabling business and societies to benefit from the ability to explore, adapt and learn. In changing contexts and urgent settings, this becomes an even more critical capability that drives creativity and enables achievement even when the goalposts continue to shift.

Drive for results. Projects are done for a reason. Resilient repositioning and repurposing allow projects to deliver enduring results and enable managers to continuously balance multiple sets of concerns and priorities focused around people, purpose, profit, planet and other emerging global concerns. This extends beyond the traditional fixation on the delivery of artefacts, enabling a real emphasis on delivering meaningful results.

Inclusive leadership. Distributed and shared leadership, responsibility and stewardship across networks of engaged participants and willing users. Empowering individuals and communities results in engagement, enhanced creativity and the development of more comprehensive and appropriate solutions. It also strengthens bonds inside and between communities and enhances relationships, providing more resilient and responsive settings that are capable of better accommodating change and emergent conditions.

On the evidence of the authors, the future seems promising, yet we are standing at a rather decisive historical point. Projects will continue to shape society and define our achievements, but there is a risk that our short-term thinking, rigid methods and long-standing rules of engagement will continue to constrain what can be accomplished. There is an even greater risk that project management may be left behind and lose its integrating role unless it is willing to engage with and learn from other disciplines and domains and benefit from the kind of informed thinking and interdisciplinary awareness shared by the authors featured in this volume.

Ultimately, projects are creative endeavours that transform societies. The role of project managers is to shape that future through critical decisions, trade-offs and adaptations. If project management can retain a creative, responsive and innovative stance as advocated throughout this volume, it can continue to take the lead in sensing, shaping and sustaining the new future. Hopefully, this book will aid reflection and offer an advantageous start to this important conversation around rethinking project management for a disruptive, dynamic and digital world.

References

APM (2019). *APM Body of Knowledge* (7th Ed.). R. Murray Webster and D. Dalcher (Eds.). Princes Risborough, UK: Association for Project Management.

Dalcher, D. (2016). Rethinking project practice: emerging insights from a series of books for practitioners. *International Journal of Managing Projects in Business, 9*(4), 798–821.

Winter, M., and Smith, C. (2006). *Rethinking Project Management, Final Report.* EPSRC Network. Manchester, UK: Manchester University.

Winter, M., Smith, C., Morris, P., and Cicmil, S. (2006). Directions for future research in project management: The main findings of a UK government-funded research network. *International Journal of Project Management, 24*(8), 638–649.

Index

A

agents, 11, 43, 96, 168, 169, 224, 238
agile, 46, 51, 54, 138, 145, 154–160, 179–181,
    188, 206, 222, 223, 226, 227, 232, 233,
    247, 286
agile development, 222, 223, 233
assumptions, 3, 13, 29, 42–46, 115, 119, 123,
    144, 213, 232, 234, 240, 241, 286, 287
authorities, 3, 201–206
authority, 49, 51, 84, 88–93, 96, 196, 197,
    200–208, 245, 254

B

balance, 11, 36, 53, 65, 69, 74, 86, 105, 106,
    145–157, 176, 219, 297
Bazaar, 225, 231
benchmark, 24–27, 37
benchmarking, 3, 24–35, 158
benchmarking paradox, 31
benefits, 6, 8, 11–15, 28, 32, 46, 57, 65, 68,
    71, 76, 96–102, 114, 120–128, 131,
    132, 136, 138, 141, 145–148, 152–158,
    164, 165, 172, 182, 195, 208, 217, 226,
    227, 238, 239, 255–257, 263–266, 276,
    285–289, 292–297
best practice, 30–32, 112, 280
brainy teams, 69, 74, 77
Brooks, Fred, 212–219, 222–225, 229, 276, 279
business priorities, 260

C

capital, 7, 37, 72, 129, 135, 150, 168, 240, 243,
    274, 275, 279
Cathedral thinking, 225
Chef, The, 48, 53–58
chief experimenters, 241, 244
clients, 33, 39, 194, 221, 294
collaboration, 6–8, 18, 29, 32, 39, 51–53, 64,
    69, 72, 79, 80, 93, 95, 106, 147, 168, 187,
    196, 198, 206, 235–239, 267, 268, 279
collaborative design, 232, 233
commercial counterurbanisation, 19
commitment, 30, 34–39, 44, 63, 64, 132, 153,
    170, 189, 195, 225, 227, 235, 236, 245,
    250, 253, 254, 257, 261, 266, 289–292
common resource systems, 253

common sense, 119, 131, 266, 283
communication, 4–7, 10, 28, 34, 37–59, 67,
    71, 81, 103–112, 115, 131, 138, 146, 164,
    165, 195, 212–215, 219, 222, 276, 277
community forms of organisation, 275
complexity, 8, 16, 21, 34, 39, 68, 77, 79, 92,
    97, 110, 117, 150, 169–173, 177–190, 198,
    201, 215, 224, 233, 294
complex systems, 67, 221
conceptual integrity, 218–225, 276
conflict, 64, 71, 154, 219, 267, 270
consumers, 99, 163, 165, 256, 262–264, 270
continuous innovation, 17, 297
convergence, 4, 69
cradle to grave, 122
cultural mindset, 244, 246
culture, 4, 8, 12–15, 21, 29–31, 34–39, 54,
    55, 70, 79, 89, 107, 109, 120, 123, 127,
    146, 156, 161, 174, 195, 198, 200, 209,
    224–232, 235, 238–247, 275, 286, 294

D

drive for results, 17, 297
Drucker, Peter, 12, 13, 19, 45, 58, 59, 91, 98,
    111, 112, 169, 171, 177, 274

E

economic perspective, 99, 101
effectuation, 175–177, 181–191, 194
effort, 30, 46, 53, 64, 66, 70, 85, 92, 106,
    120, 128, 146, 148, 152, 156, 170, 171,
    196, 197, 201, 212–218, 221, 222, 253,
    274, 276
employees, 6, 16, 17, 39, 51, 65, 125, 134,
    184–188, 194–199, 217, 236, 237, 243,
    245, 254, 265, 269, 275, 295
employees first, 195, 199
entrepreneurs, 7, 16, 168, 169, 175, 176, 179–
    183, 186, 190, 191, 194, 198, 226–229,
    232, 233, 241, 243, 251
entrepreneurship, 3, 7, 12, 13, 19, 106, 110,
    167–171, 174–178, 181, 191, 212, 226–
    229, 240, 279, 297
ethical perspective, 98
experimentation, 13, 14, 17, 66, 68, 71,
    170–175, 196, 225–229, 233, 245, 297

experiment failure, 188
extended producer responsibility, 122, 256, 258, 269, 270

F
fit, 12, 35, 50, 54, 77, 121, 134, 138, 140, 146–148, 154, 157, 161, 165, 184, 235, 245
flow, 25, 36, 37, 54, 89, 114–117, 149, 153, 206, 219, 263, 288
focus, 3–11, 15, 16, 26, 29–36, 39, 42–49, 52, 57, 58, 64–67, 75, 77, 91, 92, 95, 101, 107, 117–123, 134, 144, 147, 149, 152–158, 169, 170, 173, 174, 181, 196, 212, 216, 222–229, 237–239, 243, 246, 253, 254, 270, 275, 287–290, 294, 295
followers, 84–96, 236
followership, 3, 84–87, 91–95
Formula One, 27, 28, 32
Fourth Industrial Revolution, 21
frames, 44, 92, 224, 257
freedom, 21, 67, 99, 100, 121, 198, 219, 225, 230, 253, 288, 290
fully extended life cycles, 122, 256
future shock, 11, 21

G
Gardener, The, 48–53, 56–58, 67
gates, 125–137, 141, 190, 250
goals, 25, 34, 48, 52, 55, 56, 63–66, 70, 87–90, 102, 103, 120, 147, 150–152, 155, 162–166, 173, 175, 179–182, 185, 186, 189, 190, 195, 205, 212, 236–238, 256, 260, 265–268
Great Ormond Street Hospital for Children, 27
groups, 42, 49, 52–54, 58, 62–66, 73, 79, 81, 86, 96, 97, 103, 107–109, 114, 126, 157–159, 162, 163, 177, 198, 200, 205, 209, 218, 225, 230, 231, 234, 239–242, 253, 260–263, 268, 269, 278

H
hacker(s), 3, 20, 219–247
hacker communities, 224

hacker culture, 226–231, 235, 244, 247
hacker paradigm leaders, 232–235, 238, 241, 244
hacking, 211, 212, 220–233, 237, 244, 245
HCL Technologies, 194
heuristics, 181–190
heuristics, control-based, 182
heuristics, prediction-based, 182
hidden assumptions, 42–46
hierarchy, 51, 67, 87, 88, 93, 206, 227, 254, 279
high-performing teams, 63–65, 237
human-centred management, 92, 96–102
human-centred paradigm, 91, 96, 101, 103
Hyatt Regency Hotel, 44, 45

I
IBM, 212, 215–217, 221, 230, 276
identity, 10, 16, 48–50, 57, 59, 63, 66, 94
impact economy, 257
inclusive leadership, 297
individualism, 252–254, 259
Industrial Revolution, 4, 5, 9, 12, 18–21, 74, 279
industrious revolution, 5, 6, 9, 14, 19, 20
innovation, 2, 3, 7–21, 26, 29–35, 39, 69–75, 79–81, 99, 118–122, 144, 148–150, 153, 157–161, 169–177, 183, 196–198, 212, 219, 225–238, 241, 244–247, 274, 276, 279, 286, 292–297
institutional perspective, 100, 101
instrumental processes, 295
integrated funding, 152
integrated governance, 152
integrated justification, 152
integrated resources, 152
issue fixation, 209

K
knowing–doing gap, 120, 123, 124
knowledge, 3–9, 12–15, 18, 31, 32, 42–44, 54, 58, 67–74, 78–81, 89–92, 103–107, 115, 118–124, 127, 128, 132, 144, 145, 148, 158, 173, 176, 182, 183, 189, 198, 201, 209, 216, 220, 221, 224, 231, 232, 255, 258, 263, 265, 269, 273–294, 297

knowledge lens, 277, 281, 292
knowledge management, 3, 81, 274–281, 291

L
leadership, 8, 16, 17, 20, 21, 35–40, 46–60,
    69, 77–80, 83–99, 103, 106, 109–112,
    138, 190, 197–210, 232–234, 237–241,
    244–247, 254, 255, 265, 287, 291, 297
lean, 3, 29–40, 46, 48, 54, 119, 128, 145, 232,
    233, 240, 241, 246
lean principles, 35
lean quality, 3, 29–40
level playing field, 106, 107
life cycle(s), 17, 26, 114–124, 131–137, 141,
    173, 221, 231, 255–260, 263, 266,
    269–271, 277, 284–292, 295
life-cycle assessment, 263, 270–271
life-cycle impact, 260
life cycle mapping, 263, 266, 269–271
lovelocks, 250–252

M
maker economy, 7
maker movement, 7, 19–21, 279
McChrystal, General Stanley, 66, 67, 73
meaning, 16, 42, 43, 66, 98, 104, 134, 138,
    236, 274, 277, 295
metaphors, 46, 48
mind of the maker, 274–276, 280
Mind of the Maker, The, 276, 280
multi-stakeholder dialogues, 92, 98, 102,
    105–107
Mythical Man-Month, The, 212–215, 229, 279

N
Nayar, Vineet, 194–199

O
open-ended problem, 179
optimisation, 33, 36, 39, 148, 152, 171–173
optimiser, 170, 171, 175
optimism, 4, 213, 230, 231
outcomes, 11, 24, 29–34, 39, 51, 55, 58, 86,
    93, 97, 98, 104, 105, 126, 127, 154, 157,
    169, 173, 181–186, 200, 226, 254, 255,
    276, 281, 285

P
padlocks, 250–252
partnership, 29, 32, 64, 109, 126, 250, 254
people first, 3, 16, 194, 295
perfection trap, 119–123
physical space, 244, 245
pipeline balance, 147
pivot, 188
Popper, Karl, 86, 95
portfolio(s), 2, 3, 9, 10, 15, 18, 73, 95, 123,
    132, 143–166, 189, 230, 264, 266, 274,
    281–286, 292, 297
  compliance, 145
  execution, 153
  investment, 152
  operational, 145
  strategic, 149, 152, 165, 266
  value-creating, 145
portfolio balance, 154, 157
portfolio management, 15, 144–150, 153–166
positionality, 48, 49, 57, 58
positive organisations, 197–200, 210, 255
postheroic leadership, 92–95
post-industrial society, 6–9, 18–21
post-organisational society, 8
predictability trap, 119–123
present shock, 11
problem space, 176, 194
procurement, 44, 172, 256, 264–268
product chain, 257
product creation, 294
product goals, 265
product impacts, 260, 263
productive freedom, 225
product stewardship, 154, 255–270
product stewardship programmes, 260
product sustainability, 256
programme(s), 2, 9, 10, 15–18, 121, 123,
    144–153, 158, 160, 170, 172, 207, 215,
    218–222, 252, 260–265, 268, 269,
    274–278, 281–286, 290, 292
programme management, 160
progress, 2, 3, 10, 14, 19, 30, 35, 55, 56, 62,
    69–72, 84, 90, 93, 102, 115, 122, 123,
    172, 206–209, 212–214, 226–229, 235,
    277, 278, 294

Project Aristotle, 65–67, 205
project delivery, 29, 32–40, 114, 123, 136, 256, 281, 286, 288
project delivery method, 281, 286, 288
project framework, 125, 130–141
project leader, 201–210
project manager, 42, 49, 54, 55, 59, 126, 128, 187, 189, 214
project society, 8–11, 18, 20
project sponsor, 120, 126
project type, 134, 147, 281, 288
    going on a quest, 289, 290
    making a movie, 289
    painting by numbers, 289, 290
    walking in fog, 114, 189–290
prototyping, 121, 122, 170, 222
psychological safety, 65, 66, 71–73, 94
purpose, 4, 12–18, 28, 35, 39, 52, 63, 67, 70, 71, 87, 96, 104, 106, 116, 117, 123, 138, 154, 156, 197, 198, 204–210, 224, 232–239, 245–247, 254, 257, 261, 269, 275–277, 281, 285, 294–297

R
recovery, 176, 256, 264, 265, 268, 269
reflective practitioners, 122–256
regulatory hacking, 228, 230
responsibility, 11, 13, 27, 63, 71, 86–91, 99–101, 106–112, 122, 123, 152, 195, 196, 218, 219, 225, 250, 253–258, 261–264, 268–270, 297
responsible project management, 122, 123
Rethinking Project Management, 18, 115, 116, 119, 123, 124, 294–297
rhetorical performance, 48, 49, 57
risk society, 9, 10, 18–20
Rogers, Carl, 11, 14, 21
roles, 4, 45, 55, 66, 75, 77, 125, 126, 202–206, 224, 245, 277, 285
rollout, 189

S
scaling, 242, 243
sceptic, 170, 175
scepticism, 176
self-centrism, 252

self-organising teams, 226
social issues, 262–265
social organisations, 197, 198
social perspective, 98–101
social processes, 3, 200, 205
social space, 227, 244, 245
stages, 27, 33, 44, 115–118, 125, 127, 131–138, 141, 152, 239, 257, 263, 276, 285–288, 291, 292
stakeholder engagement, 92, 98, 105–111, 155, 198, 261, 264, 265
stakeholder management, 98, 106, 109, 110, 155, 162–165
stakeholder mapping, 262, 270
stakeholders, 33, 34, 44–46, 70, 92, 95–114, 121, 138, 146, 155, 158, 162–166, 181–185, 194, 198, 256, 260–265, 269, 270, 277, 283–291, 294
star followers, 87
start-ups, 7, 15, 227–230, 235, 245
stewardship, 3, 11, 122, 123, 154, 249, 250, 253–270, 297
strategic fit, 147, 154, 161
strategic goal alignment, 162, 164
strategic initiatives, 3, 10, 17, 151, 152, 156, 157, 164, 173
sufficiency, 147
sustainability, 5, 12, 37, 39, 69, 111, 154, 225, 256, 262–271
sustainability policy, 265
sustainable coopetive advantage, 69, 79
system, 54–58, 89, 99, 100, 215–218, 221

T
take-back, 261, 268, 269
team(s), 2, 3, 8, 15, 17, 27–29, 33, 39, 42, 45–74, 77–80, 84, 86–94, 106, 127, 141, 152, 163, 164, 172, 183, 187–189, 195, 200–219, 222–246, 253, 256, 276, 277, 284, 289–291, 294
team chemistry, 69, 77
team diversity, 69, 79
teaming, 62, 70–72, 86
team leadership, 77, 205, 206
team membership, 205, 210
team of teams, 67, 73

team transparency, 69, 80
teamwork, 3, 27, 28, 35, 62–64, 70–74, 92,
    206, 210, 225, 236
thinking small, 242
Toffler, Alvin, 11, 12, 21
Toyota, 36, 40
Toyota Way, The 36, 40
Tragedy of the Commons, 252, 258
transformation, 2, 4, 8, 12, 20, 28, 33, 37, 50,
    75, 87, 91, 102, 117, 118, 175, 183, 191,
    195–198, 215, 227
transparency, 69, 80, 146, 164, 166, 195, 225
trial-and-error, 43, 173, 222, 229
tribal mindset, 232–234, 237
trust, 4, 10, 20, 49, 50, 64–68, 71, 72, 85, 86,
    95, 106, 164, 166, 195, 200, 210, 232–
    237, 244–247, 266, 271, 279, 289
Turn the Ship Around, 89, 95

U
user value, 234, 242
utility, 147, 148, 157

V
value, 2–8, 11, 12, 16–19, 28–40, 45, 46,
    50–58, 62, 64, 67, 71–75, 79, 80, 87, 90,
    93, 100, 101, 107, 119–123, 138, 144–
    148, 152–159, 166, 169, 170, 173, 176,
    194–198, 224–226, 232–236, 240–243,
    246, 253, 256, 257, 260–264, 269, 270,
    276, 279, 281, 285, 294–297
value capture, 276
value chain, 257, 264, 276
value creation, 16, 33, 34, 100, 166, 173, 276
value creation chains, 276
values, 6, 12–14, 29–31, 34–40, 46–59, 74,
    89, 104–106, 157, 200, 202, 210, 224,
    231, 243–246, 252, 265
vehicles of change, 125

W
water cube, 70
waterfall, 51, 54, 137, 179, 180, 183, 221, 285
Who is packing your parachute?, 66
whole life cycle, 122, 255, 257
Wikipedia, 225, 226

Printed in the United States
by Baker & Taylor Publisher Services

Printed in the United States
by Baker & Taylor Publisher Services